ATLA BIBLIOGRAPHY SERIES
edited by Dr. Kenneth E. Rowe

1. *A Guide to the Study of the Holiness Movement*, by Charles Edwin Jones. 1974.
2. *Thomas Merton: A Bibliography*, by Marquita E. Breit. 1974.
3. *The Sermon on the Mount: A History of Interpretation and Bibliography*, by Warren S. Kissinger. 1975.
4. *The Parables of Jesus: A History of Interpretation and Bibliography*, by Warren S. Kissinger. 1979.
5. *Homosexuality and the Judeo-Christian: An Annotated Bibliography*, by Thom Horner. 1981.
6. *A Guide to the Study of the Pentecostal Movement*, by Charles Edwin Jones. 1983.
7. *The Genesis of Modern Process Thought: A Historical Outline with Bibliography*, by George R. Lucas Jr. 1983.
8. *A Presbyterian Bibliography*, by Harold B. Prince. 1983.
9. *Paul Tillich: A Comprehensive Bibliography . . .*, by Richard C. Crossman. 1983.
10. *A Bibliography of the Samaritans*, by Alan David Crown. 1984 (see no. 32).
11. *An Annotated and Classified Bibliography of English Literature Pertaining to the Ethiopian Orthodox Church*, by Jon Bonk. 1984.
12. *International Meditation Bibliography, 1950 to 1982*, by Howard R. Jarrell. 1984.
13. *Rabindranath Tagore: A Bibliography*, by Katherine Henn. 1985.
14. *Research in Ritual Studies: A Programmatic Essay and Bibliography*, by Ronald L. Grimes. 1985.
15. *Protestant Theological Education in America*, by Heather F. Day. 1985.
16. *Unconscious: A Guide to Sources*, by Natalino Caputi. 1985.
17. *The New Testament Apocrypha and Pseudepigrapha*, by James H. Charlesworth. 1987.
18. *Black Holiness*, by Charles Edwin Jones. 1987.
19. *A Bibliography on Ancient Ephesus*, by Richard Oster. 1987.
20. *Jerusalem, the Holy City: A Bibliography*, by James D. Purvis. Vol. I, 1988; Vol. II, 1991.
21. *An Index to English Periodical Literature on the Old Testament and Ancient Near Eastern Studies*, by William G. Hupper. Vol. I, 1987; Vol. II, 1988; Vol. III, 1990; Vol. IV, 1990; Vol. V, 1992; Vol. VI, 1994; Vol. VII, 1998; Vol. VIII, 1999.
22. *John and Charles Wesley: A Bibliography*, by Betty M. Jarboe. 1987.
23. *A Scholar's Guide to Academic Journals in Religion*, by James Dawsey. 1988.

24. *An Oxford Movement and Its Leaders: A Bibliography of Secondary and Lesser Primary Sources*, by Lawrence N. Crumb. 1988; Supplement, 1993.
25. *A Bibliography of Christian Worship*, by Bard Thompson. 1989.
26. *The Disciples and American Culture: A Bibliography of Works by Disciples of Christ Members, 1866–1984*, by Leslie R. Galbraith and Heather F. Day. 1990.
27. *The Yogacara School of Buddhism: A Bibliography*, by John Powers. 1991.
28. *The Doctrine of the Holy Spirit: A Bibliography Showing Its Chronological Development* (2 vols.), by Esther Dech Schandorff. 1995.
29. *Rediscovery of Creation: A Bibliographical Study of the Church's Response to the Environmental Crisis*, by Joseph K. Sheldon. 1992.
30. *The Charismatic Movement: A Guide to the Study of Neo-Pentecostalism with Emphasis on Anglo-American Sources*, by Charles Edwin Jones. 1995.
31. *Cities and Churches: An International Bibliography* (3 vols.), by Loyde H. Hartley. 1992.
32. *A Bibliography of the Samaritans*, 2nd ed., by Alan David Crown. 1993.
33. *The Early Church: An Annotated Bibliography of Literature in English*, by Thomas A. Robinson. 1993.
34. *Holiness Manuscripts: A Guide to Sources Documenting the Wesleyan Holiness Movement in the United States and Canada*, by William Kostlevy. 1994.
35. *Of Spirituality: A Feminist Perspective*, by Clare B. Fischer. 1995.
36. *Evangelical Sectarianism in the Russian Empire and the USSR: A Bibliographic Guide*, by Albert Wardin Jr. 1995.
37. *Hermann Sasse: A Bibliography*, by Ronald R. Feuerhahn. 1995.
38. *Women in the Biblical World: A Study Guide. Vol. I: Women in the World of Hebrew Scripture*, by Mayer I. Gruber. 1995.
39. *Women and Religion in Britain and Ireland: An Annotated Bibliography from the Reformation to 1993*, by Dale A. Johnson. 1995.
40. *Emil Brunner: A Bibliography*, by Mark G. McKim. 1996.
41. *The Book of Jeremiah: An Annotated Bibliography*, by Henry O. Thompson. 1996.
42. *The Book of Amos: An Annotated Bibliography*, by Henry O. Thompson. 1997.
43. *Ancient and Modern Chaldean History: A Comprehensive Bibliography of Sources*, by Ray Kamoo. 1999.
44. *World Lutheranism: A Select Bibliography for English Readers*, by Donald L. Huber. 2000.

45. *The Christian and Missionary Alliance: An Annotated Bibliography of Textual Sources*, by H. D. Ayer. 2001.

The Christian and Missionary Alliance

An Annotated Bibliography of Textual Sources

H. D. (Sandy) Ayer

ATLA Bibliography Series, No. 45

The Scarecrow Press, Inc.
Lanham, Maryland, and London
2001

SCARECROW PRESS, INC.

Published in the United States of America
by Scarecrow Press, Inc.
4720 Boston Way, Lanham, Maryland 20706
www.scarecrowpress.com

4 Pleydell Gardens, Folkestone
Kent CT20 2DN, England

British Library Cataloguing-in-Publication Information Available

Library of Congress Cataloging-in-Publication Data
Ayer, H.D., 1952–
The Christian and Missionary Alliance : an annotated bibliography of textual sources / H.D. (Sandy) Ayer.
p. cm. — (ATLA bibliography series ; no. 45)
Includes index.
ISBN 0-8108-3995-4 (alk. paper)
1. Christian and Missionary Alliance—Bibliography. 2. Christian and Missionary Alliance—Indexes. I. Title. II. Series.
Z7845.C48 A94 no.45 2001
[BX6700.C3]
016.2899—dc21 00-053831

™ The paper used in this publication meets the minimum requirements of American National Standard for Information Sciences—Permanence of Paper for Printed Library Materials, ANSI/NISO Z39.48-1992.
Manufactured in the United States of America.

Dedication

Dedicated to John Sawin, Christian and Missionary Alliance pastor, missionary to Vietnam, archivist, historian, and bibliographer. John's passion for early Allianceana led him to collect, organize, and catalogue, with the help of his late wife Woneta, the thousands of books, periodicals, pamphlets, tracts, and other documents that now form the basis of the special collections and archives at both the C&MA headquarters in Colorado Springs and Canadian Bible College/Canadian Theological Seminary in Regina, Sask. This volume builds on the bibliographical foundation he has laid.

Contents

Series Editor's Foreword

The American Theological Library Association Bibliography Series is designed to stimulate and encourage the preparation of reliable bibliographies and guides to the literature of religious studies in all of its scope and variety. Compilers are free to define their field, make their own selections, and work out internal organization as the unique demands of the subject indicate. We are pleased to publish this annotated bibliography of literature by and about the Christian and Missionary Alliance as number 45 in our series.

H. D.(Sandy) Ayer completed undergraduate studies in French at the University of British Columbia and earned an M.C.S. at Regent College and an M.L.S at the University of British Columbia's School of Library and Information Science. Mr. Ayer currently serves as director of library services of the Archibald Foundation Library of Canadian Bible College/Canadian Theological Seminary (CBC/CTS) in Regina, Saskatchewan, Canada. He also serves as the archivist of both CBC/CTS and the Christian and Missionary Alliance in Canada and is an active member of West Side Alliance Church.

Kenneth E. Rowe
Series Editor

Drew University Library
Madison, NJ 07940 USA

Foreword

Charles Edwin Jones

The publication of H. D. (Sandy) Ayer's *The Christian and Missionary Alliance: An Annotated Bibliography of Textual Sources*, provides for the first time access to a definitive body of material on the internal life of this mission-centered fellowship, which under the banner of the fourfold gospel—Jesus Christ: Savior, Sanctifier, Healer, and Coming King—has provided for its people a bridge over nearly every rift in the revivalistic evangelicalism of the past century. The uncomplicated design of the work—alphabetical annotated lists of books and articles and of periodical titles with personal-subject name and topical indexes—makes for quick access to more than 2,500 items relating to more than 2.4 million Christian and Missionary Alliance adherents worldwide. The objective tone of the annotations and the inclusion of sometime adherents—the Alliance did not officially become a denomination until 1974—enhance the utility of the work. The stress placed on works by the group's great spiritual leaders, A. B. Simpson and A. W. Tozer, also adds to its strength. Mr. Ayer, in short, brings to the fore the vast landscape of this unique fellowship.

Preface

Purpose

This bibliography grew out of my desire, and that of Alliance historians John Sawin and Charles Nienkirchen, to discover the universe of "Allianceana." The twofold purpose of our quest was to develop the special collection of Canadian Bible College/Canadian Theological Seminary's library and to determine which Alliance imprints need to be preserved. As doctoral students and other scholars began using the special collection these somewhat parochial concerns were augmented by a desire to make available to researchers more of the rich resources of the Alliance oeuvre in such areas of current interest as evangelicalism, missions, the divine healing movement, the Holiness movement, and evangelical spirituality. My particular personal hope is that this work will facilitate the writing of critical scholarly biographies of such Alliance luminaries as A. B. Simpson, A. W. Tozer, Paul Rader, and R. A. Jaffray.

Scope

As its title indicates this work is restricted to textual resources, i.e., primary and secondary source materials in the form of books, periodicals, articles, essays, booklets, pamphlets, tracts, and theses. Coverage extends from A. B. Simpson's first published work (1880) to the present (1999). A concerted, though unsuccessful, attempt has been made to document the entire published corpus of both Simpson and A. W. Tozer, since these Alliance luminaries are likely to be of greatest interest to scholars.

When I began this work I failed to realize that even an apparently narrow subject like the Christian and Missionary Alliance (C&MA) would prove to be so vast and so incapable of precise definition. Ultimately I decided to steal a page from A. B. Simpson by restricting my focus to the fourfold Gospel, broadly conceived. The result looks to my mind less like a universe and more like a cluster of somewhat nebulous galaxies. This is what one ought to expect, I suppose, from a phenomenon that began life as a broadly based and loosely organized parachurch movement with strong Holiness leanings and has evolved into a highly structured denomination--one that is moving in an increasingly Reformed and generically evangelical direction.

As was implied above, the bibliographical boundaries of the C&MA are ill-defined at best, and so it has been difficult to determine which subjects and which authors to include. Is a subject worthy of inclusion simply because Alliance authors have written about it? And who is an "Alliance author" anyway? Should the works of anyone who teaches in an Alliance college or seminary be included? Which of Simpson's early associates are closely enough associated with the C&MA to have their works included if they were not published by an Alliance press? Should all Alliance imprints be included? What topics ought to be regarded as being germane to the fourfold Gospel? Such questions as these are not easily answered, as my frequently changing card and computer files of deletions and tentative deletions demonstrate. At any rate, in my attempt to bring order out of bibliographical chaos I have had to make some considered yet seemingly arbitrary decisions that will not please every potential user of the work.

The following fringe (i.e., lying at the extreme edges of the fourfold Gospel, broadly conceived) subjects and material types are included:

- Missiological works of a theoretical nature
- D.Min. projects that are not merely studies of a particular congregation
- Literature (i.e., poetry and novels) that exemplifies Alliance piety
- Reprints by Alliance publishers of works by non-Alliance authors that reflect Alliance distinctives
- Selected works in church management and Christian education

The following fringe subjects and material types are not included:

- Works in the social sciences, even if written from an explicitly Christian perspective
- Works that bear an Alliance imprint but that are unrelated to Alliance themes

- Most local church histories
- Translations of works originally published in English
- Works in non-Latin alphabets (with the exception of two Chinese language works)
- Nonprint materials (including electronic resources)
- Works by Arno Clemens Gaebelein, James H. Brookes, Seth Cook Rees, and others whose connection to the Alliance seemed too tenuous to warrant their being considered "Alliance authors"
- Works published subsequent to an author's severing of ties with the Alliance, e.g. the post-departure writings of Oswald J. Smith and Paul Rader
- Articles in Alliance organs

In the context of the foregoing criteria my principles of selection also included a bias toward including works published prior to ca. 1950, since these are likely to reflect a distinctive ethos, and excluding later works.

Some entries lack annotations either because their titles may be so thoroughly descriptive as to make an annotation redundant or because I have not been able to acquire the documents to which they refer.

Sources

The special collections of the Archibald Foundation Library in Regina, Saskatchewan, and the A.B. Simpson Historical Library in Colorado Springs, Colorado, provided the majority of the materials described in this bibliography. John Sawin's voluminous notes on Alliance personages provided leads on additional writings, as did subject and known-author searches of OCLC's *FirstSearch* database; the *National Union Catalog, Pre-1956 Imprints*; the *Union List of Serials in Libraries of the United States and Canada*; *ResAnet*, the online catalogue of the National Library of Canada; the ATLA's *Religion Indexes*; *Dissertation Abstracts*; the *Dictionary Catalog of the Missionary Research Library, New York*; subject bibliographies on Pentecostalism, evangelicalism, and the Holiness movement; the "recent publications" lists in the annual reports of the C&MA; and the bibliographies and advertising supplements of works located via the sources just enumerated. The remaining entries were the result of serendipity, e.g., someone simply placing in my hands a copy of an Alliance-related work I'd never heard of before.

Arrangement

After much reflection and consultation with colleagues I decided to deviate from normal bibliographical practice and list the entries by author rather than by subject. In so doing I hope to give scholars a chance to see at a (rather extended) glance something approaching the entire corpus of major figures, such as A. B. Simpson and A. W. Tozer. This decision runs the risk of creating a rather cumbersome index, and so I have tried to assign at most two subject headings to each work. I have also divided the index into a personal name subject index and a topical index. In both indexes references to works by Simpson appear in boldface type, and those to works by Tozer appear in italics.

Concluding Appeal

I apologize for the lack of completeness of this work. I have doubtless missed a good many worthy bibliographic items, and some entries are less than complete, particularly those pertaining to Alliance periodicals. In addition, I have had to eliminate scores of potential entries that were advertised in Alliance periodicals and books but whose actual existence I have been unable to verify. Since this bibliography has been a collaborative effort from the beginning, I appeal to anyone who can provide additional entries or more complete information to existing entries to contact me so that additions and corrections can be published (likely on the Canadian Bible College/Canadian Theological Seminary web page). Thank you in advance for your help.

Acknowledgments

This bibliography is the result of more than a decade of desultory research, much of which was carried out on the job, since my original intention in undertaking the project was to provide the basis for the development of a research collection on the history and thought of the Christian and Missionary Alliance. So neither my wife Diane nor my children Adam and Hannah have been made to suffer during its compilation. In fact, during the last two of my four visits to the A.B. Simpson Historical Library in Colorado Springs they had a rather pleasant time of it while I worked frenetically days and evenings compiling entries and writing annotations.

I would like to express my gratitude to Canadian Bible College/ Canadian Theological Seminary for granting me a sabbatical during the first half of 1993, which freed me to devote myself exclusively to the project. I would also like to thank the Publication Committee of the American Theological Library Association for awarding me a grant-in-aid towards the expenses associated with the project. CBC/CTS also contributed generously towards my research expenses.

I have already mentioned my great debt to John Sawin. Charles Edwin Jones, the dean of Holiness bibliographers, has offered many helpful suggestions, sent me a number of Alliance-related publications, and served as a mentor for the project. Ken Rowe, the editor of the ATLA Bibliographies series, has provided guidance in matters of format and has also provided much encouragement, as have Bill Faupel, Bill Kostlevy, Tim Erdel, David Buschart, Charles Nienkirchen, Glen Scorgie, and Gary B. McGee. Bob Webb both cheered me on and gave selflessly of his computer skills.

The following people have provided bibliographical information and/or contributed C&MA-related library materials: Lindsay Reynolds, Charles Nienkirchen, Gordon Fairley, Jack Shannon, Barbara Volstad, Gary B. McGee, Jim Pattison, and Richard Reichert. Elvie Calig, librarian at Alliance Biblical Seminary (Manila, Philippines) and Dr. Joseph Wenninger, archivist at the A.B. Simpson Historical Library, have also been particularly helpful in this regard.

I placed hundreds of inter-library loans in the course of my research, ably aided by fellow staff members Pamela Holbrow and Donna Greenway, and by our faithful ILL couriers Kelvin and Margaret Friebel. Marion Lake and her staff at the University of Regina Library's inter-library loans division processed most of my requests and did so with conspicuous grace, perseverance, and patience. I was also helped considerably by the librarians and inter-library loan staff of the following institutions: Central Bible College, Asbury Theological Seminary, Toccoa Falls College, Nyack College, Crown College, and Simpson College. Once the entries were in something approaching final form the editorial staff at Scarecrow provided expert guidance in matters of format and style.

Finally, I would like to recognize the many contributions of my capable project assistant, Carol Petkau. Not only did she input the bulk of the records, but she also, owing to her considerable knowledge of Alliance history, brought to my attention several new items for inclusion in the bibliography and offered many helpful criticisms of the annotations.

Books, Essays, Articles, Theses, Pamphlets, and Tracts

1. *50 Years of God's Faithfulness: The Hillsdale Alliance Church Family Album*. Regina, Sask.: Hillsdale Alliance Church, 1978. 40 p.

Hillsdale is the largest C&MA church in Regina and the birthplace of the first Chinese Alliance church in Canada.

2. *A. B. Simpson Centenary, 1843-1943*. New York: Christian and Missionary Alliance, 1943. 16 p.

Four tributes to Simpson as spiritual leader, advocate of missions, writer, and evangelist.

3. Abrahamsen, Fred A. *A Brief History of the Christian & Missionary Alliance Church, Brooklyn, with the Declaration of Faith, Church Covenant, 1922-1977*. Edited by David J. Fant. New York: Clarendon Road Church, 1977. 36 p.

History of the former Brooklyn Alliance Tabernacle, now known as Clarendon Road Church.

4. Acenelli, Delfor R. *Yo fui testigo: De la campaña de salvación y sanidad del Pastor Hicks*. Buenos Aires: Librería "Alianza," 1954.

A first person account of the highly successful evangelistic and healing campaign of Pentecostal evangelist Tommy Hicks (1909-1973) in Argentina in 1954. Alliance churches in Argentina experienced rapid growth in the wake of the Hicks meetings.

5. Ackland, Donald F. *Moving Heaven and Earth: R. G. LeTourneau, Inventor, Designer, Manufacturer and Preacher*. New York: The Iverson-Ford Associates, 1949. 208 p.

Based on an extended visit with R. G. LeTourneau in 1947. Contains many photographs not found in the other two biographies of LeTourneau, i.e., 888 and 914.

6. Adams, Stephen, K. Neill Foster, and George McPeek, eds. *Voices on the Glory*. Camp Hill, Pa.: Christian Publications, 1998. 382 p.

Thirty-four meditations by C&MA pastors and workers on the glory of God.

7. Adrianoff, David (I)van. "The Church in Laos." In *Church in Asia Today: Challenges and Opportunities*, ed. Saphir Athyal, 216-25. Singapore: The Asia Lausanne Committee for World Evangelization, 1996.

The C&MA began work in northern Laos in 1928, at the invitation of the Swiss Brethren, and the two missions cooperated to establish the Lao Evangelical Church. In 1975, when the Marxist government expelled all missionaries, most of the northern churches were being led by Hmong pastors. The government suspected the Hmong of being CIA agents, and many Hmong pastors fled, leaving their churches to flounder. In the south, leadership styles were less hierarchical, and the effects of this exodus far less damaging.

8. ———. "Hmong Retribalization." Master's thesis, State University of New York at Binghamton, 1975. 156 p.

An overview of Alliance mission efforts among the Hmong (a Southeast Asian people). Argues that converts have, in effect, become retribalized.

9. *Afro-Asia Alliance Literature Conference, Hong Kong, April 8-12, 1963: Report of Proceedings*. New York: The Christian and Missionary Alliance. Foreign Department, 1964. 189 p.

Reports on literature production and distribution by the various mission fields and indigenous churches of the C&MA, together with presentations by outside contributors (among them, W. A. Smalley and Eugene Nida), that are analyzed to produce a strategy for the use of literature in Alliance missions in Africa and Asia.

10. Aghamkar, Atul Y. "Family Coherence and Evangelization in Urban India." In *God So Loves the City: Seeking a Theology for Urban Mission*, eds. Charles Van Engen and Jude Tiersma, 143-64. Monrovia, Calif.: MARC, 1994.

Christians living in cultures where the extended family is the basic social and decision-making unit must avoid an individualistic approach to evangelism and concentrate on evangelizing the leaders of the family unit. This strategy minimizes the shame associated with conversion and maximizes the potential for multiple and lasting conversions.

11. Ahl, Augustus William (1886-). *Bible Studies in the Light of Recent Research: An Introductory Manual for Higher Institutions of Learning and Thoughtful Bible Students*, rev. and enlarged ed. New York: Lemcke and Buecher, 1923. Reprint, Harrisburg, Pa.: Christian Alliance Pub. Co., 1930. 354 p.

12. Albrecht, Daniel E. "Carrie Judd Montgomery: Pioneering Contributor to Three Religious Movements." *Pneuma* 8 (fall 1986): 101-19.

Montgomery made formative contributions to the faith healing movement, the C&MA, and Pentecostalism. Appointed the first recording secretary of the Christian Alliance in 1887, she continued serving the C&MA in leadership capacities for the next three decades. A. B. Simpson invited her to address gatherings of the C&MA as late as 1918.

13. Alexander, B. H. *The Silver Key to Changsha*. New York: The Christian and Missionary Alliance, 1944. 11 p.

Changsha, capital of Hunan province, was long closed to foreigners and missionaries. The persistent efforts of the author and his Alliance coworkers resulted in the city opening to foreigners and becoming a base for mission societies and a center of theological education.

14. Allen, Russell T. *Over the River to Charlie: Highlights in the Life of C. H. Spurgeon*. Harrisburg, Pa.: Christian Publications, 1967. 88 p.

15. Allen, Tom (1954-). *I Wish You Could Meet My Mom and Dad*. Beaverlodge, Alta.: Horizon House, 1978. 121 p.

Describes the family life of Rev. and Mrs. William E. Allen. Rev. Allen pastored First Alliance Church, Mansfield, Ohio.

16. ———. *Let Him That Is without Sin: Extending the Grace of Forgiveness in Moral Failure*. Camp Hill, Pa.: Christian Publications, 1998. 17 p.

17. ———. *Spiritual Leadership Begins at Home*. Camp Hill, Pa.: Christian Publications, 1991. 19 p.

18. *L'Alliance Chrétienne Missionnaire: Après un siècle d'évangélisation mondiale*. Paris: Alliance Chrétienne et Missionnaire de France, 1987. 7 p.

A brief history of the Alliance and a description of its organizational structure.

19. *Alliance under the Cross: The Christian and Missionary Alliance in Australia*. Forestville, N.S.W.: The Christian and Missionary Alliance in Australia, 1970. 7 p.

Biographies of the pastors and missionaries of the C&MA in Australia.

20. *Alliance Witness Reader*. Harrisburg, Pa.: Christian Publications, 1975. 118 p.

Miscellaneous articles from the 1974-1975 issues of *The Alliance Witness*.

21. *The Alliance Witness Reader 2*. Harrisburg, Pa.: Christian Publications, 1976. 123 p.

Miscellaneous articles from the 1975-1976 issues of *The Alliance Witness*.

22. The Alliance World. *Bare, Beautiful Feet: And Other Missionary Stories for Children.* Camp Hill, Pa.: Christian Publications, 1992. 51 p.

23. ———. *A Happy Day for Ramona: And Other Missionary Stories for Children*. Camp Hill, Pa.: Christian Publications, 1987. 57 p.

24. ———. *The Pink and Green Church: And Other Missionary Stories for Children*. Camp Hill, Pa.: Christian Publications, 1987. 51 p.

25. ———. *The Potato Story: And Other Missionary Stories for Children*. Camp Hill, Pa.: Christian Publications, 1992. 53 p.

26. Allison, Norman E. "The Contribution of Cultural Anthropology to Missiology." *Alliance Academic Review* (1996): 85-104.

Missiologists have learned from cultural anthropologists that the message of the Gospel must be contextualized, i.e., presented in words and symbols that can be understood and appropriated by the receiving culture, for missionary work to be successful. Effective contextualization requires a proper balance between biblical relativism and biblical absolutism.

27. Anderson, E. M. (1887-1948). *From Ship to Pulpit: An Autobiography*. Grand Rapids, Mich.: Zondervan, 1942. 134 p.

A Norwegian immigrant, Anderson was trained at Nyack, ordained by A. B. Simpson, and went on to become an Alliance evangelist and an Evangelical Free Church pastor.

28. Anderson, F. Ione. "Missionary Education in the Local Church of the Christian and Missionary Alliance." Master's thesis, Wheaton College, 1964. 104 p.

Based on a survey of Alliance churches throughout North America. The most effective agencies of missionary education in Alliance churches are the Ladies' Missionary Society and the annual missionary convention. However, many churches lack a comprehensive plan for missionary education.

29. Anderson, Mavis L., ed. *Charting the Course: A Handbook for Sunday School Workers*. Harrisburg, Pa.: Christian Publications, 1955. 128 p.

30. Anderson, Robert Mapes. *Vision of the Disinherited: The Making of American Pentecostalism*. New York: Oxford University Press, 1979. 334 p.

Includes a detailed discussion of the influence of the Alliance on American Pentecostalism and of A. B. Simpson's views on glossolalia, as well as considerable biographical information on ex-Alliance Pentecostals.

31. Andre, Kouakou Kouadio. "Les Méthodes d'Évangélisation Utilisées par les Missionaires Évangéliques en Côte d'Ivoire." Licencié ès sciences thesis, Faculté Libre de Théologie Évangélique de Vaux-sur-Seine, 1975. 143 p.

An appreciative assessment of the work of Alliance missionaries in Côte d'Ivoire. The mistakes they made were "formal" and not "fundamental" in nature. Ivoirians need to take greater responsibility for leadership of the C&MA church in their country.

32. Andrews, Leslie (A)lice. "The Measurement of Adult MKs' Well-Being." *Evangelical Missions Quarterly* 31 (October 1995): 418-27.

Some of the 608 respondents were children of C&MA missionaries. Most "seemed to be doing very well with respect to their purpose and direction in life, their sense of connectedness to God and their overall spiritual well-being" (p. 426). Those who were not doing well tended to come from dysfunctional families. MK boarding schools that provide a strong nurturing environment are unlikely to have any lasting negative effects on children of strong and healthy families.

33. ———. "Perceptions of the Role of Women in the Christian and Missionary Alliance." D. Min. diss., Columbia Theological Seminary, 1976. 112 p.

Proposes various strategies to overcome the perception of women as second-class citizens and to give women a broader range of ministry within the denomination. "Either we should continue our historic practice of allowing 'liberty in non-essentials' and permit women to exercise their gifts in ministry as they feel called by God the Spirit, or we should develop definite theological bases for ordination and specific ministries which will be consistent with one another."

34. ———. "Restricted Freedom: A. B. Simpson's View of Women in Ministry." In *The Birth of a Vision*, eds. David Hartzfeld and Charles Nienkirchen, 219-40. Regina, Sask.: His Dominion, 1986.

Simpson welcomed women as co-workers, and they served as missionaries, evangelists, preachers, and officers in the Alliance. He respected their spiritual depth, intelligence, and giftedness, and he often praised them publicly. At the same time, his (at times inaccurate and inconsistent) exegesis of Scripture led him to conclude that women ought not to serve as elders or pastors.

35. Anggu, Peter. "The Role of Theological Education in Evangelism and Church Growth in the Kemah Injil Church of Indonesia." D. Min. diss., Fuller Theological Seminary, 1986. 145 p.

Includes a history of the Kemah Injil (Gospel Tabernacle, i.e., C&MA) Church of Indonesia, the world's largest Alliance church, focusing on the crucial role that Jaffray School of Theology has played in its expansion.

36. Archilla, Barbara Benjamin. "Seminario Biblico Alianza: The Impossible Community." *Urban Mission* 10 (June 1993): 50-59.

The C&MA's Spanish Ministries Department opened this seminary in New York City in 1979 to provide formal leadership training at the Bible institute level to the leaders of Hispanic churches in the Greater New York City area. Archilla, a former C&MA missionary to Ecuador, directed the seminary from 1979 to 1989.

37. Arlington Memorial Church. *Cost of Missions: Christian and Missionary Alliance Martyred Missionaries*. n.p.: Arlington Memorial Church, 1983. 16 p.

Arlington Memorial Church was named in memory of the 28 Alliance missionary martyrs whose brief biographies appear in this booklet.

38. Armstrong, Edward. *Prayer and God's Infinite Power*. New York: Christian Alliance Pub. Co., [ca. 1910]. 22 p.

Fervent prayer is a prerequisite for revival.

39. ———. *To Me to Live Is Christ*. New York: Christian Alliance Pub. Co., [ca. 1900]. 15 p.

A reflection on Phil. 1:21. "To me to live is Christ" is the testimony of one who, through being baptised in the Holy Spirit, has allowed Christ to inhabit every aspect of life.

40. Arthur, Joseph. "The Sleeping Giant: A Strategy for a Student Program of Evangelism and Church Planting in the Philippines." D. Miss. diss., Fuller Theological Seminary, 1974. 437 p.

The Philippine Student Alliance Lay Movement (PSALM) ministers more effectively to university students than most parachurch organizations because it not only has an aggressive program of evangelism, Christian nurture, and social action but also incorporates converts into the church and teaches them how to plant churches.

41. Atkinson, Harley T., and Fred R. Wilson. "Career Development Cycles and Job Satisfaction of Youth Pastors in the Christian and Missionary Alliance." *Christian Education Journal* 11 (winter 1991): 39-50.

Most Alliance youth pastors in Canada and the United States leave their positions within two years. However, few do so because they are dissatisfied with the ministry. Rather, many are prospective missionaries who resign from their churches after having satisfied the C&MA's requirements of two years of home service.

42. *Atlas Showing Mission Fields of the Christian and Missionary Alliance*. New York: The Alliance. Foreign Dept., 1922. 100 p.

Includes not only maps but, for each country or region, general statistical information, an overview of Protestant missionary activity, and a detailed description of past and present missionary work by the C&MA.

43. Atter, Gordon F. *The Third Force*, 2nd ed. Peterborough, Ont.: The College Press, 1965. 325 p.

Mentions that, during his post-Spirit-baptism ministry as an Alliance missionary in northwestern China, W. W. Simpson cleansed lepers, healed the deaf, and even raised the dead (p. 65).

44. Bachman, Anthony. *I Was a Stranger and. . . : Joyce and Morgan Ilgenfritz's Ministry to the Hurting and Homeless*. Camp Hill, Pa.: Christian Publications, 1988. 191 p.

The Ilgenfritzes open their home to poor, homeless, and otherwise disenfranchised people as a way of modeling Christ's love.

45. Bailey, Anita M., comp. *Heritage Cameos.* Camp Hill, Pa.: Christian Publications, 1987. 87 p.

Biographical sketches of more than 20 exemplary Alliance women, including Margaret Simpson ("She was willing always to submerge herself into her husband's identity" [p. 6]). This is the only published source of information on many of the biographees.

46. Bailey, Keith M., ed. *As Many as Possible.* Harrisburg, Pa.: Christian Publications, 1979.

Addresses delivered at the Leadership Evangelism Conference held at Nyack, N.Y., 26 February–2 March 1979.

47. ———. *Bringing Back the King: An Introduction to the History and Thought of The Christian and Missionary Alliance.* Nyack, N.Y.: Alliance Centers for Theological Study, Office of Specialized Ministries, Christian and Missionary Alliance, 1985. 181 p.

A textbook, for use in the in-service training of Alliance pastors, on Alliance history, missions, doctrine, and polity.

48. ———. *Care of Converts*. Harrisburg, Pa.: Christian Publications, 1979. 95 p.

A leadership training manual for discipleship. Cf. 49.

49. ———. *Care of Converts: A Comprehensive Training Tool for Discipling New Believers*. Camp Hill, Pa.: Christian Publications, 1997. 192 p.

Reprint of 48 and 53. Includes a leader's guide.

50. ———. *The Children's Bread: Divine Healing*. Harrisburg, Pa.: Christian Publications, 1977. 237 p.

Healing by supernatural intervention through prayer in the name of Jesus is primarily a benefit for the believer and only secondarily a sign to the unbeliever of the power of God. Divine healing is not so much a matter of deliverance from sickness and injury as it is a daily drawing of strength from the healing Christ for the needs of the body.

51. ———. *Christ's Coming and His Kingdom*. Camp Hill, Pa.: Christian Publications, 1981. 191 p.

A popular exposition of Alliance eschatology along standard premillennial and pretribulation rapture lines.

52. ———. *The Church Planter's Manual*. Harrisburg, Pa.: Christian Publications, 1981. 111 p.

Papers (mostly practical in nature) presented by C&MA pastors and administrators at a Church Planting Symposium held at Nyack, N.Y., in February 1980.

53. ———. *Learning to Live*. Harrisburg, Pa.: Christian Publications, 1978. 64 p.

A catechism for new believers incorporating such Alliance distinctives as the filling of the Spirit as a second work of grace, premillennial eschatology, and physical healing and health as provisions of the Atonement. Cf. 48 and 49.

54. ———. "A New Significance for the Doctrine of Healing in the Atonement." *His Dominion* 13 (summer 1987): 2-12.

The current openness of the medical community to nonmedical forms of healing has restored the credibility of divine healing in medical circles. However, the church must avoid any marriage of the sacred with the secular by continuing to insist that divine healing involves "the direct intervention of the living Christ on the basis of his [atoning] death and resurrection" (p. 12).

55. ———. *Servants in Charge*. Harrisburg, Pa.: Christian Publications, 1979. 123 p.

The pastor oversees the church (lay) elders help provide pastoral care, and deacons mostly administer ministries related to material things. These three offices either comprise, or are represented on, the executive board that governs the church. Pastors and elders are chiefly responsible for praying for the sick and for distributing the communion elements. Deacons may assist in the latter function, and deaconesses may exercise certain of the roles of the deacon.

56. ———. *Strange Gods: Responding to the Rise of Spirit-Worship in America*. Camp Hill, Pa.: Christian Publications, 1998. 254 p.

The increasing popularity of New Age religion, the growing number of immigrants from animist cultures, and the romanticization of native American religions have increased the likelihood that North American Christians will encounter demons. Hence this theology of, and manual on, spiritual warfare and exorcism. Includes reminiscences from the author's experiences as a C&MA missionary to North American Indians.

57. ———. *Ten Biblical Principles for Effective Deliverance Ministry*. Camp Hill, Pa.: Christian Publications, 1998. 31 p.

Reprint of chapter six of 56.

58. Bailey, Richard W. *The Seven Deadly Sins in the Contemporary Church*. Contemporary Christian Living Series. Camp Hill, Pa.: Christian Publications, 1993. 21 p.

Relevance has replaced revelation, flashing images have replaced a sense of God's presence, sensitivity has replaced compassion, human words have replaced God's Word, experience has replaced doctrine, psychology has replaced Christology, and pluralism has replaced proclamation.

59. Bainbridge, Harriette S. *Life for Soul and Body*. New York: Alliance Press Co., 1906. 170 p.

A manual on divine healing that places healing in the broader context of Christian holiness, i.e., as the consequence of entrusting all of one's life to the indwelling Christ whose atonement makes healing possible.

60. Baldwin, Lindley J. *African Prince*. Iloria, Nigeria: United Missionary Society, 1965. 47 p.

An adaptation of 62.

61. ———. *The Ebony Saint: Samuel Morris's Miraculous Journey of Faith*. Evesham, England: Arthur James, 1967. 125 p.

Reprint of 62.

62. ———. *The March of Faith: The Challenge of Samuel Morris to Undying Life and Leadership*. Chicago: Mary E. Baldwin, 1966. 92 p.

The fullest account of the life of Samuel Morris (1872-1893). Having miraculously escaped slavery in his native Côte d'Ivoire, Morris was led to faith by Methodist missionaries in Liberia who told him that Stephen Merritt (an early associate of A. B. Simpson) could teach him about the

Holy Spirit. But the opposite proved to be the case: Morris, having against all odds made his way to New York City, spent only a week with Merritt, but he made a lifelong impression on him. After Sammy's departure, Merritt began a remarkable ministry of healing and evangelism. Morris went on to study at Taylor University, where his St. Teresa of Lisieux-like faith inspired a revival. Cf. 60 and 61.

63. Bales, Milton. *Saved and Sealed*, 4th ed. New York: Alliance Press Co., 1905. 100 p.

Sermons on salvation and the deeper life: "there is a deeper, richer life in Jesus than the ordinary Christian is aware of" (p. 46). Conversion is comparable to Israel's escape from Egypt, the filling of the Spirit to Israel's entry into the Promised Land. The latter involves the actual indwelling of the believer by Christ. This experience must be personally appropriated—and vigorously cultivated once received.

64. ———. *Types of the Holy Spirit, and Other Addresses*. New York: Alliance Press Co., [ca. 1900]. 148 p.

Sanctification involves being saved "through and through." Conversion provides the convert with a new spirit, baptism with the Holy Spirit provides the Holy Spirit himself. The life of every truly consecrated Christian is characterized by a division between pre- and post-"Pentecostal" experience.

65. *Baliem Beachhead*. New York: The Christian and Missionary Alliance, 1954. 15 p.

Describes the first contact of C&MA missionaries with the Dani, a primitive and warlike people of Irian Jaya.

66. Ballard (J)ohn Hudson (1880-1974). "The Gift of Tongues." In *The Signs of the Times, or God's Message for To-day: A Symposium on New Theology, Christian Science, the Lord's Coming, the Gift of Tongues, and the Deeper Spiritual Life*, 138-56. New York: Alliance Press Co., 1907.

The gift of tongues is a legitimate gift of the Spirit that ought to be experienced by some of the members of each local congregation. As such, it should be welcomed, if bestowed, and not resisted. Tongues are not, however, the necessary evidence of the infilling of the Holy Spirit. They are one of the lesser gifts; their primary purpose is personal edification. Their public use should be controlled by strict scriptural guidelines.

67. ———. *Spirit, Soul and Body*. New York: Alliance Press Co., 1910. 259 p.

Scripture and experience indicate that the condition of the body profoundly affects one's sense of spiritual and mental well-being, since the inner and outer natures are essentially a unity. Hence the need to subject the heart, body, thoughts, emotions, will, soul, and spirit to the sanctifying influence of the Holy Spirit.

68. Barnes, Samuel G. *La historia de la salud del hombre*. Temuco, Chile: Imprenta y Editorial Alianza, 1959. 105 p.

An overview of salvation history.

69. Barnes, Vera F. (1900-1994). *Daybreak below the Border*. Harrisburg, Pa.: Christian Publications, 1962. 167 p.

Reminiscences from Vera F. and Samuel G. Barnes's forty-year careers as C&MA missionaries to Argentina (1920-1959).

70. ———. *Milagros en el desierto*. Buenos Aires: La Alianza Cristiana y Missionera Argentina, 1977. 147 p.

A detailed account of the missionary work of the author and her husband.

71. ———. *Miles beyond in Brazil*. Harrisburg, Pa.: Christian Publications, 1965. 134 p.

Reminiscences from the year the Barneses spent in Brazil as C&MA missionaries.

72. ———. *Yonder Horizon*. Greensboro, N.C.: Vera F. Barnes, n.d.

Further reminiscences from the Barneses' years as C&MA missionaries in Argentina.

73. Barney (G)eorge Linwood (1923-). "The Challenge of Anthropology to Current Missiology." *International Bulletin of Missionary Research* 5 (October 1981): 172-77.

God's reconciling activity in drawing self-centered human culture into relationship with himself is supracultural in nature, but needs to be appropriated in the context of culture: the Gospel, once embraced, will modify one's interpretation of experience and one's social behavior. The role of the missionary is to facilitate this process, and so missionary candidates need to be trained in ethnography.

74. ———. "The Meo—an Incipient Church." *Practical Anthropology* 4 (March-April 1957): 31-50.

An ethnography of the Hmong living around Xieng Khouang, Laos, and a brief history of the church Alliance missionaries began among them in the early 1950s. Despite mistakes made by the missionaries Christianity has been well received by this group of Hmong, and the process of acculturation is well underway.

75. ———. "The Supracultural and the Cultural: Implications for Frontier Missions." In *The Gospel and Frontier Peoples: Report of a Consultation, December 1972*, ed. R. Pierce Beaver, 48-57. South Pasadena, Calif.: William Carey Library, 1973.

Reflections on inculturation drawn from the author's experiences as a missionary to the Hmong of Indochina.

76. Barney (G)eorge Linwood (1923-), and Donald N. Larson. "How We Can Lick the Language Problem." *Evangelical Missions Quarterly* 4 (fall 1967): 31-40.

Missionary success is directly related to language skill. Therefore, missionaries should be assigned on the basis of aptitude and motivation, so that candidates with the greatest aptitude and motivation should be sent to those peoples whose languages are the most difficult (for a Westerner) to acquire.

77. Barratt, Thomas Ball (1862-1940). *When the Fire Fell, and an Outline of My Life*. Oslo: T. B. Ball, 1927. 229 p.

Barratt had a profound experience of the Holy Spirit at the Alliance guest home in New York City after attending a communion service conducted by Henry Wilson.

78. Bartleman, Frank (1871-1936). *Azusa Street*. Plainfield, N.J.: Logos International, 1980. 210 p.

Reprint of 79. Pages 105-13 record his ministry at Alliance gatherings.

79. ———. *How Pentecost Came to Los Angeles: As It Was in the Beginning,* 2nd ed. Los Angeles: by the author, 1925. 167 p.

Bartleman preached at a number of Alliance branches and conventions in 1907, including a convention at the Gospel Tabernacle in New York, which A. B. Simpson also attended. On the latter occasion, a woman sang a beautiful song in the Spirit, and Simpson was "tremendously impressed by it. He had been much opposed to the 'Pentecostal' work. Doubtless God gave it as a witness to him" (p. 109). Cf. 78 and 80.

80. ———. *Witness to Pentecost: The Life of Frank Bartleman*. The Higher Christian Life. New York: Garland Publishing, 1985. 468 p.
Includes a reprint of 79.

81. Baxter, Elizabeth. *Addresses on Divine Healing*. New York: Christian Alliance Pub. Co., [1900?].
Mrs. Baxter was the editor of the British magazine *Thy Healer*, which published several of A. B. Simpson's addresses on divine healing.

82. Baxter, Elmer. "Activities on the Field which Will Prepare Students to Re-enter Their Home Culture." In *Compendium of the International Conference on Missionary Kids: New Directions in Missions: Implications for MK's*, eds. Beth A. Tetzel and Patricia Mortenson, 149-57. West Brattleboro, Vt.: ICMK, 1986.
Covers everything from driver education to how to use a telephone. Based on the author's experience as director of Dalat School, the Alliance's boarding school in Malaysia for children of missionaries.

83. Baxter, Norman A. "A Study of the Effective Elements in the Preaching of Albert B. Simpson." S.T.B. thesis, Biblical Seminary in New York, 1947. 85 p.
Simpson was an effective preacher because he stressed both exposition and doctrine, spoke on neglected truths, and gave spiritual leadership through his sermons.

84. *Be Ready!* New York: The Christian and Missionary Alliance, [ca. 1919]. 8 p.
A compendium of evangelistically and millennially loaded Bible verses.

85. Bechtel, John (1899-). *The Chicken Devil Mystery*. Grand Rapids: Eerdmans, 1944. 102 p.
This work, and the author's other novels, are loosely based on his experiences as a C&MA missionary to Hong Kong.

86. ———. *The Dragon Boat Mystery*. Grand Rapids: Eerdmans, 1943. 88 p.

87. ———. *Fetters Fall*. Chicago: William H. Dietz, 1945. 223 p.

88. ———. *The Harrison Road Mystery*. Grand Rapids: Eerdmans, 1941. 104 p.

89. ———. *The Mystery of East Mountain Temple*. Chicago: Moody Press, 1939. 127 p.

90. ———. *The Mystery Ship*. Wheaton, Ill.: Van Kampen Press, 1952. 126 p.

91. ———. *Perla of the Walled City*. Grand Rapids: Eerdmans, 1946.

92. ———. *Pig's Birthday*. Chicago: Moody Press, 1942. 248 p.

93. ———. *The Shanghai Mystery*. Grand Rapids: Eerdmans, 1945. 88 p.

94. ———. *The Year of the Tiger*. Chicago: Moody Press, 1946. 218 p.

95. Beckdahl, Agnes N. T. (1876-1968). *A Witness of God's Faithfulness*. Lucknow, India: Lucknow Publishing House, [193-?]. 193 p.

This collection of the letters of Beckdahl, an Assemblies of God missionary to India, includes an account of her experiences as a student at Nyack during the revival of 1909.

96. Bedford, William Boyd, Jr. "A Larger Christian Life: A. B. Simpson and the Early Years of the Christian and Missionary Alliance." Ph.D. diss., University of Virginia, 1992. 373 p.

The Alliance had to sacrifice some of its original distinctives in order to resolve the tension between its outward-directed emphasis on evangelism and its inward-directed stress on holiness and physical healing. It has been successful in missions and church planting, but its most distinctive emphases, holiness and healing, figure less prominently in the life of the C&MA than they once did, largely as a result of the Alliance's reaction to Pentecostalism.

97. Bedford-Jones, T. A. *Letter to the Rev. Henry Wilson D. D., Stating Objections to His Recent Pamphlet and Submitting Other Reasons for the Apparent Decrease in Our Church Membership*. CIHM/IMCH Microfiche series, no. 10254. [Kingston, Ont.]: [British Whig], 1883. 19 p.

A response to 2331. The decrease in numbers of Anglicans in Canada is not the result of clerical incompetence, but rather of the selfishness, greed, and stinginess of the Anglican laity.

98. Bell, James B. *Divine Healing from a Medical Standpoint*. New York: Christian Alliance Pub. Co., [ca. 1900].

99. Bell, Robert W., and D. Bruce Lockerbie. *In Peril on the Sea: A Personal Remembrance*. New York: Doubleday, 1984. 284 p.

In August 1942 Ethel Bell (1893-1983), a Canadian Alliance missionary to Mali, sails for home on a freighter with her two children, Robert and Mary. The freighter is torpedoed by a U-boat and the family and the others on board spend 20 days adrift in the South Atlantic on a small raft. In the 1970s Robert contacts crew members from the U-boat and comes to terms with his need to forgive them. In 1982 he travels to Germany for a reunion of the U-boat crew. Cf. 100 and 2254.

100. ———. *In Peril on the Sea: The Story of Ethel Bell and Her Children Robert and Mary*. The Jaffray Collection of Missionary Portraits, 14. Camp Hill, Pa.: Christian Publications, 1996. 189 p.

Abridgement of 99.

101. Belsham, R. A. *God's Covenants*. Harrisburg, Pa.: Christian Alliance Pub. Co., 1931. 60 p.

Sermons on the nine covenants God makes in relation to the seven dispensations of human history. Foreword acknowledges the author's indebtedness to C. I. Scofield.

102. Benson, John T., Jr. *A History 1898-1915 of the Pentecostal Mission, Inc. Nashville, Tennessee.* Nashville, Tenn.: Trevecca Press, 1977. 238 p.

The first missionaries of the fledgling Pentecostal Mission were sent out under the auspices of the C&MA. In 1901, when it became unclear which mission they were actually responsible to, W. A. Farmer, Ada Beeson (later Ada Beeson Farmer), and Annie Goode resigned from the Pentecostal Mission and joined the South China Mission of the C&MA.

103. Best, Harold Melvin. "A Study of Some Aspects of the Theology of A. B. Simpson, the Founder of the Christian and Missionary Alliance." Master's thesis, Pacific Bible College of Azusa, 1957. 52 p.

A. B. Simpson never held to a "repressionist" or "suppressionist" view of sanctification. Holiness, in Simpson's view, describes a state higher than Adamic perfection. Neither Simpson nor Wesley preached human perfection, and there is perfect agreement between them concerning sanctification: any apparent differences derive from Simpson's avoidance of the term "eradication."

104. Beyerle, Edith, ed. *Daily Meditations, Volume 4*. Harrisburg, Pa.: Christian Publications, [ca. 1960]. 34 p.

This series of extracts from *The Alliance Witness* was published quarterly.

105. ———. *Pots of Gold*. New York: Loiseaux Brothers, 1946. 218 p.
A missionary novel by an Alliance missionary to China.

106. ———. *Rainbows*. Grand Rapids: Zondervan, 1939. 348 p.
A missionary novel.

107. Bibighaus, Alexandria Wasilewska (1908-). *From the Broadway to Narrow Way: The Testimony of a Professional Dancer*. [Nyack, N.Y.?]: Christian and Missionary Alliance, [198-?]. 75 p.

Alexandria Wasilewska was a professional dancer who performed in Broadway productions before her conversion. She became a licensed evangelist with the C&MA in 1933, serving in this capacity until 1940, when she married Alliance pastor Alexander Bibighaus.

108. Billy Graham Center. Archives. *Jazz Age Evangelism: Paul Rader and the Chicago Gospel Tabernacle, 1922-1933*. Wheaton, Ill.: Billy Graham Center, 1984. 44 p.

The catalogue of an exhibition of Rader memorabilia at the Billy Graham Center Archives: photographs of and biographical vignettes on Rader (president of the C&MA 1917-1924) and associates reveal the influence he exerted on other evangelical leaders.

109. Bingham, Rowland (V)ictor (1872-1942). *The Bible and the Body, or Healing in the Scriptures*, 2nd ed. Toronto: Evangelical Publishers, 1924. 90 p.

The Alliance doctrine that healing is provided for in the Atonement is based on a faulty interpretation of Matt. 8:17, 1 Pet. 2:24, and Isa. 53. A. B. Simpson, though a man of exemplary godliness, erred in declaring the use of means in healing to be the mark of a deficient faith. He himself used eyeglasses. The Bosworth brothers err in teaching that healing is partaken of in the Lord's Supper, and that failure to recognize this while partaking can lead to sickness or even death. Includes a refutation of 176.

110. ———. "The Bosworth Campaign in Toronto." *The Evangelical Christian*, July 1921, 199-200, 218.

Many people were either converted or filled with the Holy Spirit, but relatively few were healed during the month-long campaign, despite F. F. Bosworth's insistence that healing is "in the Atonement." Bosworth is to be commended for his overall integrity, however, and for advocating the use of "means" in healing (which teaching the C&MA itself should adopt).

111. ———. "A Great Leader Taken." *The Evangelical Christian,* December 1919, 367.

A glowing tribute to the recently deceased A. B. Simpson, whose views, except for that of "healing in the Atonement," Bingham enthusiastically shared.

112. ———. "John Salmon: A Tribute." *The Evangelical Christian,* September 1918, 236-39.

A eulogy to the recently deceased Salmon, who had been the author's mentor. Salmon receives praise for his conspicuous piety, missionary zeal, and his ultimate repudiation of Pentecostal excesses, but not for his "[overstepping] the warrant of the Scriptures in accepting the theory of the Christian Alliance that divine healing is in the Atonement" (p. 238).

113. Birrel, Frances Catlin (1869-1964). *Frances Catlin Birrel: Faithful Missionary, Wife, Mother: Her Story, with Anecdotes and Highlights*. n.p.: Barbara Ann Birrel Shockey, 1985. 89 p.

Frances Catlin went to China in 1894, married fellow C&MA missionary Matthew Brown Birrel in 1896, and served in China with him until 1927, and again from 1937 to 1940. Although she believed she had been trained well at Nyack, she also felt that its students should have been trained to study the Bible for themselves and not simply to accept the teaching of their instructors.

114. Birrel, Matthew Brown (1869-1957). *Matthew Brown Birrel, Missionary to the Chinese: Jottings, an Autobiography*. n.p., 1981. 87 p.

A Scot, who later emigrated to Canada, Birrel began his career as a C&MA missionary to China in 1892. Cf. 113.

115. Bisceglia, John B. "The Pioneer as Moody of the Italians." In *Italian Evangelical Pioneers*. Kansas City, Mo.: Brown-White-Lowell Press, 1948. 143 p.

A synopsis of the life of Michele Nardi. Cf. 1762.

116. Bixler, Virgil. "Founding Issues: The Missionary Church Association." *Reflections: A Publication of the Missionary Church Historical Society* 1 (summer 1993): 16-21.

In 1898, a group of alienated (mostly Defenseless) Mennonites who had experienced the baptism of the Holy Spirit decided not to unite with the C&MA because the C&MA was not interested in organizing local churches. Some of the founding fathers of the resulting Missionary Church Association, e.g., A. E. Funk, D. Y. Schultz, B. P. Lugibihl, and D. W. Kerr came from German-speaking C&MA churches.

117. Blackett, George Milton (1891?-1961). *The Man of Uz: A Revised Text and Exposition of the Book of Job*. [Calgary, Alta.?]: by the author, [196-?]. 110 p.

The "revised text" is actually a slightly edited version of the KJV.

118. ———. *Preparation for Church Membership*. Edited by Roy McIntyre. Calgary, Alta.: Christian and Missionary Alliance. Western Canadian District, 1968. 41 p.

Sets forth the New Testament principles of the Church, explains Alliance doctrinal distinctives, and gives a brief history of the C&MA.

119. ———. *Radio Revival Memories*. [Regina, Sask.?]: n.p., [1942?]. 23 p.

Transcripts of evangelistic sermons preached 9-13 February 1942 on the Haven of Hope Broadcast (CJRM, Regina, Sask.)

120. Blackstone (W)illiam (E)ugene (1841-1935). "God's Dealing with the Nations." In *The Signs of the Times, or God's Message for To-Day: A Symposium on New Theology, Christian Science, the Lord's Coming, the Gift of Tongues, and the Deeper Spiritual Life*, 29-51. New York: Alliance Press Co., 1907.

The political control that the Gentile nations exert over the world could end within 90 years. Some great act of deliverance for the Jewish people is at hand. It could occur in 1914, 1925, or 1933, depending on which of the various interpretations of the chronological reckoning of Israel's punishments (cf. Lev. 26) is valid.

121. ———. *Jesus Is Coming*, 3rd ed. rev. Chicago: Fleming H. Revell, 1908. Reprint, New York: Christian Alliance Pub. Co., 1908. 252 p.

The classic expression of premillennial eschatology.

122. ———. *Satan, His Kingdom and Its Overthrow*. Chicago: Fleming H. Revell, 1900. Reprint, New York: Christian Alliance Pub. Co., 1900. 54 p.

A compendium of the prophecies relating to the activity of Satan during the end times. One of these activities is Zionism, which Blackstone supported because he believed that the reestablishment of a Jewish nation in Palestine is a necessary condition for the return of Christ. Yet he had no illusions about the secular nationalism that motivated most Zionists.

123. ———. *Signs of the Lord's Coming*. New York: Christian Alliance Pub.Co., [ca. 1898-1913]. 23 p.

The signs are: the prevalence of travel and knowledge, perilous times, spiritualism, apostasy, the accumulation of wealth, and Zionism. The dates 1914, 1926, and 1933 "will [each] mark some specific great event in Israel's restoration, and . . . at the latter date all Gentile domination over them may pass away forever. . . . There remain less than seventy-five years [until] . . . the ushering in of the Millennial Kingdom" (p. 19, 21).

124. ———. The "Times of the Gentiles" and "The Time of the End." New York: Christian Alliance Pub. Co., [1921?]. 32 p.

Basically a reworking of 125 to include reflections on how the political events of 1915-1920 have coincided with biblical predictions regarding the Gentiles.

125. ———. *The Times of the Gentiles and the War in the Light of Prophecy*. New York: Christian Alliance Pub. Co., [1915?]. 32 p.

Biblical prophecies relating to the "times of the Gentiles" indicate a period in history, likely 1915 or 1916-1934 or 1935 (if a year-day interpretation of the relevant biblical prophecies is adopted) when Gentile political power will be destroyed and Israel, though terribly punished, will be restored as the center of a worldwide theocracy. The return of Christ will come sometime after these events have taken place. Cf. 124.

126. Blanchard, Charles (A)lbert (1848-1925). *The Bible Teaching concerning Sickness*. Chicago: Bible Institute Colportage Assoc., [ca. 1900]. 8 p.

Satan is the ultimate source of all sickness, but his activities are restricted by God. Sickness often results from sin: one's own or the sins of others. Some people are sick so that God, in healing them, might be glorified. Remedies, e.g., quinine in malarial areas, should be used thankfully, but sparingly. Sick Christians should confess all known sin and invite the elders of their church to anoint them with oil and pray for them.

127. ———. *The Christian and the Theatre*. Chicago: Bible Institute Colportage Assoc., [ca. 1900]. 6 p.

128. ———. *Christian Science and the Word of God*. Chicago: Bible Institute Colportage Assoc., [ca. 1900]. 15 p.

Despite the fact that people have been healed, overcome stress, and been delivered from enslaving habits through Christian Science its teachings are unbiblical, nonsensical, and evil because they are based on pantheism and thus deny the reality of evil and matter and render meaningless Christ's incarnation and atonement.

129. ———. *Christianity in the Home*. Chicago: Bible Institute Colportage Assoc., [ca. 1900]. 8 p.

If the Gospel is to be "social" in its proper sense then its effects must first be felt in the home. For this to happen, family worship needs to be revived.

130. ———. *Church and Lodge*. Chicago: National Christian Assoc., 1895. 15 p.

More than a million American men belong to a lodge of some sort. Christians must dissociate themselves from such associations, because they require secrecy, replace the Gospel with bland moral teaching, promote charity only to fellow lodge members, and conduct their affairs without any reference to Christ.

131. ———. *Getting Things from God: A Study of the Prayer Life*. Chicago: Bible Institute Colportage Assoc., 1915. 270 p.

The crassness of the title belies the author's concern that his readers be transformed through prayer and not simply have their prayers answered.

132. ———. *An Infallible Guide: Intimate Talks about Divine Guidance*. Chicago: Bible Institute Colportage Assoc., 1926. 62 p.

God is determined to guide those who seek him. Meekness is the chief prerequisite on the part of the seeker. God guides through Scripture, the Holy Spirit, and human wisdom.

133. ———. *Light on the Last Days: Being Familiar Talks on the Book of Revelation*. Chicago: Bible Institute Colportage Assoc., 1918. 22 p.

Meditations from a premillennial perspective. Arranged thematically.

134. ———. *Method in Biblical Criticism*. Chicago: Bible Institute Colportage Assoc., 1922. 30 p.

The higher criticism of the Bible must be rejected because its proponents have poisoned their minds with tobacco, alcohol, and other drugs that have impaired their judgment. Higher critics impugn the integrity and authority of the Scriptures and their conclusions are based on conjecture rather than on reason and the careful examination of evidence.

135. ———. *Modern Secret Societies*, 3rd ed. Chicago: National Christian Assoc., 1903. 310 p.

Secret societies are a menace to true faith, because in their rituals they do not acknowledge Christ as Savior or Christianity as the only true religion.They are little more than associations for mutual protection in which good men, in rubbing shoulders with bad men, lose their religious zeal.

136. ———. *An Old Testament Gospel: A Prophet's Message to Men of Today*. Chicago: Bible Institute Colportage Assoc., 1918. 130 p.

Sermons on the book of Jonah.

137. ———. *President Blanchard's Autobiography: The Dealings of God with Charles Albert Blanchard, for Many Years a Teacher in Wheaton College, Wheaton, Illinois*. Boone, Ia.: Western Christian Alliance Pub. Co., 1915. 199 p.

Mentions nothing about his involvement with the C&MA. Does not include A. B. Simpson in his list of "Men and women I have known."

138. ———. *Visions and Voices, or Who Wrote the Bible.* New York: Christian Alliance Pub. Co., 1917. 184 p.

The most reasonable explanation for the miracles that are recounted in the Bible is that they actually happened. The same God who wrought them caused the Scriptures themselves to be written, hence the Scriptures are an infallible, supremely authoritative guide. Cf. 141.

139. ———. *What Is Confession of Sin?* Chicago: Bible Institute Colportage Assoc., [ca. 1919]. 12 p.

An example of the efficacy of confession is the Day of Humiliation, Fasting and Prayer held in England and the United States (in 1918), which hastened the end of World War I.

140. ———. *What to Do with Troubles*. Chicago: Bible Institute Colportage Assoc., 1914. 8 p.

Troubles should be told to Jesus, who is a sympathetic listener. He will either remove the source of the trouble or use it to transform the Christian into his likeness.

141. ———. *Who Wrote the Bible? Has God Spoken, or Only Men.* Chicago: Bible Institute Colportage Assoc., 1917. 184 p.

Reprint of 138.

142. ———. *The World War and the Bible.* Chicago: Bible Institute Colportage Assoc., 1918. 22 p.

Germany will be defeated, and her quest for world empire quashed, because Scripture teaches that no further world empires will be established until Jesus returns to reign over the world. Many contemporary phenomena and events, especially the capture of Jerusalem by British and Arab forces, are fulfilments of prophecies connected with the imminent return of Christ.

143. ———. *The Worship of Secret Societies Offered to Satan.* Chicago: National Christian Assoc., 1902. 24 p.

All secret societies operating in the United States are modeled on Freemasonry, a society that is religious in nature and promotes a way of salvation that rejects the fundamental doctrines of Christianity and the mediatorial work of Christ. In light of 1 Cor. 10:19,20, masonic worship is, in effect, the worship of devils.

144. Blanchard, Frances Carrothers. *The Life of Charles Albert Blanchard.* New York: Fleming H. Revell, 1932. 220 p.

Blanchard, a longtime president of Wheaton College (1882-1925) frequently preached at Alliance tabernacles during his final years. "He had been asked to assume control of this work after the death of A. B. Simpson, but did not deem it advisable to do so, as he did not hold the same views as the majority of Alliance members in regard to the use of medicines and the employment of physicians. Nor did he think that physical healing was in the Atonement. But he did believe in Divine healing" (p. 197).

145. Bliss, Maurice Elias. "A Study of Inerrancy with Particular Reference to Its Meaning in the Statement of Faith of The Christian and Missionary Alliance." Master's thesis, Wheaton College, 1968. 84 p.

In 1966, the C&MA's General Council voted not to include the word "inerrancy" in the Alliance's Statement of Faith. This move is indicative of the inclusiveness of a fellowship in which it is the authority of the Scriptures that is paramount.

146. *The Blood of the Martyrs.* New York: Christian and Missionary Alliance, 1946. 14 p.

Biographical sketches of the Alliance missionaries who were martyred during World War II.

147. Blumhofer, Edith L. *The Assemblies of God: A Chapter in the Story of American Pentecostalism. Vol. 1, to 1941.* Springfield, Mo.: Gospel Publishing House, 1989. 464 p.

Enumerates the close parallels in doctrine and organization between the Assemblies of God and the early C& MA. The Alliance differed from the AOG only in rejecting tongues as the initial physical evidence of the baptism of the Holy Spirit. "The Assemblies of God owes an incalculable debt to A. B. Simpson and the Christian and Missionary Alliance" (p. 123).

148. ———. "A Confused Legacy: Reflections of Evangelical Attitudes toward Ministering Women in the Past Century." *Fides et Historia* 32 (winter/spring 1990): 49-61.

A. B. Simpson was as confused as his contemporaries vis-à-vis ministering women. On the one hand he enthusiastically supported them, and they played a prominent role in a broad range of ministries in the early Alliance. On the other hand he believed that God had not entrusted them with the ministry of ecclesiastical rule—not even with eldership. If they ministered outside their God-given sphere they lost power. Once the Alliance evolved into a denomination these limitations pushed women into the background.

149. ———. "The Overcoming Life: A Study in the Reformed Evangelical Contribution to Pentecostalism." *Pneuma* 1 (spring 1979): 7-19.

A "strongly doctrinal emphasis on the Holy Spirit among non-Wesleyan evangelicals," was an important and largely overlooked factor in the development of Pentecostalism. A. B. Simpson "more fully than the others--stressed the 'allsufficiency' of Christ as a truth the believer could only apprehend by the Holy Spirit's revelation." Hence "Assemblies of God leaders considered that Simpson, probably more than any other single evangelical, had anticipated their movement" (p. 8, 10, 16).

150. ———. *"Pentecost in My Soul": Explorations in the Meaning of Pentecostal Experience in the Assemblies of God.* Springfield, Mo.: Gospel Publishing House, 1989. 265 p.

Includes biographical information on the following Pentecostals: Carrie Judd Montgomery, J. Roswell, and Alice Reynolds Flower, Noel

Perkin, W. W. Simpson, and Victor Plymire—all of whom were associated with the Alliance in some way before joining the Assemblies of God.

151. ———. "A Woman Used by the Spirit." *Paraclete* 21 (summer 1987): 5-9.

Marie Burgess Brown became a Pentecostal in 1907. That same year she moved to New York City, where she founded Glad Tidings Hall, a mission where many students from Nyack Missionary Training Institute and many other Alliance people were first exposed to Pentecostal teaching and the Pentecostal experience.

152. Boldt, Walter. *Five Keys to Prosperity*. Saskatoon, Sask.: by the author, 1980. 24 p.

Prosperity consists in having all one needs and the capacity to enjoy this state. Total commitment to Christ, tithing, generous giving, and perseverance in trial are the keys to attaining prosperity.

153. Bollback, Anthony G. (1922-). *To China and Back*. The Jaffray Collection of Missionary Portraits, 4. Camp Hill, Pa.: Christian Publications, 1991. 130 p.

Tony and Evelyn Bollback were Alliance missionaries to China, Hong Kong, and Japan. Tony Bollback went on to become district superintendent of the Western District of the (U. S.) C&MA. Cf. 391.

154. Bollback, James Anthony (1945-). "Missions Orientation in the Christian and Missionary Alliance." Master's thesis, Alliance School of Theology and Missions, 1978. 165 p.

This survey of American C&MA churches reveals that a communication gap exists between headquarters and the local church, and between pastors and laity; that Alliance youth tend not to believe in the lostness of the unevangelized; and that the church's theology and programs of evangelism result in little actual evangelization.

155. ———. "Protestant Missionary Activity in Hunan Province, China 1875-1912: History and Analysis." Master's thesis, Cornell University, 1981. 153 p.

Deals with the Alliance, one of the first missions to enter Hunan, as well as other mission agencies such as the C. I. M.

156. Boon, Harold Watson (1910-). "The Development of the Bible College or Institute in the United States and Canada since 1880 and Its

Relationship to the Field of Theological Education in America." Ed.D. diss., New York University, 1950. 204 p.

Mentions the influence of H. Grattan Guinness and the East London Institute for Home and Foreign Missions and of various European Bible institutes on A. B. Simpson's views on the education of missionaries and Christian workers.

157. ———. "How It All Began." *Christian Life* 21 (June 1959): 36-37.

A synopsis of 156.

158. Boon, J. Henry, Mrs. *Gospel Messages for Boys and Girls*. New York: Christian Alliance Pub. Co., 1926. 126 p.

Poems and stories illustrating the fourfold Gospel.

159. Borderud, Scott Russell. "The Doctrine of Sanctification of 'The Christian and Missionary Alliance' as Represented in Its Statement of Faith of 1965-1966." Th.D. diss., University of South Africa, 1993. 349 p.

A member of the Board of Managers of the C&MA in the USA, who has himself undergone a crisis experience of sanctification, Borderud proposes a restatement of the doctrine in the C&MA statement of faith that would purge it of the unbiblical and excessively experience-oriented terms "crisis" and "subsequent to conversion" in favor of a Christological focus on holy living in response to the work of Christ. Said change would be more consistent with the Scriptures and the rest of the fourfold Gospel.

160. Bosworth (F)red (F)rancis (1877-1958). *Appropriating Faith*. River Forest, Ill.: by the author, [192-?]. 8 p.

Such faith arises from and is based on God's promises. Also published in 162.

161. ———. *Bosworth's Life Story: The Life Story of Evangelist F. F. Bosworth as Told by Himself in the Alliance Tabernacle, Toronto*. Toronto: Alliance Book Room, [192-?]. 14 p.

Highlights from his healing and evangelistic ministries.

162. ———. *Christ the Healer: Messages on Divine Healing*, 7th ed. Miami Beach: Florence N. Bosworth, 1948. 249 p.

Includes eight sermons not found in 163.

163. ———. *Christ the Healer: Sermons on Divine Healing*. River Forest, Ill.: by the author, 1924. 172 p.

Five sermons: Healing is provided for in the Atonement, is universally available, originates in the compassion of Christ, and must be personally appropriated; Paul's thorn in the flesh was not a physical ailment. Also includes 176 and accounts of miraculous healings at Bosworth's evangelistic meetings.

164. ———. *Christ the Healer: Sermons on Divine Healing*. Miami, Fla.: by the author, 1924. 189 p.

Includes seven testimonies and a supplement not found in the other 1924 ed.

165. ———. "Confirming the Word by Signs Following: Jesus Saves, Heals and Baptizes." *Latter Rain Evangel*, December 1908, 7-8.

"We have never taught the people to expect anything more than the glory and power of the Lord and the 'unknown tongue' to accompany the immersing in the Holy Spirit" (p. 7).

166. ———. *"Do All Speak with Tongues?" (1 Cor. 12:30): An Open Letter to the Ministers and Saints of the Pentecostal Movement*. New York: Christian Alliance Pub. Co., [ca. 1918]. 23 p.

Glossolalia is not the initial physical evidence of the baptism of the Holy Spirit. The gift of tongues mentioned in 1 Cor. 12-14 is the same as the gift of tongues given at Pentecost.

167. ———. *"For This Cause," or Why Many Are Weak and Sickly and Why Many Die Prematurely*. New York: Christian Alliance Pub. Co., [192-?]. 32 p.

Healing for soul and body is anticipated typologically in the Old Testament and was experienced by the heroes of the Old Testament. Christ experienced both aspects, and they have been provided for in the Atonement. They are guaranteed in the Great Commission and are present in the Lord's Supper and the other ordinances of the Church.

168. ———. *The Fulness of God's Life: The Secret of Victory*. Miami Beach: n.p., [196-?]. 11 p.

"The Holy Spirit wants to quicken us to the extent that everything he has revealed concerning us in God's Word shall be fulfilled in us" (p. 10).

169. ———. *How to Appropriate the Redemptive and Covenant Blessing of Bodily Healing*. River Forest, Ill.: by the author, [192-?].

Such appropriation comes through expectant faith that God will heal until one has lived out one's allotted lifespan. Also published in 162.

170. ———. *How to Have a Revival: Nothing Can Hinder a Revival in the Church That Prays*. New York: Christian Alliance Pub. Co., [192-?]. 32 p.

Fervent intercessory prayer is the prerequisite for revival. Pages 25-32 consist of another work, which was possibly also published separately: *Bosworth Sermonettes*.

171. ———. *How to Receive Healing from Christ, or How to Receive from Christ the Fulfillment of His Promise*. Miami Beach: by the author, [192-?]. 24 p.

Since healing is provided for in the Atonement, "As we claim the Word of promise, in faith receiving a finished work, the sword of the Spirit strikes a blow to disease," although symptoms may persist for awhile. Also published in 162.

172. ———. *The Key to the Windows of Heaven, or God's Financial Plan*. Miami Beach: by the author, [193-?]. 24 p.

An apologetic for tithing.

173. ———. *Looking at the Unseen, or the Mental Habit of Faith*. Miami Beach: by the author, [194-?]. 40 p.

A sermon on 2 Cor. 4:18. The one "soaring in contemplation and looking toward the everlasting God will attend to all the little duties which come . . . every day and enjoy them" (p. 30).

174. ———. *Meditations on the Ninety-first Psalm*. Miami Beach: by the author, [191-?]. 53 p.

The blessings enumerated in Ps. 91 are for the Spirit-filled, for these enjoy constant communion with God and will enjoy a long life. Christians can become immune to disease by faith, as were Moses, Joshua, and Caleb.

175. ———. *Paul's Thorn*. River Forest, Ill.: by the author, [192-?].

This was not sickness, but "a demon spirit sent from Satan to make trouble for him wherever he went." Also published in 162.

176. ———. *Thirty-one Questions on Divine Healing*. Toronto: Alliance Book Store, [1923?]. 8 p.

"Propounded . . . in [the] Alliance Tabernacle, Toronto, Canada." Brief refutations to common objections to divine healing. Reprinted in 162.

177. ———. *Why Some Fail to Receive Healing from Christ: Presenting Twenty Proofs of God's Will to Heal and Twenty-two Reasons for Failure to Be Healed*. Miami Beach: by the author, [192-?]. 50 p.

Most of the reasons have to do with either lack of faith or misplaced faith on the part of the subject, the subject's Christian community, or those praying for the subject. Others include improper diet, unconfessed sin, and faulty traditions such as the belief that one can glorify God more by patience in suffering than by being healed.

178. Bosworth, F. F. (Mrs.). *The "Why?" and "How?" of Salvation*. Miami Beach: by the author, [193-?]. 39 p.

An evangelistic message giving an overview of salvation history.

179. Bounds, E. M. *Purpose in Prayer*. New York: Fleming H. Revell, 1920. Reprint, New York: Christian Alliance Pub. Co., 1920. 160 p.

180. Bratvold, Eleanor Ruth (1903-1973). *The Upper Springs: Original Poems*. Edited by Deane E. D. Downey. Langley, B.C.: Trinity Press, 1977. 71 p.

Some of the poems in this collection first appeared in *The Alliance Witness*.

181. Bray, Bill. "Evangelistic Explosion in Cambodia." *World Vision*, May 1972, 4-6.

Report of the highly successful evangelistic campaign held 13-15 April 1972 in Phnom Penh, by World Vision president Stanley Mooneyham. Mentions the plans of Cambodian Evangelical Church (a product of C&MA missionary work) to catechize the converts. Cf. 1290.

182. ———. "Love amidst Hatred: Vietnam's Amazing Christians." *Moody Monthly*, February 1973, 26-27.

C&MA missionaries have complied with the request of The Evangelical Church of Vietnam that they dissociate themselves from most public expressions of involvement in the church so that Christian witness would not be linked, in the public eye, with American military presence.

183. Brennen, Katherine Alberta. *Mrs. A. B. Simpson, the Wife, or Love Stands*. n.p., [1942?]. 31 p.

This idiosyncratic "domestic history" of the Simpson family (by one of A. B. Simpson's granddaughters) sheds considerable light on the day-to-day life of the Simpson family, and the difficulties endured and sacrifices made by Margaret Simpson out of devotion to her husband.

184. Brereton, Virginia Lieson. "The Bible Schools and Conservative Higher Education, 1880-1940." In *Making Higher Education Christian: The History and Mission of Evangelical Colleges in America*, eds. Joel A. Carpenter and Kenneth W. Shipps, 110-36. Grand Rapids: Christian University Press and Eerdmans, 1987.

Condensation of 185.

185. ———. "Protestant Fundamentalist Bible Schools, 1882-1940." Ph.D. diss., Columbia University, 1981. 467 p.

Includes a chapter on the Missionary Training Institute describing how A. B. Simpson's theological and educational goals were given institutional expression and giving a vivid description of life on campus. Simpson and the Missionary Training Institute exerted a conservative and moderating influence on fundamentalism by channeling fin-de-siècle religious fervour into an inward experience, which was expressed outwardly in holy living and tireless evangelism. Cf. 186.

186. ———. *Training God's Army: The American Bible School, 1880-1940.* Bloomington: Indiana University Press, 1990. 231 p.

Abridgement of 185.

187. Bressler, Ralph E. "A Follow-up Study of Graduates and Transfer Students of the Dalat High School of Dalat, Vietnam." M.Ed. thesis, Seattle Pacific College, 1967. 163 p.

Dalat (school for children of Alliance missionaries) transfer students got basically the some grades in the United States as they did at Dalat; and they received adequate spiritual, academic, and social formation.

188. Brickensteen, E. M. *A Child's Lesson on Divine Healing*. New York: The Junior Missionary Alliance, [189-?]. 16 p.

A forty-one-point catechism on healing through prayer.

189. Brodie, Katherine H. (d. 1925). *Sickness according to the Scripture.* Nyack, N.Y.: Christian Alliance Pub. Co., 1901. 7 p.

An annotated list of the references to disease and healing in the Bible.

190. ———. *Witnesses of His Resurrection*. New York: Alliance Press Co., [1904?]. 21 p.

The resurrection of Jesus has made available to believers life for spirit, soul, and body. This address, delivered at the Old Orchard Convention of August 1904, also describes the author's miraculous healing from a respiratory ailment.

191. Brouillette, Marg. "Apology to Abused Missionary Kids Has Profound Effect." *Faith Today* 17 (July-August 1999): 42-43.

In May 1999, the C&MA formally apologized to victims of sexual, physical, and emotional abuse at Mamou Academy, an MK school the Alliance had operated (1920-1971) in Guinea. Victims accepted the apology, regarding it as a significant step forward in the healing process.

192. Brown, Hulda (1918-). *A Heart for God*. Calgary, Alta.: Sable Press, 1995. 99 p.

Biography of Carol Brown Elliott (1951-1990), Alliance missionary to Guinea, Quebec, and Côte D'Ivoire.

193. Brown, May Sundell. *The Heart of Pak (a Korean Boy)*. Omaha: Omaha Gospel Tabernacle, 1960. 25 p.

An evangelistic story for children written by the daughter-in-law of noted Alliance evangelist and radio preacher, R. R. Brown.

194. Brown, Sarah A. *A New Lesson from an Old Book*. New York: Word, Work and World Pub. Co., [1883?].

A former missionary doctor to China suffering from incurable complications from malaria receives instruction in healing prayer from a hospital matron and is healed in response to her own prayers.

195. Browning, Webster E. (1869-1942). *The Republic of Ecuador: Social, Intellectual, and Religious Conditions To-day*. New York: Committee on Cooperation in Latin America, 1920. 31 p.

The Alliance receives prominent mention as one of only a few evangelical missions working in the country.

196. Browning, Webster E. (1869-1942), John Ritchie, and Kenneth G. Grubb. *The West Coast Republics of South America*. London: World Dominion Press, 1930. 183 p.

Provides statistics on Protestant missions, mentions the C&MA's collaboration with the Evangelical Union of South America in central Peru, and praises R. B. Clark's leadership of the Alliance's Peru mission.

197. Brumback, Carl. *Like a River*. Springfield, Mo.: Gospel Publishing House, 1977. 170 p.

Reprint of Part Two of 198.

198. ———. *Suddenly . . . from Heaven*. Springfield, Mo.: Gospel Publishing House, 1961. 394 p.

The Alliance erred in rejecting the Pentecostals' initial evidence doctrine, and Simpson later regretted this decision. The Assemblies of God's debt to the Alliance includes: all of its distinctive doctrines, including the wording thereof (except, of course, the evidence doctrine); Simpson's hymns; the books of Simpson, George P. Pardington, and A. W. Tozer; the name "Gospel Tabernacle" (to which the AOG added "full"); its nonrigid organizational structure and its missionary vision; and the many AOG workers trained by the Alliance, e.g., John William Welch and John Waggoner. F. F. Bosworth, who defected to the Alliance from the AOG, receives a chapter-length treatment.

199. Bubna, Donald L. (1929-). *Building People through a Caring, Sharing Fellowship*. Wheaton, Ill.: Tyndale House, 1978. 153 p.

Describes Bubna's attempts to build true *koinonia* in the Alliance churches he has pastored.

200. ———. "Ten Reasons not to Resign." *Leadership* 4 (fall 1983): 74-80.

Liberally illustrated with anecdotes from his pastorate at Salem (Ore.) Alliance Church.

201. Bubna, Donald L. (1929-), and Al Janssen. *Encouraging People*. Wheaton, Ill.: Tyndale House, 1988. 205 p.

The illustrative anecdotes come largely from Bubna's experiences as senior pastor of Salem (Ore.) Alliance Church.

202. Bubna, Donald L. (1929-), and Sandra M. Ricketts. "Building People." *Leadership* 1 (spring 1980): 69-81.

A three chapter excerpt of 199.

203. Bubna, Paul F. *Second Corinthians: Ministry: God at Work in Me for the Good of Others*. Deeper Life Pulpit Commentary. Camp Hill, Pa.: Christian Publications, 1993. 189 p.

204. Buckley (J)ames (M)onroe (1836-1920). "Faith-Healing and Kindred Phenomena." *Century Magazine* 32 (June 1886): 221-36.

"Faith cure . . . is a pitiable superstition, dangerous in its final effects" (p. 236). Faith-healers such as A. B. Simpson, Charles Cullis, and W. E. Boardman are no more successful than their Roman Catholic, pagan, spiritualist, or mind cure counterparts. The cures they effect are less miraculous than those of Christ and the apostles, and their accomplishments can be duplicated by strictly natural means. Simpson and company also focus on the self to an unhealthy extent, promote superstition, detract attention from moral and spiritual transformation, and denigrate reason. Cf. 1714.

205. ———. "Faith Healing and Kindred Phenomena." *Century Magazine* 33 (March 1887): 781-87.

Faith healers misapply the Scriptures, and their frequent failures to bring about healing argue against the supposed supernatural origins of their successes. Many obtain donations under false pretenses, utter false prophecies, and cause grave physical and emotional harm, and even death. Indeed, a woman suffering from heart disease died a few minutes after A. B. Simpson had anointed her with oil and prayed for her.

206. ———. *Faith Healing, Christian Science and Kindred Phenomena.* New York: The Century Company, 1900. 319 p.

A. B. Simpson's views are "as wild as the weather predictions that terrify the ignorant and superstitious but are the amusement and scorn of all rational and educated persons. . . " (p. 49). For a summary of the exchange between Simpson and Buckley see 276, p. 269-92.

207. Buckman, Margaret Simpson. "The Hymns of Dr. Simpson." *Missionarian*, 1945, 17.

A. B. Simpson's daughter relates how she and her father collaborated in the writing of hymns.

208. Bullock, Mark D. "Separation Anxiety Disorder in a Missionary Child: Theoretical Considerations and Intervention Strategies." *Alliance Academic Review* (1996): 105-26.

Missionaries often must send their children to boarding schools, and their children often suffer from some form of separation anxiety as a result. The staff of boarding schools should be trained to recognize when separation anxiety becomes pathological and to offer the appropriate interventions and empathetic care.

209. Bundy, R. Craig. "A Description and Evaluation of a Church Planting Project among the Middle Class People of Buenos Aires, Argentina." D.Min. diss., Trinity Evangelical Divinity School, 1991. 352 p.

Evaluates the capital-intensive effort to plant a church based on the Lima al Encuentro con Dios model. The unexpectedly slow growth of this church could have been attributable to deficiencies in pastoral care, lack of a core group, and an insufficiently focused church planting team.

210. ———. "Religious Syncretism—a Serious Problem: With Proposed Corrective Actions for Foreign Missionaries." Master's thesis, Trinity Evangelical Divinity School, 1974. 82 p.

Most of the dangers posed by syncretism can be neutralized by diligent study and careful presentation of the Gospel.

211. Burger, Delores T. "Perfect Love Drives Out Fear." In *Women Who Changed the Heart of the City: The Untold Story of the City Rescue Mission Movement.* Grand Rapids: Kregel Publications, 1997. p. 59-74.

Emma "Mother" Whittemore, an associate of A. B. Simpson, founded the first of her Door of Hope rescue mission in New York City in 1890 (Simpson dedicated it). By the time of her death, there were 97 Doors of Hope worldwide. She and her husband Sidney co-founded the International Union of Gospel Missions in 1913.

212. Burkinshaw, Robert (K)enneth (1954-). *Pilgrims in Lotus Land: Conservative Protestantism in British Columbia, 1917-1981.* Montréal; Kingston, Ont.: McGill-Queen's University Press, 1995. 368 p.

The C&MA churches in British Columbia did not experience significant growth until after World War II, when large numbers of immigrants from Alberta and Saskatchewan swelled their ranks. Since the 1960s the Alliance has grown to become one of the largest evangelical groups in the province, thanks largely to aggressive church planting efforts, especially among the province's Chinese immigrant community, and to an influx of Mennonite Brethren (who wanted to break with Mennonite culture, but not with conservative Christianity).

213. Burns, S. Thomas. "Development of the Indigenous Church in Mali and Upper Volta." In *Missions and the Indian Church,* 1-8. Cass Lake, Minn.: Alliance Indian Publications, 1972.

The church planted by the C&MA among the Dogon in Mali in the 1920s became self-supporting, self-governing, and self-propagating by the 1950s through the prayerful determination and cultural sensitivity of both the missionaries and the national church leaders.

214. ———. "Training National Workers." In *Missions and the Indian Church*, 38-43. Cass Lake, Minn.: Alliance Indian Publications, 1972.

In developing countries theological education by extension is superior to the traditional Bible school because it provides prospective pastors with academically rigorous training within their native cultural environment.

215. Businessman, A. [G. Elgin Keefer] *God's Final Messengers, or Pharaoh's Cup Refilled.* Harrisburg, Pa.: Christian Alliance Pub. Co., 1929. 249 p.

Current political developments in Europe, North America, and the Middle East are directly connected to the fulfilment of biblical prophecies about the return of Christ. The end "is due to take place at any moment," but may not occur until after 1940. The Roman Catholic Church and the Antichrist will join forces to persecute true believers, but the former will be overthrown largely through the efforts of the Ku Klux Klan and the Freemasons.

216. Bustanoby, Andre S. *Psalms to Warm the Heart.* Harrisburg, Pa.: Christian Publications, [197-?]. 36 p.

Devotional expositions of Psalms 131, 23, 84, and 46.

217. Butcher, J. Kevin. "The Holiness and Pentecostal Labors of David Wesley Myland, 1890-1918." Th.M. thesis, Dallas Theological Seminary, 1982. 149 p.

Myland, a Canadian-born Methodist, joined the Alliance in 1890 because of his belief in spiritual healing. He left the C&MA in 1912 over the tongues issue and later became a leader in the Pentecostal movement.

218. Bynum, Alton Clark. "Albert B. Simpson, Hymn Writer, 1843-1919." *The Hymn* 30 (April 1979): 108-12.

"Few hymn writers since Charles Wesley have had a more profound and lasting influence upon the denomination with which they were associated" (p. 108). Simpson wrote his first hymns not as songs but as poetic enhancements to his sermons, and only later had them set to music. Though they were often too long, difficult to sing, and far from being poetical masterpieces, Simpson's hymns were nevertheless able to convey the fourfold Gospel in a way that powerfully moved the first generation of Alliance people and contributed to the success of the Alliance itself.

219. ———. "Music Programs and Practices of the Christian and Missionary Alliance." Ed.D. diss., New Orleans Baptist Theological Seminary, 1975. 212 p.

Some of A. B. Simpson's 157 hymns continue to be sung in Alliance churches, almost 90% of which use *Hymns of the Christian Life* as their principal hymnal, despite the fact that 91% of the respondents expressed dissatisfaction with the latest edition. Includes an overview of Alliance hymnody; biographical sketches of all known Alliance hymn writers; and a listing, by subject and hymnal, of the titles of all documented Alliance hymns.

220. C. F. M. *The Question of the Sabbath*. New York: Christian Alliance Pub. Co., [ca. 1900]. 7 p.

The frequent references in Scripture to the assembling of the disciples on the first day in obedience to the Lord of the Sabbath should be enough to convince Christians to keep Sunday, rather than Saturday, as the Lord's day.

221. Cable, John (H)enry (1883-1948). *Christ in the Four Gospels*. New York: Christian Alliance Pub. Co., 1926. 375 p.

A chiefly devotional commentary by an instructor at the Missionary Training Institute. It does, however, deal with the question of the authorship of the Gospels, and it also takes Jesus' humanity seriously (cf. p. 42-49).

222. ———. *The Fulness of God: An Exposition of Ephesians from the Greek*. Chicago: Moody Press, 1945. 160 p.

223. ———. *A History of the Missionary Training Institute, the Pioneer Bible School of America*. New York: [The Institute?], 1933. 44 p.

Issued on the 50th anniversary of the Institute. Includes many photographs.

224. Cadman, Grace Hazenberg. *Pen Pictures of Annam and Its People*. New York: Christian Alliance Pub. Co., 1920. 124 p.

An account of the life of the typical missionary to Vietnam, the social life and customs of the Vietnamese, the history of Vietnam, and the history of the C&MA mission (established in 1911), which for many years was the only Protestant mission in the country.

225. Cairns, Earle E. *V. Raymond Edman: In the Presence of the King*. Chicago: Moody Press, 1972. 255 p.

Although best known as president of Wheaton College (1941-1965), Victor Raymond Edman (1900-1967) also served as an Alliance missionary to Ecuador (1923-1928), taught at the Missionary Training Institute, pastored the New York Gospel Tabernacle (1935-1936), and edited *The Alliance Witness* (1965-1967).

226. Calas, Th. "Le Protestantisme en Annam." *Bulletin paroissal*. April 1929. 1 ff.

227. Calkins, Loren. "The Pragmatics of Elder Rule in the Alliance." *His Dominion* 14 (winter 1988): 2-8.

Most U. S. C&MA churches have a governing board to oversee finances, administration, and building maintenance; and elders to assist the pastor in the spiritual governance of the church. About a quarter of the churches surveyed had combined these two functions into a governing board of elders. Many churches, regardless of their system of government, were having difficulty finding spiritually qualified elders.

228. "Cambodia: Brittle and Delicate." *World Vision*, November 1973, 4-8.

Includes a description of the cooperative relief efforts in which World Vision, the medical personnel of the C&MA mission, and the Khmer Evangelical Church (C&MA) were engaged.

229. *"Cambodia" News Bulletin* Staff. *"Light in Their Dwellings": A History of Forty Years of Missions in Cambodia.* n.p., 1963. 44 p.

A history of the C&MA mission to Cambodia (begun in 1923) and the development of the indigenous church.

230. Campbell, Henry D. *The Congo.* Missionary Series. New York: Christian and Missionary Alliance, [ca. 1900]. 8 p.

A description of life in the Congo and a detailed account of Alliance mission work there.

231. ———. *A Congo Chattel: The Story of an African Slave Girl.* New York: Christian Alliance Pub. Co., 1917. 213 p.

The women of the Congo are treated as little better than slaves in their native cultures. However, when Congolese men and women respond to the Gospel the resulting spiritual freedom brings with it a restoration of dignity to both sexes.

232. ———. *The Congo Mission of the Christian and Missionary Alliance.* New York: Christian Alliance Pub. Co., 1916. 12 p.

An overview of the geography, religion, and culture of the region of the Congo for which the C&MA has missionary responsibility. Although "the natives need to be taught improved methods of cultivation and profitable handicrafts and also given a knowledge of books" (p. 8), the C&MA is devoting its efforts to the proclamation of the Gospel.

233. Campbell, William. *A History of Knox Presbyterian Church, Hamilton, Ontario.* n.p., 1967. 32 p.

Includes excerpts from the church's minutes with respect to the induction and ordination (12 September 1865) and resignation (20 December 1873) of A. B. Simpson (this was his first pastorate). Also mentioned are the session's vigorous endorsement of missions during Simpson's tenure, and Simpson's return visits of 1894 and 1915.

234. *Captain John Coutts: A True Story*. New York: Soldiers' and Sailors' Alliance for Fellowship and Service; Christian Alliance Pub. Co., [19–?]. 5 p.

A dying sea captain becomes a Christian through reading Isa. 53.

235. Carlsen, William D. *Tibet: In Search of a Miracle*. Nyack, N.Y.: Nyack College, 1985. 70 p.

Chapters four and five cover Alliance missions in Tibet, centering on the work of Robert B. Ekvall. Includes many photographs.

236. Carlson, David Axel. *A Glimpse of 14 Years in the Arkansas Ozarks*. [Batesville, Ark.?]: by the author, 1949. 78 p.

The last 10 of those years were spent as a C&MA pastor.

237. Carner, E. R. *E. D. Whiteside, the Praying Man of Pittsburgh*. Pittsburgh, Pa.: Gospel Tabernacle of the Christian and Missionary Alliance, 1929. 174 p.

Edward Drury Whiteside (1848-1927), a pious and influential Alliance pastor, served as a mentor to many future leaders of the C&MA, including Paul Rader. Cf. 238.

238. ———. *The Life of E. D. Whiteside, the Praying Man of Pittsburgh*. Harrisburg, Pa.: Christian Publications, 1963. 140 p.

Reprint of 237, with new introduction, but without photographs.

239. Carter, Joan Elsie. "Interpersonal Skills in Cross-cultural Effectiveness: A Descriptive Study of Christian and Missionary Alliance Missionaries." Ph.D. diss., Marquette University, 1987. 155 p.

One's ability to adapt to a new culture depends to a great extent on one's ability to relate well with others. The 170 C&MA missionaries and 33 C&MA missions administrators in the sample were rated on self-disclosure, listening and responding, and challenging. The latter interpersonal skill was identified as being the most underdeveloped in the respondents.

240. Carter (R)ussell Kelso (1849-1928). *Alpha and Omega or, the Birth and Death of the World, the Science of the Creation, the Coming Crisis and the Golden Age*. San Francisco: O. H. Elliott, 1894. 613 p.

241. ———. *Amor Victor: A Novel of Ephesus and Rome, 95-105 A. D.* New York: Frederick A. Stokes Company, 1902. 424 p.

Written under the pseudonym Orr Kenyon.

242. ———. *The Atonement for Sin and Sickness, or a Full Salvation for Soul and Body*. Boston: Willard Tract Repository, 1884. 243 p.

Christ's atonement includes divine healing: the fully consecrated Christian who does not abuse his or her body out of ignorance can expect God to keep it free from disease without the use of medical means. (Carter had been healed of heart disease without "means" in 1879.)

243. ———. *Behold! The Bridegroom!* New Britain, Conn.: n.p, [189-?]. 20 p.

244. ———. *Caleb Koons, a 'Postle of Common Sense*. Boston: C. M. Clark Pub. Co., 1910. 453 p.

245. ———. *The Coming Physical Transformation of the Earth: A Scientific Study of the Millennium*. New York: n.p., 1892. 24 p.

246. ———. "Divine Healing, or Faith Cure." *Century Magazine*, n.s. 11 (March 1887): 777-80.

From the time of the Exodus, the Israelites were promised freedom from disease if they kept the covenant. Likewise, Christ's atonement applies to both soul and body (Matt. 8:16-17). The indwelling Christ gives those Christians who appropriate it the power to fulfill their vocation until death. Faith healers believe in means: the laying-on of hands, anointing with oil, and the prayer of faith.

247. ———. "Divine Healing." *Thy Healer and Faith Witness* 4 (1887): 212-17.

Reprint of 246.

248. ———. *Divine Healing, or the Atonement for Sin and Sickness*, new ed., rewritten and enlarged. New York: J. B. Alden, 1888. 189 p.

This revised edition of 242 also includes the full text of 246. Also added are appendices on John Wesley's views on divine healing and the differences between Carter's views and those of the cults and Eastern religions.

249. ———. *Faith Healing Reviewed after Twenty Years*. Boston: Christian Witness Company, 1897. 168 p.

After a prolonged bout of neurasthenia, against which healing prayer unaccompanied by "means" was ineffective, Carter began to take medicine and quickly made a remarkable recovery. From this experience he concluded that God can heal with or without means and that " to claim that ALL the results of the Atonement are NOW open to the present living Christian is a grave mistake" (p. 167). For the response of John Alexander Dowie, see 442.

250. ———. *Pastor Blumhardt: Selections from His Life and Ministry*. New York: Christian Alliance Pub. Co., [19–?]. 102 p.

Christoph Blumhardt was a pioneer in the divine healing movement in Germany who exerted a formative influence on the American divine healing movement.

251. ———. *Russell Kelso Carter on "Faith Healing."* New York: Garland Publishing, 1985. 415 p.

Reprint of 242 and 249.

252. ———. *The Sleeping Car "Twilight," or Motherhood without Pain. The Whole Truth about "Twilight Sleep" and the New Anesthesia; the Marvelous French Discovery, the Most Wonderful of All; and a Special Chapter for Every Man on the Conquest of Pain*. Boston: Chapple, 1915. 181 p.

———. *The Supernatural Gifts of the Spirit*.

See 532.

253. ———. *The Tree of Knowledge: A Startling Scientific Study of the Original Sin of Angels, with a History of Spiritism in All Ages*. San Francisco: O. H. Elliott, 1894. 423 p.

254. ———. *What God Hath (Not) Joined Together*. New York: Dodge Pub. Co., 1905. 383 p.

255. ———. "What the Law Could Not Do." *Thy Healer* 2 (1885): 348-49.

A sermon on self-renunciation and absolute trust in God.

256. Carter (R)ussell Kelso (1849-1928), and A. B. Simpson, eds. *Hymns of the Christian Life: New and Standard Songs for the Sanctuary, Sunday Schools, Prayer Meetings, Mission Work and Revival Services*. New York: Christian Alliance Pub. Co., 1891. 320 p.

The first Alliance hymnal (454 hymns). Mostly gospel songs, and most of these are by Simpson or Carter. Carter's contributions outnumber Simpson's. Also includes hymns by Charles Wesley, Isaac Watts, and others. Cf. 772.

257. ———, eds. *Hymns of the Christian Life (words only): New and Standard Songs for the Sanctuary, Sunday Schools, Prayer Meetings, Mission Work and Revival Services*. New York: Christian Alliance Pub. Co., 1891. 150 p. Cf. 1878.

258. Carter (R)ussell Kelso (1849-1928), and (H)enry (L)ake) Gilmour (1836-1920). *The Silver Trumpet: A Collection of New and Selected Hymns for Use in Public Worship, Revival Services, Prayer and Social Meetings and Sunday Schools*. Philadelphia: J. J. Hood, 1889. 160 p.

259. Carter (R)ussell Kelso (1849-1928), and John R. Sweeney, eds. *Songs of Perfect Love*. Philadelphia: J. J. Hood, 1886. 128 p.

260. Cartmel, Daryl Westwood (1925-1985). "Mission Policy and Program of A. B. Simpson." Master's thesis, Hartford Seminary, 1962. 200 p.

Simpson had always been an advocate of missions. He envisioned the Gospel Tabernacle as "a church which had within it the life and function of a mission" (p. 42). Poor planning and various administrative problems contributed to the failure of a number of the Alliance's early missions ventures, but during the 1890s it began to experience the phenomenal growth that would later force it to reconsider its nondenominational status.

261. ———. "Partnership in Mission." D.Miss. diss., Fuller Theological Seminary, 1980. 163 p.

Examines the contributions made by Louis L. King to the development and implementation of the C&MA's missions policy. As the C&MA's foreign secretary (1956-1978), King placed particular emphasis on indigenization and on partnership between the indigenous church and the mission.

262. Cassidy, Bertha (E)rnestine (1884-1980). *China Adventure.* Brookline, Mass.: American Advent Missionary Society, 1962. 128 p.

William Cassidy, a native of Toronto, sailed for China in 1887 as the first Alliance missionary to that country. He died en route in Kobe, Japan. Undaunted, his wife Elizabeth took his place, studying at the Missionary Training Institute and departing with her two daughters for China ca. 1890. She married Alliance missionary Charles Beak in 1894. They served with the Alliance in China until 1901, when they joined the American Advent Missionary Society.

263. Castillo, Metosalem Quillupras (1935-). *The Church in Thy House.* Manila: Alliance Publishers; OMF Literature, 1982. 138 p.

Revision of 264.

264. ———. "'The Church in Thy House': A Study of the House Church Concept as it Relates to Christian Mission." D.Miss. diss., Fuller Theological Seminary, 1976. 327 p.

The house church model is well-suited to Filipino culture, which is much more family-oriented and far less individualistic than North American culture.

265. ———. *Evangelism in Philippine Context.* Cebu City, Philippines: Target 400 Committee, 1977. 33 p.

Describes Project 400, an attempt by CAMACOP (Christian and Missionary Alliance Churches of the Philippines) and the C&MA Mission to plant 400 new churches and make 40,000 new converts within two years by establishing houses churches and evangelizing families.

266. ———. *Let's Plant Churches: A Manual for Church Planting.* Manila: Alliance Publishers, 1991. 90 p.

Specially adapted to the Philippine context.

267. ———. "Missiological Education: A Proposed Curriculum for the Alliance Graduate School of Church Growth and Missions." Master's thesis, Fuller Theological Seminary, 1975. 175 p.

Alliance Graduate School of Church Growth and Missions later became Alliance Biblical Seminary, Manila.

268. ———. "Towards Greater Equivalence in the CAMACOP." In *Readings in Dynamic Indigeneity*, eds. Charles Kraft and Tom N. Wisley, 239-52. Pasadena, Calif.: William Carey Library, 1979.

The CAMACOP appears to be a completely indigenized church, but it continues to use Western church structures. It still needs to develop a Filipino hymnody and liturgy, use vernacular translations of the Bible, conduct worship services in Filipino languages, govern itself according to Filipino leadership and decision-making practices, and formulate a culturally relevant theology.

269. Cathey, Gordon M. "Missionary Passion Builds Great Church." *United Evangelical Action* 15 (15 September 1956): 22, 36.

North Side Christian and Missionary Alliance Church (Pittsburgh), founded by E. D. Whiteside in 1894, has been experiencing a resurgence of vitality.

270. *Celebration in Song*. Camp Hill, Pa.: Christian Publications, 1983. 144 p.

A compilation of 137 hymns and Gospel songs, mostly from *Hymns of the Christian Life*, for use at the Alliance's centennial General Council (1987).

271. Chapell (F)rederic (L)eonard (1836-1900). *Biblical and Practical Theology*. Philadelphia: H. Chapell, 1901. Reprint, New York: Christian Alliance Pub. Co., 1912. 315 p.

272. ———. *The Eleventh-Hour Laborers: A Series of Articles from The Watchword*. South Nyack, N.Y.: Christian Alliance Pub. Co., [1898?]. 124 p.

The emergence of nondenominational Bible schools, city missions, and mission agencies staffed by zealous workers (many of whom are women) with only basic, practically oriented, theological training is a sign of the last days. The C&MA epitomizes these phenomena, and it is "unprecedented in its financial, numerical and geographic expansion" (p. 106). Reissued in 1899 as vol. 1, no. 7 of the Alliance Colportage Library.

273. Chapman (C)harles P. *With the Bible among the Andes*. Kansas City: Gospel Missionary Union, [1949?]. 111 p.

The Gospel Missionary Union (GMU) founded in 1892 in Topeka, Kansas, was initially associated with the C&MA: the GMU was to recruit volunteers whom the C&MA would oversee on the field. This relationship was soon terminated, however. Nevertheless, the Alliance and the GMU have always had a close working relationship in Ecuador and Colombia.

274. Chapman, Katharine Elise. *CHUMS*. New York: Christian Alliance Pub. Co., 1914. 92 p.

A novel about the conversion and reform of a criminal.

275. ———. *Following the Glory*. New York: Christian Alliance Pub. Co., 1918. 170 p.

A novel about the advent of the millennial reign of Christ.

276. Chappell, Paul G. "The Divine Healing Movement in America." Ph.D. diss., Drew University, 1983. 400 p.

A. B. Simpson was the most influential of Charles Cullis's disciples in the healing movement. Thousands experienced divine healing at Alliance conventions, Simpson's Friday healing meetings, and the C&MA's healing home. Simpson also published extensively on the subject and ably defended divine healing against its detractors, such as James M. Buckley; and against extremists, such as John Alexander Dowie. Unlike most of his contemporaries in the movement, Simpson left behind a structure, the C&MA, to perpetuate (among other things) the teaching and practice of divine healing. Cf. 206.

277. ———. "Origins of the Divine Healing Movement in America." *Spiritus* 1 (winter 1985): 5-18.

Focuses on R. Kelso Carter, Ethan O. Allen, and Charles Cullis.

278. *Charles Hamilton Pridgeon*. Gibsonia, Pa.: The Evangelization Society of Pittsburgh Bible Institute, 1963. 210 p.

Pridgeon married Louise Shepard, an associate of A. B. Simpson in late 1899. That December Shepard left the Alliance to found a more strictly faith-based ministry along the lines of that of George Müller. Her desires were realized in 1901, when she and Pridgeon co-founded Pittsburgh Bible Institute (cf. also 915).

279. Charter, Miriam L. "Theological Education for New Protestant Churches of Russia: Indigenous Judgments on the Appropriateness of Educational Methods and Styles." Ph.D. diss., Trinity Evangelical Divinity School, 1997. 324 p.

The results of ethnographic interviews conducted by the author, an Alliance missionary, of the students and faculty of Donetsk Christian University, St. Petersburg Christian University, and Lampados Bible College (the official college of the Christian Missionary Union [C&MA] in Russia). Includes proposals for indigenizing Protestant theological education in Russia.

280. Chavan, Raghuel P. "Evangelism and the Lord's Imminent Return." In *One Race, One Gospel, One Task: World Congress on Evangelism, Berlin, 1966, Vol. 2*, ed. Carl F. H. Henry and W. Stanley Mooneyham, 72-73. Minneapolis: World Wide Publications, 1967.

The return of the Lord is imminent. The only condition that must yet be fulfilled is the proclamation of the Gospel to all nations.

281. ———. "Mission—and Foreign Missions." In *The Church's Worldwide Mission: An Analysis of the Current State of Evangelical Missions and a Strategy for Future Activity,* ed. Harold Lindsell, 151-61. Waco, Tex.: Word Books, 1966.

The indigenous church should be an organization separate from the mission if it is to mature. Only then will native Christians take responsibility for evangelism and the cultivation of their own piety. The C&MA's pioneering of self-support in India provides a good example of indigenization.

282. Choy, Leona. *The Holy Spirit and His Work: An "Interview" with A. B. Simpson*. Camp Hill, Pa.: Christian Publications, 1991. 35 p.

Reprint of the chapter on A. B. Simpson in 283.

283. ———. *Powerlines: What Great Evangelical Leaders Believed about the Holy Spirit, 1850-1930*. Camp Hill, Pa.: Christian Publications, 1990. 321 p.

Mock interviews with the 24 subjects provide a synopsis of their beliefs. The chapter on A. B. Simpson (p. 235-61) is a distillation of five of his pneumatological works. Cf. 282.

284. *Christ on the Battlefield: The Italian Soldier*. Nyack, N.Y.: The Missionary Institute, [ca. 1914-1918?]. 4 p.

An Italian soldier is converted after reading the Italian translation of the tract *Come to Jesus* and dies happily on the battlefield two days later.

285. *Christ Pour la Vie*. Sainte-Foy, P.Q.: Alliance Chrétienne et Missionaire, [198-?]. 4 p.

A salvation tract.

286. *Le Christ, toujours nécessaire et pleinement suffisant*. Sainte-Foy, P.Q.: Alliance Chrétienne et Missionaire, [198-?]. 7 p.

A brief presentation of the fourfold Gospel.

287. "The Christian and Missionary Alliance." *The Independent*, 22 June 1899, 1710-11.

Letters to the editor from several different countries allege that some C&MA missionaries are suffering acutely as a result of neglect. Furthermore, contributed funds are evidently put into Mrs. A. B. Simpson's personal bank account, and the C&MA is thus also guilty of financial mismanagement. It is difficult to get a straight answer on these questions from A. B. Simpson, "a man of peculiarly magnetic, almost hypnotic power."

288. "The Christian and Missionary Alliance." *The Independent*, 6 July 1899, 1840-43.

Includes a letter from the Board of Managers of the C&MA denying the allegations made in the issue of 22 June. The religion editor of *The Independent* responds: "The Alliance sends out ignorant, untrained missionaries . . . with so little regard to . . . their support that missionary circles are full of the stories of their suffering."

289. *The Christian and Missionary Alliance after Three-quarters of a Century*. New York: The Alliance, [1963?]. 7 p.

Rev. ed. of 1861.

290. The Christian and Missionary Alliance. *Bringing in the Sheaves: Gleanings from the Mission Fields of the Christian and Missionary Alliance*. New York: The Alliance, 1898. 30 p.

An illustrated report, intended for use as a fund-raising tool, on the state of Alliance missions worldwide.

291. ———. *The Christian and Missionary Alliance: A Statement regarding Its History, Government, Message, Policy, Scope*. New York: The Alliance, 1934. 7 p.

Born in 1887, the Alliance is governed by its members via their delegates. It believes and teaches "all the evangelical doctrines of the church" (p. 4). International in scope, it seeks to avoid sectarianism and to cooperate with all individuals and groups who desire to use it as an agency for the worldwide propagation of the Gospel.

292. ———. *The Christian and Missionary Alliance Leadership Conference on Evangelism, Nov. 28 to Dec. 1, 1966*. New York: Christian and Missionary Alliance Home Department, 1966. 218 p.

Addresses (uneven in quality) on the theory and practice of evangelism. In one of the better ones, "Evangelism and Church Growth,"

Samuel Stoesz laments that church growth in the C&MA has been retarded because the Alliance has labored under the illusion that it is not a church.

293. ———. *Convention Songs: A Selection of 84 Hymns and Choruses, New and Old, Including Many Famous Copyrights, Especially Prepared for Missionary Conventions and Evangelistic Campaigns*. Harrisburg, Pa.: Christian Publications, [193-?]. 66 p.

294. ———. *Convention Songs: Selections from Hymns of the Christian Life Nos. 1, 2 and 3*. New York: Christian Alliance Pub. Co., [192-?]. 167 p.

Some of the 247 songs, such as Paul Rader's "Only Believe," are not found in previous Alliance hymnals.

295. ———. *An Explanation of Alliance Methods of Missionary Support.* New York: Christian Alliance Pub. Co., 1912. 7 p.

The Alliance's policy of pooling missions contributions and distributing them evenly among its missionaries is not only in harmony with the society's principles but also best meets the needs of both supporter and missionary.

296. ———. *Finance Manual for Alliance Church Treasurers (and Pastors)*. Colorado Springs: The Alliance, 1991. 91 p.

297. ———. *Hymns of the Christian Life: Conference Edition*. Harrisburg, Pa.: Christian Publications, 1966. 159 p.

Nineteen of the 170 hymns are by Alliance hymn writers; 10 of these are by A. B. Simpson.

298. ———. *Look on the Fields: A Brief Outline of the Foreign Work of The Christian and Missionary Alliance*. New York: Christian and Missionary Alliance, [1911?]. 14 p.

Alliance missions seek to evangelize hitherto unevangelized peoples and to establish self-governing and self-propagating churches.

299. ———. *Lost behind the Ranges*. New York: The Alliance, 1953.

"Behind the Ranges" is an Alliance epithet for the remote interior of Irian Jaya (cf. the periodical of the same name).

300. ———. *The Missionary Institute of the Christian and Missionary Alliance*. Nyack, N.Y.: The Alliance, 1911.

301. ———. *A New Heart for Stone Age People*. Nyack, N.Y.: The Alliance, 1974.

On missions to Irian Jaya.

302. ———. *Report and Retrospect of the Work of the Christian and Missionary Alliance*. New York: The Alliance, 1897. 110 p.

Covers 1 October 1895 to 1 April 1897 (the latter date being that of the merger of the Christian Alliance and the International Missionary Alliance) and includes a brief history of the Alliance. Field reports comprise the bulk of the document, for "the pre-eminent work of the Alliance has been the evangelization of the world" (p. 19).

303. ———. *The Revived Tongues Movement, "Seek Not, Forbid Not": The Official Position and Statement of the Christian and Missionary Alliance*. New York: The Alliance, 1963. 8 p.

A reprint from the 1 May 1963 issue of *The Alliance Witness*, of a statement unanimously adopted by the Board of Managers. Warns against the excesses of Pentecostalism, affirms that tongues is a legitimate gift of the Holy Spirit, but denies both that it is "the sign of having been filled with the Holy Spirit" and that all Christians ought to seek it. "[T]he attitude toward the gift of tongues held by pastor and people should be 'seek not, forbid not.' This we hold to be the part of the wisdom of the hour." Cf. 645.

304. ———. *Salvation Comes to Shangri-La*. New York: The Alliance, [1961?]. 14 p.

Sequel to 701. Recounts the mass conversions (1954-1960) of tribes in the Baliem River Valley of Irian Jaya, Indonesia.

305. ———. *Souvenir and Survey of the Work of the Christian and Missionary Alliance, 1899*. [New York?]: [The Alliance?], [1899?]. 32 p.

A considerably abbreviated annual report. Largely devoted to extended responses to the harsh criticisms that had been made against the C&MA in the American press. Many of these involved alleged financial improprieties and the accusations of former C&MA missionary to Argentina, Emilio Olsson.

306. ———. *Statistics of The Christian and Missionary Alliance: Mission Fields and National Churches*. Nyack, N.Y.: The Alliance, [1970?]. 246 p.

Covers 1915-1969.

307. ———. *Statutes of The Christian and Missionary Alliance Enacted since the Adoption of the Constitution in 1912.* New York: The Alliance, 1933. 37 p.

308. The Christian and Missionary Alliance. Central China Mission. *Central China Mission Report for 1907.* [New York?]: The Alliance, [1908?]. 30 p.

Includes photographs.

309. The Christian and Missionary Alliance. Committee to Study the Role of Women in Ministry. *Report of the Committee to Study the Role of Women in Ministry.* Colorado Springs: The Alliance, 1995. 187 p.

Exegetical, theological, and historical essays commissioned by the 1994 General Council of the C&MA (in the USA). The Committee recommended that the Alliance not restrict the ministry of unordained men and women, and that each local C&MA church be given the right to reflect in its bylaws its own convictions and practice regarding the role of women in ministry. The latter recommendation was rejected by the 1995 General Council.

310. The Christian and Missionary Alliance. Division of Church Ministries. Office of Church Growth. *Churches Planting Churches.* Nyack, N.Y.: The Division of Church Ministries, Christian and Missionary Alliance, 1987. 74 p.

A compendium on the theology and practice of church planting designed to be used in conjunction with the C&MA's "1000 More by '94" church planting campaign.

311. The Christian and Missionary Alliance. Division of Overseas Ministries. *The Education of Missionary Children in the Christian and Missionary Alliance.* Nyack, N.Y.: The Alliance, 1986. 10 p.

Alliance missionaries should not expect to home school their children, since both husband and wife are expected to serve full-time as missionaries. Since their children will likely return to their home country as adults, the best option for their education is either an inexpensive local international school or a boarding school for children of missionaries. Surveys indicate that most Alliance missionaries prefer the boarding school option and that parents remain the most important shapers of values for children attending such schools.

312. The Christian and Missionary Alliance. Foreign Department. *Atlas Showing Mission Fields of the Christian and Missionary Alliance*, rev. ed. New York: The Alliance, 1924. 111 p.

An updated version of the original (1922) ed. Cf. 1945.

313. ———. *Bringing It All Together: A Current World View of Alliance Missions.* New York: The Alliance, 1973. 24 p.

Includes general statistics, theological education, media ministries, youth work, ministries of compassion, and a report on how contributions for missionary support are allocated.

314. ———. *Central China: The Work of the Christian and Missionary Alliance on This Field.* New York: The Department, [ca. 1900]. 7 p.

Statistics by province and district.

315. ———. *Report of the Asia Conference, Bangkok, Thailand, October 26-November 5, 1955.* New York: The Alliance, 1956. 126 p.

Consists mostly of discussions with respect to the level of self-support that has been achieved in the churches of the Philippines, Thailand, Indonesia, and Laos.

316. ———. *Hearts Aflame in a World on Fire: A Story of God's Working through Devoted Missionaries and Nationals in the Foreign Fields of The Christian and Missionary Alliance.* New York: The Alliance, 1942. 79 p.

A separately published annual report of the C&MA (on the state of Alliance missions as of 31 December 1941).

317. ———. *"The Lord Hath Need . . . .": The Use of Consecrated Funds in the Foreign Fields of the Christian and Missionary Alliance.* New York: The Alliance, [192-?]. 8 p.

318. ———. *Missionary Atlas: A Manual of the Foreign Work of the Christian and Missionary Alliance.* Harrisburg, Pa.: The Alliance, 1950. 155 p.

Rev. ed. of 1945. Cf. 319.

319. ———. *Missionary Atlas: A Manual of the Foreign Work of the Christian and Missionary Alliance*, rev. ed. Harrisburg, Pa.: Christian Publications, 1964. 207 p.

Rev. ed. of 318.

320. The Christian and Missionary Alliance. Forty-third [sic] General Council. *The New Crusade Songs*, souvenir ed. Harrisburg, Pa.: Christian Publications, 1940. 98 p.

A selection of hymns compiled for use at the 53rd General Council of the C&MA (1940). Sixteen of the 106 selections were written by Alliance hymn writers; seven by A. B. Simpson.

321. The Christian and Missionary Alliance. Home Department. Christian Education Office. *Administration of Christian Education in the Local Church*. New York: The Alliance, 1966. 23 p.

A checklist for Christian education committees.

322. ———. Christian Education Office. *Christian Education Agencies*. New York: The Office, [196-?]. 47 p.

Covers Sunday schools, youth work, children's clubs, vacation Bible Schools, music, missionary education, audio-visuals, and library.

323. ———. *Operation Harvest: What Made Your Church Grow?* [Nyack, N.Y.?]: Operation Harvest, 1973. 22 p.

A compilation of extracts of letters from 57 Alliance pastors who responded to the survey question, "What made your church grow?" (in 1972).

324. The Christian and Missionary Alliance in Canada. *How, Why, What to Think about Abortion: An Alliance Response*. Toronto: The Alliance, [198-?]. 16 p.

Abortion violates Scripture and promotes humanistic values.

325. The Christian and Missionary Alliance in South China. *The Publication Work of the Christian and Missionary Alliance in South China*. [Wuzhou, China?]: C&MA in South China, 1917. 20 p.

The annual report of the activities of the South China Alliance Press for 1916.

326. Christian Publications, Inc. *How to Use Your Hymnal*. Harrisburg, Pa.: Christian Publications, [1978?]. 16 p.

A guide to the use of 771.

327. Christie, William (1870-1955). *Alliance Work in Western China and Tibet*, rev. ed. New York: The Alliance, 1913. 12 p.

A survey and history of Alliance missions in these areas. Originally published ca. 1908.

328. ———. *The Beginnings of Harvest on the China-Tibetan Border.* New York: Christian and Missionary Alliance, 1918. 13 p.

A history of the work of the Alliance's Kansu-Tibetan border mission since its inception in 1895.

329. ———. "Personal Character and Spiritual Attainments." In *A. B. Simpson Centenary: 1843-1943,* 3-6. New York: Christian and Missionary Alliance, 1943.

A. B. Simpson was God-fearing, intelligent, industrious, large-hearted, and strong willed. His life exemplified his teachings on salvation, sanctification, and healing.

330. Chu, Peter. "Single Church Evangelistic Crusades in Asia." In *The Work of an Evangelist: International Congress for Itinerant Evangelists, Amsterdam, the Netherlands,* ed. J. D. Douglas, 407-9. Minneapolis: World Wide Publications, 1984.

Lists in point form: the advantages and disadvantages of this kind of outreach, how to overcome barriers to non-believers, how to involve church members in outreach, and suggestions for publicity.

331. Clark, R. B. *Under the Southern Cross: The Story of Alliance Missions in South America.* Harrisburg, Pa.: Christian Publications, 1938. 232 p.

Covers Argentina, Chile, Ecuador, Colombia, and Peru. Provides, for each country, information on geography and history, a history of Protestant missions, and a history of the C&MA mission.

332. Clement, Saint. [Arthur Clermont Peck]. *Christ's Return: The Key to Prophecy and Providence.* New York: Christian Alliance Pub. Co., 1906. 166 p.

An overview of premillennial eschatology from a pretribulation rapture perspective. Considers the papacy to be the embodiment of the Antichrist.

333. ———. *The Masterpiece of Satan.* New York: Christian Alliance Pub. Co., [ca. 1911]. 14 p.

A fictitious conversation in which Satan reveals his latest plan to divert worship from Christ to himself: Christian Science.

334. ———. *Who Is Sufficient.* Tracts for the Times: Deeper Life Series. New York: Christian Alliance Pub. Co., [ca. 1900]. 8 p.

The deeper life consists not in the imitation of Christ by an unregenerate human, but rather in the voluntary crucifixion of the old nature. This leads to the experience of the Apostle Paul: "it is no longer I who live, but Christ who lives in me" (Gal. 2:20).

335. Cleveland Colored Quintette. *The Coloured Quintette: A Brief Narrative of God's Marvellous Dealings with the Cleveland Gospel Quintette, and Their Personal Testimony.* Kilmarnock, Scotland: John Ritchie, 1937. 37 p.

A narrative of the travels and ministry of this very popular Afro-American quintette, all five of whom were converted through the Alliance. They toured extensively in North America and Europe and sang at meetings conducted by such Alliance notables as F. F. Bosworth and Paul Rader.

336. ———. *The Coloured Quintette: A Narrative of God's Marvellous Dealings with the Cleveland Gospel Quintette, and Their Personal Testimony*, silver jubilee ed. Kilmarnock, Scotland: John Ritchie, 1945. 84 p.

Includes many photos not in 335, as well as an account of their tour through the British Isles and Europe.

337. Cline, Edward A., and Bill Bray. "The Khmer Republic (Cambodia)." In *The Church in Asia*, ed. Donald E. Hoke, 349-67. Chicago: Moody Press, 1975.

A history of the church in Cambodia, which is largely the product of C&MA mission efforts, and an overview of the country's history and culture.

338. Cocjin, Cleotilde L. "The Literacy Work of the Christian and Missionary Alliance Churches of the Philippines among the Selected Tribes of Mindanao and Sulu." Master's thesis, Manuel L. Quezon University, 1969.

339. Coleman, Robert E. *Evangelism in Perspective.* Harrisburg, Pa.: Christian Publications, 1965. 109 p.

"Presented as the L. W. Pippert Memorial Lectures October 1974, Alliance School of Theology and Missions, Nyack, N.Y."

340. Collier, Leonard John. "Interpersonal Skills among Pastoral Workers with the Christian and Missionary Alliance of Australia." D.Min. diss., Canadian Theological Seminary, 1994. 251 p.

The interpersonal skills of Australian C&MA clergy are less than adequate. The C&MA in Australia must therefore establish an acceptable standard, develop a tool by which to measure the relational skills, and establish a training program for the improvement of the interpersonal skills of its clergy.

341. Collins, Harold M. "Planting C. & M. A. Churches in Australia." B.D. thesis, Alliance College of Theology, 1978. 68 p.
The most complete history of the C&MA in Australia. Proposes a church growth strategy appropriate to Australian culture.

342. Collitt (F)rank B. *The Future Unveiled in the Light of Revealed Prophecy*. Vermillion, Ohio: by the author, [193-?]. 38 p.

343. ———. *A Great Revival*. Vermilion, Ohio: by the author, [ca. 1940]. 35 p.
The nature of revival, the need for revival in the contemporary church, and ways of facilitating revival.

344. ———. *Our Lord's Message of Truth*. Beulah Beach, Ohio: by the author, 1951. 31 p.
Meditations on Jesus as the Word of truth.

345. ———. *The Truth of the Holy Spirit Made Plain.* Vermilion, Ohio: by the author, [ca. 1939]. 38 p.
The filling of the Holy Spirit is for both power and holy living. It is received as a result of a crisis subsequent to conversion.

346. ———. *The War and the Bible*. Vermilion, Ohio: by the author, 1940. 34 p.
World War II in the light of biblical prophecy.

347. *Colombia's New Day*. New York; Toronto: The Christian and Missionary Alliance, 1955. 11 p.
Chronicles the planting and growth of Alliance churches in Colombia in the face of opposition and persecution by the Roman Catholic Church.

348. Conley, William W. *The Kalimantan Kenyah: A Study of Tribal Conversion in Terms of Dynamic Cultural Themes*. Nutley, N.J.: Presbyterian and Reformed, 1973. 494 p.
The 35,000 Kenyah of Indonesian Kalimantan converted to Christianity between 1930 and 1965, but the basic "themes" of their

culture: supernaturalism, communalism, status and rank, the importance of children, rice agriculture, and riverine orientation remained intact, although the animistic core was replaced by a Christian core. The author worked among the Kenyah for most of his 13 years as a C&MA missionary.

349. Constance, Helen (1912-1995). *Stepping Out on Faith: The Story of Colombia Missionaries George and Helen Constance.* Camp Hill, Pa.: Christian Publications, 1988. 157 p.

Ohioans George (1906-1996) and Helen Constance served in Colombia from 1935 to 1953, experiencing the dangers and rigors of jungle life as well as persecution at the hands of the Catholic Church. Written largely from the perspective of a mother of young children who must endure frequent absences by her husband and be constantly vigilant for her children's safety.

350. *Constitution for Christian and Missionary Alliance Churches.* Harrisburg, Pa.: Christian Publications, [1976?]. 14 p.

Adopted at the May 1976 General Council.

351. Cook, Arnold (L)orne (1932-). "The Biblical and Ethical Implications of Latin American Marriage Problems." D.Miss. diss., Fuller Theological Seminary, 1979. 193 p.

Church disciplinary rulings on (Latin American) marriage problems must be made according to biblical principles, conform to the requirements of civil law, be minimally socially disruptive, and be acceptable to a local church. Uses case studies drawn from the author's experience as a C&MA missionary in Colombia, Peru, and Argentina.

352. ———. "Partnership for Finishing the Job." *His Dominion* 15 (July 1989): 27-42.

The C&MA has provided subsidies, technical assistance, and human resources to C&MA churches overseas that are attempting to establish their own missions. It has also funded indigenous missionaries to do church planting in their own countries. Some fledgling indigenous Alliance missions have established partnerships with other indigenous missions.

353. ———. *Why Be Missionary: A Prophetic Message to the Christian and Missionary Alliance.* Classic Christian Living series. Camp Hill, Pa.: Christian Publications, 1996. 19 p.

The church is missionary by nature, but even in the C&MA, a supposedly missionary denomination, nominalism threatens the missionary vision.

354. Cook, Frank S. *Seeds in the Wind: The Story of The Voice of the Andes, Radio Station HCJB, Quito, Ecuador*, rev. ed. Miami: World Radio Missionary Fellowship, 1974. 203 p.

HCJB was founded by Reuben Larson, a former Alliance missionary to Ecuador, and Clarence Jones (1915-1986) who received much spiritual nurture from Alliance people. HCJB and the C&MA mission in Ecuador have always had a close working relationship.

355. Corbin, Linda. *Seven Ways to Pray for Spiritual Leaders: Joining the Battle to Win the World.* Camp Hill, Pa.: Christian Publications, 1995. 34 p.

356. Cormack, Don. *Killing Fields, Living Fields*. Crowborough, England: OMF International; MARC, 1997. 463 p.

The Khmer Evangelical Church, i.e., the Protestant church in Cambodia, was founded by C&MA missionaries in 1922, and was, until the 1970s, the only non-Roman Catholic Christian group in the country. The C&MA and OMF International began a partnership in Cambodia in 1974 at the request of the Cambodian church. The church continues to grow despite the devastating effects of the Khmer Rouge's reign of terror.

357. Cowles, Deborah. *Alliance History and Beliefs*. Manila: Alliance Publishers, 1984. 390 p.

A programmed learning text designed for use in theological education by extension.

358. ———. *Psalms*. Manila: Alliance Publishers, 1982. 388 p.

Same format as 357.

359. Cowles, H. Robert. *Opening the New Testament.* Camp Hill, Pa.: Christian Publications, 1985. 158 p.

A survey course for adult Sunday school classes.

360. ———. *Opening the Old Testament.* Camp Hill, Pa.: Christian Publications, 1980. 158 p.

Same format as 359.

361. ———. *Operation Heartbeat*. Harrisburg, Pa.: Christian Publications, 1976. 265 p.

A compilation of news reports, letters, interviews, and articles from *The Alliance Witness* chronicling the withdrawal of C&MA missionaries from Indochina after the fall of Vietnam and the establishment of churches for Indochinese refugees in North America.

362. ———. *Prime Time: 366 Devotions for Seniors*. Camp Hill, Pa.: Christian Publications, 1991. 379 p.

A devotional calendar based on the author's reflections on life and Scripture.

363. ———, ed. *Questions and Answers for Young Disciples: Truth for Children Straight from Scripture*. Camp Hill, Pa.: Christian Publications, 1993. 46 p.

A thorough revision of 1315 that is less didactic in tone and different in emphasis (e.g., the eschatology is less explicitly millennarian) than its predecessor.

364. Cowles, H. Robert, and K. Neill Foster, eds. *Holiness Voices: A Practical Theology of Holiness*. Camp Hill, Pa.: Christian Publications, 1995. 314 p.

Thirty commentaries on holiness by Alliance clergy and laypersons.

365. ———, eds. *Prayer Voices: A Popular Theology of Prayer*. Camp Hill, Pa.: Christian Publications, 1993. 308 p.

Twenty reflections on prayer by Alliance clergy and laypersons.

366. Cowles, H. Robert, K. Neill Foster, and David P. Jones, eds. *Missionary Voices: A Popular Theology of Missions*. Camp Hill, Pa.: Christian Publications, 1996. 279 p.

Brief articles on a variety of topics related to missions.

367. Crawford, Don. *Miracles in Indonesia: God's Power Builds His Church*. Wheaton, Ill.: Tyndale House, 1972. 160 p.

A popular account of the remarkable growth of the Indonesian church during the 1960s and early 1970s. Includes a chapter-length interview of a C&MA missionary.

368. Crawford (J)ohn Charles McKay (1859-1936). *Be Ye Holy: Teaching on the Sanctified Life*. Boone, Ia.: Boone Biblical College, 1913. 53 p.

Meditations on 1 Pet. 1:16.

369. ———. *Examples of the Spirit Filled Life, and What the Holy Spirit Is to Believers*. Boone, Ia.: Boone Biblical College, 1923. 53 p.

Sermons on New Testament characters and the sanctifying, teaching, and intercessory work of the Holy Spirit.

370. ———. *The Holy Spirit and Holy Living*. Boone, Ia.: Boone Biblical Ministries, 1984. 251 p.

Reprint of 368, 369, and 371.

371. ———. *Led of the Spirit: Testimony and Teaching Showing the Leading of the Holy Spirit Is Practical*. Boone, Ia.: Boone Biblical College, 1913. 71 p.

Crawford's spiritual autobiography.

372. Crawford, Lois (1893 or 1894-). *Papa and I: The Story of J. Charles Crawford*. Boone, Ia.: n.p., 1981. 231 p.

John Charles McKay Crawford, known as the George Müller of Iowa, founded Boone Biblical College and the ministries associated with it. The college was once affiliated with the Alliance (1905-1916). Crawford served as superintendent of the Western District of the C&MA from 1910 to ca. 1916.

373. Cressman, Norman M. *Revelation As a Missionary Sees It*. Washington, D.C.: Gospel Tabernacle, [ca. 1940]. 31 p.

Meditations, by a C&MA missionary to Cambodia, from a premillennial, pretribulation-rapture perspective, with frequent allusions to oriental wedding customs.

374. *Crisis in Viet Nam*. New York; Toronto: Christian and Missionary Alliance, [196-?]. 6 p.

An appeal for prayer, money, and more missionaries to meet the challenges of an undersupply of national pastors and an unnamed "liberal" organization.

375. Crockett, William V., ed. *Four Views on Hell*. Grand Rapids: Zondervan, 1992. 190 p.

The editor is professor of New Testament at Alliance Theological Seminary.

376. Crockett, William V. "The Metaphorical View." In *Four Views on Hell*, ed. William Crockett, 43-76. Grand Rapids: Zondervan, 1992.

The images of heaven and hell presented in the Bible should not be taken literally, but heaven and hell are real places. The Christians of the second century believed that hell is a place of eternal, conscious torment.

377. ———. "Will God Save Everyone in the End?" In *Through No Fault of Their Own?: The Fate of Those Who Have Never Heard*, eds. William V. Crockett and James G. Sigountos, 159-66. Grand Rapids: Baker, 1991.

Some Pauline texts seem to suggest that Paul is a universalist, but Paul's constant use of "insider-outsider" language indicates that outsiders must trust in Christ if they are to be included in the people of God..

378. ———. "Wrath That Endures Forever." *Journal of the Evangelical Theological Society* 34 (June 1991): 195-202.

The writings of Paul the Apostle indicate that once the wicked go so far as to place themselves under eschatological wrath God will withdraw his love from them forever

379. Crockett, William V., and James G. Sigountos, eds. *Through No Fault of Their Own?: The Fate of Those Who Have Never Heard*. Grand Rapids: Baker, 1991. 278 p.

Evangelical scholars discuss, from the perspective of history, biblical exegesis, and missiology, the fate of those who have never heard the Gospel.

380. *Crusade Songs: Purposefully Selected for Evangelistic Campaigns, Bible Conferences, and Missionary Conventions*. Harrisburg, Pa.: Christian Publications, 1937. 96 p.

381. Cullis, Charles. *More Faith Cures, or Answers to Prayer in the Healing of the Sick*. Boston: Willard Tract Repository, 1881. 105 p.

Includes an account of the healing of R. Kelso Carter (p. 44-48).

382. Cummings, Marjorie J. *Sunrise Furlough*. Philadelphia: Dorrance and Company, 1969. 187 p.

A biography of C&MA missionaries Paul and Priscilla Johnson, who were murdered by bandits in Thailand in 1952. Cf. 567.

383. Cunningham, John A. *Building My Church*. Edmonton, Alta.: China Alliance Press (Canada), 1992. 171 p.

A popular exposition of the Acts of the Apostles.

384. ———. *The Ministry of the Holy Spirit*. Edmonton, Alta.: by the author, [1986?]. 36 p.

Being filled with the Holy Spirit involves a crisis that leads to a process. An excerpt from 385.

385. ———. *Understanding God's Truth: How Progressive Revelation Can Help You Understand the Bible*. Beaverlodge, Alta.: Buena Book Services, 1981. 175 p.

Homespun reflections, often including illustrations from his more than 50 years as a C&MA pastor. Cf. 384.

386. Cunningham, Raymond J. "From Holiness to Healing: The Faith Cure in America, 1872-1892." *Church History* 43 (December 1974): 499-513.

A. B. Simpson's healing services and his Berachah Home led to his being "recognized as a leader of the faith-cure school, second only to Charles Cullis" (p. 503).

387. Curtis, Carolyn. *A Man for All Nations: The Story of Clyde and Ruth Taylor*. The Jaffray Collection of Missionary Portraits, 20. Camp Hill, Pa.: Christian Publications, 1998. 207 p.

Clyde Willis Taylor (1904-) best known for his service with the National Association of Evangelicals (1944-1974) began his career in ministry at 19, as the youngest missionary ever sent overseas by the C&MA. He worked among the Campo Indians of Peru (1925-1929). In 1932 the Taylors were posted to Colombia, where they served until 1941.

388. Cutts, Gracie B. (1924-). *Angel at the Bridge*. Toccoa Falls, Ga.: Toccoa Falls College Press, 1997. 207 p.

The story of Alice, a Moni from Irian Jaya, whom C&MA missionaries Bill and Gracie Cutts adopted while on the field, illustrates the differences between Western and Moni cultures and the impact of the Gospel on Moni social life and customs.

389. ———. *Let My People Go*. The Junior Jaffray Collection of Missionary Stories, book 1. Camp Hill, Pa.: Christian Publications, 1991. 29 p.

A retelling, for children, of 2151.

390. ———. *On Call.* The Junior Jaffray Collection of Missionary Stories, book 3. Camp Hill, Pa.: Christian Publications, 1991. 30 p.

A retelling, for children, of 2070.

391. ———. *To China and Back.* The Junior Jaffray Collection of Missionary Stories, book 4. Camp Hill, Pa.: Christian Publications, 1991. 27 p.

A retelling, for children, of 153.

392. ———. *"Weak Thing" in Moni Land.* The Junior Jaffray Collection of Missionary Stories, book 2. Camp Hill, Pa.: Christian Publications, 1991. 29 p.

A retelling, for children, of 393.

393. Cutts, William A. (1915-). *"Weak Thing" in Moni Land: The Story of Bill and Gracie Cutts.* The Jaffray Collection of Missionary Portraits, 2. Camp Hill, Pa.: Christian Publications, 1990. 164 p.

The Cuttses served as Alliance missionaries to the Moni people of Irian Jaya from 1950 to 1985. Bill, seriously deformed from birth, nevertheless managed to serve with distinction as a pioneer missionary. Cf. 392.

394. Dahms, John (V)oelzing (1919-1998). "Christian and Missionary Alliance Church Growth in Australia." *His Dominion* 10 (winter 1984): 17-23.

A history of the C&MA in Australia from its establishment in 1969 to 1992.

395. ———. "The Social Interest and Concern of A. B. Simpson." In *The Birth of a Vision*, eds. David F. Hartzfeld and Charles Nienkirchen, 49-74. Regina, Sask.: His Dominion, 1986.

A. B. Simpson rightly placed evangelism above social concern, but his intention to work among "the neglected classes," led him and his co-workers to establish rescue homes for women, schools for the poor, orphanages, rest homes, medical missions, and industrial missions; and to engage in famine relief and temperance work. He deplored the oppression of the poor and the harshness and selfishness of American society, yet he condemned socialism. Unfortunately, the Alliance began to de-emphasize social concern after 1908, perhaps in response to the social gospel of contemporary liberalism.

396. Dale, Daryl. *Children's Coordinator Notebook.* Colorado Springs: The Christian and Missionary Alliance, 1993. 130 p.

397. ———. *Teaching Basics, Adult: A Teacher Certification Book.* Camp Hill, Pa.: Christian Publications, 1985. 80 p.

398. ———. *Teaching Basics, Junior: A Teacher Certification Book.* Camp Hill, Pa.: Christian Publications, 1984. 73 p.

399. ———. *Teaching Basics: Primary.* Camp Hill, Pa.: Christian Publications, 1985. 77 p.

400. ———. *Teaching Basics, Youth: A Teacher Certification Book.* Camp Hill, Pa.: Christian Publications, 1985. 80 p.

401. ———. *Youth Worker's Manual.* Camp Hill, Pa.: Christian Publications, 1987. 125 p.

402. Damboriena, Prudencio. *Tongues As of Fire: Pentecostalism in Contemporary Christianity.* Cleveland, Oh: Corpus Books, 1969. 256 p.

Classifies the C&MA as a Holiness group; regards A. B. Simpson's doctrine of sanctification as the most thorough of any advocate of Holiness; and considers his repudiation of the Pentecostals' "evidence doctrine" (1907) as the first response by the Holiness movement to Pentecostalism.

403. Damron, Troy. *A Tree God Planted.* Toccoa, Ga.: Cross Reference Books, 1982. 207 p.

A history of Toccoa Falls College.

404. Davey, James A. *God Is the Superintendent: Seventy-five Wonderful Years: A Historical Narrative of the North Side Church of the Christian & Missionary Alliance, Pittsburgh, Pa., 1894-1969.* Harrisburg, Pa.: Christian Publications, 1969. 68 p.

The church was founded by A. B. Simpson as the first "branch" of the C&MA in Pittsburgh. Its first pastor was E. D. Whiteside. The founding members of the church were former rescue mission workers.

405. Davey, James E. *The Riches of Grace.* Harrisburg, Pa.: Christian Publications, 1974. 64 p.

Meditations on knowing Christ.

406. David, Ira E. *Christ Our Coming King*. Alliance Colportage Series. Harrisburg, Pa.: Christian Alliance Pub. Co., 1928. 116 p.

Sermons on premillennial eschatology.

407. ———. *Not I, but Christ.* New York: Christian Alliance Pub. Co., 1901. 114 p.

A meditation on "entire consecration" as exemplified in the life and ministry of Jesus and the Apostle Paul. Chapter one recounts the author's own experience of self-surrender.

408. David, V. D. *The Life More Abundant.* South Nyack, N.Y.: Christian Alliance Pub. Co., [ca. 1900]. 32 p.

A Tamil itinerant evangelist recounts his conversion and baptism in the Holy Spirit. Includes a report on the results of a deeper life convention for Syrian Orthodox Christians in Travancore, India (at which women preached).

409. Davidson, Jack. "Hmong Ethnohistory: An Historical Study of Hmong Culture and Its Implications for Ministry." D.Miss. diss., Fuller Theological Seminary, 1993. 240 p.

Includes a history of the Hmong church, which began in 1950 as a result of C&MA missionary work in Laos. As of 1993, more than 115,000 Hmong were residing in the United States, of whom 20,000 were attending C&MA churches.

410. Davis, George (T)hompson (B)rown (1873-). *China's Christian Army: A Story of Marshall Feng and His Soldiers*. New York: Christian Alliance Pub. Co., 1925. 136 p.

411. Davis, George W. *Gleams from the Morning Star and Gleams from the Sun of Righteousness*. Los Angeles: Premier Pub. Co., [ca. 1914]. 196 p.

Sermons on the Second Advent. Originally delivered in the Gospel Tabernacles of Los Angeles and Pasadena.

412. Davis, Kenneth Robert (1943-). "100 Churches in a Single Day!" D.Min. diss., Fuller Theological Seminary, 1992. 443 p.

Analyzes Easter 100, a project involving the planting of 101 churches in the United States and Puerto Rico. The project would have been more successful if its leaders had been properly trained to deal with the challenges of ministering to the previously unchurched.

413. *Dawn among the Dyaks*. New York: The Christian and Missionary Alliance, 1947. 30 p.

A brief history of Alliance missions in Kalimantan, Indonesia (1928-1947).

414. Dayton, Donald Wilber. "The Rise of the Evangelical Healing Movement in Nineteenth Century America." *Pneuma* 4 (spring 1982): 1-18.

A. B. Simpson was second only to Charles Cullis as a leader of the divine healing movement of his day. Simpson was more Christocentric than most others in the movement, and his rejection of "means" made him more radical. He and R. Kelso Carter were later forced by the ill health of some of their most saintly colleagues to moderate their position.

415. ———. *Theological Roots of Pentecostalism*. Grand Rapids: Francis Asbury Press, 1987. 199 p.

A. B. Simpson was such an important forerunner of Pentecostalism that "when Pentecostalism did emerge, some observers thought it a split within the Christian and Missionary Alliance" (p. 176).

416. de Jesus, Benjamin P. "A Study of the Aspects of the Church Program of the Christian and Missionary Alliance Churches of the Philippines with Implications for Christian Education." Ed.D. thesis, Southwestern Baptist Theological Seminary, 1978. 296 p.

CAMACOP churches tend to be leader-centered and to stress worship and teaching over fellowship and service.

417. de Jesus, Benjamin P., and Deborah Cowles. *A Man Sent from God*. Manila: Alliance Publishers, 1986. 134 p.

Biography of Rev. Florentino Deterra de Jesus, Sr., former head of the Christian and Missionary Alliance Churches of the Philippines (CAMACOP) and the Philippine Council of Evangelical Churches.

418. de Vries, Henri (1847-1932). *The Incarnate Son of God: A Series of Devotional Studies on the Person of Christ*. New York: Christian Alliance Pub. Co., 1921. 273 p.

Lectures on Christology originally delivered at Nyack Missionary Institute and other Bible schools in New York City.

419. ———. *The Lord's Anointed Prophet, Priest and King: A Series of Devotional Studies on the Redemptive Work of Christ*. London: Marshall Brothers, 1925. 400 p.

420. Decision Magazine. *Great Churches of Today: Outstanding Congregations, Their Leaders, Their Program, Their People.* Minneapolis: World Wide Publications, 1973. 147 p.

First Alliance Church, Mansfield, Ohio, is the subject of chapter 11.

421. Deegan, Charles. "Understanding Indian Culture and the Minnesota Chippewa Indian in the City." In *Missions and the Indian Church*, 22-37. Cass Lake, Minn.: Alliance Indian Publications, 1972.

Native Americans value human relationships above all else and will subordinate material and employment-related interests to the interests of family and friends. The Christian Indian needs to become like Christ in an authentically Indian way.

422. Deem, Fred. *"In Modern Setting" and Another Story: "If the Miracles of the New Testament Took Place in Our Day, How Would They Be Received?"* New York: Christian Alliance Pub. Co., [ca. 1900]. 76 p.

This retelling (set in contemporary Kansas) of two of the miracles of healing recounted in Acts suggests that such blessings of the kingdom of God can be appropriated in the here and now.

423. *The Deeper Life Pulpit Commentary.* Camp Hill, Pa.: Christian Publications, 1993-.

A commentary series that aims to combine both expository soundness and an emphasis on the deeper life within a homiletical framework. The contributors are Alliance pastors.

424. Denton, Joseph (1896-1963). *Gun-Pit to Pulpit: Autobiography of Joseph Denton, Evangelist.* Akron, Ohio: by the author, [193-?]. 32 p.

Denton was a former British soldier who became a Christian at the Akron Gospel Tabernacle.

425. Derk, Francis H. *Heart Beats.* n.p., [ca. 1970]. 25 p.

The author's collected poems.

426. ———. *"Write the Vision, Make It Plain"* n.p., 1973. 32 p.

Biography of Georgia L. Derk (d. 1966), founder of the Women's Missionary Prayer Fellowship (WMPF).

427. *The Development of the Indigenous Church.* New York: The Christian and Missionary Alliance, [1957?]. 11 p.

The Alliance is more concerned with principle than method. It seeks to foster independence and to avoid anything that would create dependence. However, some national workers, e.g., translators, will always need to work under the oversight of the mission and be paid by the mission.

428. Dholakia, Nerius Peter. "A Survey and Critical Evaluation of the Christian and Missionary Alliance Ministries in Gujarat." M.Th. thesis, South Asia Institute of Advanced Christian Studies, 1990.

Deals at length with the manifestations, in C&MA settings, of the 1905-1906 revival in India.

429. Diener (W)illiam. *Medio siglo de testimonio para Cristo: Obra de la Alianza Cristiana y Misionera en Chile*. Temuco, Chile: Imprenta Alianza, 1947.

A history of the C&MA in Chile, 1897-1947.

430. Dieter, Melvin Easterday. *The Holiness Revival of the Nineteenth Century*, 2nd ed. Studies in Evangelicalism, no 1. Lanham, Md.: Scarecrow Press, 1996. 319 p.

A. B. Simpson's fourfold Gospel, and in particular his articulation of the themes of divine healing and premillennialism, served as the doctrinal standard for many emerging holiness churches, among them the Pilgrim Holiness church founded by Seth Cook Rees and Martin Wells Knapp (both of whom left the Alliance in 1897).

431. Dinwiddie, Howard B. (d. 1925). *Report of a Missionary Survey of the Republic of Ecuador, South America*. New York: Christian and Missionary Alliance, 1924. 40 p.

An account of the author's fact-finding mission to Ecuador. Covers geography, climate, and constituent ethnic groups. Also assesses the possibilities for the expansion of the C&MA mission.

432. Dirks, Randall Philip. "Styles and Stages of Relationships between Missionaries and Leaders of the Churches: Reflections from Adult Developmental Theory." Ph.D. diss., Trinity Evangelical Divinity School, 1995. 288 p.

Attempts to gain a clearer understanding, through ethnographic interviews, of the relationships between North American missionaries and the leaders of the C&MA churches in South America. Includes an integrated model for the formation of church leaders in Latin American churches of the C&MA.

433. Dittmar, John W. *What Are Your Answers?* Baltimore: by the author, [ca. 1960]. 25 p.

Questions for a survey of the North American Alliance constituency on how the Alliance should go about meeting its goals for extension.

434. *The Diversion of Missionary Forces and Resources*. New York: Christian Alliance Pub. Co., 1912. 16 p.

Laments the fact that an alarming number of Christians are supporting independent missionaries. The missionaries of established missions like the C&MA are usually more qualified, have better (and more efficient and cost-effective) support structures, and are generally more effective than the independents.

435. Dixon, Bertha Pinkham. *A Romance of Faith*. n. p., [193-?]. 206 p.

Bertha Pinkham Dixon and her husband W. T. Dixon were Quakers who became attracted to the holiness movement and ultimately joined the Alliance. They went on to establish Alliance branches in Southern California.

436. Dixon, Mary (1908-1994). *A White Lady Doing Nothing in the Tropics: The Story of Herman and Mary Dixon*. The Jaffray Collection of Missionary Portraits, 15. Camp Hill, Pa.: Christian Publications, 1996. 189 p.

The Dixons served as C&MA missionaries to the Dyaks of East Kalimantan, Indonesia, 1933-1945 and 1948-1951 (the latter period is the subject of the present work.)

437. Dobbin, Murray. *Preston Manning and the Reform Party*. Toronto: James Lorimer and Co., 1991. 230 p.

Characterizes Manning's home church, First Alliance Church (Calgary, Alta.) as a close (if not closed) community of well-to-do, mostly middle-aged people who believe in the inerrancy of the Bible, the subordination of women, and the utter sinfulness of homosexuality; but who, at the same time, glorify individualism and free enterprise.

438. Donle, Charles B. *How to Interest the Young in Bible Truths*. New York: The Book Stall, 1919. 113 p.

439. ———. *"Uncle Charlie's" 25 Bible Objectalks for Children and Young People*. New York: The Book Stall, 1922. 145 p.

440. Dowdy, Homer E. *The Bamboo Cross: Christian Witness in the Jungles of Viet Nam*. New York: Harper and Row; Harrisburg, Pa.: Christian Publications, 1964. 239 p.

An account of a group of Montagnards who had been evangelized by C&MA missionaries and who must now live out their faith in the face of the increasing menace of the Viet Cong.

441. Dowie, John Alexander (1847-1907). "The Great Neglected Chapter." *Leaves of Healing*, 25 September 1897, 763-67.

Many of the healings reported by A. B. Simpson and his associates are fraudulent, and especially the healing (reported in *The Christian Alliance* of 3 July 1891) of a Mr. Weeks, who later confessed to being an escaped criminal and to feigning the paralysis of which he was supposedly cured. Simpson has failed to acknowledge publicly his error. He further errs in requiring people for whom he prays to claim healing in spite of overwhelming indications that they have not in fact been healed.

442. ———. "The Great Neglected Chapter." *Leaves of Healing*, 12 March 1898, 388-93.

R. Kelso Carter's account (in his *Faith Healing Reviewed after Twenty Years*) of Dowie's unsuccessful prayers on his behalf for healing fails to mention that the real cause of Carter's failure to be healed was his own sin of abandoning his wife. Carter, like many holiness preachers, is a hypocrite. "Divine healing has been cursed by many of its advocates, and especially by R. Kelso Carter and A. B. Simpson" (p. 393).

443. Downey, Murray (W)illiam (1910-1992). *The Art of Soul-Winning*. Grand Rapids: Baker, 1963. 176 p.

A textbook on personal evangelism. Includes arguments (with proof texts) to use in witnessing to communists, Roman Catholics, and the major cults.

444. ———. *The Art of Soul-Winning*, 2nd ed. Grand Rapids: Baker, 1989. 196 p.

Includes additional chapters on witnessing to Freemasons, members of the Worldwide Church of God, and followers of the New Age Movement.

445. ———. *The Book of Books*. Harrisburg, Pa.: Christian Publications; Beaverlodge, Alta.: Horizon House, [1976-ca. 1980]. 10 vols.

An introductory textbook on the Bible designed for use in theological education by extension.

446. ———. *Dare to Share: A Manual on Soul-Winning*. Grand Rapids: Baker, 1972. 31 p.
Reprint of 451.

447. ———. "The Day of the Lord." Master's thesis, Wheaton College, 1955. 157 p.
The events associated with the Day of the Lord in the Old Testament are the same as those associated with the term in the New Testament. The resurrection of believers and the "rapture" are also interchangeable terms.

448. ———. *James: A Practical Faith*. Chicago: Moody Press, 1972. 143 p.
A textbook that includes a commentary, sermon outlines, and Bible study aids.

449. ———. *Learning to Care, Daring to Share*. Harrisburg, Pa.: Christian Publications, [1972?] 32 p.
A reprint of 451. Adapted for use by churches of the C& MA.

450. ———. *Living in the Eye of the Storm: Another Look at the Day of the Lord*. Burlington, Ont.: Welch Pub. Co., 1989. 214 p.
Develops to their logical conclusion the ideas set forth in 447, i.e., the rapture of the church will occur at Christ's return, after the great tribulation mentioned in Rev. 7:9-14.

451. ———. *A Manual on Soul-Winning: A Condensation of 10 Lessons from the Author's Book, "The Art of Soul-Winning."* Grand Rapids: Baker, 1958. 23 p.
Cf. 446.

452. ———. *Sermons on Christian Commitment or, What Is a Christian?* Grand Rapids: Baker, 1963. 100 p.

453. ———. "Triumph out of Tragedy." *The Evangelical Christian*, November 1956, 525-26.
Persecution will be a fact of life for Christians until the Lord returns, but Jesus will soon return to inaugurate the day of the Lord. Repentance on the part of the church could lead to a revival that would result in the evangelization of the world in this generation.

454. Downey, Raymur (J)ames (1941-). "Leadership Training in African Context." *His Dominion* 12 (summer 1986): 18-24.

A description, drawn from the author's 12 years as a C&MA missionary to the Democratic Republic of the Congo, of Congolese Protestant church culture. Includes suggested strategies for the training of African church leaders.

455. ———. "Ministerial Formation in Africa: Implications of the Experiential Component for Training Zairian Alliance Church Leadership." Ph.D. diss., Fuller Theological Seminary, 1985. 325 p.

Proposes a contextualized experience-centered program of ministerial formation. Includes a history of theological education in the Communauté Évangélique de l'Alliance de Zaire (CÉAZ).

456. ———. "Old Testament Patterns of Leadership Training: Prophets, Priests, and Kings." Master's thesis, School of World Mission, Fuller Theological Seminary, 1981. 131 p.

Suggests that CÉAZ Churches stress apprenticeship, recognize nonformal education, and encourage creativity in the process of developing church leaders.

Draper, Ken, joint author. "A. B. Simpson and World Evangelization." In *The Birth of a Vision*, eds. David F. Hartzfeld and Charles Nienkirchen, 195-219.

See 2060.

457. Dugan, Richard. *How to Know You Are Born Again*. Van Nuys, Calif.: Bible Voice, Incorporated, 1978. 166 p.

Describes how to become a Christian and gain assurance of salvation. Cf. 458.

458. ———. *How to Know You'll Live Forever!* Minneapolis: Bethany House, 1984. 166 p.

Reprint of 457.

459. Dupont, Anthony Paul (1966-). "Divine Healing in the Experience, Thought, and Ministry of Albert Benjamin Simpson." Master's thesis, Asbury Theological Seminary, 1993. 74 p.

Simpson vigorously promoted divine healing, but he considered it to be less important than either salvation or sanctification.

460. Dyer, Helen S. *A Life for God in India: Memorials of Mrs. Jennie Fuller of Akola and Bombay*. New York: Alliance Press Co., [ca. 1904]. 190 p.

Jennie Frow (1851-1903) went to India as a Methodist missionary in 1877. She and her husband Marcus B. Fuller joined the Alliance in 1892. Her ministry included writing, teaching, famine relief, and caring for orphans. She died of cholera contracted from the ailing missionaries she was nursing.

461. ———. *Revival in India: "Years of the Right Hand of the Most High."* New York: Gospel Publishing House, 1907. 158 p.

Chapter 13 recounts the ways in which the revival of 1905-1906 manifested itself at Alliance conferences, orphanages, and mission stations: visions, restitution of stolen property, sacrificial giving, and an overwhelming sense of the presence of the Holy Spirit.

462. Dyer, Wayne Robert. "The Role and Function of the District Superintendent for Support and Effective Ministry from the Perspective of the Local Congregation in the Christian and Missionary Alliance." D.Min. diss., Drew University, 1984. 209 p.

Unless the present structure is altered, district superintendents of the C&MA in the USA will continue to spend most of their time in crisis management and will therefore be unable to help churches that have either declined or stagnated.

463. Dys, Pat, and Linda Corbin. *He Obeyed God: The Story of Albert Benjamin Simpson.* Camp Hill, Pa.: Christian Publications, 1986. 75 p.

Focuses on the role obedience played in Simpson's life.

464. Easton, T. C. *The Precious Blood.* Christian Alliance Tracts. New York: Christian Alliance Pub. Co., [1898?]. 27 p.

The text of an address on the Atonement given at the Old Orchard Convention, August 1898.

465. Edman (V)ictor Raymond (1900-1967). *But God!: Little Lessons of Large Importance Learned from the Holy Scriptures, with Poems by Annie Johnson Flint.* Grand Rapids: Zondervan, 1962. 152 p.

466. ———. "Christian Ethics." In *The Word for This Century*, ed. Merrill C Tenney, 131-52. New York: Oxford University Press, 1960.

The Scriptures present an absolute and authoritative, though unsystematic, form of ethics based on the ministry and teaching of Jesus and the writings of the apostles.

467. ———. "The Conflict of the Spirits." In *One Race, One Gospel, One Task: World Congress on Evangelism, Berlin, 1966, Official Reference Volumes*, eds. Carl F. H. Henry and W. Stanley Mooneyham, 2:38-9. Minneapolis: World Wide Publications, 1967.

Missionaries should expect to engage in spiritual warfare.

468. ———. *Crisis Experiences in the Lives of Noted Christians*. Minneapolis: Bethany Fellowship, [ca. 1970]. 96 p.

His own crisis with respect to his decision to become an Alliance missionary to Ecuador is recounted on p. 9-18.

469. ———. *The Delights of Life*. Chicago: Scripture Press, 1954. 268 p.

Meditations on Scripture.

470. ———. *The Discipline of Duty*. Wheaton, Ill.: Scripture Distribution Society, [193-?]. 14 p.

471. ———. *The Disciplines of Life*. Chicago: Scripture Press, 1948. 254 p.

Devotional thoughts on 31 spiritual disciplines.

472. ———. *Fear Not: A Book of Devotions*. Wheaton, Ill.: Scripture Press, 1957. 63 p.

473. ———. *Finney Lives On: The Man, His Revival Methods, and His Message*. New York: Fleming H. Revell, 1951. 250 p.

Charles Finney's principles of revival are still applicable in modern America.

474. ———. "For Years I Prayed for Them, Now They Pray for Me." *Christian Life*, January 1963, 30-31.

While a C&MA missionary in Ecuador, Edman had heard of the fierce Auca tribe and he later trained the first missionaries sent to them—all of whom the Auca later murdered. After a church was established among the tribe, Edman learned that the Auca had begun to pray for him.

475. ———. *Great Is Thy Faithfulness: A Book of Devotions*. Wheaton, Ill.: Scripture Press, 1954. 64 p.

476. ———. *He Leadeth Me: Lessons on God's Gracious Guidance in the Lives of Those Who Love and Trust Him.* Wheaton, Ill.: Scripture Press, 1959. 95 p.

477. ———. *In Quietness and Confidence: A Book of Devotions.* Wheaton, Ill.: Victor Books, 1953. 64 p.

478. ———. *In Step with God.* London: Oliphants, 1965. 62 p.

479. ———. *Just Why? A Little Book to Help Find the Answer to One of Life's Most Perplexing Problems—Why? Often This Question Is Asked in the Bible and Here Are the Explanations Given in the Scriptures.* Wheaton, Ill.: Scripture Press, 1956. 88 p.

480. ———. *The Light in Dark Ages: Eighteen Centuries of Missions from the Giving of the Great Commission to the Beginning of Modern Missions under William Carey.* Wheaton, Ill.: Van Kampen Press, 1949. 451 p.

481. ———. *Look unto the Hills.* Chicago: Moody Press, 1968. 61 p.
Meditations on biblical place names.

482. ———. *Not Ashamed: A Book of Devotions.* Wheaton, Ill.: Scripture Press, 1955. 64 p.

483. ———. *Not Somehow, but Triumphantly: Lessons Shared with Young Hearts at Wheaton College These Many Years, and Learned by Them So That They Might Become More Than Conquerors through the Savior.* Grand Rapids: Zondervan, 1965. 214 p.

484. ———. *Out of My Life: Lessons Learned from the Scriptures on the Presence of God with His Own, and on the Promises Made by the Most High.* Grand Rapids: Zondervan, 1961. 224 p.
Some of the autobiographical information in these accounts relates to Edman's involvement with the C&MA.

485. ———. "The Person and Work of the Holy Spirit." *Foundations of the Faith: Twelve Studies in the Basic Christian Revelation*, 121-31. Westwood, N.J.: Fleming H. Revell, 1951.
An overview of the biblical teaching on the personality, divinity, work, gifts, and fruits of the Holy Spirit. Mentions, but does not dwell on, the enduement of power for service.

486. ———. *Signs of the Second Coming*. Camp Hill, Pa.: Christian Publications, [1969?].

A collection of articles originally published in *The Alliance Witness*.

487. ———. *Storms and Starlight*. Wheaton, Ill.: Van Kampen Press, 1951. 240 p.

Meditations on Christ.

488. ———. *Sweeter than Honey: A Little Book of Deep and Personal Devotion to the Saviour, with Poems from John Oxenham's Bees in Amber, and Meditations from Bible References to Honey*. Chicago: Scripture Press, 1956. 96 p.

489. ———. *Swords and Plowshares*. Chicago: Van Kampen Press, 1967. 31 p.

490. ———. "Ten Marks of the Spirit-filled Christian" *Christian Life* 20 (January 1959): 14-15.

These are: fruitfulness, love, joy, peace, long-suffering, gentleness, goodness, faithfulness, meekness, and temperance.

491. ———. *Then and There: The Touch of the Eternal upon Human Hearts*. Grand Rapids: Zondervan, 1964. 224 p.

492. ———. *They Found the Secret: Twenty Transformed Lives That Reveal a Touch of Eternity*. Grand Rapids: Zondervan, 1960. 159 p.

Each of the biographees had had a crisis experience that moved him or her out of Christian mediocrity and into the Spirit-filled life. The only one with Alliance connections is Edman himself; his story is recounted in the epilogue.

493. ———. *Windows in Heaven*. Chicago: Moody Press, 1967. 61 p.

494. ———. *Wiser Than They Thought*. Wheaton, Ill.: Scripture Press, 1960. 142 p.

Meditations on the Christmas story.

495. ———. *Your Personal Problems Answered: Questions and Answers Selected from the "Personal Problem Clinic" Conducted in Christian Life Magazine*. Wheaton, Ill.: Scripture Press, 1959. 64 p.

496. Edman (V)ictor Raymond (1900-1967), and Robert A. Laidlaw. *The Fullness of the Spirit*. Harrisburg, Pa.: Christian Publications, 1966. 36 p.

The sealing of the Spirit provides assurance of salvation and the ability to live a holy life; the Spirit's anointing, discernment; the Spirit's filling, power for service.

497. Edman (V)ictor Raymond (1900-1967), and Robert Edwin Nicholas (1882-). *Midnight Meditations*. n.p., 1957. 57 p.

498. Edwards, Jonathan. *The Life of David Brainerd, Missionary to the Indians, Taken from His Diary and Other Private Writings*. Edited and abridged by Homer W. Hodge. New York: Christian Alliance Pub. Co., 1925. 201 p.

499. Edwards, Kenneth Bruce. "The Development of a Learning Network in the Christian and Missionary Alliance of Canada." Ph.D. diss., University of Alberta, 1995. 361 p.

Respondents to the survey wanted to see courses in theology, pastoral studies, counseling, education, liberal arts, and communications and media delivered in intensive modules in a group setting using delivery methods compatible with the respondents' schedules. They were, however, unwilling to increase their financial support of the denomination's educational institutions.

500. Edwards, Mildred. *Elocile, or the King's Return*. New York: Christian Alliance Pub. Co., [ca. 1910]. 176 p.

An epic poem about the Second Advent.

501. Ekvall, David (P)aul (d. 1912). *Outposts, or Tibetan Border Sketches*. New York: Alliance Press Co., 1907. 227 p.

A history of the C&MA's Kansu-Tibetan Border Mission (Gansu province, China and southwestern Tibet) in commemoration of its tenth anniversary (1905).

502. Ekvall, Robert (B)rainerd (1898-1983). *Cultural Relations on the Kansu-Tibetan Border*. Chicago: University of Chicago Press, 1939. 103 p.

Pages 1-3 give an account of Ekvall's (C&MA) missionary work and scholarly research in the region.

503. ———. *Gateway to Tibet: The Kansu-Tibetan Border*. Harrisburg, Pa.: Christian Publications, 1938. 198 p.

Brings the history of the C&MA's Kansu-Tibetan Border Mission (cf. 501) up to date. (Author is the son of David P. Ekvall).

504. ———. *God's Miracle in the Heart of a Tibetan*. New York: The Alliance, 1936. 29 p.

Biography of Legs Bshad Rgya Mtso, a Tibetan scholar who became a Christian through the influence of Ekvall.

505. ———. *Monologues from the Chinese*. Harrisburg, Pa.: Christian Publications, 1939. 38 p.

Various responses of the Chinese to the Gospel, rendered in poetic form, and replete with references to Chinese social life and customs.

506. ———. *Tibetan Sky Lines*. New York: Farrar, Straus and Young, 1952. 240 p.

Incidents from the Ekvall family's missionary sojourn in Tibet that shed light on Tibetan culture.

507. ———. *Tibetan Voices*. New York: Harper and Brothers, 1939. 63 p.

A collection of poetry based on the author's experiences as a missionary.

508. Ekvall, Robert (B)rainerd (1898-1983), et al. *After Fifty Years: A Record of God's Working through the Christian and Missionary Alliance*. Harrisburg, Pa.: Christian Publications, 1939. 284 p.

A laudatory history of the C&MA, 1887-1937, the bulk of which is devoted to an overview of Alliance mission fields. Includes comprehensive lists of all Alliance educational institutions, deceased home workers, and deceased missionaries.

509. Eldridge, George N. (1847-1930). *Personal Reminiscences*. Los Angeles: West Coast Publishing Company, [ca. 1930]. 52 p.

Eldridge joined the C&MA in 1896, and served for a number of years as a district superintendent. He joined the Pentecostals in 1910 (the year his wife, under the ministry of John Salmon, received the baptism of the Holy Spirit with tongues), and played a key role establishing the Assemblies of God in California. He maintained his Alliance credentials until 1916.

510. Ellenberger, John (D)avid. "The Beginnings of Hymnology in a New Guinea Church." *Practical Anthropology* 9 (November-December 1962): 263-67.

The stages involved in the development of the hymnody of the Uhunduni people of Irian Jaya (among whom the author served as a C&MA missionary) were: the importation of hymnody from an adjacent culture, the use of local tunes to convey lyrics composed by a missionary, and the composition of indigenous tunes and lyrics.

511. ———. "Evangelistic Outreach in Irian Jaya." In *Church Growth in the Third World*, ed. Roger E. Hedlund, 279-82. Bombay: F. C. Durham for Gospel Literature Service, 1977.

Between 1957 and 1962 the Damals, an animistic people of Irian Jaya, decided as a group to follow Christ. To remain vital they must evangelize their own second and third generations and other people and tribes beyond their cultural borders. They must also reevangelize nominal Christians within their own cultural borders to prevent a resurgence of animism.

512. ———. *How to Pray for Your Missionaries*. Camp Hill, Pa.: Christian Publications, [198-?]. 12 p.

Based on the author's experience as a C&MA missionary in Irian Jaya.

513. ———. "The Impact of Damal World View on the Formation of a Local Theology in Irian Jaya." D.Miss. diss., Fuller Theological Seminary, 1996. 495 p.

Based on the author's attempt to contextualize theology among the Damal.

514. ———. "Is Hell a Proper Motivation for Missions?" In *Through No Fault of Their Own?: The Fate of Those Who Have Never Heard*, eds. William V. Crockett and James G. Sigountos, 217-27. Grand Rapids: Baker, 1991.

Jesus considered saving people from hell to be part of his ministry, but he evangelized above all as a lover. The disciples evangelized because they believed Jesus to be the only answer to humankind's lostness. Besides, they believed that the end of the age was near and that the discipling of all nations was a prerequisite for Jesus' return. For them, the threat of judgment was subordinated to Jesus' demand for Lordship.

515. ———. "Multi-individual Conversions in West Irian." *Evangelical Missions Quarterly* 1 (fall 1964): 31-34.

Missionaries from the individualistic West had to come to terms with the fact that, within the highland societies of Irian Jaya, decisions involving social change are made by the kinship group as a whole. Careful presentation of the Gospel—and especially of biblical eschatology—and circumspect behavior on the part of missionaries should prevent new converts from succumbing to native Melanesian millennialist movements.

516. ———. "The Planting of the Church among the Damals of West Irian." In *The Gospel and Frontier Peoples: Report of a Consultation, December, 1972,* ed. R. Pierce Beaver, 160-68. South Pasadena, Calif.: William Carey Library, 1973.

Deals with the planting of churches in the Ilaga Valley of Irian Jaya, concentrating on factors related to communication.

517. Elliott, David R. "Knowing No Borders: Canadian Contributions to American Fundamentalism." In *Amazing Grace: Evangelicalism in Australia, Britain, Canada and the United States*, eds. George A. Rawlyk and Mark A. Noll, 349-74. Montreal; Kingston, Ont.: McGill-Queen's University Press; Grand Rapids: Baker Books, 1994.

A summary of 518.

518. ———. "Studies of Eight Canadian Fundamentalists." Ph.D. diss., University of British Columbia, 1989. 466 p.

Simpson, perhaps the most successful Canadian fundamentalist, had a direct influence on P. W. Philpott, Aimee Semple MacPherson, L. E. Maxwell, and Oswald J. Smith; and an indirect influence on William Aberhart. He became a fundamentalist, not so much because of his ecclesiastical or theological background, but rather because of his emotional instability. Like Oswald J. Smith, he was a neurotic who required psychiatric treatment. More specifically, he suffered from severe depressions, psychosis, and psychosomatic illnesses. He also had schizophrenic tendencies. Philpott had an informal relationship with the Alliance. He had been ordained by the C&MA, healed in an Alliance meeting, and occasionally filled Alliance pulpits, but the Associated Gospel Churches (which he helped to found) did not adopt the fourfold Gospel, and he himself rejected "healing in the Atonement." Cf. 517.

519. Ellison, Craig W. (1944-). "Addressing Felt Needs of Urban Dwellers." *Urban Mission* 4 (March 1987): 26-42.

The evangelical church needs to combine ministries of compassion (tailored to the needs of a particular community) with evangelistic proclamation and programming if it expects to make an impact in the city.

520. ———. "Attitudes and Urban Transition." *Urban Mission* 2 (January 1985): 14-26.

Frequent change characterizes urban life and ought to be accepted and planned for by those involved in urban churches. A vital urban church will be allocentric, and neither overly attached to property nor afraid to take risks.

521. ———. "Growing Urban Churches Biblically." *Urban Mission* 6 (November 1988): 7-18.

Corporate prayer, contextualization, caring and compassion, commitment, courage, and cell groups are the marks of biblically based and growing urban churches such as the thriving C&MA church in Tokyo, Japan, led by Rev. Sam Kim.

522. Enlow, David (R)oland (1916-). *Church Usher: Servant of God.* Camp Hill, Pa.: Christian Publications, 1980. 64 p.

523. ———. "Lessons from a Twentieth Century Prophet." *Moody Monthly,* September 1980, 32-34.

A wide-ranging biographical snapshot that covers everything from A. W. Tozer's sense of humor to the vow he made at the time of his ordination.

524. Enlow, David (R)oland (1916-), and Dorothy Enlow. *Saved from Bankruptcy: The Story of the Boatbuilding Meloons*. Chicago: Moody Press, 1975. 111 p.

The Meloons founded Correct Craft. Company president Walter O. Meloon is a licensed worker with the C&MA.

525. Enns, Arno W. "The Christian and Missionary Alliance." In *Man, Milieu and Mission in Argentina: A Close Look at Church Growth.* Grand Rapids: Eerdmans, 1971. 258 p.

The C&MA churches in Argentina have (despite some periods of exceptional vitality) experienced slow growth because of tensions between the missionaries and the indigenous church, an overemphasis on evangelizing middle- and upper-class Argentines, the concentration of missionary effort on the Buenos Aires Bible Institute, a failure to develop lay leadership, and the excessive influence of the missionaries.

526. Ens, Marie (1934-). *Journey to Joy: The Story of Norman and Marie Ens*. The Jaffray Collection of Missionary Portraits, 11. Camp Hill, Pa.: Christian Publications, 1994. 175 p.

Norman (1934-1991) and Marie Ens served as C&MA missionaries to Cambodia from 1960 to 1975, with brief stints in Thailand during wartime. They later worked with Cambodian refugees in Thailand and then, from 1978 until Norm's death, as missionaries to Cambodian expatriots in Paris, France. Cf. 1017.

527. ———. *A Time for Mercy: Touching Stories of Open Arms and God's Love in the Streets and Alleys, Homes and Hospitals of Cambodia*. Camp Hill, Pa.: Christian Publications, 1998. 168 p.

Reminiscences of a former missionary to Cambodia (1960-1975) who returned to Phnom Penh in 1994, serving as an evangelist, director of the C&MA's women's ministry in Cambodia, and a relief worker, until the forced evacuation of all C&MA missionary personnel during the political unrest of July 1997.

528. Eramo, Rose Marie. "A Teacher Training Course for an African Bible School." Master's thesis, Wheaton College, 1970. 92 p.

Originally written as a textbook in the Bambara language for Ntoroso Central Bible School, Mali.

529. Erdel, Paul Arthur. "The Development of the Iglesia Misionera in Ecuador." D. Miss. diss., Trinity Evangelical Divinity School, 1985. 168 p.

Includes an account of the disagreement that arose between the Missionary Church Association and the C&MA with respect to their jointly administered mission in the province of Esmeraldas.

530. ———. "Henry Zehr: Never Sound Defeat." *Reflections: A Publication of the Missionary Church Historical Society* 2 (spring 1994): 8-11.

Henry Zehr (1877-1904) was the first missionary to be sent overseas by the Missionary Church Association. He served on the C&MA's South China field from 1902 until his death.

531. Erdman, Fred. *Why I Am Not a Christian Scientist*. New York: Christian Alliance Pub. Co., [ca. 1900]. 15 p.

Christian Science denies the reality of matter, evil, pain, and sickness. Among the 45 reasons for the author's rejection of the movement is the fact that its leader is a woman: nothing good has ever come from movements led by women.

532. Erskine, Thomas (1788-1870). *The Supernatural Gifts of the Spirit.* Edited by R. Kelso Carter. Philadelphia: Office of "Words of Faith," 1883. 48 p.

The supernatural gifts of the Spirit, and especially glossolalia and healing, are still valid and ought to be appropriated by all sincere believers. Comprises chapter five of Erskine's *The Brazen Serpent* and editorial commentary by Carter.

533. Eskridge, Larry K. "Only Believe: Paul Rader and the Chicago Gospel Tabernacle, 1922-1933." Master's thesis, University of Maryland, 1985. 278 p.

Under Rader's presidency (1919-1923) the C&MA expanded both its missionary force and its financial base, and Rader himself helped to raise a good deal of money for missions by speaking at missionary conferences. However, such C&MA luminaries as E. D. Whiteside (Rader's former mentor) and R. H. Glover thought him unfit for the leadership of the C&MA, and the latter resigned from the C&MA's Board of Managers in 1921 over the issue. By 1922, Rader's frequent absences from Board meetings, and his preoccupation with the Chicago Gospel Tabernacle and other outside interests began to trouble the rest of the leadership of the C&MA. The inevitable rupture occurred in December 1923. In the ensuing years, Rader's various organizations had cordial relationships with the C&MA, and the two groups often cooperated in mission ventures.

534. Espada-Matta, Alberto. "The Christian and Missionary Alliance of Puerto Rico: Indigenous Leadership in Partnership in Mission in the Caribbean." D.Miss. diss., Fuller Theological Seminary, 1992. 341 p.

A history of the Alliance in Puerto Rico. The development of indigenous leadership was a key factor in the growth of the church.

535. Estrada, María Alban, and Juan Pablo Muñoz. *Con Dios todo se puede: La invasión de los sectos al Ecuador*. Quito: Editorial Planeta, 1987. 206 p.

Since the 1960s, many Ecuadorians have become adherents of sects, among them the C&MA, which have introduced into a communitarian society an individualistic form of religion that focuses on the hereafter, eschews social action, and disrupts family relationships. Includes an interview with two adherents of the C&MA who recount experiences of persecution at the hands of Catholics and explain the differences between Catholicism and evangelicalism (p. 38-41).

536. Evearitt, Daniel (J)oseph. *Body & Soul: Evangelism and the Social Concern of A.B. Simpson*. Camp Hill, Pa.: Christian Publications, 1994. 164 p.

A reworking of the author's Master's thesis. The efforts of Simpson and his associates, although they did not address to any great extent the structural ills underlying social problems, should serve as an inspiration for today's socially conscious evangelicals.

537. ———. "Jewish Christian Missions to Jews, 1820-1935." Ph.D. diss., Drew University, 1988. 400 p.

Includes a discussion of the C&MA's efforts to evangelize Jews.

538. ———. "The Social Aspects of the Ministry and Writings of Albert B. Simpson." Master's thesis, Drew University, 1980. 148 p.

The "social activity of Simpson and his followers, while flowing from deep compassion and love, was always seen by them as a stop-gap effort to meet needs until Christ's return. . . . [I]t does not reflect the rigid self-isolation of fundamentalism, or the benign neglect of some evangelicals" (p. 131-32).

539. ———. "The Social Gospel vs. Personal Salvation: A Late Nineteenth-Century Case Study: Walter Rauschenbusch and A. B. Simpson." *Alliance Academic Review* (1997): 1-18.

Rauschenbusch (1861-1918) and Simpson both served churches in the impoverished Hell's Kitchen district of New York City. Rauschenbusch believed that the church was to be the catalyst for the gradual realization of the kingdom of God on earth. Simpson championed a personalist view of salvation that included a social dimension: the regenerate individual, freed from bondage to selfishness, would seek to meet the temporal needs of others in order to facilitate their conversion to Christ. But Simpson fully expected that social conditions would steadily deteriorate until the return of Christ. Nevertheless, he was even more involved in ministry to the poor than was Rauschenbusch. However, toward the end of his life he placed less and less emphasis on social action.

540. Ewart, Frank J. *The Phenomenon of Pentecost*. Houston, Tex.: Herald, 1947.

Pages 68-69 recount the Spirit-baptism of Sarah Coxe and other Alliance people in India during the revival of 1905-1906.

541. Fairley, Donald A. (1905-1990). *Hunting Pygmy Hunters*. Findlay, Ohio: Fundamental Truth Publishers, [ca. 1945]. 85 p.

A narrative of the author's ministry as a C&MA missionary (1924-ca.1945) among the Babongo pygmies of Gabon.

542. Fairley, Dorothy (M)illicent (1907-1982). *In God's Time, His Provision*. Salem, Ore.: Faith Press, 1982. 87 p.

Reminiscences taken mostly from her life (with husband Donald Fairley) as a C&MA missionary to Gabon (1929-1969); cf. 2069, which draws heavily on this work.

543. "Faith Healing." *The Christian*, 18 June 1885, 5.

Criticizes A. B. Simpson for implying in his article "The Principles of Faith Healing" (see 1803) that the redemption of the body can be achieved before the Lord's return.

544. Fant, David (J)ones (1868-1965). *A Railroad Engineer's Testimony*. New York: the Christian and Missionary Alliance, [ca. 1939]. 11 p.

The speech given by Fant, 22 September 1939, on the occasion of his retirement after 52 years as a railroad engineer (cf. 547).

545. Fant, David (J)ones (1897-1982). *A. W. Tozer: A Twentieth Century Prophet*. Harrisburg, Pa.: Christian Publications, 1964. 180 p.

An appreciation of Tozer as prophet, scholar, mystic, theologian, pastor, missionary, poet, author, and editor. Includes many quotations from both Tozer's works and those of writers who influenced him. Cf. 1954.

546. ———. *The Advance of Rome on America: The Political and Religious Significance of the Eucharistic Congress Held at Chicago, Illinois, June 20-24, 1926*. New York: Christian Alliance Pub. Co., 1926. 32 p.

America's 20,000,000 Roman Catholics are the best organized political force in the country, and their power has steadily increased as a result of Protestantism's loss of evangelistic zeal and its drift towards modernism and ritualism. Catholic dogma is pernicious, unbiblical, and un-Christian; and the Eucharistic Congress is part of the papacy's plan to attain worldwide political and religious control.

547. ———. *Ambassador on Rails: David J. Fant—Engineer Evangelist*. Harrisburg, Pa.: Christian Publications, 1948. 160 p.

Incidents from the life of David J. Fant, Sr. (1868-1965), a railroad engineer who joined the Alliance in 1901 and served the C&MA thereafter as a lay evangelist and preacher (cf. 544).

548. ———. "Early Associates of A. B. Simpson: A Reprint of the Biographical Articles Written by David J. Fant, Jr." *Southeastern District Report of the Christian and Missionary Alliance*, special ed., May 1977, 3-17.

Thorough biographical sketches, enriched by photographs and the author's personal reminiscences, of 25 of A. B. Simpson's co-workers.

549. ———. "Early Associates of A. B. Simpson: A. W. Roffe." *Southeastern District Report of the Christian and Missionary Alliance*, October-November 1977, 4-5.

Alfred William Roffe (1866-1947) was a former Salvation Army officer who joined the C&MA ca. 1919, serving as the superintendent of the Canadian District and establishing the Missionary Rest Home near Toronto. He was the father of Alliance missionary Ethel Bell (cf. 100).

550. ———, ed. *Foundations of the Faith: Twelve Studies in the Basic Christian Revelation*. Westwood, N.J.: Fleming H. Revell, 1951. 189 p.

An exposition of the Apostles' creed by leading evangelicals, including V. Raymond Edman and A. W. Tozer.

551. ———. *How Can Others Know You Are Saved?: The Way to Influence Made Plain*. Harrisburg, Pa.: Christian Publications, 1945. 13 p.

552. ———, ed. *Modern Miracles of Healing: Personal Testimonies of Well-known Christian Men and Women to the Power of God to Heal Their Bodies*. Harrisburg, Pa.: Christian Publications, 1943. 160 p.

The biographees are mostly prominent members of the C&MA.

553. ———. "The Pen of a Ready Writer." In *A. B. Simpson Centenary 1843-1943,* 10-13. New York: Christian and Missionary Alliance, 1943.

Simpson's prodigious output as a speaker and author can be directly attributed to the increased mental acuity that accompanied his physical healing. But he was more of a preacher than a writer; most of his books consist of transcribed sermons.

554. ———. *"Uncle" Gus Woerner: With Signs and Wonders*. Toccoa Falls, Ga.: Toccoa Falls College, 1978 . 156 p.

Biography of Gustave Woerner (1896-1978), C&MA missionary to South China, Indonesia, and Malaya, and instructor in missions at Toccoa Falls College (1944-1975). Based on Woerner's diary.

555. Fant, David (J)ones (1897-1982), and Addie Marie French. *All about the Sunday School: Instructions for the Conduct of an Average Sunday School—Courses of Study, Methods of Teaching, Departmental Grading, Accessories, and Literature*, 2nd ed. rev. Harrisburg, Pa.: Christian Publications, 1947. 192 p.

556. Farmer, Wilmoth Alexander (1877-1970). *Ada Beeson Farmer: A Missionary Heroine of Kwang Si China*. Atlanta: Foote & Davies, 1912. 325 p.

Ada Beeson (1871-1911) came to China in 1902 as the second missionary appointed by the Pentecostal Mission (Nashville, Tenn.) and sent under the jurisdiction of the C&MA. Her future husband (1904), Wilmoth Alexander Farmer, had been the first. Both resigned from the Pentecostal Mission and joined the Alliance in 1902 because they judged it unwise to splinter the existing work by joining the Pentecostal Mission's newly established mission board (1902) (cf. 102). This is also a good firsthand account of early C&MA work in Guangxi.

557. Farr, Frederic (W)illiam (1860-1939). *Alliance Arrows*. New York: Alliance Press Co., 1900. 163 p.

Seventeen sermons on various aspects of the Christian life.

558. ———. *The Christ You'll Have to Know*. Los Angeles: American Prophetic League, 1939. 112 p.

Sermon notes on the person of Christ, which were published after the author's death as a tribute to him by the American Prophetic League.

559. ———. "The City of God." In *Timely Prophetic Considerations*, 47-52. Los Angeles: American Prophetic League, 1940.

Ancient Greek mythology conceives of heaven as a pastoral paradise, but the Christian conception begins in a garden and ends in a city. At the return of Christ, heaven will come down to earth, and God will establish the celestial metropolis in which the righteous, in their new spiritual bodies, will live, work, and worship God for eternity.

560. ———. "I Say unto You: Watch." In *Timely Prophetic Considerations*, 71-76. Los Angeles: American Prophetic League, 1940.

This command, addressed to the church during the tribulation (Rev. 16:15) serves as an exhortation to the church in every age to maintain unswerving devotion to the Lord, because his return is imminent.

561. ———. "The Literal and the Mystical Bodies." In *Timely Prophetic Considerations*, 17-24. Los Angeles: American Prophetic League, 1940.

Christ has a material human body in which he lived and died for our salvation, which was resurrected, and in which he ascended to heaven. His mystical body, composed of Christian believers, remains on earth in intimate union with him to finish his work of redemption.

562. ———. *A Manual of Christian Doctrine*. New York: The Alliance Press, [ca. 1900]. 182 p.

A textbook in systematic theology based on various standard works (as well as the lectures of F. L. Chapell) but in which Alliance distinctives shine through; e.g., the "habitation" theory of sanctification is preferred to the eradicationist or suppressionist theories. Based on lectures delivered at the New York Missionary Training Institute, where the author was an instructor.

563. ———. "The Marriage of the Lamb Is Come." In *Timely Prophetic Considerations*, 64-70. Los Angeles: American Prophetic League, 1940.

Rev. 19:9 foretells the marriage supper of the Lamb, which will commemorate the victory of God over the powers of evil and the eternal union of the bride (faithful believers) and the bridegroom (Christ).

564. ———. *The Representative Christ*. New York: Raff, 1896. 219 p.

Twenty-one Christological sermons published on the occasion of the beginning of Farr's pastorate at Bethlehem Baptist Church, Philadelphia.

565. ———. *Spiritual Jewels from the Pen of a Preacher of Beloved Memory*. Los Angeles, Calif.: American Prophetic League, 1940. 39 p.

Sermons.

566. Farr, Frederic (W)illiam (1860-1939), Howard W. Kellogg, and Keith L. Brooks. *Timely Prophetic Considerations*. Los Angeles: American Prophetic League, 1940. 78 p.

"Twelve papers from the research files of the American Prophetic League, Inc.," four of which are by Farr.

567. *Father Forgive Them*. New York: The Christian and Missionary Alliance, 1953. 11 p.

The story of the martyrdom of Paul and Priscilla Johnson, Alliance missionaries to Thailand, who were killed by bandits in 1952 (cf. 382). Includes photographs.

568. Faupel, D. William. *The Everlasting Gospel: The Significance of Eschatology in the Development of Pentecostal Thought*. Sheffield: Sheffield Academic Press, 1996. 326 p.

A. B. Simpson influenced the development of Pentecostalism through his "Keswickian" doctrine of sanctification, his teaching on divine healing, his premillennialism, and his identification of Jesus as the Jehovah of the Old Testament. His associate George B. Peck introduced proto-Pentecostal Frank Sandford to British Israelism.

569. Fenton, W. J. *Letter to Rev. A. B. Simpson, President of the Christian and Missionary Alliance, New York, Replying to His Strictures on the Promotion of Companies*. Toronto: the author, 1902. 31 p.

A response to Simpson's editorial in the *Christian and Missionary Alliance* of 8 February 1902, denouncing Christians who become involved in "get rich quick" schemes. Fenton asks whether Simpson is obliquely referring to his (Fenton's) own business activities, since John Salmon and others have been slandering him by questioning his business practices and accusing him of mistreating his wife. He denies these accusations and claims that Salmon had forced him out of the Alliance and that Salmon had become an advocate of both sinless perfection and John Alexander Dowie's extreme views on healing.

570. Ferris, Robert W. "Canadian Bible College." In *Renewal in Theological Education: Strategies for Change*, 45-56. Wheaton, Ill.: The Billy Graham Center, Wheaton College, 1990.

Canadian Bible College (CBC) and Canadian Theological Seminary (CTS) have demonstrated an attentiveness to the needs of the church in their internship program, Doctor of Ministry program (CTS), curriculum review (CBC), commitment to provide alternative delivery systems (CTS), and outcomes assessment (CTS).

571. Fessenden, David E. "Present Truths: The Historical and Contemporary Distinctives of the Christian and Missionary Alliance." *Alliance Academic Review* (1999): 1-30.

Although other denominations may have adopted the elements of Simpson's fourfold Gospel, they lack the Christocentric focus of the

Alliance, e.g., the Assemblies of God lack "a practical and functional understanding of the active and present ministry of Christ as Sanctifier" (p. 5). The C&MA is also characterized by the following emphases, which set it apart from many other denominations: "innovation and 'Evangelical Ecumenicity'. . . balance and tolerance . . . simplicity in organization, adaptability in structure. . . ." (p. 23-25) and the extensive involvement of the laity in ministry. The C&MA's stress on balance may explain the conflicts between Paul Rader and the Board of Managers: "Where Rader sought a rejection of institutionalized churches in favor of loosely organized urban tabernacles, the rest of the Alliance leadership wanted the small, mostly rural church to work side-by-side with the tabernacles" (p. 24).

572. ———. *The Waiting Missionary*. Missionary—That's Me! Series. Camp Hill, Pa.: Christian Publications, 1995. 29 p.

Introduces children to the prerequisites for effective missionary service.

573. Fiedler, Klaus. *The Story of Faith Missions*. Oxford: Regnum Lynx, 1994. 428 p.

A. B. Simpson's Evangelical Missionary Alliance prospered only when the Christian Alliance embraced the cause of missions. The vitality of the two organizations depended on the spiritual truths embodied in Simpson's fourfold Gospel. The C&MA's organizational structure, like that of many faith missions, combined Bible school, fellowship movement, and mission. But it also included an atypical element, the independent congregation, that provided the catalyst for the C&MA's eventual evolution from fellowship movement to free church. In the move towards Calvinism that accompanied the C&MA's reaction to Pentecostalism the formal ministry of women became increasingly restricted. Racism also affected the C&MA. In the 1920s, the Alliance had more American blacks in its missionary force than any other mission, but a decade later it decided to stop accepting blacks for missionary service. The next black American C&MA missionary was not sent until 1979.

574. *Fifteenth Anniversary Exercises of the New York Missionary Training Institute*. New York: The Missionary Training Institute, 1897. 6 p.

575. *Fifty Years for Christ in Chile*. Temuco, Chile: [Christian and Missionary Alliance in Chile], [1947?]. 24 p.

The history of the Christian and Missionary Alliance in Chile, published on the 50th anniversary of the arrival of the first Alliance missionaries.

576. *Fire on the Frontier.* New York: Christian and Missionary Alliance, 1959. 11 p.

Recounts the mass conversions of the Uhunduni people of Irian Jaya and describes C&MA missionary activity among neighboring peoples.

577. First Alliance Church, Calgary, Alta. *40-year History of First Alliance Church, The Christian and Missionary Alliance, 1938-1978.* Calgary, Alta.: First Alliance Church, ca. 1978. 60 p.

578. Fitzstevens, John A. "The History of Dalat School, Dalat, Viet Nam." Master's thesis, Stetson University, 1966. 95 p.

Dalat School, which has since been moved to Penang, Malaysia, is the Alliance's boarding school for the children of its missionaries to Asia.

579. Fleagle, Arnold R. *First Peter: Strategic Imperatives for Suffering Saints.* The Deeper Life Pulpit Commentary. Camp Hill, Pa.: Christian Publications, 1997. 239 p.

580. Fletcher (R)ebecca I. "Bethany Home, Toronto." *Triumphs of Faith,* May 1890, 105-8.

The story of the founding of an Alliance healing home.

581. ———. "Himself Hath Done It, or How the Lord Taught Me Divine Healing." *Triumphs of Faith,* January 1890, 15-19.

John Salmon and A. B. Simpson figure prominently in her testimony.

582. Flower, Alice Reynolds (1890-). *Grace for Grace: Some Highlights of God's Grace in the Daily Life of the Flower Family.* Springfield, Mo.: by the author, 1961. 179 p.

Mary Alice Reynolds, the author's mother, helped establish the C&MA Gospel Tabernacle in Indianapolis. Under the leadership of George N. Eldridge, it soon became the largest Alliance branch in the Midwest. In 1907 the Reynolds family experienced Spirit-baptism with tongues and left the Gospel Tabernacle to help found a Pentecostal church. Alice and her husband, Joseph James Roswell Flower (1888-1970) were associated with the ministry of D. Wesley Myland from 1911 until 1914, when the Flowers were asked to help found Gospel Publishing House.

583. *For Courage and Fortitude: The Philippine Internment of an Alliance Missionary*. New York: The Christian and Missionary Alliance, [1945?]. 19 p.

William F. Christie (1903-1990) son of C&MA missionary William Christie, and 12 other Alliance missionaries to the Philippines were interned by the Japanese from 28 January 1943 to 3 February 1945.

584. Ford, Jerry. "Mission to the Montagnards." *World Vision*, May 1971, 22-23, 28.

A brief history of missionary work among the ethnic minorities of Vietnam, most of which was carried out by the C&MA, the pioneer mission to these peoples.

585. Forder, Archibald (1865-1934). "Alone in the Desert." In *Yarns of the Near East*, ed. Basil Mathews, 72-80. London: United Council for Missionary Education, 1922.

An excerpt from *With the Arabs in Tent and Town* that recounts Forder's journey to Jauf in northern Saudi Arabia.

586. ———. *The Branded Foot: The Story of Life and Experiences among the Arabians*. New York: Christian Alliance Pub. Co., 1921. 234 p.

A novel, based on the author's own experiences, for the purpose of both arousing interest in missions to Arabs and demonstrating how to evangelize Muslims.

587. ———. "The Friend of the Wild Arab." In *Yarns of the Near East*, ed. Basil Mathews, 62-71. London: United Council for Missionary Education, 1922.

An excerpt from 589 that recounts Forder's journey to Kef in the Jordanian desert.

588. ———. *Ventures among the Arabs in Tent and Town: Thirteen Years of Pioneer Missionary Life with the Ishmaelites of Moab, Edom and Arabia*. Boston: W. N. Hartshorn, 1905. 304 p.

Recounts Forder's adventures as a colporteur to the Arabs of Moab and Arabia, including some already recounted in 589. Includes an account of the reasons for his leaving the Church Missionary Society (he was a Wesleyan Methodist and refused to be confirmed as an Anglican).

589. ———. *With the Arabs in Tent and Town: An Account of Missionary Work, Life and Experiences in Moab and Edom and the First*

Missionary Journey into Arabia from the North. London: Marshall Brothers, 1902. 257 p.

Forder spent five years in Palestine and Arabia as an independent colporteur/medical missionary among the Arabs before being expelled by the Turkish forces of occupation in 1897. That year he began a career as an Alliance missionary to Arabia that was fraught with hair-raising adventures and narrow escapes from death.

590. Foster, K. Neill. "Dangers in the Deliverance Ministry." *Alliance Academic Review* (1996): 171-82.

Among these are: failure to distinguish between true and false deliverances; the possibility of sustaining physical, spiritual, or emotional injury while performing an exorcism; constructing a methodology for, or a theology of, exorcism based on isolated Scriptures or experiences; emphasizing exorcism to the exclusion of more important aspects of ministry; and attributing all sinful behavior to the influence of demons.

591. ———. *The Discerning Christian: How the Believer Detects Truth from Error in the Midst of Today's Religious Confusion.* Harrisburg, Pa.: Christian Publications, 1981. 164 p.

"The more loving you are, the more discerning you are certain to be" (p. 100).

592. ———. "Discernment, the Powers and Spirit-Speaking." Ph.D. diss., Fuller Theological Seminary, 1988. 268 p.

Glossolalia may be of divine or demonic origin. The Scriptures strongly imply that glossolalia, when interpreted, constitutes prophecy. Therefore the procedure outlined in 1 John 4:1-3 for testing the spirits of prophecy should be applied to glossolalia as well. Those who have done so report that, in the overwhelming majority of cases involved, the spirit underlying a particular manifestation of glossolalia was, in fact, demonic. This experiential evidence refutes the claim of Pentecostals that tongues-speaking is the initial physical evidence of the baptism of the Holy Spirit. Cf. 595.

593. ———. *Fasting: The Delightful Discipline.* Camp Hill, Pa.: Christian Publications, 1995. 14 p.

"The absence of the miraculous among many of today's Christians could be traceable to the lack of this forgotten discipline" (p. 8). Reprint of chapter six of 596.

594. ———. *Gardez-vous des faux prophètes*. Camp Hill, Pa.: Christian Publications, 1991. 23 p.

Sermons preached in June 1990 at L'Église d'Avéa II in Libreville, Gabon, on the nature of false prophecy and on the principles of discernment believers can use to protect themselves from deception.

595. ———. "Glossolalia and the Ruark Procedure: Distinguishing between True and False Utterances." *Alliance Academic Review* (1997): 155-74.

A condensation of 592.

596. ———. *The Happen Stance*. Beaverlodge, Alta.: Horizon House, 1977. 159 p.

A popular treatise on spiritual warfare. Liberally spiced with autobiographical anecdotes.

597. ———. *Help! I Believe in Tongues: A Third View of the Charismatic Phenomenon*. Minneapolis: Bethany Fellowship, 1975. 160 p.

Proposes a set of biblical criteria that can be used to test manifestations of glossolalia to determine whether they originate with the Holy Spirit or an evil spirit. Glossolalia is one of the gifts of the Holy Spirit, but not the initial physical evidence of the baptism of the Holy Spirit. (The author received the gift of tongues in the course of writing this book.) Cf. 598 and 602.

598. ———. *I Believe in Tongues, But*. . . . Eastbourne, England: Victory Press, 1976. 160 p.

Reprint of 597.

599. ———. "Implicit Christians: An Evangelical Appraisal." *Alliance Academic Review* (1998): 123-46.

The popular belief that some people will attain eternal life without expressly confessing Jesus Christ must be rejected because it implies that "holy pagans" must exhibit good works in order to be saved.

600. ———. *Lessons Learned When a Teenager Was Liberated from LSD, or the Weapons of Our Warfare*. Beaverlodge, Alta.: Evangelistic Enterprises Society, 1971. 35 p.

Lists of topically arranged Bible verses (along with brief explanatory comments) on the subject of spiritual warfare.

601. ———. *A Revolution of Love.* Minneapolis: Dimension Books 1973. 92 p.

A first-person account of the western Canadian revival (1971-1972) in which C&MA evangelists Ralph and Lou Sutera figured prominently.

602. ———. *The Third View of Tongues: Calm for the Charismatic Controversy.* Beaverlodge, Alta.: Horizon House, 1982. 160 p.

Reprint of 597.

603. ———. *Twenty-three Reasons Why Some Are Not Healed.* Kamloops, B.C.: n.p., [1964?]. 12 p.

604. ———. *Warfare Weapons.* Camp Hill, Pa.: Christian Publications, 1995. 176 p.

Reprint of 596.

605. Foster, K. Neill, and Paul L. King. *Binding & Loosing: How to Exercise Authority of the Dark Powers.* Camp Hill, Pa.: Christian Publications, 1998. 352 p.

The scriptural prerogatives of binding and loosing should not be restricted to matters of church discipline and authority, for God desires to share his authority and power with all believers in all situations involving spiritual warfare. Yet such authority needs to be exercised in the context of Bible-based discerning prayer, lest it degenerate into the excesses of the Faith Movement, or be used indiscriminately as a panacea for problems that ought to be confronted in a different way.

606. Foster, K. Neill, with Eric Mills. *Dam Break in Georgia: Sadness and Joy at Toccoa Falls.* Beaverlodge, Alta.: Horizon House, 1978. 159 p.

The story of the flood of 6 November 1977, that killed 41 people and caused widespread damage on the campus of Toccoa Falls College (a college affiliated with the C&MA).

607. Foster, Marilynne E., comp. *Walk Around the World: Healings, Miracles, Power Encounters and Other First Person Accounts from Earth's Frontiers.* Camp Hill, Pa.: Christian Publications, 1996. 154 p.

Vignettes, by Alliance missionaries, about life on the mission field.

608. Francis, Mabel (1880-1975). *Filled with the Spirit . . . then What?* Harrisburg, Pa.: Christian Publications, 1974. 61 p.

The filling of the Holy Spirit is not intended to be an ecstatic experience that never wears off, but rather the entry into a life of increasing union with Christ through the often painful annihilation of selfish desires.

609. Francis, Mabel (1880-1975), with Gerald B. Smith. *One Shall Chase a Thousand*. Harrisburg, Pa.: Christian Publications, 1968. 119 p.

New Englander Mabel Francis served as a C&MA missionary to Japan (1909-1964). Her ministry included teaching, preaching, evangelism, feeding the hungry, and caring for the sick. Twice (in 1929 and 1941) she chose to remain in Japan after the C&MA had ordered its missionaries to return home. In 1962 she became the first living person to receive Japan's highest civilian award, the Fifth Order of the Sacred Treasure. (The Order is normally conferred posthumously.)

610. ———. *One Shall Chase a Thousand: The Story of Mabel Francis*. The Jaffray Collection of Missionary Portraits, 9. Camp Hill, Pa.: Christian Publications, 1993. 148 p.

Includes four appendices not found in 609, otherwise identical to it. Cf. 737.

611. Frank, Douglas. *Less than Conquerors: How Evangelicals Entered the Twentieth Century*. Grand Rapids: Eerdmans, 1986. 320 p.

A. B. Simpson represents a transition between the old heroism of character and the new heroism of power—the new hero being "somewhat less of an earnest moral struggler."

612. Freligh, Harold (M)eredith (1891-). *The Eight Pillars of Salvation*. Minneapolis: Bethany Fellowship, 1962. 123 p.

A textbook on soteriology. The initial experience of salvation is usually so narrowly focused on forgiveness of sin that the "law of sin" that causes us to sin is not dealt with. Hence the need for sanctification, a post-conversion crisis experience that gives us "deliverance from self and sin and [shows] us God's way of victory" (p. 94). Foreword by A. W. Tozer.

613. ———. *Job—an Early Document of Fundamental Doctrines*. Harrisburg, Pa.: Christian Publications, 1947. 91 p.

The book of Job sets forth the fundamental doctrines of angels and Satan, God, human being, and sin. It also points forward to the coming of Christ. Cf. 614.

614. ———. *Newborn: A Basic Handbook on Salvation for Personal or Group Study*. Minneapolis: Bethany Fellowship, 1975. 123 p.
Reprint of 613.

615. ———. *Say unto This Mountain*. Harrisburg, Pa.: Christian Publications, 1966. 40 p.
Five articles on intercessory prayer, some of which were originally published in the *Alliance Witness*.

616. ———. *Studies in Revelation*. Harrisburg, Pa.: Christian Publications, 1969. 4 v.
A commentary and study guide for adult Sunday school classes.

617. Fried, Ralph (1892-). *Pilgrims—Whither Bound?* New York: Christian and Missionary Alliance, 1945. 11 p.
A history of Alliance missions in Palestine to Jews, Muslims, and nominal Christians.

618. ———. *Reaching Arabs for Christ*. Grand Rapids: Zondervan, 1947. 125 p.
Vignettes from the Frieds' sojourn in Palestine as C&MA missionaries (1926-1948).

619. Friesen, Kenneth Leroy. "A Study of the Doctrine of Holiness in the Thought of A. W. Tozer." M. Div. thesis, Western Evangelical Seminary, 1971. 217 p.
Tozer believed that holiness involves "the full restoration of the fulness of God to the whole of the Christian in actual experience" (p. 198) via self-surrender and the baptism of the Holy Spirit.

620. Frodsham, Stanley Howard. *With Signs Following: The Story of the Pentecostal Revival in the Twentieth Century*, rev. ed. Springfield, Mo.: Gospel Publishing House, 1946. 279 p.
Includes accounts of Pentecostal visitations among adherents of the C&MA (p. 45-47) and Alliance missionaries (p. 134-36).

621. Frost, A. J. *The Victorious Sacrifice of Christ*. Living Truths, vol. 1, no. 26. Nyack, N.Y.: Christian Alliance Pub. Co., 1901. 22 p.
An exposition of Isa. 53:1-12.

622. Frost, Henry W. *Miraculous Healing: A Personal Testimony and Biblical Study*. Westwood, N.J.: Fleming H. Revell, 1952. 125 p.

God grants healing to some Christians through prayer, to other Christians via rest or medical means. A. B. Simpson's doctrine of "healing in the Atonement" cannot bear the scrutiny of either Scripture or logic.

623. Fuller, Jennie Frow (1851-1903). *The Ideal Missionary*. [New York]: Christian and Missionary Alliance, [189-?]. 14 p.

Exhorts the Christians of the homeland to embrace and live out the same ideal of supernatural Christian life that they expect of missionaries.

624. ———. *The Ministry of Prayer*. Nyack, N.Y.: Christian Alliance Pub. Co., 1901. 31 p.

Mostly on intercessory prayer.

625. ———. *Texts Illuminated, or God's Care*. New York: Christian Alliance Pub. Co., 1898. 166 p.

A series of autobiographical illustrations of Scriptures that speak of God's care for his people. Originally published serially in *The Christian and Missionary Alliance.*

626. ———. *The Wrongs of Indian Womanhood*. New York: Fleming H. Revell, 1900. 302 p.

A catalogue, based on Indian sources, of the degradation—child marriage, prostitution, enforced widowhood, and other injustices—that was the lot of contemporary Indian women. The real remedy for these wrongs is the Christian Gospel, because it elevates women in a way that culture and civilization alone cannot.

627. Fuller, Mary Lucia Bierce (1882-1923). *The Triumph of an Indian Widow: The Life of Pandita Ramabai*. New York: The American Auxiliary of the Ramabai Mukti Mission, 1928. 72 p.

The author was the daughter of Ramabai's spiritual mentor, C&MA missionary Jenny Fuller. Ramabai (1858-1922) regarded the C&MA as the mission closest to her Mukti Mission in vision; and so in her will she arranged that the Alliance would administer the work of the Mukti Mission on the retirement of her successor.

628. Funé, Jean Émile Roger (1902-2000). *Feet Dipped in Oil!* Hillsboro, Ore.: George Funé, 1994. 192 p.

Quebecker Jean Funé spent 42 years as a C&MA missionary to Vietnam and Cambodia.

629. *Gabon's Glorious Hour*. New York: The Christian and Missionary Alliance, [1960?]. 4 p.

An account of the recent expansion of the churches planted by the Alliance in Gabon.

630. Gaebelein, Arno Clemens (1861-1945). *The Healing Question: An Examination of the Claims of Faith-Healing and Divine Healing Systems in the Light of Scriptures and History*. New York: Publication Office "Our Hope," 1925. 132 p

The advocates of divine healing have misunderstood the Scriptures, and the testimonies used in the promotional literature of healer-evangelists such as F. F. Bosworth turn out, on investigation by physicians, to be untrue. If obedience leads to freedom from sickness, then well-known healers who became sick and died must have been harboring unconfessed sin. Indeed, since A. B. Simpson was afflicted both mentally and physically during his last two years of life he must have, as certain of his followers claimed, departed in some way from a fully consecrated life. God often does heal the sick in response to prayer, but just as often such prayers seem to go unanswered. This mystery can best be explained with reference to the sovereignty of God.

631. Gainforth, Mary (1857-1930). *The Life and Healing of Mrs. Mary Gainforth*. Trenton, Ont.: Jarrett Printing and Pub. Co., [ca. 1930]. 75 p.

The founder of Faith Mission, Trenton, Ont., which became an Alliance branch in 1914. She met A. B. Simpson at the 1902 convention of the Alliance in Toronto: "Dr. Simpson assured [her] that it was right for women to anoint and pray for the sick, until God raised up men elders and then to stand at their side and help" (p. 39).

632. Gangel, Kenneth. "The Bible College: Past, Present, and Future." *Christianity Today*, 7 November 1980, 34-35.

In an 1880 editorial in "The Gospel in All Lands," A. B. Simpson made a plea for a college to train missionaries. He answered his own call by founding the Missionary Training Institute.

633. Gardiner, Gordon P. *Champion of the Kingdom: The Story of Philip Mauro*. New York: Bread of Life, 1961. 79 p.

Philip Mauro (1859-1952) the noted evangelical author, Bible teacher, and lawyer was converted in 1903 in A. B. Simpson's Gospel Tabernacle in New York City. His first three books were published by the Alliance.

634. Garrison, Eze(k)iel (D)ay (1887-1960). *An Outcaste Transformed.* New York: The Christian and Missionary Alliance, 1937. 29 p.

The story of Sagunabai, a low-caste Hindu of Maharashtra state, who became a Christian through the influence of C&MA missionaries. Through her life of hope amid poverty and suffering, and especially through the many miraculous healings that occurred in response to her prayers, many Indians of both high and low castes became Christians.

635. Garrison, John Marcus. *The Garrison of Faith.* Golden, B.C.: by the author, 1997. 111 p.

The history of Marcus Irenaus Garrison (1847-1897), Elizabeth Day Garrison (1856-1933), and of those of their three generations of descendants who have been involved in some form of cross-cultural ministry. Marcus and Elizabeth Garrison were among the first Alliance missionaries to India, arriving in 1893. Their children Ruth (1891-1973), (A)llelujah (I)renaeus (1885-1954), and Kiel D. (Ezekiel Day) 1887-1960) also served as Alliance missionaries to India; as did the author, the son of A. I. Garrison.

636. Gee, Donald (1891-1966). *After Pentecost.* Springfield, Mo.: Gospel Publishing House, 1945. 111 p.

Credits A. B. Simpson with originating the fourfold Gospel. Pentecostals appropriated the concept, substituting baptism in the Holy Spirit for sanctification.

637. Gerig, Ezra S. *La plenitud del Espíritu Santo.* Camp Hill, Pa.: Christian Publications, 1985. 31 p.

A standard Holiness presentation of the fullness of the Holy Spirit.

638. Gesswein, Armin (R)ichard. *How to Overcome Discouragement.* Camp Hill, Pa.: Christian Publications, 1991. 19 p.

Recognition and refusal, combined with dependence on God, are the proposed strategies.

639. ———. *With One Accord in One Place.* Harrisburg, Pa.: Christian Publications, 1978. 93 p.

The Holy Spirit's fullness and power are encountered preeminently in the church as an assembled body.

640. Gibbons, Alice. *The People Time Forgot.* Chicago: Moody Press, 1981. 347 p.

"The people time forgot" are the Dani and Ahundini peoples of Irian Jaya, among whom Dan and Alice Gibbons served as C&MA missionaries.

641. Gibbud, H. B. *Sermonizing Sophie, or Sophie's Second Sermon.* Springfield, Mass.: by the author, 1906. 16 p.

Sequel to 643.

642. ———. *Sophie's Second Sermon.* New York: Loizeaux Brothers, [ca. 1906]. 30 p.

Reprint of 641.

643. ———. *Sophie's Sermon, or Called to Scrub and Preach.* Springfield, Mass.: by the author, 1893. 16 p.

A wide-ranging stream-of-consciousness autobiographical sermon in broken English, based on the utterances of Sophie Lichtenfels (1843-1919), a German immigrant scrubwoman-evangelist, who was an influential member of Simpson's Gospel Tabernacle.

644. Gifford, Ronald. *Zechariah: A Gift of Vision.* The Deeper Life Pulpit Commentary. Camp Hill, Pa.: Christian Publications, 1998. 296 p.

645. *The Gift of Tongues: Seek Not, Forbid Not: A Critique of the Revived Tongues Movement.* Nyack, N.Y.: Christian and Missionary Alliance, [196-?]. 7 p.

Updated version of 303. Includes an addendum by A. W. Tozer.

646. Gilbertson, Richard Paul. "Albert Benjamin Simpson's View of the Baptism of the Holy Spirit, 'a View Distinct Though Not Unique': A Study in Historical Theology." M.Th. thesis, Regent College, 1988. 291 p.

Simpson differed from his Holiness contemporaries in stressing Spirit-baptism as a fulfillment of the "new covenant" promises of Jer. 31 and Ezek. 36. Simpson also more fully explored the relationship between water baptism and Spirit-baptism, the nature of the believer's union with Christ and the Spirit's role in mediating this union, and the work of the persons of the Trinity in relation to the Christian life. Cf. 647.

647. ———. *The Baptism of the Holy Spirit: The Views of A. B. Simpson and His Contemporaries.* Camp Hill, Pa.: Christian Publications, 1993. 351 p.

Rev. ed. of 646.

648. Gilbreath, Edward. "The 'Jackie Robinson' of Evangelism." *Christianity Today*, 9 February 1998, 52-55, 57.

A native of Cleveland, Howard O. Jones graduated from Nyack College in 1944, after which he pastored Alliance churches in Harlem and Cleveland. He later began a radio ministry to Liberia, Ghana, and Nigeria before becoming the Billy Graham Evangelistic Association's first black associate evangelist in 1957. He retired from the BGEA in 1994.

649. Girolimon, Michael Thomas. "A Real Crisis of Blessing: Part I." *Paraclete* 27 (winter 1993): 17-26.

A. B. Simpson and the early Pentecostals had similar doctrinal convictions regarding salvation, sanctification, healing, and the return of Christ. Unlike many of his dispensationalist contemporaries, Simpson did not believe that spiritual gifts had ceased, but rather that they were about to be restored to the church.

650. ———. "A Real Crisis of Blessing: Part II." *Paraclete* 27 (spring 1993): 1-6.

Simpson rejected the Pentecostal doctrine of glossolalia as the initial physical evidence of the baptism of the Holy Spirit because it called into question the claim of non-tongues-speakers to have been baptized in the Spirit, and because he disagreed with the Pentecostal exegesis of the relevant Scriptures. Even if he had supported the Pentecostal view he would have had a difficult time convincing his loosely organized constituency to accept it as a formal doctrine.

651. Glass, Clyde McLean. "Mysticism and Contemplation in the Life and Teaching of Albert Benjamin Simpson." Ph.D. diss., Marquette University, 1997. 434 p.

A. B. Simpson was mystic in the apophatic tradition of St. Augustine, Brother Lawrence, St. Francis de Sales, and the Quietists. He was one of only a handful of mystics who have managed to blend mysticism, activism, and evangelical theology. He emphasized the believer's union with Christ to a greater degree than any of the other leaders of the Holiness or Deeper Life movements. However, in formulating doctrine, he tended to invest his own experience of God with inordinate authority, e.g., since he himself had experienced divine healing he therefore believed that divine healing must be available to all believers.

652. Glover, Robert Hall (1871-1947). *Ebenezer: A Record of Divine Deliverances in China*. New York: Alliance Press Co., 1905. 106 p.

A catalogue of the persecutions suffered by Alliance missionaries and their converts during the establishment of the Alliance's mission work in China. Treats the Boxer Rebellion at length.

653. ———. *Missions: Charity or a Debt, Which?* New York: Christian Alliance Pub. Co., [ca. 1910]. 4 p.

Missions ought to be regarded as a debt in response to one's own salvation, one's loyalty to Christ, and one's consequent compassion for the unevangelized.

654. ———. *The Real Heart of the Missionary Problem.* New York: The Christian and Missionary Alliance, 1915. 15 p.

The heart of the problem is not primarily personnel, money, or method, but love for Christ. An address delivered at the New York Convention of the C&MA, October 1911.

655. ———. *Trustees of the Gospel.* New York: Christian Alliance Pub. Co., [ca. 1910]. 4 p.

Christians have been entrusted with the Gospel. They are the only means at God's disposal for its worldwide propagation.

656. *God Visits the Tribesmen.* New York: Christian and Missionary Alliance, 1952. 10 p.

A history of the Alliance's missionary activity in Laos, 1929-1952.

657. *God's Chosen People.* Home Missions Series. New York: Christian and Missionary Alliance, 1956. 4 p.

Describes the Alliance's evangelization of Jews in the United States.

658. *The Gods Have Heavy Ears.* World Missions Series. New York: The Christian and Missionary Alliance, 1947. 31 p.

A thorough account, rich in biographical data, of the Alliance mission in India, 1887-1947.

659. Goetz, William R. *Apocalypse Next.* Beaverlodge, Alta.: Horizon House, 1991. 391 p.

A best-selling futurist *Late Great Planet Earth*-like interpretation of biblical prophecies in light of current events. Author was a Canadian C&MA pastor. Originally published in 1980.

660. ———. *The Economy to Come: And Other Signs of the Earth's Impending Climax.* Beaverlodge, Alta.: Horizon House, 1988. 394 p.

Focuses on the economic aspects of biblical prophecy that are, in the author's opinion, being fulfilled in contemporary developments such as the increasing use of credit cards and the increasing concentration of political and economic power. This edition updates the 1983 original.

661. ———. *Holiness and the Gray Areas: Distinguishing between Liberty and Legalism*. Camp Hill, Pa.: Christian Publications, 1997. 10 p.
Christians should seek to glorify God and to avoid harming their bodies, compromising their loyalty to Christ, and causing other Christians to stumble.

662. ———. *Missions Today*. High School Selectives. Wheaton, Ill.: Scripture Press, 1970. 15 p.
Basic information, for teenagers interested in missions, on the nature of missionary work and the qualifications required of prospective missionaries.

663. ———. *UFO's: Friend, Foe or Fantasy?* Camp Hill, Pa.: Horizon Books, 1997. 306 p.
UFO's exist and are demonic in origin. Christians can resist abductions by UFO's in the same way that they would resist any other demonic attack: by rebuking the potential abductor by the authority of Jesus Christ.

664. Goffin, Alvin Matthew. "Protestantism in Ecuador: A Case Study in Latin American Church History, 1895-1980s." Ph.D. diss., Florida State University, 1990. 264 p.
Protestants took advantage of social distress to make evangelistic inroads in Ecuador. They made many worthwhile contributions in health care, education, communications, and disaster relief, but these benefits came at the expense of traditional ways of life (especially among indigenous peoples). Protestant groups, including the C&MA and HCJB Radio, also did little to alleviate the social problems plaguing Ecuador. Cf. 665.

665. ———. *The Rise of Protestant Evangelism in Ecuador, 1895-1990*. Gainesville, Fla.: University Press of Florida, 1994. 203 p.
Revised and updated version of 664.

666. Gold, Leon B. "Thailand." In *The Church in Asia*, ed. Donald E. Hoke, 625-41. Chicago: Moody Press, 1975.

Covers the work of the Alliance and the other missions working in Thailand. The Alliance mission, which works in the 19 eastern provinces, began in 1928.

667. *Golden Anniversary of Hoover Heights Christian and Missionary Alliance Church, 1900-1950*. New Castle, Pa.: n.p., 1950. 20 p.

The church began as an interdenominational Sunday School, became a house church, and took the name Pentecostal Mission on the dedication of its building in 1900. After searching for a worthy group with which to affiliate itself, the church joined the C&MA in 1902.

668. *The Golden Anniversary of the Christian and Missionary Alliance: 1887-1937*. New York: The Alliance, [1937?]. 15 p.

A celebration of 50 years of missions and evangelism by the still-interdenominational society, which had recently (1934) grudgingly concluded that "there were localities where the organization of a New Testament church by the Society was unavoidable" (p. 10).

669. Gordon (A)doniram (J)udson (1836-1895). *Brother Moses, or "I Kicks Agin It, Sah!"* n.p., [ca. 1893]. Reprint, New York: Christian Alliance Pub. Co., [ca. 1910]. 30 p.

Brother Moses's, (a black acquaintance of A. J. Gordon's) railings against church amusements and fundraising activities set the stage for Gordon's more systematic attack on church amusements.

670. ———. *Christian Science Tested by Scripture*. New York: Christian Alliance Pub. Co., [ca. 1918]. 15 p.

Christian Science is a pantheistic parody of Christianity that has strong affinities with Theosophy. The healings that its practitioners effect are real, but it has a heretically deficient view of God, Satan, and the human person. Reprint of an article originally published in *The Congregationalist.*

671. ———. *The Holy Spirit in Missions: Six Lectures*. New York: Fleming H. Revell, 1893. Reprint, Harrisburg, Pa.: Christian Alliance Pub. Co., [1925?]. 241 p.

672. ———. *The Ministry of Healing: Miracles of Cure in All Ages*. New York: Fleming H. Revell, 1882. Reprint, New York: Christian Alliance Pub. Co., [ca. 1900].

673. Gorton, Dennis L. *A 31-Day Prayer Venture for Every Believer*. Camp Hill, Pa.: Christian Publications, 1994. 33 p.

Includes instructions on what to pray for and how to pray. Adapted from the writings of Andrew Murray.

674. ———. *Church Development and Resource Manual*. Toledo, Ohio: West Central District, Christian and Missionary Alliance, 1983. 148 p.

An omnibus resource for the planting and administration of new churches that was intended to help the American C&MA attain its goal of doubling its membership by 1987.

675. ———. *Growing Together: A Local Church Membership Manual for Churches of the Christian and Missionary Alliance*. Camp Hill, Pa.: Christian Publications, 1988. 58 p.

676. ———. *Oaks of Righteousness: A Pastoral Ministries Guide*. Nyack, N.Y.: Christian and Missionary Alliance, 1988. 196 p.

A manual on pastoral methods for Alliance pastors, covering everything from C&MA polity to personal prayer.

677. *The Gospel Abroad during the World War*. New York: Christian and Missionary Alliance, 1918. 31 p.

Identical to the narrative statistical report presented by the Foreign Secretary at the 1919 General Council of the C&MA.

678. *Gospel Quintet Songs*. Chicago: Thoro Harris, 1930. 192 p.

This is apparently the repertoire of the Cleveland Colored Quintette. Many of the 155 songs were composed or arranged by Thoro Harris. Includes some songs by A. B. Simpson and B. B. Bosworth, as well as a discography of the Colored Quintette.

679. *Gospel Quintet Songs*. Chicago: Thoro Harris, [193-?]. 188 p.

Evidently a revision of 678. Nearly half of the 229 songs are by Thoro Harris; only one is by A. B. Simpson.

680. Gospel Tabernacle, New York City. *Fifty Golden Years: 1882-1932*. New York: Gospel Tabernacle, [1932?]. 24 p.

A history of the first Alliance church, the (New York) Gospel Tabernacle, founded in February 1882 as a result of evangelistic meetings conducted by A. B. Simpson November 1881-January 1882.

681. Gosselin, Blanche. "A. B. Simpson: The Man behind the Work." *Fundamentalist Journal* 4 (September 1985): 42-3.

A brief but comprehensive biographical sketch that concentrates on the years 1843 to 1881.

682. Gould, Louella, and Miriam Charter. "Women's Involvement in the Church Should Provide a Broader Basis for a Wider Ministry." *His Dominion* 6 (winter 1979): 10-3.

The Women's Missionary Prayer Fellowship (now Alliance Women) of Circle Drive Alliance, Saskatoon, Sask., has expanded its vision beyond prayer and financial support for missionaries to include a local program of evangelistic outreach.

683. Govett, R. *The Twofoldness of Divine Truth.* Harrisburg, Pa.: Christian Publications, [195-?] 23 p.

Humankind is active with respect to God's justice and passive with respect to God's sovereignty.

684. Graf, Jonathan L., comp. and ed. *Healing: The Three Great Classics on Divine Healing.* Camp Hill, Pa.: Christian Publications, 1992. 376 p.

Reprint of 1171, 672, 1635.

685. ———. *The Personal or Group Study Guide to A. W. Tozer's "The Pursuit of God."* Camp Hill, Pa.: Christian Publications, 1992. 85 p.

686. Graffam, Alan Edward. "On the Persistence of Denominational Evangelical Higher Education: Case Studies in the History of Geneva College, Roberts Wesleyan College, Nyack College and Houghton College (Pennsylvania, New York)." Ph.D. diss., State University of New York at Buffalo, 1986. 275 p.

Includes a brief history of each college and its parent denomination. All four colleges have maintained their denominational and evangelical distinctives through strong presidential leadership and by ensuring that their theological beliefs and mission statements were consistent with those of the parent denomination.

687. Graham, Billy. *Just As I Am.* Grand Rapids: Zondervan, 1997. 760 p.

Graham's first formal ministry experience occurred in a C&MA church, and he numbers C&MA pastor John Minder among his mentors. Graham served as Minder's assistant pastor at Tampa Gospel Tabernacle

(1940) and as vice-president of the C&MA's youth ministries in Florida in the late 1930s.

688. Grauer, O. C., comp. and ed. *Fredrik Franson, Founder of The Scandinavian Alliance Mission of North America: An Evangelist and Missionary in World-wide Service*. Chicago: Scandinavian Alliance Mission, 1939. 240 p.

More hagiographical than 2104 and covers much of the same ground, though in less detail. Contends that Franson (1852-1908) was let down by A. B. Simpson and the C&MA, and that the intellectual snobbery of Alliance missionaries in China contributed to funding being withheld from 155 potential additional Swedish Alliance missionaries to that country. Includes many photographs.

689. Gray, James (M)artin (1851-1935). *The Bulwarks of the Faith: A Brief and Popular Treatise on the Evidences of Christianity; or the Authenticity, Truth and Inspiration of the Holy Scriptures, Arranged with Questions for Use in Bible Institutes and Training Schools*. Nyack, N.Y. and New York: Christian Alliance Pub. Co., 1899. 161 p.

The gist of the author's lectures on the subject. He was a sometime lecturer at the Missionary Training Institute.

690. *Great Things He Hath Done*. Windsor, Ont.: n.p., 1946. 36 p.

A history of the C&MA in Windsor to 1946.

691. Green, Louise. "Robert Jaffray: Man of Spirit, Man of Power." *His Dominion* 16 (March 1990): 2-14.

Jaffray was devoted to prayer: contemplative prayer, healing prayer, and what would today be termed "spiritual warfare prayer." He sought and received power for service through the baptism of the Holy Spirit. He also received the gift of tongues, which he gratefully incorporated into his prayer life without considering it to be the initial physical evidence of Spirit-baptism. Despite being a diabetic, and suffering from a weak heart and a gastric ulcer, he pioneered Alliance mission efforts in Indonesia by relying on the Lord as the source of his health.

692. Grubb, Kenneth G. *The Northern Republics of South America: Ecuador, Colombia and Venezuela*. London: World Dominion Press, 1931. 149 p.

The Alliance's 29 missionaries in Ecuador in 1929 comprised 71% of the total missionary force there, and the 190 in attendance at Alliance churches represented 68% of the total attendance at evangelical churches in the country.

693. ———. *The Northern Republics of South America: Review of Ten Years' Evangelical Progress to 1938.* London: World Dominion Press, 1939. 157 p.

In Ecuador, "Church organization is facilitated by the predominant position that the Christian and Missionary Alliance hold in the country" (p. 4).

694. Grunlan, Stephen (A)rthur (1941-). *Serving with Joy: A Study in Philippians*. Camp Hill, Pa.: Christian Publications, 1985. 117 p.

695. Guang, Enrique. "Missionary Action Is an 'In the Meantime.'" In *Evangelical Missions Tomorrow*, eds. Wade T. Coggins and E. L. Frizen, 36-50. South Pasadena, Calif.: William Carey Library, 1977.

Criticizes the methods employed by evangelical missionaries thus far. Advocates an advisory role for missionaries and the speedy indigenization of church life and ministry. Provides examples of initiatives in which missionaries have followed this model, among them the Lima al Encuentro con Dios project of the Alliance in Peru.

696. Guinness, H. Grattan, Mrs. "Faith Healing and Missions."*The Regions Beyond* 12 (November 1890): 411-20.

A response to the deaths, in Sierra Leone, in July 1890, of three members of the Kansas Mission to the Soudan. They had fallen ill, but had refused medical assistance believing than God would heal them without means. Although some people are healed in response to prayer, means must also be used in dealing with organic disease. Besides, no instance of divine healing has yet been medically verified. This implicit critique of the teaching of Simpson becomes explicit in subsequent articles.

697. ———. "Faith Healing and Missions (Continued)." *The Regions Beyond* 12 (December 1890): 465-70.

Reports that the three deceased missionaries mentioned in her original article had acquired their views of divine healing during a layover in New York City, where " the notorious Dr. Simpson, who has already sent others to die in Africa and elsewhere from a similar cause—got hold of them and infused into them his fanatical views on the subject" (p. 466).

698. ———. "Faith-Healing and Missions (Continued)" *The Regions Beyond* 12 (January 1891): 24-32.

Rejects Simpson's contention (expressed in an editorial in *The Christian Alliance*) that he was not directly responsible for the deaths of the three missionaries to the Soudan, and gives a point by point refutation of *The Gospel of Healing*. Concludes "that [Simpson] teaches foolish, false and very mischievous doctrines; that he is himself the victim of gross delusion, and that his practical counsels are misleading and dangerous."

699. Haagen, Paul C. *Second Timothy: A Father's Final Counsel*. Madras: Evangelical Literature Service, 1964. 84 p.

700. Hall, A. Eugene, comp. *A Caring Church*. Colorado Springs: Office of Special Ministries, C&MA Division of Church Ministries, [1989?]. 141 p.

Contributions by Alliance clergy and laity and the theory and practice of caring for the handicapped and their families in the context of the local church.

701. Hall, Clarence W. *The White Man Comes to Shangri-La*. New York: The Christian and Missionary Alliance, [1957?]. 9 p.

A reprint of an article that was published in the February 1957 issue of *The Reader's Digest* on the arrival of C&MA missionaries in the Baliem Valley of Irian Jaya, the hardships the missionaries had to face, and the cultural adjustments they had to make.

702. Hall, Douglas. *Not Made for Defeat: The Authorized Biography of Oswald J. Smith*. Grand Rapids: Zondervan, 1969. 192 p.

Interviews of Smith and contemporary newspaper accounts of his ministry enhance the basic narrative already provided in 1938.

703. Hallman, H. S. (1881-). *The Law of Faith*. New York: Christian Alliance Pub. Co., [ca. 1910]. 14 p.

Sermons on faith preached at the Gospel Tabernacle, New York City.

704. Hamilton, Keith E. *Church Growth in the High Andes*. Lucknow, India: Lucknow Publishing House, 1962. 154 p.

Commends the Alliance for making their Ecuadorian church self-supporting (1960) and, in their work with the Quechua Indians, for requiring their missionaries to learn Quechua, for using Quechua-language recordings of the Gospel, and for developing Quechua evangelists.

705. Handoc, Teofilo. "A Study on the Influences of the Christian Alliance Mission upon the Socio-Cultural Life of the Manobos of Kdapawan." Master's thesis, Central Mindanao College, 1974.

706. Harris (E)leanor Lynn. *The Mystic Spirituality of A. W. Tozer, a Twentieth-Century American Protestant.* San Francisco: Mellen Research University Press, 1992. 173 p.

Revision of 707.

707. ———. "The Thought of Aiden Wilson Tozer: An Analysis and Appraisal with Special Emphasis on His Mysticism and Conceptual Approach to the World." Ph.D. diss., New York University, 1980. 236 p.

Tozer was clearly in the mainstream of the mystical tradition of Western Christianity. His mysticism made him a fringe figure within evangelicalism, however, even though it is marked by evangelical distinctives such as bibliocentrism, Christocentrism, marked moralism, and service. The goal of his writings was to initiate the laity into the mystical life, into union with God in Christ. Cf. 706.

708. Harrison, Robert M. *Taiwan: Second Special Taiwan Report.* n.p.: Christian and Missionary Alliance, China-Taiwan Field, 1975. 91 p.

709. Hartley, Fred. *"Holy Spirit, Fill Me!"* Camp Hill, Pa.: Christian Publications, 1992. 25 p.

Instructions on how to be filled with the Holy Spirit (total surrender to Christ, total receptivity to the Holy Spirit) and know it. Includes the testimony of the author, an Alliance pastor.

710. Hartzfeld, David F. "Appropriating the Dynamic of the Christian Life." *His Dominion* 13 (spring 1987): 29-34.

A. B. Simpson's autobiographical writings indicate that, ultimately, it was his "thorough and absolute obedience to Christ" rather than his experience of either water or Spirit-baptism (pivotal though they were) that enabled him to "appropriate the dynamic of the Christian life."

711. Hartzfeld, David F., and Charles Nienkirchen, eds. *The Birth of a Vision.* Regina, Sask.: Canadian Theological Seminary, 1986. 321 p.

Twelve essays on the ministry and thought of A. B. Simpson. Although the quality of the contributions is uneven, this is the best (and until recently, the only) collection of essays by Alliance scholars on Alliance themes. Conspicuously absent is a treatment of Simpson's views on divine healing.

712. Harvey, David P. "The Urban Challenge of Côte d'Ivoire: Toward an Effective C&MA Strategy of Evangelizing Ivoirian Cities." D.Min. diss., Columbia Biblical Seminary and Graduate School of Missions, 1994. 189 p.

An effective strategy would include fervent prayer, variety in evangelistic method, cell group ministry, and theological education.

713. Harvey, Richard H. (1905-1992). *70 Years of Miracles*. Beaverlodge, Alta.: Horizon Books, 1977. 185 p.

Autobiographical anecdotes, many of which deal with miraculous answers to prayer, by a veteran Alliance pastor. Includes biographical information on C&MA evangelist Cora Rudy Turnbull (under whose ministry he was converted) and pastor E. D. Whiteside.

714. Haskins, Doug. "Journey to an Indigenous Church: The History of the Christian and Missionary Alliance Work with Native Americans."*Alliance Academic Review* (1998): 1-30.

The work, which began in 1925, continues to struggle, and progress toward indigenization has been slow. Inadequate leadership training; the unrealistic requirement, on the part of the Division of Church Ministries, that the Native American District become self-supporting before it becomes self-governing; and the failure of Native believers to take fiscal responsibility for their churches have all contributed to the problem.

715. Hassey, Janette. *No Time for Silence: Evangelical Women in Public Ministry around the Turn of the Century*. Grand Rapids: Academie Books, 1986. 269 p.

The section "Nyack and the C.& M. A." gives an overview of the ministry of women in the early days of the Alliance, with particular emphasis on their involvement as educators in Bible institutes.

716. Hatch, Ellen (1840?-1895). *How the Lord Healed Me, or Taking God at His Word*. Buffalo: Triumphs of Faith; Toronto: The Willard Tract Repository, [1886?]. 20 p.

Hatch was a vice-president of the Toronto branch of the Alliance in the late 1880s.

717. Hatton, Eleanor Beard. *The Banished King and His Kingdom.* Butler, Ind.: The Higley Press, 1945. 127 p.

Bible stories for children.

718. ———. *Follow Thou Me.* New York: Christian Alliance Pub. Co., 1916. 261 p.

The (fictional?) diary of a godly pastor who is forced to come to terms with the "fanatical" teaching of the "eleventh hour labourers" and ends up deciding to become a missionary to China.

719. Hawkins, May Anderson (1847-1917). "The 'Latter Rain' and its Counterfeit." In *The Signs of the Times, or God's Message for To-day: A Symposium on New Theology, Christian Science, the Lord's Coming, the Gift of Tongues, and the Deeper Spiritual Life*, 114-37. New York: Alliance Press Co., 1907.

A holy quietness evidenced in a consistent and godly life is the mark of the Spirit-filled Christian. True and counterfeit revival exist side by side, and so the church needs to pray for spiritual discernment lest it fall into one or more of the following errors: exalting the gift of tongues as the necessary evidence of the baptism of the Holy Spirit, pursuing the spectacular and the sensational instead of Christ, and distorting Scripture to support misguided theories.

720. ———. *Lights and Shadows in the Life of Canaan.* Anderson, Ind.: Anderson Gospel Tabernacle, [ca. 1900]. 95 p.

A spiritual autobiography, in epistolary form, focusing on the author's experience of sanctification: "although [one may have been] cleansed and empowered for service in an instant, it takes long years of discipline in God's school to mould the entire being to Christ-likeness" (p. 53).

721. ———. *The Sun Bathed Life.* The Alliance Colportage Library, vol. 2, no. 2. New York: Christian Alliance Pub. Co., 1900. 108 p.

Regardless of external circumstances, there is a quiet abiding-place mediated by the Holy Spirit, close to the heart of God, for those who consecrate themselves entirely to Christ.

722. Hefley, James. *By Life or by Death: The Dramatic Story of the Valiant Missionary Martyrs Who Have Lived and Died for Christ in War-torn Viet Nam.* Grand Rapids: Zondervan, 1969. 208 p.

Six of the ten martyrs, and three of the five prisoners of war covered in this account, were C&MA missionaries.

723. Hefley, James, and Marti Hefley. *By Their Blood: Christian Martyrs of the 20th Century*. Milford, Mich.: Mott Media, 1979. 636 p.

Considerable information on martyred C&MA missionaries, including an account of the martyrdom of R. A. Jaffray.

724. ———. *No Time for Tombstones: Life and Death in the Vietnamese Jungle.* Harrisburg, Pa.: Christian Publications, 1974. 132 p.

An account, in novelized form, of the ordeal of C&MA missionary Betty Olsen, Wycliffe Bible Translators missionary Hank Blood, and agronomist Mike Benge, who were captured by the North Vietnamese during the Tet Offensive of 1968. Of the three, only Benge survived.

725. ———. *Prisoners of Hope*. Harrisburg, Pa.: Christian Publications, 1976. 241 p.

A novel-like reconstruction of the 234-day captivity of Alliance missionaries Richard and Lillian Phillips; Betty Mitchell; Norman and Jean Johnson; and Carolyn, John, and (their daughter) LuAnne Miller. The seven had been captured by North Vietnamese soldiers.

726. Henry, R. C. *The Holy City: The Eternal Home of the Children of God*. Birmingham, Ala.: by the author, 1955. 75 p.

Thirteen sermons on Rev. 21-22 from the daily radio program of the author (who was pastor of West End Alliance Church of the C&MA in Birmingham, Ala.)

727. Henry, Robert T. *Live a Day in My Shoes: Theological Concerns Regarding the Handicapped.* Nyack, N.Y.: Christian and Missionary Alliance, Specialized Ministries, [198-?]. 36 p.

A biblical theology of disabilities, prepared for the C&MA's Handicap Ministries Task Force.

728. Herber, Ruth, and Ralph Herber. *Crossing Frontiers with Christ: The Life Story of R. S. Roseberry*. Toccoa Falls, Ga.: Toccoa Falls College Press, 1997. 179 p.

A revision of the unpublished autobiography of (R)obert (S)herman Roseberry (1883-1976). After serving as C&MA missionaries to Sierra Leone (1909-1919) he and his wife Edith were among the group of C&MA workers who pioneered Protestant missions in French West Africa. He also served as field director of the C&MA's French West Africa mission (1919-1953).

729. Herendeen, Dale Sims (1926-). "Conversion and Indigeneity in the Evangelical Church of Viet Nam. D.Miss. diss., Fuller Theological Seminary, 1975.

The Evangelical Church of Vietnam was planted by C&MA missionaries and became an official body in 1927. The conversions of the 150 members of the ECVN interviewed met the criteria of dynamic equivalence, i.e., they were truly biblical, culturally appropriate, and effectively synthesized the biblical and the cultural. The church itself, however, tends to rely too heavily on Western forms of expression in worship, organization, education, theology, and proclamation. Hence the ECVN could be said to be only moderately indigenized.

730. ———. "Missionary Describes Siege at Dalat." *Christianity Today* 15 March 1968, 36-37.

Herendeen (of the C&MA) was one of 34 North American missionaries who survived the Viet Cong attack on Dalat.

731. ———. "A Model Bible School Program for Vietnam." Master's thesis, Pasadena College, 1964. 259 p.

Includes a brief history of the Alliance's Bible school in Nhatrang.

732. Hess, Robert Reuel. "Mid Crucifix, Crescent and Shrine: Alliance Mission in Southern Mindanao and Sulu." B.D. thesis, National Bible School (Wichita, Kans.), 1941. 104 p.

The mission experienced steady growth from 1902 to 1941, despite opposition from Catholics, Muslims, and pagans.

733. Hibschman, Barbara. *Edge of Conflict*. The Junior Jaffray Collection of Missionary Stories, book 8. Camp Hill, Pa.: Christian Publications, 1993. 31 p.

A retelling for children of 2038.

734. ———. *A Heart for Imbabura*. The Junior Jaffray Collection of Missionary Stories, Book 6. Camp Hill, Pa.: Christian Publications, 1992. 30 p.

A retelling for children of 1488.

735. ———. *I Want to Be a Missionary: The Go, Show, and Tell Book*. Missionary—That's Me! series. Camp Hill, Pa.: Christian Publications, 1990. 29 p.

736. ———. *No Sacrifice Too Great.* The Junior Jaffray Collection of Missionary Stories, book 7. Camp Hill, Pa.: Christian Publications, 1993. 27 p.

A retelling for children of 766.

737. ———. *One Shall Chase a Thousand.* The Junior Jaffray Collection of Missionary Stories, book 9. Camp Hill, Pa.: Christian Publications, 1993. 31 p.

A retelling for children of 610.

738. ———. *Please Leave Your Shoes at the Door.* The Junior Jaffray Collection of Missionary Stories, book 5. Camp Hill, Pa.: Christian Publications, 1992. 32 p.

A retelling for children of 1434.

739. Hildebrandt, Edward. "A History of the Winnipeg Bible Institute and College of Theology, 1925-1960." Th.M. thesis, Dallas Theological Seminary, 1965. 202 p.

The school was founded by Harry L. Turner, a former C&MA missionary (and future president of the C&MA) but personal problems forced him to leave Winnipeg at the end of the first academic year.

740. *Himnos de la vida cristiana: Una colección de antiguos y nuevos himnos de albanza a Dios*. Camp Hill, Pa.: Christian Publications, 1967. 380 p.

Some of the 350 hymns were written by Latin American evangelicals, but most are translations of hymns (including Alliance standards by A. B. Simpson and R. Kelso Carter) that had appeared in *Hymns of the Christian Life.*

741. Hitchcock, Mary (1865-). *The First Soprano*. New York: Christian Alliance Pub. Co., 1912. 187 p.

A novel, set in New Laodicea, on the theme of entire consecration.

742. ———. *The Gift of the Holy Spirit: A Series of Studies*. New York: Christian Alliance Pub. Co., 1924. 29 p.

An interpretation, from a Holiness perspective, of the Scriptures pertaining to the gift/baptism of the Holy Spirit which, "with all that it embraces, is the unique feature of New Testament salvation" (p. 3).

743. ———. *One Christmas*. New York: Christian Alliance Pub. Co., 1928. 32 p.

744. Hitchcock, Ruth. *The Good Hand of Our God*. Elgin, Ill.: David C. Cook, 1975. 240 p.

The story of Hebron Mission, Inc., a small independent mission to Guangdong, China (1920-1951), whose remnants merged with the C&MA's Hong Kong mission in 1962.

745. Hitt, Russell T. *Cannibal Valley*. Harrisburg, Pa.: Christian Publications, 1962. 253 p.

A thorough descriptive history of the C&MA missionary effort that resulted in mass conversions among the tribal people of the interior of Irian Jaya.

746. Hjersman, Carl. *Christ the Great Physician*. Oakland: by the author, 1946. 160 p.

Acknowledges A. B. Simpson's profound influence on the divine healing movement and regards him as being "probably the first man to define healing as provided in the Atonement" (p. 87).

747. Ho, Phy Xuan. "The Church in Vietnam." In *Church in Asia Today: Challenges and Opportunities*, ed. Saphir Athyal, 201-15. Singapore: The Asia Lausanne Committee for World Evangelization, 1996.

The Evangelical Church of Vietnam (ECVN) is largely the product of the C&MA mission, which began to bear fruit in the 1920s. Other Protestant missions began to operate in Vietnam in the late 1950s, but their contributions to the growth of the ECVN were relatively modest. The ECVN continues to grow, despite persecution at the hands of the government, and it remains one of the most successful of the C&MA's mission endeavors.

748. Hollingshead, Margaret Alene. "Yesterday, Today, Forever: An Ethnographic Study of the Culture and Legitimation Process of Canadian Bible College." Ph.D. diss., Walden University, 1996. 214 p.

The spiritual emphasis at Canadian Bible College (CBC) appeals to both students and staff, and the school does a good job of whole-person formation. However, "paternalistic" behavioral guidelines for students, the lack of job opportunities for women in C&MA churches, a sense of powerlessness on the part of students and staff regarding how decisions are made, and a number of other factors threaten the viability of CBC's culture.

749. Hope, Evangeline [pseud.]. *Daisy: The Fascinating Story of Daisy Smith, Wife of Oswald J. Smith, Missionary Statesman and Founder of the Peoples Church, Toronto*. Grand Rapids: Baker, 1980. 260 p.

Daisy Billings was raised in a C&MA church, attended Nyack, and served as a home missionary in West Virginia before becoming a deaconess at Dale Presbyterian Church (Toronto) where she met Oswald J. Smith, whom she married in 1916. She was largely responsible for Smith's interest in missions and his desire to seek the filling of the Holy Spirit. The author is the daughter of Daisy (1891-1972) and Oswald J. Smith.

750. Houts, Richard Franklin (1929-). "Sect or Denomination: The Experience of the Christian and Missionary Alliance." Th.M. thesis, Golden Gate Theological Seminary, 1965. 81 p.

Gives a good summary of why the Alliance, which officially became a denomination in 1974, had well before that date become a de facto denomination, i.e.,: "an established sect chosen voluntarily, exclusive in certain distinctive modes of doctrine and polity." Alliance distinctives include a Baptist view of the church and its ordinances and a Presbyterian understanding of church polity.

751. "How God Reached Down in Viet Nam: In the Midst of Political Unrest and Persecution, the Spirit of God Has Prepared a Witness to Southeast Asia." *Christian Life* 20 (May 1959): 27-29.

The story of Le Hoang Phu, a pastor in the Evangelical Church of Viet Nam (C&MA).

752. Howard, Dale Dwight. "The Pastor as Leader: Personality Strengths and Church Expectations, Factors in Pastoral Length of Ministry with the Individual Church." Ed.D. diss., University of Alabama, 1985. 142 p.

Based on a survey of 250 C&MA pastors.

753. Howard, Edna. "Personality Strengths and Temperament Traits: Factors in Continued and Discontinued Missionaries." Ph.D. diss., University of Alabama, 1984. 112 p.

Continuing missionaries (i.e., those who did not "drop out") tended to be "dependent riskers" who trusted and drew strength from others as they took the risks that the missionary vocation requires.

754. Howland, William (H)olmes (1844-1893). "Women Preaching: A Sign of the Last Days." *Faithful Witness*, 14 June 1890. 162-63.

The prophecy of Joel repeated in Acts 2:17-18 is being fulfilled in this present age (in part) by the extraordinarily effective evangelistic ministries being carried out by Spirit-filled women. Howland was mayor of Toronto (1886-1888) and a founder of the C&MA in Canada (cf. 1382).

755. Huling, Franklin G. *What Is the Difference between Mormonism and Biblical Christianity? A Kindly Word of Distinction.* New York: Christian Alliance Pub. Co., 1927. 38 p.

The teachings of the two "are as different as day and night" (p. 35).

756. Hunt, Garth. *God Is Not Hiding*. Harrisburg, Pa.: Christian Publications, 1973. 63 p.

A manual, by an Alliance missionary to Vietnam, on how to be filled with the Holy Spirit. Complete renunciation of sin and complete consecration to God are the main prerequisites. Those who seek to be filled but lack assurance of having been filled need to repent of unconfessed sin. Reprint of 757, 758, and a third pamphlet *Life from Above*, with an introduction by Billy Graham.

757. ———. *The Path to Fulfillment: A Study on How to Obtain the Fullness of the Spirit.* [Vietnam?]: n.p., 1972. 30 p.

Cf. 756.

758. ———. *The Promise of the Father: A Study on the Meaning of Pentecost and the Fullness of the Holy Spirit.* [Vietnam?]: n.p., 1972. 17 p.

Cf. 756.

759. Hunter, Harold D. *Spirit Baptism, a Pentecostal Alternative.* Lanham, Md.: University Press of America, 1983. 322 p.

A. B. Simpson believed that the baptism of the Holy Spirit serves above all a purificatory function. Agnes Ozman (1870-1937), the first person to speak in tongues at Charles Parham's school in Topeka, Kans., had studied at the Missionary Training Institute in Nyack, N.Y.

760. Hunter, James Hogg (1890-). *Adrift: The Story of Twenty Days on a Raft in the South Atlantic.* Grand Rapids: Zondervan, 1943. 127 p.

Recounts the raft ordeal of the Bell family, but in less detail than 99.

761. ———. *Beside All Waters: The Story of Seventy-five Years of World-wide Ministry— the Christian and Missionary Alliance.* Harrisburg, Pa.: Christian Publications, 1964. 245 p.

A general history of C&MA missions, 1887-1962. Also includes a brief overview of the North American ministries of the Alliance.

762. Hunter, John. *Knowing God's Secrets: The Secret of the Effective Christian Life.* Grand Rapids: Zondervan, 1965. Reprint, Akola, India: Alliance Publications India, 1965. 151 p.

The secret is utter dependence on God.

763. Hussey, A. H. *Confessing Christ.* New York: Christian Alliance Pub. Co., [ca. 1918]. 13 p.

Christians should tell others what Christ has done for them because the Scriptures command them to, because it strengthens their faith, and because it is an effective means of evangelism. They often fail to do so out of ingratitude, fear, and pride.

764. ———. *Divine Healing in Mission Work.* Nyack, N.Y.: Christian Alliance Pub. Co., 1902. 65 p.

Divine healing, besides being the Christian's birthright, testifies to the transcendence and power of God and provides openings for the presentation of the Gospel. Includes testimonies by C&MA missionaries.

765. ———. *Perfect in Christ.* New York: Christian Alliance Pub. Co., [ca. 1918]. 13 p.

The baptism of the Holy Spirit burns up the carnal nature and frees one from sin, enabling growth toward Christian perfection.

766. Hutchins, Ruth Presswood. *No Sacrifice Too Great: The Story of Ernest and Ruth Presswood.* The Jaffray Collection of Missionary Portraits, 7. Camp Hill, Pa.: Christian Publications, 1993. 205 p.

Focuses on the experiences of Ruth Presswood (Hutchins), Darlene Deibler (Rose), Margaret Jaffray (and other female C&MA missionaries) from 1942 to 1945 in a Japanese internment camp in Kalimantan, Indonesia (cf. 1414); and on the postwar visit of Ernest (1908-1946) and Ruth Presswood to the Dyak people of Kalimantan to whom Ernest had ministered from 1930 until his internment. Ernest died on 1 February 1946 during this visit. Cf. 736.

767. Hyde (P)eter (R)ichard (1891-1954). *Notes on the Book of Revelation. Part One: Fourteen Lessons on Chapters One to Three.* [Meadville, Pa.?]: P. R. Hyde, 1933. 47 p.

Based on presentations originally given in the Gospel Tabernacle of Meadville, Pa.

768. *Hymns of the Christian Life.* New York: Christian Alliance Pub. Co., [ca. 1914]. 128 p.

A selection of hymns taken from 1883. Also includes newer hymns (including several by A. B. Simpson), some of which have copyright dates as recent as 1914.

769. *Hymns of the Christian Life: A Book of Worship in Song Emphasizing Evangelism, Missions and the Deeper Life.* Harrisburg, Pa.: Christian Publications, 1936. 480 p.

The 5th ed. of the Alliance hymnal.

770. *Hymns of the Christian Life: A Book of Worship in Song Emphasizing Evangelism, Missions and the Deeper Life*, rev. and enlarged ed. Harrisburg, Pa.: Christian Publications, 1962. 663 p.

The 6th ed. of the Alliance hymnal.

771. *Hymns of the Christian Life: A Book of Worship in Song Emphasizing Evangelism, Missions and the Deeper Life.* rev. and enlarged ed. Harrisburg, Pa.: Christian Publications, 1978. 698 p.

The 7th and most recent ed. of the Alliance hymnal.

772. *Hymns of the Christian Life Nos. 1 and 2.* Nyack, N.Y.: Christian Alliance Pub. Co., [1902?]. 620 p.

A combined edition of 256 and 1698. Cf. 1764.

773. Indochina Mission of the C&MA. *La Mission Évangélique, sa raison d'être.* Hanoi: Imprimerie Évangelique, 1932.

774. Inkster, John Gibson. *The Letters to the Seven Churches.* New York: Christian Alliance Pub. Co., 1926. 83 p.

The seven churches of Revelation all have their counterparts in the modern era, e.g., the Philadelphian church has the modern evangelical and missionary movement as its contemporary counterpart. The modern church needs to repent of its lost love.

775. *International Outreach: A Ministry of The Christian and Missionary Alliance*. Nyack, N.Y.: The Alliance, [198-?]. 30 p.

A handbook for the friendship evangelism of foreign students studying in the United States.

776. Irish, Carolyn (F)ritz (1903-), and Elizabeth Irish Wright. *Sharing Good Tidings in Zion: An Account of God's Faithfulness to Mideast Missionaries*. Columbus, Ga.: Brentwood Christian Press, 1995. 152 p.

Recounts the missionary work of Leigh and Carolyn Irish, who served with the C&MA in Palestine (1924-1961) working among both Arabs (1924-1931) and Jews (1940-1961).

777. Irish, L. F. *Light on the Prophetic Word: Therefore Watch and Be Sober*. n.p. [1950?]. 10 p.

The establishment of the state of Israel in 1948 is the restoration of Israel prophesied in the Bible. Includes a list of prophecies about Israel that have been fulfilled.

778. Irvin, Maurice R. (1930-). *Consider This: Thoughts for the Serious Christian*. Nyack, N.Y.: Alliance Life, 1989. 158 p.

Editorials published in *Alliance Life,* 1984-1988.

779. ———. *Eternally Named*. Harrisburg, Pa.: Christian Publications, 1975. 117 p.

Sermons on the names and titles of Jesus. Originally delivered at Simpson Memorial Church, Nyack, N.Y.

780. ———. *From Condemnation to Glory: An Exposition of Romans 8*. Camp Hill, Pa.: Christian Publications, 1996. 138 p.

781. ———. "The Second Coming and Salvation." *His Dominion* 14 (fall 1987): 23-26.

The doctrine of the second coming of Christ is both the substance of the Christian hope and an incentive to conversion.

782. ———. *The Tragedy of Ignoring the Creator: And Other Essays on Christian Life and Ministry*. Camp Hill, Pa.: Christian Publications, 1995. 126 p.

A collection of 52 editorials that appeared in *Alliance Life*, 1988-1993.

783. Irwin, E. F. *With Christ in Indo-China: The Story of Alliance Missions in French Indo-China and Eastern Siam.* Harrisburg, Pa.: Christian Publications, 1937. 164 p.

784. Jacober, Virginia. *The Promise: The Story of Ed and Virginia Jacober.* The Jaffray Collection of Missionary Portraits, 10. Camp Hill, Pa.: Christian Publications, 1994. 212 p.

Edward G. (1919-1984) and Virginia Jacober served as C&MA missionaries in India (1950-1975) and then in Israel, where Ed served from 1975 until his death, and Virginia from 1975 until her retirement in 1990. Cf. 1018.

785. Jacobson, S. Winnifred. *The Pearl and the Dragon: The Story of Alma and Gerhard Jacobson.* The Jaffray Collection of Missionary Portraits, 17. Camp Hill, Pa.: Christian Publications, 1997. 198 p.

The Jacobsons served as Alliance missionaries to China: Alma (d. 1965) 1921-1934, Gerhard (1889-1972) 1921-1945. Gerhard was serving as a missionary to European Jews in Shanghai prior to his internment by the Japanese during World War II.

786. Janes, Burton K. *The Lady Who Came: The Biography of Alice Belle Garrigus, Newfoundland's First Pentecostal Pioneer, Volume One, 1858-1908.* St. John's, Nfld.: Good Tidings Press, 1982. 135 p.

Alice Belle Garrigus (1868-1949) founded the Pentecostal movement in Newfoundland in 1910. Seeking a deeper experience of God, she attended the Alliance's Old Orchard convention of 1907. There she met A. B. Simpson's associate Minnie Draper and accompanied her to a tarrying meeting where she received the Pentecostal baptism of the Holy Spirit.

787. Janzen, James David. "The Role of Music in the Christian and Missionary Alliance Schools for Missionary Children 1924-89." M.Mus. thesis, University of Calgary, 1993. 292 p.

"[Traces] the growth and development of music education within four overseas boarding schools of the . . . Alliance from their inception to 1989" (p. iii).

788. Jeffrey, Ruth Goforth (1898-1972). *Amazing Grace: A Brief Account of My Life in China and Vietnam.* Stouffville, Ont.: D. I. Jeffrey, [1972?]. 59 p.

The author was a C&MA missionary to Vietnam and the daughter of well-known Canadian missionaries to China Jonathan and Rosalind Goforth.

789. Jensen, Evelyn. "Advocating for Women in Development." In *Christian Relief and Development: Developing Workers for Effective Ministry*, ed. Edgar J. Elliston, 269-83. Dallas: Word Publishing, 1989.

The concerns of women are usually neglected in development planning in the Third World. Development workers need to be taught to "conceptualize, analyze, and appreciate both the male and female worlds in a given culture" (p. 297).

790. Johnson, Gilbert H. *The Pilgrimage of Joseph Douglas Williams: A Brief Portrayal of His Life*. Harrisburg, Pa.: Christian Publications, 1952. 30 p.

During his more than 40 years as an Alliance minister, Williams (1870-1949) served as a district superintendent, a member of the Board of Managers, and the president of four Alliance educational institutions.

791. Johnson, Ruth I., and Ord L. Morrow. *Teen Talks from the Studio: Bible Talks Given by Theodore H. Epp, Ord L. Morrow and G. Christian Weiss on the Back to the Bible Youth Broadcast*. Lincoln, Neb.: Back to the Bible, 1966. 128 p.

792. Jones, Charles E. "People to Meet, Books to Read." *Fundamentalist Journal* 5 (January 1986): 35-36.

Jones credits A. W. Tozer's *The Pursuit of God* with enabling him to overcome his resentment towards his critics.

793. Jones, Clarence W. (1915-1986). *Radio: The New Missionary*. Chicago: Moody Press, 1946. 147 p.

The history of Radio Station HCJB, the first missionary radio station, which began broadcasting in 1931 from its base in Quito, Ecuador. Alliance missionaries were directly involved in its founding, and the C&MA and HCJB continue to have a close working relationship.

794. Jones, Howard O. (1921-). "The Evangelist's Use of Radio and Television." In *The Calling of an Evangelist: The Second International Congress for Itinerant Evangelists, Amsterdam, the Netherlands,* ed. J. D. Douglas, 287-91. Minneapolis: World Wide Publications, 1987.

795. ———. *For This Time: A Challenge to Black and White Christians.* Chicago: Moody Press, 1966. 160 p.

Reprint of 797.

796. ———. "The Impact of Materialism in Africa." In *One Race, One Gospel, One Task: World Congress on Evangelism, Berlin, 1966,* eds. Carl F. H. Henry and W. Stanley Mooneyham, 2: 268-71. Minneapolis: World Wide Publications, 1967.

The improvement of social conditions must accompany the presentation of the Gospel if Africa is to be evangelized effectively. Moreover, the pay of African pastors will need to be increased to ensure the vitality of the African church.

797. ———. *Shall We Overcome?: A Challenge to Negro and White Christians.* Westwood, N.J.: Fleming H. Revell, 1966. 146 p.

The black church in America has been weakened by moral laxity, discord, lack of trained leadership, and an inability to pass on the faith to succeeding generations. Black churches need to renew their zeal for holiness, evangelism, missions, and stewardship. Racism has done much to discredit American missionary work in Africa and to sap the potency of the American church in general. Billy Graham's courageous stand against racism should be emulated by all American Christians. Includes several anecdotes from Jones's days as a C&MA minister. Cf. 795.

798. ———. *White Questions to a Black Christian.* Grand Rapids: Zondervan, 1975. 215 p.

Poses, and answers, from a Christian perspective, a variety of questions with respect to race relations in the United States. Jones is perhaps the most influential person of color associated with the C&MA.

799. Jones, Howard O. (1921-), et al. *Heritage & Hope: The Legacy of the Black Family in America.* Wheaton, Ill.: Victor Books, 1992. 201 p.

Chapter one contains a brief biography of the ancestors of Howard and Wanda Jones.

800. Jones, Ruth A. *The St. Paul Bible College, 1916 . . . Decades of Training.* n.p., 1962.

801. Jones, Wanda (1923-), with Sandra Pickleshimer Aldrich. *Living in Two Worlds: The Wanda Jones Story.* Grand Rapids: Zondervan, 1988. 164 p.

Covers Wanda and Howard Jones's childhood, their student days at Nyack (which, despite the racism they sometimes encountered, were a positive experience) their ministry with the C&MA, and their subsequent ministry as evangelists with radio station ELWA in Liberia and the Billy Graham Evangelistic Association.

802. Jordan, W. F. *Ecuador: A Story of Mission Achievement*. New York: Christian Alliance Pub. Co., 1926. 130 p.

Describes the visit made to Ecuador by Jordan, a representative of the American Bible Society, in 1925. Alliance mission work and the work of Bible Society colporteurs figure prominently in the narrative.

803. Julian, Helen. *Key to Abundant Living*. Harrisburg, Pa.: Christian Publications, 1977. 48 p.

A Bible study using Hannah Whitall Smith's *The Christian's Secret of a Happy Life* as a commentary on the book of Colossians.

804. Kageler, Len (1950-). *On Being a Good Dad*. Grand Rapids: Fleming H. Revell, 1992. 230 p.

Groucho Marx (1891-1977) was a far better father than A. B. Simpson (p. 73-76).

805. Kaye, James R. *Calvary, the Crisis of History: A Sermon Delivered in Jerusalem, Palestine*. New York: Christian Alliance Pub. Co., [19–?]. 24 p.

All history converges on the death and resurrection of Christ. Christianity is unique in being the only religion in which "the person and work of founder are indispensable to the religion itself" (p. 24).

806. Keidel, Paul R. "Pedagogical Principles for Training Pastors in West Africa." D.Miss. diss., Trinity Evangelical Divinity School, 1994. 221 p.

A study of the Bible institute and theological education by extension programs currently overseen by both the C&MA mission in Guinea and the C&MA national church (l'Église Protestante Évangélique de Guinée). Proposes a model for the training of pastors that would be more congruent with the learning styles of Guineans and the example of Jesus.

807. Kelly, Eugene. "Churches Expand in Peru." *His Dominion* 5 (spring 1978): 10-12.

An interview with Kelly, who was the senior C&MA missionary on the leadership team of the Lima al Encuentro con Dios saturation evangelism campaign.

808. Kennedy, H. D. *Does God Care? or the Face of God As Seen in the Story of Esther*. New York: Christian Alliance Pub. Co., 1920. 182 p.

In Esther's case, as is the case for all of God's people, all things work together for good because God is in the story.

809. Kenyon, Don J. *The Double Mind: An Expository and Devotional Study from the Epistle of James.* Grand Rapids: Zondervan, 1959. Reprint, Harrisburg, Pa.: Christian Publications, 1980. 83 p.

810. ———. *The Glory of Grace: An Interpretation of the Epistle of Paul the Apostle to the Romans, Volume 2: Romans 7-16.* Harrisburg, Pa.: Christian Publications, 1979. 199 p.

811. ———. *He That Will Love Life*. Harrisburg, Pa.: Christian Publications, 1968. 376 p.

"A daily-reading commentary on the First Epistle of Peter" (p. 7).

812. ———. *Kiss the Son: Missionary Meditations on the Second Psalm.* Harrisburg, Pa.: Christian Publications, 1961. 102 p.

The meditations are guided by the author's belief that Psalm 2 "presents in germinal form all of the great revelatory concepts which relate Jesus Christ to the great commission" (p. 8).

813. ———. *The Triumph of Truth: An Interpretation of the Epistle of Paul to the Romans, Volume 1: Romans 1-6.* Harrisburg, Pa.: Christian Publications, 1978. 191 p.

814. Kerr (D)aniel (W)arren (1856-1927). *Waters in the Desert.* Springfield, Mo.: Gospel Publishing House, 1925. 139 p.

A "spontaneous theology" from a deeper life/Pentecostal perspective. Many chapters conclude with a poem by A. B. Simpson.

815. Kerr, William W. "Cost of Living Structure of the Christian and Missionary Alliance." In *1969 Retreat Report: Papers Presented to the 18th Annual Mission Executives Retreat, October, 1969,* eds. Clyde W. Taylor and Wade T. Coggins, 101-9. Wheaton, Ill.: Evangelical Missions Information Service, 1969.

Missionaries annually submit a monthly cost of living report (foodstuffs, utilities, cost of one servant) to the C&MA Foreign Department. These reports are used in determining future cost of living allowances. Fringe benefits, e.g., educational allowances for children, are added to the basic allowance. A proposed amendment to the formula would also factor in official cost-of-living statistics compiled by international monitoring agencies.

816. ———. "Policies and Practises of the West Irian Christian and Missionary Alliance (KINGMI) Church regarding Polygamy." In *1969 Retreat Report: Papers Presented to the 18th Annual Mission Executives Retreat, October, 1969*, eds., Clyde W. Taylor and Wade T. Coggins, 123-32. Wheaton, Ill.: Evangelical Missions Information Service, 1969.

Those who were polygamists before conversion may be baptized, take communion, and become church members, but they may not hold a church office. After conversion, believers are not permitted to take any more wives or husbands. The previously unmarried may only marry one wife or husband. A complete transition to monogamy from polygamy seems to be taking place.

817. Kessler, J. B. A. *A Study of the Older Protestant Missions and Churches in Peru and Chile with Special Reference to the Problems of Division, Nationalism, and Native Ministry.* Goes, the Netherlands: Oosterbbaan and le Cointre, 1967. 381 p.

Includes a chapter on C&MA work to 1964 that gives a thorough critical analysis of the C&MA's application of indigenous principles (the mission tried to indigenize too quickly) and the mission's involvement in and separation from the Iglesia Evangélica Peruana.

818. Kincaid, Ray L., and Bernard Palmer. *His! Not Mine*. Camp Hill, Pa.: Buena Book Service, 1991. 209 p.

Kincaid, an Alliance layman, has striven to put Christian principles into practice in all aspects of his business, ranging from how he treats his employees to how much money he gives to his church.

819. Kincheloe, Raymond McFarland (1909-1986). *Encouragement for the Newly Spirit-filled Christian*. Holy Spirit Series. Regina, Sask.: CBC/CTC, 1973. 8 p.

Newly Spirit-filled believers are apt to be tempted to believe that their experience was a delusion, but the tempted believer can use the experience of exemplary Christians such as D. L. Moody, A. B. Simpson, and Madame Guyon, in combination with the promises of Scripture regarding the Holy Spirit, to effectively resist such temptation.

820. ———. "Experiencing Miracle Health." D.Min. thesis, Luther Rice Seminary, 1981. 187 p.

An idiosyncratic apologetic for healing in the Atonement based on Scripture, personal experience, and the experience of other Christians (most of whom are associated with the C&MA). "Miracle health" comes not only through the prayer of faith, but also by way of a healthy diet and, very occasionally, medical intervention.

821. ———. *Is the Holy Spirit a Person?* Holy Spirit Series. Regina, Sask.: CBC/CTC, 1977. 12 p.

Yes.

822. ———. *A Personal Adventure in Prophecy: Understanding Revelation*. Wheaton, Ill.: Tyndale House, 1974. 224 p.

A study of Revelation "from a premillenarian, modified-futuristic viewpoint" (p. ix). Concludes that "the rapture" will occur in phases.

823. ———. *What Is the Difference between Spiritual Gifts and Christian Ministries?* Holy Spirit Series. Regina, Sask.: CBC/CTC, 1977. 21 p.

All of the spiritual gifts mentioned in Scripture, even the controversial ones, should function in the life of the Church today, albeit within certain guidelines.

824. ———. *What the Holy Spirit Does for You*. Holy Spirit Series. Regina, Sask.: CBC/CTC, 1977. 21 p.

Sanctification is the second step a believer takes along the path of following Christ. At salvation one is sanctified positionally. When one asks the Father for the Holy Spirit sanctification becomes experiential. Complete sanctification will come at the Parousia.

825. King, Fred G. *The Church Planter's Training Manual*. [Nyack, N.Y.]: The Christian and Missionary Alliance. Division of Church Ministries, 1988. 224 p.

A "how-to" manual for planting a C&MA church.

826. ———. *Effective Church Planting Models*. Colorado Springs: The Christian and Missionary Alliance, Division of Church Ministries, Office of Church Growth, 1993. 125 p.

The seven models covered are: church-driven, need-driven, pastor-driven, lay-driven, Christian-education-driven, technique-driven, and district-driven. Concludes with a chapter on how to start an Alliance church.

827. ———. *Fold In, Send Out: A Training Guide for Small Group Leaders*. Colorado Springs: The Christian and Missionary Alliance, Division of Church Ministries, Office of Church Growth, 1992. 56 p.

828. ———. *Getting Behind Closed Doors: Four Proven Strategies to Successfully Start and Grow a Church*. Colorado Springs: The Christian and Missionary Alliance, Division of Church Ministries, Office of Church Growth, 1993. 136 p.

The strategies are: sacrificial prayer, expository preaching, Bible teaching via radio, and involvement in law enforcement and institutional chaplaincy.

829. King, Louis L. (1915-). "Bible Translation and Distribution in an Ecumenical Era." In *1969 Retreat Report: Papers Presented to the 18th Annual Mission Executives Retreat, October, 1969,* eds. Clyde W. Taylor and Wade T. Coggins, 133-57. Wheaton, Ill.: Evangelical Missions Information Service, 1969.

Records a candid discussion between representatives of the Evangelical Foreign Mission Association, the Interdenominational Foreign Mission Association, and the American Bible Society with respect to the participation of evangelicals in Bible translation and distribution projects in which Roman Catholics would be involved

830. ———. "The Indigenous Church Policy of the Christian and Missionary Alliance in the Orient." In *The Indigenous Church: A Report from Many Fields*, 20-42. Chicago: Moody Press, 1960.

Summarizes the policy and the history of its development, and gives examples of how it has been applied in the Alliance's Asian missions.

831. ———. "Indigenous Hymnody of the Ivory Coast." *Practical Anthropology* 9 (November-December 1962): 268-70.

In the church that Alliance missionaries planted among the Baouli tribe of Côte d'Ivoire, indigenous hymns find greater acceptance and are far more effective in conveying Christian truth than are translated Western hymns set to Western tunes.

832. ———. "The Keynote Address: God's Gift to the Church." In *The Church's Worldwide Mission: An Analysis of the Current State of Evangelical Missions and a Strategy for Future Activity*, ed. Harold Lindsell, 18-26. Waco, Tex.: Word Books, 1966.

A summary of evangelical ecclesiology emphasizing Christ as Head of the Church.

833. ———. *The Lostness of Mankind: One Motivation for Evangelism.* Camp Hill, Pa.: Christian Publications, 1991. 29 p.

Scripture and the church's major confessions of faith teach unequivocally that those who have never heard the Gospel will not be saved but will spend eternity in conscious torment. Hence the pressing need to evangelize the world.

834. ———. "Miracle in New Guinea." *United Evangelical Action* 19 (March 1960): 8-10.

An account of the mass conversion of the warlike Dani and Uhunduni peoples and the subsequent pacification, civilization, and catechesis of both groups.

835. ———. "Mission/Church Relations Overseas, Part I: In Principle." In *Missions in Creative Tension: The Green Lake '71 Compendium*, ed. Vergil Gerber, 154-78. South Pasadena, Calif.: William Carey Library, 1971.

Discusses the missiological strategies of partial vs. full integration and regular vs. modified dichotomy and finds both lacking. Advocates the independence of the national church from the control of the mission, but recognizes that the national church and the mission must work together to fulfill the Great Commission.

836. ———. "Mission/Church Relations Overseas, Part II: In Practice." In *Missions in Creative Tension: The Green Lake '71 Compendium*, ed. Vergil Gerber, 179-88. South Pasadena, Calif.: William Carey Library, 1971.

For an indigenous church and a mission to maintain a wholesome relationship the mission must ensure that the indigenous church becomes self-sufficient as quickly as possible; and both parties must participate in open forums, establish administrative bridges, and negotiate documented agreements.

837. ———. "New Universalism: Its Exponents, Tenets and Threats to Missions." *Evangelical Missions Quarterly* 1 (summer 1965): 2-12.

Universalism not only blunts the missionary enterprise but it also errs in equating love (as humanly understood) with God.

838. ———. "Report on a New Missionary Thrust." *United Evangelical Action* 22 (March 1963): 15, 30-31.

Churches that have been planted by missionaries are now sending missionaries themselves. Among these new sending agencies are the

Chinese Foreign Missionary Union (founded by R. A. Jaffray and Chinese Alliance leaders in 1929), which may well be the first Chinese missionary organization in history, and the Foreign Missions Society of the Christian and Missionary Alliance Church Union in Hong Kong.

839. ———. "A Rising Tide of Expectation." *Church Growth Bulletin* 16 (September 1979): 291-94.

Evangelistic programs have contributed greatly to the remarkable growth of the C&MA church in Peru, Zaire, the Philippines, and (in a more limited way) North America. Evangelistic programs will therefore continue to play a leading role in the C&MA's denominational strategy.

840. ———. "Where Are the Missionary Candidates?" *United Evangelical Action* 22 (March 1964): 11-12, 26, 32, 41-45.

The C&MA's outstanding missionary record (one missionary for every 80 members) stems from its origin as a mission that gave birth to a church. The annual missionary convention is the focal point of the C&MA church year. It is the principal vehicle for the recruitment of missionaries and the raising of funds for missions.

841. King, Louis L. (1915-), and Arthur Glasser. "Who Controls the Missionary? Two Missions Executives State Alternative Views." *His Magazine,* May 1968, 14-16, 21-23, 26-27.

King maintains that the Scriptures do not indicate whether church and mission structures should be kept separate. Yet there are functional and practical reasons for keeping them so: it eliminates unhealthy dependence by the national church on the resources of the mission, it helps avoid the stigma of colonialism, and it contributes to the indigenization of every aspect of church life. Glasser contends that the New Testament seems to argue against a massive parallel structure (the mission) that is distinct from the church; and that often the reason for maintaining the distinction is a desire for control on the part of the mission.

842. King, Paul. "Early Alliance Missions in China." In *The Birth of a Vision*, eds. David F. Hartzfeld and Charles Nienkirchen, 261-78. Regina, Sask.: His Dominion, 1986.

Alliance missionaries entered China in 1888. They encountered intense opposition and persecution, which they attributed to the activity of Satan. However, had they been more aware of the reasons for the xenophobia of the Chinese, e.g., the unequal treaties imposed on China, they would perhaps have changed their offensive policies and procedures. Nevertheless, their dedication and sacrifice led to the establishment of indigenous churches in several parts of the country by the time of the communist takeover in 1949. Cf. 843.

843. ———. "Early Alliance Missions in China." *His Dominion* 11 (spring 1985): 17-23.
The basis of the more extensive treatment found in 842.

844. King, Paul L. "A. B. Simpson and the Modern Faith Movement." *Alliance Academic Review* (1996): 1-22.
A. B. Simpson, John A. MacMillan, T. J. McCrossan, and F. F. Bosworth have exerted a strong influence on the "word of faith" movement through their teaching that healing has been provided in the Atonement, that the power and the gifts of the Holy Spirit are still available, and that believers must exercise spiritual authority. However, the Alliance's views on these subjects are more healthy and balanced.

———, joint author. *Binding & Loosing: How to Exercise Authority of the Dark Powers.*
See 590.

845. ———. "Holy Laughter and Other Phenomena in Evangelical and Holiness Revival Movements." *Alliance Academic Review* (1998): 107-22.
The revivals that occurred in the C&MA around the turn of the century were accompanied by most, if not all, of the phenomena associated with the Toronto blessing. The approach of early Alliance leaders to such phenomena is still relevant today: do not accept them as the necessary accompaniment to revival or reject them as demonic in origin but rather pray for discernment.

846. ———. "The Restoration of the Doctrine of Binding and Loosing." *Alliance Academic Review* (1997): 57-80.
The doctrine of binding evil powers and releasing their captives (especially within the context of exorcism) was widely taught and practiced in the early church. It was revived by the Holiness movement, with A. B. Simpson being one of its chief advocates. One of the most influential writers on the topic in the twentieth century was John A. MacMillan, a C&MA missionary to China.

847. King, Philip J. *A Parable of Hell.* Camp Hill, Pa.: Christian Publications, 1995. 17 p.
"A graphic portrayal of the condition of a lost soul in eternity."

848. Klassen, Jacob (P)eter (1934-). "A. B. Simpson and the Tensions in the Preparation of Missionaries." In *The Birth of a Vision*, eds. David F. Hartzfeld and Charles Nienkirchen, 241-60. Regina, Sask.: His Dominion, 1986.

The Missionary Training College for Home and Foreign Workers, founded by A. B. Simpson in 1883, was modelled on the East London Training Institute for Home and Foreign Workers. Its one-year training course was designed to crank out "irregulars" to meet the urgent demand for missionaries. Renamed the New York Training Institute in 1894, it moved to Nyack, N.Y., in 1897, where it was known as the Missionary Training Institute. Its alumni include Rowland Bingham (founder of the Sudan Interior Mission) and Peter Cameron Scott (founder of the Africa Inland Mission).

849. ———. "Fire on the Paramo: A New Day in Quechua Receptivity." Master's thesis, Fuller Theological Seminary, 1975. 250 p.

A history and analysis of the remarkable responsiveness of the Mountain Quechua of Ecuador to the Gospel during the late 1960s and early 1970s. The Quechua had been largely unresponsive during the first 60 years of Protestant missionary work, which was largely carried out by the Gospel Missionary Union, the C&MA, and the Berean Mission.

850. ———. "Fire on the Paramo: Spreading Fire in Chimborazo, Ecuador, South America." *Global Church Growth* 29 (April-June 1992): 11-12.

An account of the mass conversions to Christ among the Quechuas of Ecuador.

851. ———. "Quito, Ecuador: Transferable Principles of Urban Outreach." *Urban Mission* 3 (September 1985): 32-40.

Describes how the strategy of the Lima al Encuentro con Dios program—evangelistic campaigns overseen by a committee of C&MA missionaries and local church leaders, bolstered by prayer cells, and followed up with a formal program for instructing new converts—was adapted to fit the situation in Quito.

852. ———. "The Restructured Board of Elders: Bane or Blessing?" *His Dominion* 14 (winter 1988): 9-12.

The responses to the author's survey of five Canadian C&MA churches suggest that it is too early to determine whether the (1984) decision of the C&MA in Canada to amalgamate the functions of the executive committee with those of the elders has been beneficial.

853. Klein, Carol M. *We Went to Gabon*. Harrisburg, Pa.: Christian Publications, 1974. 184 p.

Autobiography of Carol and George Klein, C&MA missionaries to Gabon (1936-1962). Includes an account of their visits with Albert Schweitzer (1875-1965).

854. Knauss, Elizabeth. *The Rising Tide: A Novel Dealing with the Spread of Bolshevism and Atheism Throughout America*. New York: Christian Alliance Pub. Co., 1927. 248 p.

855. Knight, E. P. *The Names of the Lord*. Living Truths, vol. 1, no. 5. Nyack, N.Y.: Christian Alliance Pub. Co., 1900. 21 p.

A sermon on Prov. 18:10.

856. Knowlton, Grace. *For You . . . Today, Vol. 1*. [Afton, N.Y.?]: by the author, 1972. 99 p.

Sermonettes on the spiritual life.

857. ———. *For You . . . Today, Vol. 2*. Bainbridge, N.Y.: The Broadcaster Press, 1973. 108 p.

858. ———. *A String of Moni Beads*. Harrisburg, Pa.: Christian Publications, [196-?]. 84 p.

A popular account of the establishment by C&MA missionaries of a church among the Moni people of the remote interior of Irian Jaya.

859. Koch, Kurt E. *Revival Fires in Canada*. Grand Rapids: Kregel Publications, 1973. 102 p.

A collection of eyewitness accounts about the Western Canadian revival of 1971-1972, in which Alliance evangelists Ralph and Lou Sutera figured prominently.

860. Koffi, Diéké. "Mass Evangelism in the Ivory Coast." In *One Race, One Gospel, One Task: World Congress on Evangelism, Berlin, 1966*, eds. Carl F. H. Henry and W. Stanley Mooneyham, 2: 506-8. Minneapolis: World Wide Publications, 1967.

Discusses eight methods that were used successfully in Côte d'Ivoire.

861. Kooiman, Helen W. "Evelyn LeTourneau: Wife of R. G. LeTourneau." In *Silhouettes: Women Behind Great Men*. Waco, Tex.: Word Books, 1972.

862. ———. "You May Abound." In *Cameos: Women Fashioned by God*. Wheaton, Ill.: Tyndale House, 1968.

A biographical sketch of Wanda Jones.

863. Kraft, Charles, and Thomas Noel Wisley. *Readings in Dynamic Indigeneity*. Pasadena, Calif.: William Carey Library, 1980. 347 p.

Wisley's contributions are based on his experience as a C&MA missionary to the Philippines.

864. Krishnan, Sunder. *World Christians: Living on the Wavelength of the Great Commission*. Burlington, Ont.: Welch, 1989. 149 p.

Sermons, by the preaching pastor of Rexdale Alliance Church (Toronto, Ont.) on the missionary nature of the church.

865. Kucharsky, David E. "Viet Nam: The Vulnerable Ones." *Christianity Today,* 1 March 1968, 16-19.

An account of the killing of C&MA missionaries Ruth Wilting, Robert Zeimer, C. Edward and Ruth Thompson, and Leon and Carolyn Griswold by the Viet Cong at Banmethuout during the Tet Offensive of 1968.

866. Kuglin, Robert J. *Dancing in the Spirit: What Does the Old Testament Say?* Contemporary Christian Living Series. Camp Hill, Pa.: Christian Publications, 1997. 16 p.

There is no scriptural precedent for the contemporary phenomenon, associated with the Toronto Blessing, of "dancing the Spirit." King David's dance (2 Sam. 6:14-20) must not be used as a precedent, since he was not under the control of the Spirit at the time. Besides, dancing in the Spirit has often led to sexual immorality.

867. ———. *Handbook on the Holy Spirit: Clear and Heartwarming Guidance on His Work in the Believer's Life*. Camp Hill, Pa.: Christian Publications, 1996. 213 p.

Reprint of 869, with an added appendix on spiritual pride.

868. ———. *I Was the Devil's Egg*. [Regina, Sask.?]: by the author, 1986. 96 p.

The autobiography of a juvenile delinquent who went on to become an Alliance pastor.

869. ———. *A Layman's Handbook on the Holy Spirit*. Beaverlodge, Alta.: Buena Book Services, 1983. 191 p.

Stresses the nature, gifts, and fruit of the Spirit, mentioning crisis-sanctification only in passing. Includes many illustrations from the author's ministry as a C&MA pastor and evangelist.

870. ———. *The Toronto Blessing: What Would the Holy Spirit Say?* Camp Hill, Pa.: Christian Publications, 1996. 270 p.

The Toronto Blessing is not a genuine revival because a number of the prophecies associated with it have been shown to be false; because it minimizes prayer, the Scriptures, and personal repentance; because it promotes unbiblical and possibly demonic manifestations such as animal noises, laughter, and being slain in the Spirit; and because its leaders have been influenced by people of questionable character.

871. Lake, John (G)raham (1870-1935). *The New John G. Lake Sermons*, ed. Gordon Lindsay. Dallas: Christ for the Nations, 1979. 61 p.

C&MA pastors D. W. Myland and George D. Watson exerted a formative influence on Lake, according to the first two of these largely autobiographical sermons.

872. Landis, R. M. *The Holy Spirit and the Believer*. Dubuque, Ia.: Dubuque Presbyterian Press, [194-?]. 47 p.

Addresses, first delivered in 1936, on the filling of the Holy Spirit as a necessary step in Christian growth—and one that must be appropriated subsequent to conversion. The author was an Alliance missionary.

873. Lanpher, Bill W. "Establishing a Missions Strategy for New Districts of the Christian and Missionary Alliance." D.Min. thesis, Drew University, 1984. 365 p.

The author's "Manual for Discovery of District Conditions and Resources" (p. 134-61) was successfully field tested by the Puerto Rico District of the C&MA.

874. Lao Christian Service. *Life after Liberation: The Church in the Lao People's Democratic Republic*. Nakhon Sawan, Thailand: Lao Christian Service, 1987. 50 p.

Includes a chapter on the history of the Hmong church, a church that was planted by C&MA missionaries.

875. Larsen, David L. *The Company of the Preachers: A History of Biblical Preaching from the Old Testament to the Modern Era*. Grand Rapids: Kregel, 1998.

During his lifetime, A. B. Simpson was one of the "soundest and most exegetical" preachers in New York City, and his sermons were "models of structural perfection." (p. 660-61) Clarity, precision, and vivid illustration characterized the laser-like prophetic preaching of A. W. Tozer (p. 844-45).

876. Larson, Margaret, and William A. Smalley. "Practical Problems." *Practical Anthropology* 4 (summer 1957): 195-99.

In the fall of 1956, Kapauku tribesmen attacked an Alliance mission station in Irian Jaya, killing several people (none of them Westerners). Christian anthropologists must determine the factors that contributed to this incident so that a better strategy for inculturating the Gospel among the Kapauku may be developed.

877. Lecaro, Miguel. *Mi lejano ayer!* Guayaquil, Ecuador: n.p., 1995.

Autobiography of the influential pastor of the C&MA's flagship church in Guayaquil, Ecuador.

878. Lee, Mark Wilcox. "The Biblical View of the Doctrine of the Holy Spirit in the Writings of Albert B. Simpson." Master's thesis, Wheaton College, 1952. 115 p.

Simpson's works are often hard to understand because they are full of sermonic overstatement. Moreover, the literalness with which he interpreted the Bible often "strains credulity." His doctrine of sanctification is at odds with certain Pauline principles, and he never clearly states how one may attain the sanctified life. His doctrine of divine health seems little more than a description of God's providence applied to health, and he does not make a convincing case for healing being included in the Atonement. Yet Simpson's teachings have borne lasting and abundant fruit, largely because of the consistency of his teachings and his ability to communicate them forcefully in the common idiom.

879. ———. *Finishing Well.* Camp Hill, Pa.: Christian Publications, 1996. 193 p.

Reflections on biblical texts relating to Christian maturity.

880. Leese, Marianne B. "Nyack College: 100 Years of Missionary Training." *South of the Mountains* 26 (October-December 1982): 3-10.

A brief but thorough overview that includes some information not found in 1453.

881. LeLacheur (D)avid W. (1841-1901). *The Land of the Lamas: The Opening of Tibet to the Gospel.* South Nyack, N.Y.: Christian Alliance Pub. Co., [ca. 1897]. 63 p.

An account of a seven-month trip the author took in 1896 from Wuhu, China, to Mongolia and Tibet. George Shields and William Christie accompanied him to Tibet, where they obtained permission to establish a (C&MA) mission in Pao-an. Christie and Shields began the mission the following year.

882. ———. *Limiting God & Other Addresses.* New York: Christian Alliance Pub. Co., [ca. 1900]. 130 p.

Twelve sermons on such Alliance themes as divine healing, the filling of the Holy Spirit, and missions.

883. Lemon, William Richard. "A Comparative Investigation of the Differing Responses to the Good News of the Gospel among the Highland and Jungle Quechua Indians of Ecuador." Master's thesis, University of the Pacific, 1969. 72 p.

Missionaries should learn Quechua and should use the appropriate cultural referents in communicating the Gospel. They should also train indigenous leaders and refrain from using affluence as a criterion by which to evaluate the success of an evangelistic effort.

884. Leno, Garth. *Hebrews: The Superiority of Christ.* The Deeper Life Pulpit Commentary. Camp Hill, Pa.: Christian Publications, 1996. 378 p.

885. Leno, Patty. *Living with a Broken Dream.* Belleville, Ont.: Essence Publishing, 1995. 22 p.

The mother of a child with Rett Syndrome reflects on suffering as a means of grace. The author is the wife of C&MA pastor Garth Leno.

886. Leonard (L)eonard J. *Christ for China.* New York: Alliance Press Co., 1904. 22 p.

An appeal, on behalf of the China Board of the Nyack Missionary Training Institute, for workers for the C&MA's China field.

887. Lesko, Basil. *"Something More than Gold": The Personal Testimony of Evangelist Basil Lesko.* Jamesville, Wis.: Alliance Gospel Press, [192-?]. 7 p.

A former acolyte at St. Michael's Russian Orthodox Church, Portage, Pa., Lesko failed to receive physical healing via the Orthodox rites of healing. In desperation he attended the evangelistic healing meetings of

F. F. Bosworth. He received healing, had a conversion experience, left the Orthodox Church, and joined the Alliance.

888. LeTourneau (R)obert (G)ilmour (1888-1969). *Mover of Men and Mountains: The Autobiography of R. G. LeTourneau*. Chicago: Moody Press, 1967. 296 p.

This reprint, with added epilogue and eulogy, of the original edition (Prentice-Hall, 1960) is more comprehensive than either 5 or 914.

889. ———. *R. G. Talks about . . . : the Industrial Genius, Practical Philosophy and Christian Commitment of Robert G. LeTourneau (1888-1969)*. Edited by Louise LeTourneau Dick. Longview, Tex.: LeTourneau Press, 1985. 264 p.

LeTourneau's musings on a variety of topics, ranging from his inventions to Christian stewardship.

890. ———. "Up from Bankruptcy." In *The Wesleyan Message Bearing Fruit: Addresses Delivered at the 13th and 14th Sessions of the Ministers' Conference of Greenville College, April 1940-1941*, 140-45. Winona Lake, Ind.: Light and Life Press, 1942.

A brief account of his deliverance from moral, spiritual, financial, and physical bankruptcy.

891. Lewer, Mary E. "50 Years of Pentecostal Blessing." *The Pentecostal Evangel*, 26 January 1958, 7.

Lewer and her husband were Pentecostal missionaries to China. She received the baptism of the Holy Spirit via A. B. Simpson at a camp meeting in 1905. In the fall of 1906, while she was a student at Nyack, news came of the Azusa Street revival. An all-night prayer meeting ensued, and a similar revival began at Nyack.

892. Lewis, A. Rodger (1923-1999). *The Battle for Bali: The Story of Rodger and Lelia Lewis*. Camp Hill, Pa.: Christian Publications, 1999. 213 p.

The Lewises served as C&MA missionaries to Bali (1953-1994).

893. ———. *Karya Kristus di Indonesia: Sejarah Gereja Kemah Injil Indonesia sejak 1930*. Bandung, Indonesia: Kalam Hidup, 1995. 503 p.

A history of Gereja Kemah Injil Indonesia (the C&MA Church of Indonesia) and the C&MA mission to Indonesia, 1930-1990. Text in Bahasa Indonesia.

894. ———. *Ringkasan sejarah Gereja Kemah Injil Indonesia 1928-1987* (The Concise History of the C.M.A. Church of Indonesia). Bandung, Indonesia: Kalam Hidup, 1987.

Text in Bahasa Indonesia.

895. Lichtenfels, Sophie (1843-1919). *An Elevator for a Tenement House for Daily Use*. New York: by the author, [19–?]. 6 p.

An exposition of Ps. 37:1-6. The orthography reflects the author's broken, German-accented English.

896. ———. *An Elevator for a Tenement House for Daily Use*, 2nd ed. New York: by the author, [19–?]. 8 p.

Adds two brief messages, "God's Promises" and "Pearls by Sophie," to the original text.

897. ———. *A Telegram Message to the Lost World*. New York: by the author, [189-?]. 16 p.

Evangelistic messages by this pious German immigrant scrubwoman who became an effective lay evangelist and promoter of missions for the Alliance. The text preserves the colorful broken English of the messages on which it is based.

898. Lightbody, C. Stuart. "Great Cities: An Analysis of Special Project Giving in Canada." *His Dominion* 16 (July 1990): 20-27.

An account of a successful campaign on the part of the churches of the C&MA in Canada to raise funds for the construction of large church buildings in Buenos Aires and Manila. These edifices were to be used as bases for a campaign of saturation evangelism.

899. ———. "A Management Model of Fund Raising for Church Planting in Manila, Philippine Islands, by the Churches of the Christian and Missionary Alliance in Canada." D.Min. diss., Trinity Evangelical Divinity School, 1985. 264 p.

The funds raised were used to build a large cathedral-like church and to fund evangelistic campaigns to fill it.

900. ———. "New Strategies for a New Era: The Story of a Denominational Mission Turning Urban." *Urban Mission* 3 (January 1986): 30-34.

An overview of the major projects in evangelism the Alliance has initiated in 12 of the world's largest cities.

901. Lindberg, Beth M. *A God-Filled Life: The Story of William E. Blackstone*. Chicago: American Messianic Fellowship, [1957?]. 46 p.

Focuses on Blackstone's Zionist activities and on his work with the Chicago Hebrew Mission, which he founded. Mentions in passing his address at the 1886 Old Orchard convention that inspired A. B. Simpson to found the Christian Alliance the following year.

902. Lindenberger (S)arah A. (1852-1922). *A Cloud of Witnesses*. New York: Christian Alliance Pub. Co., 1900. 137 p.

Testimonies by recipients of divine healing.

903. ———. *Streams from the Valley of Berachah*. New York: Christian Alliance Pub. Co., 1893. 160 p.

A manual on the spiritual life that is replete with C&MA themes—healing in the Atonement, the filling of the Holy Spirit, union with Christ, and preparation for Christ the Coming King—and is also partly a spiritual autobiography. Also includes illustrations from the author's ministry as the overseer of the Berachah Home, the Alliance's healing home in New York City.

904. Linn (J)ason S. *The Life of Dr. R. A. Jaffray*. Hong Kong: The Alliance Press, 1962. 138 p.

Text in Chinese. Linn was a co-worker of R. A. Jaffray's.

905. ———. *The Life of Dr. R. A. Jaffray,* rev. ed. Hong Kong: China Alliance Press, 1981. 155 p.

906. ———. *Pioneering in Dyak Borneo*, 2nd ed. Singapore: Far Eastern Bible College, 1973. 247 p.

A history of the Chinese Foreign Missionary Union's work among the Dyaks of Kalimantan, Indonesia. R. A. Jaffray co-founded (with Leland Wang) the CFMU in 1929 as an Alliance-affiliated mission for Chinese who wanted to serve as foreign missionaries. Includes considerable biographical material on both Linn and Jaffray.

907. Livingston, C. Jeter. "Where Souls Still Sit in Heathen Darkness: Christian and Missionary Alliance Missionaries as Interpreters of African Culture: An Investigation of Their Writings, 1881-1997." Ph.D. diss., Trinity Evangelical Divinity School, 1998. 283 p.

Up until about 1965 the writings of C&MA missionaries portrayed Africans and African culture in at best a paternalistic way. By the 1990s, however, this attitude had changed, and African Christians began to replace missionaries as heroes of the faith.

908. Livingston, Jean Ann (1931-). *Tears for the Smaller Dragon: The Story of Jim and Jean Livingston*. The Jaffray Collection of Missionary Portraits, no. 18. Camp Hill, Pa.: Christian Publications, 1997. 197 p.

James Healey (Jim) (1931-) and Jean Livingston served as Alliance missionaries to Vietnam; teachers and chaplains at the C&MA's Dalat school for children of missionaries in Penang, Malaysia; and missionaries to Vietnamese in refugee camps in the Philippines.

909. Lockerbie, Jeanette W. *When Blood Flows the Heart Grows Softer*. Wheaton, Ill.: Tyndale House; Harrisburg, Pa.: Christian Publications, 1976. 232 p.

An account, compiled from interviews of (mostly C&MA) missionaries and indigenous workers, of the rapid growth of the church in Cambodia between 1971 and the Khmer Rouge takeover in 1975.

910. Lockyer, Herbert. *The Healer and Healing Movements*. Stirling, Scotland: Drummond's Tract Depot, [ca. 1925]. 63 p.

Advocates prayer for healing "if there is the clear indication that such healing is God's will for one." Rejects A. B. Simpson's contention that medical means are "God's second best," and laments Simpson's departure from his mentor, Charles Cullis, on this point: "the logical conclusion of such teaching is that we can possess a kind of physical immortality in this life."

911. Lombard, Victor. *Victor Lombard of Geneva: A Story of Healing & Spiritual Transformation*. New York: Alliance Press Co., 1906. 61 p.

Testimony of a Swiss advocate of divine healing.

912. Long, Charles E. (1935-). *To Vietnam with Love: The Story of Charlie and EG Long*. Camp Hill, Pa.: Christian Publications, 1995. 217 p.

Charlie and (E)lma (G)race (1933-) Long served as C&MA missionaries to the Jarai of the Vietnamese highlands (1958-1974). They finished translating the New Testament into Jarai and compiling a Jarai hymnal just before the fall of Vietnam. Long's passionate biography is also a history of Alliance missions in Vietnam during the Vietnam War and a lament over the U. S. pull-out: "The anti-war people, who persuaded America to abandon Southeast Asia to the communists, have the blood of a million Cambodians and hundreds of thousands of Vietnamese and Laotians on their consciences" (p. 11). Cf. 1019.

913. "Looking Back in the Southeastern District." *Southeastern District Report of the Christian and Missionary Alliance, Special Edition*, May 1977, 18-22.

Biographical sketches of the six superintendents of the Southeastern District: R. A. Forrest, John Minder, W. I. McGarvey, T. F. Mangam, Richard H. Harvey, T. J. Spier, and Paul Alford. The sketch of John Minder includes observations by his former protégé, Billy Graham, who served briefly as Minder's assistant pastor at the Tampa Gospel Tabernacle in 1940. This pastorate was Graham's first church assignment. A. B. Simpson's writings had a profound influence on Graham, and he occasionally preached some of Simpson's sermons.

914. Lorimer, Albert W. *God Runs My Business: The Story of R. G. LeTourneau*. New York: Fleming H. Revell, 1941. 192 p.

LeTourneau was an inventor, businessman, and Alliance lay preacher who became a successful manufacturer of road-building and other specialized equipment. He set aside 90% of the stock of his company, using it to promote missions, evangelism, and Christian higher education via the R. G. LeTourneau Foundation.

915. *Louise Shepard Pridgeon*. Pittsburgh: The Evangelization Society of Pittsburgh Bible Institute, 1955. 176 p.

A former society belle and opera singer, Louise Shepard was converted in the Gospel Tabernacle in December 1890. During the following nine years, she spoke and sang at Alliance meetings, served as assistant editor of the Alliance's weekly periodical, and was an effective and sought-after evangelist and advocate for the deeper life. On 14 July 1891, at a conference of the C&MA held at Round Lake, N.Y., she offered her jewellery for missions. Thus began an outpouring of gifts of jewellery among Alliance people that raised over $80,000 for missions between 1891 and 1899. Shepard left the Alliance on 27 December 1899, but she remained on good terms with A. B. Simpson (cf. 278).

916. Lugibihl, Walter H. (1883-), and Jared F. Greig. *The Missionary Church Association: Historical Account of Its Origin and Development*. Berne, Ind.: Economy Printing Concern, 1950. 164 p.

The evangelistic efforts of A. E. Funk and A. B. Simpson led to the establishment of a German branch of the Christian Alliance in 1888. This group merged with other German Holiness groups in 1898 to form the

Missionary Church Association, with Funk as president. The MCA embraced the Alliance's fourfold Gospel and its missionary fervor in their entirety and, until 1945, relied on the Alliance to supervise its missionaries on the field. A proposed merger between the Alliance and the MCA, to be called the Missionary Alliance Church, was approved by the Alliance in 1960, but rejected by the MCA shortly thereafter.

917. Lutzer, Erwin W. *Flames of Freedom*. Chicago: Moody Press, 1976. 191 p.

Probably the most thorough account of the Canadian revival of the early 1970s that was facilitated by Alliance evangelists Ralph and Lou Sutera. Many Alliance churches were affected by the revival, especially University Drive Alliance Church in Saskatoon, Sask.

918. Ma, Nancy K. W. "Chinese Missionaries in Indonesia." Master's thesis, Columbia Bible College, 1962. 141 p.

A history of the missionaries of the Chinese Foreign Missionary Union, a mission organized by R. A. Jaffray to send Chinese missionaries to Indonesia.

919. Mabiala, Justin. "Called to Obey." In *One Race, One Gospel, One Task: World Congress on Evangelism, Berlin, 1966,* eds. Carl F. H. Henry and W. Stanley Mooneyham, 2: 35-7 Minneapolis: World Wide Publications, 1967.

Laments the lack of evangelistic zeal among African Christians and proposes various strategies for evangelizing the world.

920. Mabille, Georges. *L'appel du Soudanais: Voyage en A.O.F., carnet de route*. Paris : Société des Missions Évangéliques, [1945?]. 167 p.

The travel diary of Mabille, who was one of the representatives of La Société des Missions Évangéliques de Paris who traveled to French West Africa to persuade the colonial authorities to end their harsh treatment of C&MA missionaries.

921. MacArthur, William (T)elfer (1861-1949). *Ethan O. Allen*. Philadelphia: Office of the Parlor Evangelist, [1924?]. 19 p.

Allen was one of the first North American exponents of divine healing. He influenced A. B. Simpson and many others in the movement. This account includes the story of how Allen cast a demon out of a girl and into a pig some miles distant.

922. ———. *The Philistines' Cows*. New York: Christian Alliance Pub. Co., [189-?]. 15 p.

A sermon, based on Phil. 3:10 and 1 Sam. 4-6, on the need to efface self if one is to attain true communion with God.

923. ———. *Practical Righteousness*. New York: Alliance Press Co., [ca. 1906]. 34 p.

Holiness of personal conduct is an essential feature of the Christian life. It involves constantly yielding to the Holy Spirit, doing everything one can to make restitution for sins one has committed, and discerning right from wrong.

924. ———. *Practical Righteousness*, new and enlarged ed. New York: Christian Alliance Pub. Co., [1918?]. 46 p.

Includes sermons not found in 923.

925. ———. *The Translation of the Saints*. Evangel Tracts, no. 35. Chicago: The Evangel Publishing House, 1917. 18 p.

A sermon on Rev. 12.

926. ———. *Travel Letter*. Chicago: Evangel Publishing House, [1925-1926?].

MacArthur's five travel letters recount his visits to Alliance mission stations in Japan, Central China, Indochina, and India (1925-1926).

927. ———. *The Turkey Story and Other Incidents*. New York: Christian Alliance Pub. Co., [ca. 1935]. 51 p.

A reprint of 924 with an additional sermon, "The Turkey Story."

928. ———. *Twenty Sermonettes*. Oak Park, Ill.: by the author, [1935?]. 77 p.

Articles on Alliance themes, e.g., "The Genius of the Alliance," that were originally published in *The Alliance Weekly*.

929. Macaw, Mrs. Alexander. *Congo: The First Alliance Mission Field*. Harrisburg, Pa.: Christian Publications, 1937. 168 p.

The Alliance's Congo mission, which was established in 1885, has operated almost exclusively in the southwestern part of the present-day Democratic Republic of the Congo. Includes a history of the Gabon field, which C&MA missionaries from the Congo founded in 1934, and a list of deceased C&MA missionaries to the Congo.

930. Mackenzie, Kenneth (1853-1943). *An Angel of Light.* New York: Christian Alliance Pub. Co., 1917. 294 p.

Essentially an expansion of 934, with a more extended treatment of the history and beliefs of the new cults. Only a repentant church can expect to have the power needed to counter the threat they pose.

931. ———. *Anti-Christian Supernaturalism.* New York: Christian Alliance Pub. Co., 1901. 191 p.

An exposé of New Thought, Spiritualism, Theosophy, Christian Science, and other monistic Satan-inspired religions to which many professing Christians attending spiritually insipid churches have naively turned to fulfill their longing for an experience of the supernatural.

932. ———. *Divine Life for the Body.* New York: Christian Alliance Pub. Co., 1926. 175 p.

God may use sickness as a means of testing and humbling the Christian, but he does not desire it as a permanent condition. The focus of healing prayer should be Christ, who is the source of life for the body, and not healing for healing's sake. Christ bestows divine health only to those who have entirely consecrated their lives to him.

933. ———. *Elijah, a Character Study.* New York: Christian Alliance Pub. Co., 1921. 40 p.

Elijah is an example of strength being perfected in weakness.

934. ———. *Faith and Fanaticism.* New York: n.p., [ca. 1885]. 7 p.

935. ———. *The Minister's Home, Health and Habits.* Harrisburg, Pa.: Christian Publications, [193-?]. 30 p.

Covers such topics as dress, family devotions, proper eating habits, physical hygiene, sermon preparation, visitation, and private prayer.

936. ———. *Our Physical Heritage in Christ.* New York: Fleming H. Revell, 1923. 222 p.

An apologetic for the doctrine of "healing in the Atonement" by an Episcopalian associate of A. B. Simpson for whom the Eucharist is a symbol of Christ as the source of life and health. Claims that Simpson differed from John Alexander Dowie in believing that God can use sickness to chasten people. Includes Mackenzie's testimony of his own healing.

937. ———. "Present-day Supernaturalism." In *The Signs of the Times, or God's Message for Today: A Symposium on New Theology, Christian Science, The Lord's Coming, the Gift of Tongues, and the Deeper Spiritual Life*, 138-56. New York: Alliance Press Co., 1907.

Materialism and rationalism are gradually being replaced as the chief opponents of Christianity by a revived paganism that is masquerading as a modernizing of Christianity. Cf. 931.

938. ———. *Redemption: A Study*. New York: Christian Alliance Pub. Co., 1903. 83 p.

Christ's atoning death not only makes believers righteous before God, but it also takes away that "terror of God [that] is the foundation of man's alienation from his best Friend" (p. 79). But sanctification is the necessary prerequisite for this experience of freedom, for by it believers are "absolutely separated from [their] old bond-master and unto God, our present, loving Possessor" (p. 73).

939. ———. *The Secret*. New York: Christian Alliance Pub. Co., [ca. 1910]. 4 p.

Abiding in Christ, not frenzied pleading or spasmodic intercession, is the key to effectual prayer.

940. ———. *The Silent Unity*. New York: Christian Alliance Pub. Co., [ca. 1900]. 22 p.

A critique of New Thought, which later became known as the Unity School of Christianity

941. ———. *The Spirit of Fearfulness*. New York: Christian Alliance Pub. Co., [ca. 1900]. 8 p.

A critique of Christian Science and New Thought, both of which claim to eliminate fear by denying the reality of evil. Jesus, by contrast, eliminates fear by dealing with it at the cross: fear is incompatible with the redemption and eternal life he promises to the believer.

942. MacKinnon, Ronald P. "Open Doors: A Program of Theological Education by Extension and Lay Preacher's Institutes for the Christian and Missionary Alliance Church (and Mission) of the Philippines." M.A. thesis, Fuller Theological Seminary, 1975. 128 p.

943. MacMillan, John A. (1873-1956). *The Authority of the Believer*. Camp Hill, Pa.: Christian Publications, 1997. 176 p.

A reprint of 944 and 947.

944. ———. *The Authority of the Believer: A Compilation of the Authority of the Believer and the Authority of the Intercessor*. Harrisburg, Pa.: Christian Publications, 1980. 96 p.

A reprint of 945 and 946.

945. ———. *The Authority of the Believer: Principles Set Forth in the Epistle to the Ephesians.* Harrisburg, Pa.: Christian Publications, [193-?]. 23 p.

Christian authority is delegated power, conferred on the believer by Jesus, over the powers of evil. Humble use of this power in dependence on its source gives release from demonic oppression of the body and the world; victory over outbursts of anger; and authority over fear, demons, and those who oppose the truth.

946. ———. *The Authority of the Intercessor: And Other Studies in the Co-operation of the Overcomer with His Lord*. Harrisburg, Pa.: Christian Publications, 1942. 20 p.

God shares "with human hands the throttle of divine power" (p. 5) and the spiritual warfare waged by the intercessor "is directing the throne-power of Christ against Satan and his hosts" (p. 20).

947. ———. *Encounter with Darkness*. Harrisburg, Pa.: Christian Publications, 1980. 116 p.

A considerably expanded version of 948.

948. ———. *Modern Demon Possession: The Increasing Menace of These Latter Days in Spiritism and Its Attendant Evils*. Harrisburg, Pa.: Christian Publications, 1949. 24 p.

First published in 1948 as articles in *The Alliance Weekly.* An explication of the three ways in which demons attack people: oppression, obsession, and possession; followed by guidelines for conducting an exorcism. The author was a C&MA missionary to China and the Philippines, and much of his firsthand knowledge of demons came from his ministry to animists in the latter country. Cf. 947.

949. Magnuson, Norris A. (1932-). *Salvation in the Slums: Evangelical Social Work, 1865-1920.* Metuchen, N.J.: Scarecrow Press and the American Theological Library Association, 1977. 315 p.

Includes an extensive catalogue of the C&MA's social ministries, which were "a by-product of the deeper spiritual life Simpson and his associates sought to cultivate" (p. 18).

950. Mains, Karen Burton. "Up from the Misty Lowlands." *Christian Herald*, November 1980, 17-22.

Tozer's evangelical mysticism accords completely with the six characteristics proposed by Georgia Harkness in *Mysticism: Its Meaning and Message*. His is a communicable mysticism that speaks prophetically against the rationalism, materialism, and soul-less activism to which evangelicals often succumb. It is most eloquently expressed in 2123 and 2176.

951. Mallory (O)son (E)rskine (1835-1923). *Lips Touched with Fire, or Pentecost for Me.* New York: Christian Alliance Pub. Co., [1898?]. 179 p.

The baptism of the Holy Spirit is a definite experience subsequent to conversion for the purpose of granting power and holiness to the recipient, but "for us to be looking for the gift of tongues now and charge it to the apostasy of the church that we do not see it is not warranted by scripture." God can, however, give this gift today if he chooses to, just as he still gives the gifts of miracles and healing.

952. ———. *The Signs of the Times*. New York: Christian Alliance Pub. Co., [ca.1910]. 12 p.

A meditation on Matt. 24:3 in the light of current events.

953. Mangham, T. Grady. "Aftermath to Persecution." In *Christ and Caesar in Christian Missions*, eds. Edwin L. Frizen Jr. and Wade T. Coggins, 61-74. Pasadena, Calif.: William Carey Library, 1979.

The C&MA experience in Vietnam indicates that missionaries should withdraw before a communist takeover, since they would not be able to minister thereafter and would be an embarrassment to indigenous church leaders; avoid contact with the U. S. military and the U. S. government so as to avoid allegations of collusion; and avoid expressing their opinions on both communism and politics.

954. ———. "Developing Church Responsibility in Vietnam." In *Church/Mission Tensions Today*, ed. C. Peter Wagner, 163-84. Chicago: Moody Press, 1972.

Credits the successful relationship between the C&MA mission and the Evangelical Church of Vietnam to: the establishment of firm policies, well-defined channels of communication, a willingness to negotiate, continuing emphasis on church planting and evangelism, and the opportunity for dialogue afforded by the C&MA's Asia conferences.

955. ———. "English Language Ministries." In *1969 Retreat Report: Papers Presented to the 18th Annual Mission Executives Retreat, October, 1969*, eds. Clyde W. Taylor and Wade T. Coggins, 72-75. Wheaton, Ill.: Evangelical Missions Information Service, 1969.

Missionaries working in non-English-speaking countries often neglect to present the gospel to English-speaking expatriates. The C&MA has attempted to redress this imbalance by planting churches called simply "The International Church of [city X]." Such churches operate independently of the C&MA, but their constitutions require that their pulpits be filled by Alliance personnel. Such churches are also required to have fraternal relations with both the C&MA mission and the (C&MA) national church.

956. Mangham, T. Grady, and Phil Butler. "New Optimism in Viet Nam." *Moody Monthly*, September 1967, 41-45.

Mangham, field director for the C&MA mission in South Vietnam, believes that the church in Vietnam will prosper and grow despite the suffering it has had to endure because of the war.

957. Mangham, William F., Jr. "A Study of the History and Strategy of the Movement 'Lima to an Encounter with God,' 1973-1986." Master's thesis, Columbia Biblical Seminary and Graduate School of Missions, 1987. 144 p.

Probably the most exhaustive treatment of this highly successful church growth initiative. The Encounter project has served as a model for all subsequent urban missionary work by the Alliance.

958. Mantle (J)ohn Gregory (1852-1925). *Abraham My Friend, or Lessons in the School of Faith*. Louisville, Ky.: Pentecostal Pub. Co., 1918. 127 p.

959. ———. *According to the Pattern*. London: Marshall Brothers, 1898. 255 p.

Christians should not be satisfied with anything less than a life characterized by the pursuit of holiness by faith—a life in which Jesus Christ serves not only as the example, but also as the source of power.

960. ———. *"Better Things": A Series of Bible Readings on the Epistle to the Hebrews,* 3rd ed. New York: Christian Alliance Pub. Co., 1921. 237 p.

A devotional commentary with study questions at the end of each chapter, in keeping with its use as a textbook at the Missionary Training Institute. Cf. 961.

961. ———. *Better Things from Above*. Harrisburg, Pa.: Christian Publications, 1971. 207 p.
Reprint of 960.

962. ———. *Beyond Humiliation: The Way of the Cross*. Minneapolis: Dimension Books, 1975. 248 p.
Reprint of 971.

963. ———. *Consecrated Husks*. London: W. G. Wheeler, [ca.1900-1930]. 100 p.

964. ———. *The Counterfeit Christ, and Other Sermons*. New York: Fleming H. Revell, 1920. 203 p.

965. ———. *God's To-morrow*. London: Marshall Brothers, 1902. 246 p.
Miscellaneous sermons preached at the West London Mission.

966. ———. *Guarding the Outposts: A Book for Young Men*. New York: Fleming H. Revell, 1919. 128 p.
Abridged reprint of 970. Lacks the chapters referring to World War I.

967. ———. *"My Servant Job," or Lessons in the School of Suffering*. Louisville: Pentecostal Pub. Co., [191-?] 111 p.
Job suffered so that he might be cleansed of pride, self-righteousness, and self-trust; and that he might be brought into complete subjection to God.

968. ———. *The Romance of the Missionary Institute at Nyack-on-Hudson, New York*. [New York]: n.p, [1921?]. 32 p.
A promotional piece consisting mostly of photographs, including one of the last taken of A. B. Simpson. Written anonymously, but a comment in 224 indicates that Mantle is the author.

969. ———. *Saul, a Type of the Self-Life*. Synopsis of Sermon, no 1. Louisville: Pentecostal Pub. Co., [191-?]. 8 p.

Saul became king as a result of Israel's self-will. His rule provides an example of how self-will usurps the sovereignty of God; leads to enslavement to self interest; and exercises its dominion with great power, subtlety, and stubbornness. Self-will can be eliminated only by a radical annihilation in submission to God as epitomized in Samuel's hacking Agag to pieces before the Lord.

970. ———. *Taps: A Book for the Boys in Khaki*. New York: Fleming H. Revell, 1917. 265 p.

Miscellaneous admonitions and object lessons for young men (and especially for soldiers) on how to be a "soldier for Christ."

971. ———. *The Way of the Cross: A Contribution to the Doctrine of Christian Sanctity,* 6th ed. rev. and enlarged. New York: Christian Alliance Pub. Co., 1922. 269 p.

The sanctified life consists in utter self-abandonment to Christ in light of the cross. Cf. 962.

972. Mar, Jacqueline. "Fulfillment: An Integrative Synthesis of Psychological and Christian Perspectives." Psy.D. diss., Biola University, 1984. 175 p.

Synthesizes the views of fulfillment of psychologists Carl Rogers, Abraham Maslow, Rollo May, and Sidney Jourard with those of contemporary spiritual writers A. W. Tozer, Thomas Merton, Adrian Van Kaam, and Thomas Horn.

973. Marsh (F)rederick (E)dward (1858-1931). *125 Sermon Outlines and Bible Readings*. Dollar Sermon Library Books. Grand Rapids: Baker, 1969. 88 p.

Reprint of selected passages from 985.

974. ———. *500 Bible Study Outlines*. Grand Rapids: Kregel Publications, 1986. 384 p.

Reprint of 985.

975. ———. *1000 Bible Study Outlines*. Grand Rapids: Kregel, 1970. 493 p.

976. ———. *1000 New Bible Readings: For the Help of Students and Workers*. London: Pickering and Inglis, 1925. 493 p.

Brief topical studies together with outlines to facilitate Bible study and sermon preparation. Foreword by F. B. Meyer.

977. ———. *The Believer's Hope, or Christ Coming for His People.* New York: Gospel Publishing House, [ca.1900-1917]. 15 p.

On the personal return of Christ.

978. ———. *Caught Up.* Nyack, N.Y.: Christian Alliance Pub. Co., 1900. 19 p.

A sermon on the resurrection of the body, based on 1 Thess. 4:17.

979. ———. *Challenging Sermon Outlines and Bible Readings.* Dollar Sermon Library. Grand Rapids: Baker, 1971. 80 p.

980. ———. *The Christian Worker's Equipment.* New York: Christian Alliance Pub. Co., 1900. 390 p.

A reprint of 15 of the 17 chapters in 1014, with additional meditations on the pastoral ministry.

981. ———. *Christ's Atonement.* New York: Christian Alliance Pub. Co., 1898. 152 p.

Nine sermons.

982. ———. "The Coming Super-Man of Sin, or the Masterpiece of Satan." In *Aids to Prophetic Study, No. 20*, 56-75. London: Charles J. Thynne, 1921.

An extended word study on "the man of sin" (2 Thess. 2:3). He will come to earth physically as a representative of Satan and will be destroyed by Jesus Christ at the Parousia.

983. ———. *Devotional Bible Studies.* Grand Rapids: Kregel, 1980. 302 p.

Reprint of 996.

984. ———. *Emblems of the Holy Spirit.* Grand Rapids: Kregel Publications, [ca. 1905]. 257 p.

Explains, in somewhat "stream-of-consciousness" fashion, fourteen figures of speech used in the Bible to describe the Holy Spirit.

985. ———. *Five Hundred Bible Readings, or Light from the Lamp of Truth,* 4th ed. Glasgow: Pickering and Inglis; New York: Alliance Press Co., [19–?]. 366 p.

Each Bible reading consists of a topic, e.g., "the Ark," that is explained by a sort of extended exercise in theological and biblical word association.

986. ———. *Flashes from the Lighthouse of Truth, or Bible Readings on the First Three Chapters of the Epistle to the Church at Thessalonica.* Stirling, Scotland: Drummond's Tract Depot, 1893. 271 p.
Cf. 997.

987. ———. *"Glorious Person."* In *The New Heavens and the New Earth (Revelation XXI) Together with a Survey of European and Near East Conditions.* Aids to Prophetic Study, no. 24, eds. S. H. Wilkinson and E. Bendor Samuel. London: Charles J. Thynne, 1923. 74 p.
The Holy City/Bride of Christ is not the church as a whole, but rather the consecrated, Spirit-filled Old and New Testament saints. Includes a reference to God as "many-breasted" (p. 43).

988. ———. *The Greatest Book in Literature.* London: Hulbert Pub. Co., 1929. 156 p.
Lectures on the doctrine of Scripture that were originally delivered as part of the Bible Doctrine course at the Missionary Training Institute, Nyack, N.Y.

989. ———. *The Greatest Theme in the World.* New York: Alliance Press Co., 1908. 161 p.
A somewhat idiosyncratic analysis, under a multitude of categories, buttressed by a multitude of biblical quotations, of the Atonement. Cf. 1009.

990. ———. *Illustrated Bible Studies.* New York: Fleming H. Revell, [191-?]. 267 p.

991. ———. *Illustrated Bible Study Outlines.* Grand Rapids: Kregel, 1978. 267 p.
Reprint of 990.

992. ———. *Living God's Way.* Grand Rapids: Kregel, 1981. 229 p.
Reprint of 1003.

993. ———. *Major Bible Truths.* Grand Rapids: Kregel, 1979. 458 p.
Reprint of 1004.

994. ———. *Night Scenes of the Bible.* [New York?]: Alliance Press Co., 1904. 131 p.
Sermons on various topics that are in some way connected to literal or figurative darkness, e.g., the Exodus.

995. ———. *One Hundred New Bible Readings*. New York: The Book Stall, 1924. 134 p.

Brief meditations on a variety of topics related to the Christian life.

996. ———. *Pearls, Points and Parables*. New York: Gospel Pub. House, 1908. 297 p.

About 250 sermonettes keyed to an index of biblical texts. Cf. 983.

997. ———. *Practical Truths from First Thessalonians*. Grand Rapids: Kregel, 1986. 271 p.

Reprint of 986.

998. ———. *The Resurrection of Christ: Fact or Fiction?* London: Pickering and Inglis, 1904. 230 p.

Identical in content to 1006.

999. ———. "The Secrets of the Kingdom of Heaven." In *Aids to Prophetic Study No. 34*, 51-61. London: Charles J. Thynne and Jarvis, [1928?].

The "secrets" mentioned in Dan. 2:27-30 are intended to be revealed, hence the need to study prophecy thoroughly to understand the revelation as it applies to Israel and the nations and, ultimately, to the return of Christ.

1000. ———. *Select Sermon Outlines and Bible Readings*. Grand Rapids: Baker, 1970. 74 p.

1001. ———. "The Signs of the Times." In *The Signs of the Times, or God's Message for Today: A Symposium on New Theology, Christian Science, The Lord's Coming, the Gift of Tongues, and the Deeper Spiritual Life*, 52-86. New York: Alliance Press Company, 1907.

The signs are: apostasy, rationalism, the gullibility of religious people, counterfeit Gospels (such as Christian Science), widespread death by accident and violence, natural disasters, widespread moral decline, and the intense desire on the part of devout Christians for revival.

1002. ———. *Sin and Salvation*. New York: Gospel Pub. House; London: Morgan & Scott, [1912?]. 58 p.

An exhaustive catalogue, with brief explanatory notes, of the relevant biblical passages.

1003. ———. *The Spiritual Life, or Helps and Hindrances.* London: by the author, [191-?]. 225 p.

The cultivation of the inner life requires entire consecration, the baptism of the Holy Spirit, the avoidance of sin, and the diligent study of the Bible.

1004. ———. *The Structural Principles of the Bible, or How to Study the Word of God.* Fincastle, Va.: Bible Study Classics, [192-?]. 458 p.

An elementary textbook in hermeneutics intended for use in Bible colleges and seminaries.

1005. ———. *Topics for the Times.* New York: Alliance Press Co., 1904. 189 p.

Addresses originally given at the Gospel Tabernacle, New York City. Introduction by A. B. Simpson. Affirms that: the Bible is the word of God, the wicked will suffer eternal punishment, the unrighteous dead are in Hades, and that the righteous dead are "with the Lord" awaiting the redemption of their bodies.

1006. ———. *What Does the Resurrection of Christ Mean?* London: Marshall Brothers; New York: Bass and Company, 1904. 230 p.

An extended meditation on "the fact of Christ's Resurrection and the consequent influence it should have on our lives" (p. vii). Cf. 998.

1007. ———. *What Is Heaven?* London: Marshall Brothers, [189-?]. 119 p.

Heaven is summed up in Christ, who lives there, opens access to heaven to humankind, and will make its inhabitants like himself.

1008. ———. *What Will Take Place When Jesus Returns?* London: S. E. Roberts, [191-?]. Reprint, New York: Christian Alliance Pub. Co., [191-?]. 258 p.

A comprehensive eschatology, like 1213, but more popular and sermonic in form.

1009. ———. *Why Did Christ Die? or the Greatest Theme in the World.* London: Marshall Brothers, 1921. 199 p.

Reprint of 989. Includes two additional chapters.

1010. ———. *Why Will Christ Come Back?: Advent Addresses.* London: Pickering and Inglis, [191-?]. 152 p.

Twelve addresses, from a premillennialist perspective, delivered in London at monthly meetings of the Advent Testimony Movement.

1011. ———. *Will the Church, or Any Part of It, Go Through the Great Tribulation?: An Address Delivered at the Liverpool Convention, November 1894.* London: W. G. Wheeler; New York: Gospel Publishing House, 1894. 16 p.
No.

1012. ———. *Words to Christian Workers*. London: Drummond's Tract Depot, 1890. 279 p.
Meditations on Scriptures that bear on the pastoral ministry.

1013. Marsh (F)rederick (E)dward (1858-1931), and C. M. Mackay. *The Millennial City and Temple: Ezekiel XL-XLVII.* Aids to Prophetic Study, no. 29. London: Charles J. Thynne and Jarvis, 1925. 80 p.
Papers presented at the meeting of the Prophecy Investigation Society, 2 April 1925.

1014. Marsh (F)rederick (E)dward (1858-1931), and E. A. Rawlence. "Will Babylon Be Rebuilt?" In *The Millennial City and Temple: Ezekiel XL-XLVII.* Aids to Prophetic Study, no. 29, 43-59. London: Charles J. Thynne and Jarvis, 1925.
Babylon will be rebuilt because Scripture promises that it will be, and because economic and political factors are propitious to its rebuilding. The new Babylon will be the embodiment of materialism, and Christians must shun the idolatrous covetousness that the city symbolizes.

1015. Marshall, Alex. *God's Way of Salvation: Set Forth Simply by Illustration, Comparison and Contrast.* New York: Christian Alliance Pub. Co., [192-?]. 31 p.
Attempts to answer objections raised by non-Christians when confronted with the demand of the Gospel to repent and believe in Jesus.

1016. Marston, Hope. *By an Unfamiliar Path*. Junior Jaffray Collection of Missionary Stories, book 13. Camp Hill, Pa.: Christian Publications, 1995. 28 p.
A retelling, for children, of 1270.

1017. ———. *Journey to Joy*. The Junior Jaffray Collection of Missionary Stories, book 11. Camp Hill, Pa.: Christian Publications, 1994. 31 p.
A retelling, for children, of 526.

1018. ———. *The Promise.* The Junior Jaffray Collection of Missionary Stories, book 10. Camp Hill, Pa.: Christian Publications, 1994. 32 p.

A retelling, for children, of 784.

1019. ———. *To Vietnam with Love.* Junior Jaffray Collection of Missionary Stories, book 12. Camp Hill, Pa.: Christian Publications, 1995. 29 p.

A retelling, for children, of 912.

1020. Martin, Alvin. *Fulfilled Prophecy in Israel Today: A Series of Prophetic Messages Delivered over "Tabernacle Tidings" during the Month of January, 1956.* Moose Jaw, Sask.: The Southand Press, [1956?]. 44 p.

"Tabernacle Tidings" was broadcast over CHAB Moose Jaw, Saskatchewan.

1021. Martin, Keith. *Beginning at Jerusalem: The Christian and Missionary Alliance in the Holy Land.* Jerusalem: The Christian and Missionary Alliance in Israel, 1990. 32 p.

The text of a videorecording that was produced to commemorate the centenary of Alliance missions in Palestine. Includes the names of missionaries and national workers who are not mentioned in the video.

1022. Martin, Ruth Mildred. "The Canadian Bible College—History from 1941 to 1962." Master's thesis, Winona Lake School of Theology, 1962. 213 p.

Includes a list of CBC alumni currently serving as missionaries.

1023. Martinez, Joel. "An Evaluation of Church Planting Methods Used by the Churches of The Christian and Missionary Alliance in Barcelona, Spain." Master's thesis, Columbia Graduate School of Bible and Missions, 1983. 86 p.

1024. Masa, Jorge O. *The Angel in Ebony, or the Life and Message of Sammy Morris.* Upland, Ind.: Taylor University Press, 1928. 131 p.

Somewhat less thorough and more florid than 62.

1025. Matthews, Douglas K. "Approximating the Millennium: Premillennial Evangelicalism and Racial Reconciliation." *Alliance Academic Review* (1998): 71-106.

Properly understood, premillennialism offers hope for the future and leads to concern for all of creation, including cultural life. What is to take place at the end of the age, namely, the realization of the kingdom of God in the form of an earthly utopia, should be the model for what believers ought to be doing now. Since racism will be done away with when Christ returns, Christians ought to be working for racial reconciliation now.

1026. ———. "Approximating the Millennium: Toward a Coherent Premillennial Theology of Social Transformation." Ph.D. diss., Baylor University, 1992. 498 p.

Classifies A. B. Simpson and the Alliance as "symptomatic or relief-oriented" in their social concern. Simpson excelled at all kinds of relief work, but his adoption of a premillennial eschatology led him to regard social degeneration as inevitable and to distrust attempts to change social structures. He did not believe that society could be changed by reforming individuals, but he did believe in treating the victims of social ills. He spoke out prophetically against vices such as drunkenness, but didn't expect to stop the inexorable slide towards Armageddon (p. 63-64).

1027. Mauro, Philip (1859-1952). *Concerning the Sabbath.* New York: Christian Alliance Pub. Co., 1915. 56 p.

Christ did not command his followers to keep the Sabbath, but Christians should abstain from all avoidable work on the first day of the week, so as to make it a day of fellowship, good works, and worship—as was, apparently, the practice of the early church.

1028. ———. *Man's Day.* London: Morgan and Scott; New York: Alliance Press Company, [191-?]. 267 p.

The idea of the inevitability of human progress to perfection flies in the face both of human experience and the Word of God. The bondage under which supposedly autonomous humankind is living can only be broken by trusting in Christ and placing one's hopes in the day of the Lord.

1029. ———. *The Present State of the Crops.* New York: Alliance Press Co., 1906. 32 p.

The present state of the world (everything worth doing has already been done) indicates that it is ripe for harvest and that, therefore, the return of the Lord is imminent. This address was given at the Old Orchard Convention of the C&MA, 8 August 1906.

1030. ———. "Progress of 'the Apostasy.'" In *The Signs of the Times, or God's Message for To-day: A Symposium on New Theology, Christian*

Science, the Lord's Coming, the Gift of Tongues, and the Deeper Spiritual Life, 7-28. New York: Alliance Press Co., 1907.

A catalogue of the contemporary evidences of apostasy: new religious movements, higher criticism, and the liberalism that is rampant in the established denominations. This widespread falling away is a sure sign that Christ's return is imminent.

1031. ———. *Reason to Revelation*. New York: Alliance Press Co., 1904. 102 p.

Introduction by A. B. Simpson. Reason rightly used will lead a seeker after truth to accept the Christian Scriptures as God's revelation and to submit to them. Reason wrongly used demands to see before it believes.

1032. ———. *Salvation and the Mortal Body*. New York: Alliance Press Co., 1905. 105 p.

Christians, when sick, should obey the injunction of James 5 and call on the elders to lay on hands and pray. Scripture does not support the use of medical "means," and so Christians should not use them.

1033. ———. *A Testimony*. London: Morgan and Scott, 1910. 30 p.

Reprinted from *The Christian*. The author became a Christian in 1903 as a result of several visits to the Gospel Tabernacle in New York City.

1034. ———. *The Truth about Evolution*. New York: Christian Alliance Pub. Co., [192-?]. 29 p.

The internal inconsistencies in the theory make it logically untenable. It is based on the mere speculations of people in rebellion against the Creator.

1035. ———. *Watch. Be Ready: The Parable of the Ten Virgins*. New York: Gospel Publishing House, 1918. Reprint, New York: Christian Alliance Pub. Co., 1919. 41 p.

Jesus' exhortation to his followers to be vigilant and to live according to his teachings takes on increased significance in the light of World War I, which undoubtedly is a sign that the end of the age is near.

1036. ———. *Why We Separated from the World*. New York: Alliance Press Co., 1908. 32 p.

Mauro withdrew from his parish church because many in the congregation were either nominal Christians or entirely unregenerate people who did not live under the authority of the Scriptures.

1037. ———. *The World and Its God*. New York: Alliance Press Co., 1906. 104 p.

"The object of these pages . . . is to rouse the indifferent and callous soul to the making of a choice between Satan's world and God's" (p. 79).

1038. Mauro, Philip (1859-1952), et al. *The Signs of the Times, or God's Message for Today: A Symposium on New Theology, Christian Science, the Lord's Coming, the Gift of Tongues, and the Deeper Spiritual Life.* New York: Alliance Press Co., 1907. 226 p.

A collection of essays on a variety of "end-time" themes by A. B. Simpson, other leaders of the Alliance, and non-Alliance people sympathetic to the fourfold Gospel.

1039. Maust, John. "At 20, Church Growth Plan in Lima Encountering Success." *Pulse* 28 (21 May 1993): 4.

A brief history of the Lima al Encuentro con Dios movement and a listing of its 12 principles.

1040. Maxwell (L)eslie (E)arl (1895-1984), and Ruth C. Dearing. *Women in Ministry*. Wheaton, Ill.: Victor Books, 1987. Reprint, Camp Hill, Pa.: Christian Publications, 1987. 167 p.

"That God does choose to call and qualify some women for positions of leadership is proof that women are not intrinsically debarred from such offices because of their womanhood" (p. 146-47). Maxwell founded Prairie Bible Institute. His mentor during his Bible school training was A. B. Simpson's associate W. C. Stevens.

1041. McBirnie, William Stuart. "History of the St. Paul Bible Institute." B.D. thesis, Bethel Theological Seminary, 1945. 40 p.

1042. McClurkan, James (O)ctavius (1861-1914). *Behold He Cometh!: A Series of Brief Lessons on the Second Coming of Christ.* Nashville: Pentecostal Book and Tract Depository, 1899. 179 p.

1043. ———. *Chosen Vessels: Twenty-one Biographical Sketches of Men and Women, Most of Whom Have Been Used of God in the Pioneering of Some Great Pentecostal Movement.* Nashville: Pentecostal Mission Pub. Co., 1901. 199 p.

The sketches stress the biographees' personal appropriation of the experience of sanctification. Subjects include Alliance luminaries Mrs. E. M. Whittemore and Henry Wilson. McClurkan, a leader in the Holiness movement, was a sometime associate of A. B. Simpson. Originally published as articles in *Zion's Outlook.*

1044. ———. *How to Keep Sanctified.* Nashville: Pentecostal Book and Tract Depository, 1900. 29 p.

1045. ———. *Wholly Sanctified: What It Is and How It May Be Obtained.* Nashville: Pentecostal Mission Pub. Co., 1895. 127 p.

The result of regeneration is salvation and forgiveness of sins committed, that of sanctification both freedom from original sin and entire consecration to God. Holiness people stand in the tradition of Ignatius of Antioch, Chrysostom, Molinos, Madame Guyon, Fenelon, the Moravians, and Wesley in maintaining that sanctification is a crisis experience received by faith. The persistence of "medieval theology" in all branches of the church has led most Christians to balk at entering the promised land of sanctification because they believe that the wilderness of feeble struggle against sin is good for them.

1046. McCrossan (T)homas (J)ames (1867-1960). *Are All Christians Baptized with the Holy Ghost at Conversion?* Seattle: n.p., 1932. 85 p.

No. They receive a derivative "exousia," but not the unrestrained soul-winning "dunamis" power of the Spirit-baptized believers of Acts. Contemporary Christians should follow the example of A. B. Simpson who waited and prayed fervently until the Holy Spirit filled him.

1047. ———. *The Bible and Its Eternal Facts.* Seattle: by the author, 1947. 428 p.

An apologetic for various doctrines—e.g., the inspiration of the Bible, the Holy Spirit, the return of Christ—that have been challenged by modernists.

1048. ———. *The Bible, Its Christ and Modernism.* New York: Christian Alliance Pub. Co., 1925. 212 p.

Introduction by Kenneth Mackenzie. Defends the inspiration of the Scriptures and orthodox Christology against the counter-claims of liberal revisionists.

1049. ———. *The Bible, Its Hell and Its Ages.* Seattle: by the author, 1941. 144 p.

Restorationists err in assuming that the punishment meted out at the Last Judgment will be of limited duration and that all sinners, and even Satan himself, will be restored to heaven.

1050. ———. *Bodily Healing and the Atonement*. Seattle: by the author, 1930. 117 p.

"Christ died to atone for our sicknesses as well as our sins" (p. 16). The baptism of the Holy Spirit can produce the expectant faith needed for healing. The Apostle Paul was eventually healed of his thorn in the flesh.

1051. ———. *Christian Science and Christianity Compared: 20 Great Fundamental Differences Clearly Proven*. New York: Charles E. Cook, [191-?]. 58 p.

Christian Science denies the most important doctrines of the Bible. Mary Baker Eddy is a liar, a deceiver, and an anti-Christ. Cf. 1052.

1052. ———. *Christian Science and the Bible Compared: 23 Great Fundamental Differences Clearly Proven*. Seattle: by the author, 1923. 73 p.

A slightly updated version of 1051.

1053. ———. *Christ's Paralyzed Church X-rayed*. Youngstown, Ohio: C. E. Humbard, 1937. 341 p.

No one with a proper understanding of Greek grammar could ever teach that all Christians are baptized in the Holy Spirit at conversion, that bodily healing is not part of the Atonement, or that glossolalia is the only true evidence of Spirit-baptism.

1054. ———. *The Great Tribulation: Are We Now in It? The Rapture: Who Will Be Taken? The Tribulation Saints: Are They Church Members?* Seattle: by the author, 1940. 32 p.

The present world crisis is not the great tribulation, because it is the work of Satan and his agents. The great tribulation will be the direct work of God Himself. The whole church will be taken in the rapture, not just Spirit-filled believers. The tribulation saints have attained eternal life by confessing Christ during the tribulation, but they will not have the privilege of being members of Christ's church, which was complete before the rapture.

1055. ———. *Jesus Christ as a Higher Critic*. Seattle: by the author, [193-?]. 29 p.

Jesus Christ ought to be our supreme authority on the Old Testament because he came from God, was God, represented God, and declared himself to be above the Old Testament. The theories of higher criticism ought to be rejected because they have been based on the assumptions of rationalists, atheists, and infidels.

1056. ———. *Speaking with Other Tongues: Sign or Gift, Which?* New York: Christian Alliance Pub. Co., 1927. 53 p.

Speaking in tongues is a gift that has been restored to the church, but Christians seeking to be baptised in the Holy Spirit should allow the Spirit to manifest himself as he will. A deeply felt inner experience that is outwardly manifested in love is the true sign of Spirit-baptism.

1057. ———. *The True Sabbath: Saturday or Sunday, Which?* 5th ed. Seattle: by the author, [193-?]. 32 p.

Sunday: even in the Old Testament Saturday could not always have been the Sabbath, for certain work days and Sabbaths had to fall on the same date every year. Old Testament prophecies point to a new day "that the Lord has made," which is fulfilled in the New Testament's honoring of Sunday above all days in commemoration of the Resurrection.

1058. ———. *The World's Crisis and the Coming Christ.* Seattle: by the author, 1934. 253 p.

The rapture of the church will precede the great tribulation. Scriptural prophecies regarding the return of Christ, when correlated with current events, indicate that Christ will return in the generation of those now living. Matt. 24:14 refers not to the end of this age and the beginning of the millennium (as A. B. Simpson taught) but to the end of the millennial age.

1059. McDonnell, Kilian, ed. *Presence, Power, Praise. Documents on the Charismatic Renewal. Volume 1—Continental, National, and Regional Documents, Numbers 1 to 37, 1960-1974.* Collegeville, Minn.: The Liturgical Press, 1980.

Includes the "Seek Not, Forbid Not" document on glossolalia adopted by the C&MA in 1963 (p. 63-69).

1060. McFedries, Annie. *Healed by Him Alone*. Pittsburgh: Christian and Missionary Alliance, [1921?]. 8 p.

In 1889 the author was healed of a chronic knee ailment after becoming convinced, on the basis of Matt. 8:17, that healing is provided for in the Atonement. Her subsequent life was devoted to the C&MA's ministry to the poor of Pittsburgh.

1061. McGee, Gary B. "Assemblies of God Mission Theology: A Historical Perspective." *International Bulletin of Missionary Research* 10 (October 1986): 166, 168-69.

Until the early 1920s, more Assemblies of God missionaries had been trained at the Nyack Missionary Training Institute than at any other institution. It was there that they learned the indigenous church principles of John Nevius and S. J. Burton that became one of the cornerstones of AOG mission theology.

1062. ———. "For the Training of . . . Missionaries." *Central Bible College Bulletin*, February 1984, 4-5.

Five of the main buildings on the campus of Central Bible College (CBC) are named after early C&MA leaders who later joined the Assemblies of God (AOG). Some of these had been trained at Nyack. They brought with them the Alliance's premillennial theology and passion for missions, both of which characterize CBC and the AOG to this day.

1063. ———. "Historical Background." In *Systematic Theology: A Pentecostal Perspective*, ed. Stanley M. Horton, 9-37. Springfield, Mo.: Logion Press; Gospel Publishing House, 1994.

"A. B. Simpson . . . strongly emphasized Spirit baptism and had a major impact on the formulation of Assemblies of God doctrine" (p. 12).

1064. ———. "Pentecostal Awakenings at Nyack." *Paraclete* 18 (summer 1984): 22-28.

A well-documented refutation of John Thomas Nichol's contention (1201, p. 37) that the Azusa Street revival of 1906 did not contribute to the revival that occurred in the Alliance in 1907. Includes lists of ex-Alliance AOG worthies and the ways in which the C&MA and Nyack Missionary Training Institute contributed to the AOG.

1065. ———. "The Pentecostal Movement and Assemblies of God Theology: Exploring the Historical Background." *Assemblies of God Heritage* 13 (winter 1993-1994): 10-12, 28-29.

Acknowledges the debt that the Pentecostals owe to Simpson. Cf. 1063.

1066. ———. *"This Gospel Shall Be Preached": A History and Theology of Assemblies of God Foreign Missions to 1959*. Springfield, Mo.: Gospel Publishing House, 1986. 288 p.

Expands on Carl Brumbach's lists of ways in which the C&MA contributed to the development of the AOG (cf. 198). Includes a list of former C&MA missionaries who joined the AOG (p. 62-63).

1067. McGraw, Gerald E. "A. B. Simpson, 1843-1919: From Home Missions to a World Missionary Movement." *Mission Legacies: Biographical Studies of Leaders of the Modern Missionary Movement*, eds. Gerald H. Anderson, et al., 37-47. Maryknoll, N.Y.: Orbis Books, 1994.

Reprint of 1071.

1068. ———. "A. B. Simpson as a Missions Advocate." *Alliance Academic Review* (1997): 1-25.

Reprint of 1071.

1069. ———. "The Doctrine of Sanctification in the Published Writings of Albert Benjamin Simpson." Ph.D. diss., New York University, 1986. 727 p.

Sanctification receives more emphasis in Simpson's oeuvre than any other topic. His teaching is quite internally consistent: he rejects both the "eradicationist" and "suppressionist" in favor of what could be termed a "habitationist" understanding of sanctification. He regards this experience as the entry into the "deeper life," which includes power for service, holy living, physical healing, growth towards union with Christ, and the fullness of the Holy Spirit.

1070. ———. "An Effective Deliverance Methodology: Then and Now." *Alliance Academic Review* (1996): 151-70.

The Gospels do not provide a detailed methodology for exorcism, but Jesus' healing of the Gadarene demoniac and the boy at the foot of the Mount of Transfiguration suggest the following sequence: preparatory counseling, prayers of intercession, commands to demons, testing the spirits, expulsion, invitation of the Holy Spirit to occupy those areas of the counselee's life that were formerly under demonic control, and ongoing instruction on how to live under the control of the Holy Spirit.

1071. ———. "The Legacy of A. B. Simpson." *International Bulletin of Missionary Research* 16 (April 1992): 69-71, 74-77.

Though somewhat lacking in analysis, this is a thorough description of Simpson as an organizer, innovator, and theorist in the field of missions. Includes a lengthy catalogue of Simpson's accomplishments and an extensive bibliography. Cf. 1067 and 1068.

1072. ———. *The Mystery of Jesus' Indwelling: A Centennial Investigation of A. B. Simpson's Christocentric Sanctification*. Evangelical Theological Society Papers, ETS-0405. 23 p.

1073. ———. "Oil in Your Vessel: A. B. Simpson's Concept of a Partial Rapture." Evangelical Theological Society Papers, ETS-1178. 21 p.

A thoroughly documented overview of the views of A. B. Simpson and his contemporaries on the pretribulation rapture of sanctified (as opposed to unsanctified) believers.

1074. McIntyre, Joe. *E. W. Kenyon and His Message of Faith: The True Story*. Orlando, Fla.: Creation House, 1997. 371 p.

Credits A. B. Simpson with having had a profound influence on E. W. Kenyon's understanding of both divine healing and sanctification.

1075. McKaig, Charles Donald. "The Educational Philosophy of A. B. Simpson, Founder of the Christian and Missionary Alliance." Ph.D. diss., New York University, 1948. 254 p.

Simpson was an idealist as far as his philosophy and views on education are concerned. Of the 84 active Bible schools affiliated with the Evangelical Teacher Training Association, 11 owe their existence to Simpson's work, as do 21 Bible schools overseas. Simpson's educational philosophy continues to govern the program of the C&MA's Bible schools.

1076. ———, comp. *Simpson Scrapbook*. n.p., 1971. 374 p.

Includes an autobiography dealing with Simpson's early life, reminiscences by Simpson's friends, his letters to his wife (May-August 1871) a diary (10 November 1879-3 March 1880) newspaper clippings from the 1870s to 1897, and miscellaneous biographical documents.

1077. McKinney, F. J., Mrs. F. J. McKinney, and (R)obert (S)herman Roseberry (1883-1976). *Among the Cliff Dwellers of French West Africa.* New York: Christian and Missionary Alliance, 1936. 31 p.

The McKinneys were the first missionaries ever to evangelize the Habbe people of southern Mali. The first church was established in 1931, after the Habbe, having unsuccessfully invoked their gods, appealed to the McKinneys to pray for rain to end a devastating drought. After their prayer, rain clouds appeared out of a cloudless sky, ending the drought.

1078. McKinney, Mrs. F. J. *God's Light in an African Heart: The Story of Monbalu, First Habbe Native Worker.* Harrisburg, Pa.: Christian Publications, 1946. 61 p.

Monbalu Habbe Kodio was a member of the cliff-dwelling Habbe tribe of southern Mali. A sequel to 1077.

1079. McKinney, Larry (J)ames. *Equipping for Service: A Historical Account of the Bible College Movement in North America*. Fayetteville, Ark.: Accrediting Association of Bible Colleges, 1997. 258 p.

The movement traces its origins to the first Bible college to survive to the present: the Missionary Training Institute for Home and Foreign Missionaries and Evangelists (now Nyack College) founded by A. B. Simpson in 1883. Simpson was influenced by the East London Institute for Home and Foreign Missions, established in 1872 by Mr. and Mrs. H. Grattan Guinness. Harry L. Turner, a C&MA missionary who later became president of the Alliance, exerted a formative influence on the Bible College movement in western Canada. He was the first president (1925) of Winnipeg Bible Training School (now Providence College and Theological Seminary), one of whose early graduates, Henry Hildebrand, founded Briercrest Bible Institute in 1935.

1080. ———. "An Historical Analysis of the Bible College Movement during Its Formative Years: 1882-1920." Ed. D. diss., Temple University, 1985. 456 p.

Includes a much more thorough account of the development of A. B. Simpson's Missionary Training Institute than does 1079, e.g., notes that the move to Nyack was precipitated as much by a desire for separation from the world as it was by the astronomical cost of building an expanded facility in New York City.

1081. McLeod, Christian [Anna Christian Ruddy] (1861-). *The Heart of the Stranger: A Story of Little Italy*. The Italian American Experience. New York: Fleming H. Revell, 1908. Reprint, New York: Arno Press 1975. 221 p.

A distillation, in novel form, of the author's experiences as a C&MA worker among the Italian immigrant poor of East Harlem.

1082. Mead, Ruth. *No One Wins Like a Loser*. Harrisburg, Pa.: Christian Publications, 1976. 163 p.

Meditations.

1083. Meloon, Walter O., with David Enlow. *Men Alive: Miracles through Yielded Men*. Harrisburg, Pa.: Christian Publications, 1982. 120 p.

Recounts the involvement of Alliance Men International (the official men's ministry of the C&MA) in Alliance missions projects around the world.

1084. Meminger, Mrs. Wilbur F. *The Little Man from Chicago*. New York: Alliance Press Co., 1910. 200 p.

Biography of Wilbur Fisk Meminger (1851-1909), a former Methodist Episcopal minister whose life epitomized the fourfold Gospel. He became superintendent of the C&MA's West and Northwest districts in 1897 and was eventually put in charge of the Alliance work in Chicago. Introduction by A. B. Simpson.

1085. Mendoza, Bayani Y. *The Philippine Christian Alliance: First Seventy-eight Years*. [Manila?]: by the author, 1985. 171 p.

A history of the C&MA mission and the Christian and Missionary Alliance Churches of the Philippines (CAMACOP) 1900-1978. Includes recommendations for the strengthening of the church and a copy of the 1978 Tetuan Working Agreement between CAMACOP and the C&MA mission.

1086. Mendoza, César G., and Richard P. Reichert. *Un siglo de avance: El nacimiento, desarrollo y madurez de la Iglesia Alianza Cristiana y Misionera en el Ecuador*. Quito, Ecuador: [Iglesia Alianza Cristiana y Misionera en el Ecuador?], 1997. 604 p.

A descriptive and at times strongly partisan (e.g., p. 342) history of the C&MA in Ecuador, 1897-1997. Includes brief biographies of national leaders and C&MA missionaries to Ecuador.

1087. Menzies, William W. *Anointed to Serve: The Story of the Assemblies of God*. Springfield, Mo.: Gospel Pub. House, 1971. 436 p.

Pages 70-72 deal with the outpouring of the Spirit that took place in certain Alliance branches in 1907 and the subsequent response of A. B. Simpson and the Alliance.

1088. ———. "The Non-Wesleyan Origins of the Pentecostal Movement." In *Aspects of Pentecostal-Charismatic Origins*, ed. Vinson Synan, 81-98. Plainfield, N.J.: Logos International, 1975.

Regards Simpson and his associates as non-Wesleyans. Credits the Alliance with providing many of the leaders who shaped the theology of the Assemblies of God (AOG). The AOG adopted much of the doctrinal statement of the C&MA with little or no revision, and it also borrowed heavily from Alliance polity.

1089. Merrill, Dean. "The Church: Healing's Natural Home?" *Leadership* 6 (spring 1985): 116-26.

An interview on the healing ministry of the church with four prominent pastors whose churches incorporate prayer for physical and emotional healing into their services: John Wimber, John Lavender, Don Williams, and Don Bubna. Bubna, an Alliance pastor, insists, over Wimber's objections, that healing is one of the provisions of the Atonement.

1090. Merritt, Stephen (1834-1917). *Not a Word.* Los Angeles: Free Tract Society, n.d. 3 p.

A plea for the discipline of holy silence as a means of hearing God and witnessing for him. Includes an abridged version of 1799.

1091. ———. *Samuel Morris, "The Kru Boy."* Black Mountain, N.C. : C. C. Howerton, n.d. 8 p.

A brief biography of the saintly African (d. 1893) who had such a profound influence on both Merritt and Taylor University. Cf. 1093.

1092. ———. *Stephen Merritt's Experience: A One Hundred and Thirty-Eight Degree Freemason.* Chicago: National Christian Association, [ca. 1900?]. 8 p.

Membership in the Masonic Lodge is inconsistent with Christian faith in that Masonry teaches that a moral life is all that is required of one.

1093. Merritt, Stephen (1834-1917), and T. C. Reade. *An Hour with Sammy Morris: A Spirit-filled African Boy*, 3rd ed. Grand Rapids: Zondervan, [194-?]. 26 p.

Reprint of 1091, with extensive additional material by the former president of Taylor University.

1094. Meyer (F)rederick (B)rotherton (1847-1929). *The Blessed Life.* Camp Hill, Pa.: Christian Publications, 1941. 50 p.

1095. ———. *Christian Living.* New York: Fleming H. Revell, 1892. Reprint, New York: Christian Alliance Pub. Co., [189-?]. 160 p.

1096. ———. *The Present Tenses of the Blessed Life.* New York: Fleming H. Revell, 1892. Reprint, Harrisburg, Pa.: Christian Alliance Pub. Co., [1929?]. 163 p.

1097. ———. *Through Fire and Flood.* London: Marshall Bros., 1896. Reprint, Harrisburg, Pa.: Christian Alliance Pub. Co., [1929?] 162 p.

1098. Mickelson, Einar H. *God Can: The Story of God's Faithfulness to a Pioneer Missionary Explorer in New Guinea.* Manila: Far Eastern Broadcasting Co., 1966. 301 p.

A history of C&MA mission work among the Dani people of Irian Jaya. Includes an extensive account of the author's exploratory journeys to the Baliem Valley (home of the Dani).

1099. Milburn, E. (I)saac (1882-). *Sermon on Hell.* [Altoona, Pennsylvania?]: Altoona Tribune Press, [19–?]. 23 p.

The text is Luke 16:23.

1100. Miller, Donald A. *Medicine for Depression.* Contemporary Christian Living Series. Camp Hill, Pa.: Christian Publications, 1994. 33 p.

Christians are just as subject to depression as non-Christians. To deal effectively with depression requires understanding its cause, taking appropriate action, and holding tenaciously to God. Includes an account of a lengthy depression the author suffered while serving as a C&MA pastor.

1101. ———. *Songs in the Night: How to Have Peace under Pressure.* Contemporary Christian Living Series. Camp Hill, Pa.: Christian Publications, 1993. 23 p.

Song as a metaphor for the consolation God gives in the midst of tragedy and suffering.

1102. Miller (H)erbert (S)umner (1867-). *The Christian Workers' Manual*, 5th ed. Harrisburg, Pa.: Christian Alliance Pub. Co., 1928. 254 p.

Essential doctrines of the Bible simplified.

1103. ———. *The Inspiration of the Scriptures.* New York: Christian Alliance Pub. Co., 1917. 64 p.

Argues in favor of the plenary verbal inspiration of the original documents of the Bible.

1104. ———. *Outline of the Book of Hebrews.* Wilkes-Barre, Pa.: White, 1901. 76 p.

1105. Miller, Robert V. *The Confession of the Hope: Outlines of Bible Studies in Unfulfilled Prophecy.* Colportage Library. New York: Alliance Press Co., 1904. 79 p.

A premillennialist interpretation that leans toward the partial rapture theory, but yet cautions against dogmatism with respect to any theory of the rapture.

1106. ———. "This Present Age." In *The Signs of the Times, or God's Message for Today: A Symposium on New Theology, Christian Science, the Lord's Coming, the Gift of Tongues, and the Deeper Spiritual Life*, 87-94. New York: Alliance Press Co., 1907.

According to Matt. 16:1-3 we are, eschatologically speaking, living in the night, but the "dawn" of Christ's return is at hand.

1107. Minder, Lorene. *John Minder: A Man Sent from God*. St. Louis: Creative Concepts, 1988. 153 p.

A brief biography followed by a collection of historical documents, photographs, and poetry. Minder (1898-1980) was a minister in the Southeastern District of the C&MA and served as its superintendent (1930-1934). Includes biographical data on Billy Graham, who served under Minder as youth pastor, and later as assistant pastor, of Tampa Gospel Tabernacle.

1108. *A Ministry of Mercy: Leprosy Work on Foreign Fields of the Christian and Missionary Alliance*. New York: The Alliance, 1958. 10 p.

Concentrates on work in West Africa, Thailand, and Indochina.

1109. *Missionary Vision and Blueprint*. New York: The Christian and Missionary Alliance, 1954. 11 p.

Describes the strategies for worldwide mission that the C&MA has developed as a result of the original missionary vision of A. B. Simpson.

1110. *Missions and the Indian Church*. Cass Lake, Minn.: Alliance Indian Publications, 1972. 63 p.

The six articles cover topics ranging from the development of a national church in Mali and Burkina Faso to understanding First Nations culture in Minnesota.

1111. Mitchell, L. David. *Liberty in Jesus!: Evil Spirits and Exorcism Simply Explained*. Edinburgh: The Pentland Press, 1999. 215 p.

Includes accounts of exorcisms performed while the author was serving as a C&MA pastor.

1112. Moghabgab, Faddoul. *The Shepherd Song on the Hills of Lebanon: The Twenty-Third Psalm Illustrated and Explained*. Harrisburg, Pa.: Christian Publications, [195-?]. 128 p.

A former shepherd explains the psalm in the light of Middle Eastern customs, practices, and geography.

1113. Montgomery, Carrie Judd (1858-1946). *All Things Reconciled to Christ*. Oakland: Office of Triumphs of Faith, [190-?]. 5 p.

An exposition of Col. 1:20.

1114. ———. *Divine Healing in Relation to the Use of Our Lips*. Oakland: Office of Triumphs of Faith, [190-?]. 15 p.

"[We] find so many Christians who get out of the place of blessing through the wrong use of their tongues, and the Lord [allows] them to be sick because they have not used their tongues to His glory" (p. 3).

1115. ———. *Faith's Reckonings*. Oakland: Office of Triumphs of Faith, [190-?]. 11 p.

"After each venture of faith, look steadfastly at Jesus without regard to your apparent weakness, and you will surely receive according to your faith and not according to your feelings" (p. 10).

1116. ———. *God's Messengers to the Sick*. Oakland: Office of Triumphs of Faith, [19–?]. 20 p.

A meditation on Job 33:23: God allows sickness to make us dependent on him. He heals us so that we may bring healing and salvation to others. "I believe in these last days . . . Satan is trying to destroy the bodies of the saints so that there will be none left for translation, when Jesus comes for His own" (p. 19).

1117. ———. *God's Word about Witchcraft and Kindred Errors*. Oakland: Office of Triumphs of Faith, [191-?]. 20 p.

Recounts the biblical prohibitions against spiritualism and witchcraft, and relates an incident in which the author cast out a demon that was troubling a Christian who had had contact with spiritualists.

1118. ———. *Have Faith in God*. Oakland: Office of Triumphs of Faith, 1912. 21 p.

Reprint of the introductory chapter of 1125, which recounts her miraculous healing.

1119. ———. *Heart Melody*. Oakland: Office of Triumphs of Faith, 1922. 102 p.

Poetry.

1120. ———. *Heart Whisperings*. Oakland: Office of Triumphs of Faith, 1897. 73 p.

Poetry.

1121. ———. *Life and Teachings of Carrie Judd Montgomery*. New York: Garland Publications, 1985. 319 p.

Reprint of 1125 and 1129.

1122. ———. *The Life of Praise*. New York: Christian Alliance Pub. Co., 1900. 146 p.

Meditations on the Christian life, with special emphasis on the role of praise and faith, that were originally published as editorials in her periodical *Triumphs of Faith*.

1123. ———. *Lilies from the Vale of Thought*. Buffalo, N.Y.: H. H. Otis, 1878. 109 p.

"[P]oems composed after the fourteenth and after the nineteenth year of their author," p. iii.

1124. ———. *The Power of the Tongue*. Rochester, N.Y.: Elim Publishing House, [192-?]. 8 p.

The tongue that has not been submitted to God's control can act like a deadly poison. A loose tongue or the keeping of grudges may prove to be the cause of sickness or an obstacle to healing.

1125. ———. *The Prayer of Faith*. New York: Fleming H. Revell, 1880. 163 p.

A treatise on divine healing that includes the author's testimony of her recent (1879) healing from an extended illness. Cf. 1121.

1126. ———. *Secrets of Victory*. Oakland: Office of Triumphs of Faith, 1921. 168 p.

Editorials from *Triumphs of Faith* on healing and the deeper life.

1127. ———. *The Steps of Faith*. Beulah Heights, Calif.: Office of Triumphs of Faith. 24 p.

True faith conforms to God's will and word. God, who has both the father-heart and the mother-heart, will teach his children to walk in faith, although they can expect faith to be tested. God strengthens the faith of those who, by faith, empty themselves to receive the baptism of the Holy Spirit.

1128. ———. *To My Beloved.* Oakland: Office of Triumphs of Faith, 1912. 10 p.

Poems written on the death of the author's mother.

1129. ———. *"Under His Wings": The Story of My Life.* Oakland: Office of Triumphs of Faith, 1936. 256 p.

Montgomery had a lifelong friendship with her mentor, A. B. Simpson. She was the first recording secretary of the Christian Alliance and often spoke at Alliance conventions, even after becoming a Pentecostal. Simpson once invited her to join him in his work in New York City, but she declined. She was also a friend of many of Simpson's associates, including Henry Wilson and Kenneth Mackenzie. Wilson "always said that the deep truths that Dr. Simpson taught were to be found within the covers of the Prayer Book" (p. 126). Cf. 1121.

1130. ———. *Zaida Eversey, or Life Two-fold.* Buffalo, N.Y.: H. H. Otis, 1881. 234 p.

A novel.

1131. Montgomery, James H., and Donald A. McGavran. *The Discipling of a Nation.* Santa Clara, Calif.: Global Church Growth Bulletin, 1980. 175 p.

Chapter 10, "C&MA Target 400," is an account of Alliance church growth in the Philippines.

1132. Moore, David H. "How the C&MA Relates to Overseas Churches." *His Dominion* 15 (July 1989): 7-18.

The C&MA's overseas national churches are independent and autonomous. The C&MA mission and the overseas national church work together either as partners, in which case the mission functions as an elder sibling that helps usher the church into the responsibilities of adulthood; or as co-participants, in which case the mission functions as a consultant to the national church. All national churches function as equal members in The Alliance World Fellowship.

1133. Moore, Robert C. *Los Evangélicos en marcha en América latina.* Santiago: Librería el Lucero, 1959. 176 p.

An overview from a Baptist perspective of the work of evangelical missions, including the C&MA, in Latin America. Mentions Baptist/Alliance cooperative efforts in Chile around the turn of the century.

1134. Moothart, Phillis Lorene (1912-). *Achieving the Impossible. . . with God: The Life Story of Dr. R. A. Forrest*. Toccoa Falls, Ga.: Toccoa Falls Institute, 1956. 224 p.

Richard Alexander Forrest (1881-1959) is best known as the founder (1911) of Toccoa Falls College.

1135. ———. *Heartbeat for the World: The Story of Gustave and Pauline Woerner*. The Jaffray Collection of Missionary Portraits, 22. Camp Hill, Pa.: Christian Publications, 1999. 187 p.

Less thorough than 555, but it has more information on Pauline (Kohn) Woerner (d. 1978) and on the Woerners' final years.

1136. ———. *Outstandingly His: The Life Story of Paul and Mary Williams (Uncle Paul and Aunt Mary)*. Toccoa Falls, Ga.: Toccoa Falls Press, 1993. 205 p.

Paul I. (Paul Isaac) Williams (1903-1977) and Mary H. (Mary Helen Nealy) Williams (1907-1977) were staff members at Toccoa Falls College from 1947 until their deaths in the Toccoa Falls flood.

1137. ———. *Sunbursts: True Adventures of Toccoa Falls College Missionaries*. Toccoa Falls, Ga.: Toccoa Falls College, 1992. 229 p.

Brief autobiographical accounts, mostly by C&MA missionaries.

1138. Morgan, G. L. *Sketch of My Life: With Some of My Experiences in Evangelistic Work*. n.p., [1940?]. 68 p.

Recounts mostly his experiences as a healer and evangelist, including dreams and visions. His selected letters, reprinted from *The Messenger*, the organ of the Northwest District of the C&MA, are included in an appendix.

1139. Morrow, Abbie (C)lemens. *Christian Science, "Falsely So-called": An Exposé of New Errors under an Old Name*. Louisville: Pentecostal Pub. Co., [190-?]. 86 p.

Falsely so-called because it is not Christian, not scientific, not scriptural, and not true.

1140. ———. *Out of and Into*. Louisville: Pickett Pub. Co., [189-?]. 161 p.

1141. ———. *Questions on Divine Healing*. New York: Christian Alliance Pub. Co., [ca. 1900]. 8 p.

Poses 17 questions and answers them, mostly with quotations from the Bible. Physicians fare poorly: they originated in (worldly) Egypt; Asa sought them instead of the Lord; and they only made the woman with the issue of blood worse. Luke may be the beloved physician "but the Word is . . . silent about any ministry of pills and powders" (p. 8).

1142. ———. *"Transformed": The Life of Jerry MacAuley*. Alliance Colportage Library, vol. 3, no. 1. Nyack, N.Y.: Christian Alliance Pub. Co., 1901. 232 p.

Jeremiah "Jerry" McAuley (1839-1884) was a reformed criminal who started two rescue missions in New York City.

1143. Morrow, Ord L. *Behold He Cometh*. Lincoln, Neb.: Back to the Bible, 1963. 75 p.

Radio sermons, as are all other works by this Alliance pastor listed below.

1144. ———. *Counsel on the Christian's Problems*. Lincoln, Neb.: Back to the Bible, 1974. 128 p.

1145. ———. *The Devil in Our Day*. Lincoln, Neb.: Back to the Bible, 1961. 72 p.

1146. ———. *Does It Matter What You Believe?* Lincoln, Neb.: Back to the Bible, 1962. 64 p.

1147. ———. *The Faithful Witness: Reflections from Revelation 2 & 3*. Lincoln, Neb.: Back to the Bible, 1981. 87 p.

1148. ———. *Giants in Your Life*. Lincoln, Neb.: Back to the Bible, 1976. 126 p.

1149. ———. *Hindrances to Answered Prayer*. Lincoln, Neb.: Back to the Bible, 1965.

1150. ———. *A Life That Pleases God*. Lincoln, Neb.: Back to the Bible, 1979. 140 p.

1151. ———. *Poems for Sunshine and Shadow*. Lincoln, Neb.: Back to the Bible, 1962. 2 volumes.

1152. ———. *Puzzles of Job*. Lincoln, Neb.: Back to the Bible, 1965. 123 p.

1153. ———. *The Puzzles of Life*. Lincoln, Neb.: Back to the Bible, 1973. 123 p.

1154. ———. *Seven Who Found Life*. Lincoln, Neb.: Back to the Bible, 1966. 96 p.

1155. ———. *Shattered Hopes and Mended Lives*. Lincoln, Neb.: Back to the Bible, 1978. 94 p.

1156. ———. *Straight Thinking about God*. Lincoln, Neb.: Back to the Bible, 1976. 92 p.

1157. ———. *Straight Thinking about Spiritual Growth*. Lincoln, Neb.: Back to the Bible, 1977. 93 p.

1158. ———. *What Follows Death? and Other Messages*. Lincoln, Neb.: Back to the Bible, 1963. 79 p.

1159. ———. *What if Christ Had Not Come?* Lincoln, Neb.: Back to the Bible. 62 p.

1160. ———. *When God Laughs*. Lincoln, Neb.: Back to the Bible, 1956. 47 p.

1161. ———. *When God Speaks*. Lincoln, Neb.: Back to the Bible, 1960. 64 p.

1162. ———. *Your Sin and God's Forgiveness, or the Revelation of Redemption*. Lincoln, Neb.: Back to the Bible, 1967. 95 p.

1163. Moseley, Eva M. *MO TA-IU "Man of Great Plans": The Biography of Dr. Thomas Moseley, Missionary-Educator*. Harrisburg, Pa.: Christian Publications, 1963. 224 p.

Moseley (1886-1959) served as a missionary to China with the C&MA's Kansu-Tibetan Border Mission (1915-1940) and as president of Nyack Missionary College (1941-1958).

1164. Moser, Alvin J. *An Objective Analysis of the Offerings of Our Schools, Including Curriculum Offerings, Course Enrollments and Outcomes*. n.p.: by the author, 1969. 24 p.

The General Council of the C&MA rescinded in 1963 its resolution of 1944 that forbade the Missionary Training Institute to become a liberal arts college. By 1967 all Alliance colleges had added enough liberal arts courses to offer B.A.'s that would satisfy the American Association of Theological Schools requirement for pre-seminary education. However, by 1970 the Alliance still had only one seminary, Canadian Theological College (Regina, Sask.).

1165. Mullen, Mary B. (1867-1920). *The Dark Soudan*. Missionary Series. New York: Christian and Missionary Alliance, [191-?]. 7 p.

Deals with the difficulties faced by missionaries serving in West Africa—and especially with the tendency of Africans to imitate whites—and the negative effects of providing Africans with financial support (most become proud and fall away).

1166. Müller, George. *Believing God*. Philadelphia: Philadelphia Branch, Christian and Missionary Alliance, [ca. 1900]. 3 p.

Reprint.

1167. *Multitudes on the March*. New York: The Christian and Missionary Alliance, 1955. 11 p.

A short history of the Alliance mission in the Democratic Republic of the Congo.

1168. Murdoch, Elmer H. *Shattering Religious Boredom*. Harrisburg, Pa.: Christian Publications, 1973. 132 p.

Sermons by the pastor of Omaha Gospel Tabernacle.

1169. ———. *Training Book for the Use of Step Up to Life*. Harrisburg, Pa.: Christian Publications, 1972. 42 p.

A handbook for personal evangelism that emphasizes conviction, repentance, and the Lordship of Christ.

1170. Murphree, Jon Tal. *The Love Motive: A Practical Psychology of Sanctification*. Camp Hill, Pa.: Christian Publications, 1990. 114 p.

A Methodist (who teaches at Toccoa Falls College) explains sanctification by reflecting on his own experience: the crisis dimension involves moving to a point of full surrender where one's deepest desire becomes that of pleasing Christ. Growth in sanctity follows as a process of disciplined response to the leading of the Spirit.

1171. Murray, Andrew (1828-1917). *Divine Healing: A Series of Addresses*. New York: Christian Alliance Pub. Co., 1900. 189 p.

A classic presentation of "healing in the Atonement." Sickness is connected to sin, and the sanctified believer should expect to be free from sickness and to live at least 70 years.

1172. ———. *Divine Healing: A Series of Addresses*. [Part 1] Alliance Colportage Library, vol. 2, no. 3. Nyack, N.Y.: Christian Alliance Pub. Co., 1900. 110 p.

Chapters 1-17 of the original.

1173. ———. *Divine Healing: A Series of Addresses*. [Part 2] Alliance Colportage Library, vol. 2, no. 10. Nyack, N.Y.: Christian Alliance Pub. Co., 1900. 119 p.

Chapters 18-33 of the original.

1174. ———. *The Holiest of All: An Exposition of the Epistle to the Hebrews*. New York: Fleming H. Revell, 1894. Reprint, New York: Christian Alliance Pub. Co., 1921. 567 p.

1175. ———. *Jesus Himself*. New York: Fleming H. Revell, 1893. Reprint, Harrisburg, Pa.: Christian Publications, 1928. 68 p.

1176. ———. *Jesus Himself: A Call to Spiritual Intimacy*. New York: Fleming H. Revell, 1893. Reprint, Camp Hill, Pa.: Christian Publications, 1996. 34 p.

1177. Murray, Frank S. *The Sublimity of Faith: The Life and Work of Frank W. Sandford*. Amherst, N. H.: The Kingdom Press, 1981. 951 p.

Frank Sandford (1862-1948), founder of the Shiloh movement, regarded A. B. Simpson "as a prophet and spiritual father" (p. 73). While with the Alliance Sandford experienced divine healing and was filled with the Spirit. His wife was a former C&MA missionary to Japan, and A. B. Simpson officiated at their wedding. Simpson regarded Sandford's World's Evangelization Crusade highly, and he never criticized Sandford, for though Simpson "had gone far with God . . . he could see when someone else had gone farther" (p. 191).

1178. Musgrove, Sarah (M)inot C. (1839-1933). *History of Twenty-five Years' Four-fold Gospel Work in Troy N.Y. As Given by Sara M. C. Musgrove on the Twenty-fifth Anniversary, April 12, 1908.* [Troy, N.Y.?]: n.p., [1908?]. 16 p.

The independent work at Troy became associated with the C&MA in 1889.

1179. *My Experience in Christian Science.* New York: Christian Alliance Pub. Co., [ca. 1911]. 20 p.

Arthur Clermont Peck's Tract *The Masterpiece of Satan* helped set the author free from the deception that had bound her to Christian Science. She began to realize that Scientists could only heal psychosomatic illness, that they were cold and unfeeling as people, and that their beliefs are contrary to Scripture.

1180. Myland (D)avid (W)esley (1858-1943). *Full Redemption Songs: For Conventions, Camp Meetings, Revivals and Pentecostal Work*, 2nd ed. Cleveland, Ohio: Gospel Union, 1896. 142 p.

1181. ———. *The Latter Rain Covenant.* Billings, Mont.: A. N. Trotter, 1973. 177 p.

A reprint of the 1910 edition, omitting the introduction, preface, rain chart of Palestine, and letter from Palestine.

1182. ———. *The Latter Rain Covenant and Pentecostal Power, with Testimony of Healings and Baptism.* Chicago: Evangel Publishing House, 1910. 215 p.

An apologetic for the Pentecostal baptism of the Holy Spirit, which Myland began to preach after his own Pentecostal baptism (recorded here, along with some of his experiences as a C&MA pastor) in 1906. He believed that contemporary outpourings of the Spirit were fulfillments of Old Testament prophecies related to the latter rain, and even cites precipitation statistics from Palestine (rainfall increased considerably during the 1890s) as physical evidence of his theory.

1183. ———. *Latter Rain Songs.* Columbus, Ohio: Peace Pub. Co., 1907.

1184. ———. *The Revelation of Jesus Christ: A Comprehensive Harmonic Outline and Perspective View of the Book.* Chicago: Evangel Publishing House, 1911. 255 p.

A lecture series that attempts to blend the preterist, historic, and futurist views of Revelation. Advocates a pretribulation rapture.

1185. ———. *Songs of the Spirit: Suitable for Evangelistic Work, Gospel Meetings, Conventions and All Church Services*. Cleveland, Ohio: by the author, 1902. 256 p.

Includes many songs by Myland and James Kirk, and a few by A. B. Simpson.

1186. Myland (D)avid (W)esley (1858-1943), and James M. Kirk. *Redemption Songs for Conventions, Camp Meetings, Revivals, and Pentecostal Work*, 3rd ed. Cleveland, Ohio: The Gospel Union, 1898. 220 p.

Songs are mostly by Myland and Kirk. Frontispiece has a photo of the Ohio Quartette, which consisted of Myland, Kirk, D. W. Kerr (all of whom were associated with the Alliance), and E. L. Bowyer.

1187. ———. *Redemption Songs No. 2: As Used by the "Ohio Quartette," Specially Adapted for Conventions, Camp-meetings, Revivals and Pentecostal Work.* Cleveland, Ohio: by the author, 1900. 240 p.

Includes mostly songs by Myland and Kirk, along with a few by A. B. Simpson.

1188. Myland (D)avid (W)esley (1858-1943), and Thoro Harris. *Gospel Praise*. Columbus, Ohio: Peace Pub. Co., 1911.

1189. Nanfelt, Peter Norris (1937-). "A Restructuring of the Administrative Procedures Governing the Missionary Program of the Christian and Missionary Alliance." Master's thesis, Fuller Theological Seminary, 1991. 222 p.

The procedures suggested are intended to enable the C&MA to adapt to changing conditions, e.g., the rising financial cost of mission work, so that it may remain a missions-centered church.

1190. Naraval, Thelma F. *The Southern Cross: A History of the Christian and Missionary Alliance Churches of the Philippines, Inc. and the Ebenezer Bible College, Vol. 1*. Cagayan de Oro City, the Philippines: Thelma F. Naraval, 1978. 51 p.

The first history of the CAMACOP by a Filipino. Alliance work in the Philippines began in 1902, and Ebenezer Bible College was established in 1928.

1191. Naylor, Henry (Mrs.). *The Great Physician*. New York: Word, Work and World Pub. Co., [1883?].

This former superintendent of the Berachah Mission of the C&MA found salvation and was healed from a terminal lung condition through the ministry of Dr. Charles Cullis.

1192. Neely, Lois. *Come Up This Mountain: The Miracle of Clarence W. Jones and HCJB*. Wheaton, Ill.: Tyndale House, 1980. 194 p.

Jones was converted under Paul Rader's ministry, and the C&MA played a pivotal role in the establishment of HCJB.

1193. ———. *Fire in His Bones: The Official Biography of Oswald J. Smith*. Wheaton, Ill.: Tyndale House, 1982. 317 p.

Fleshes out the skeletal autobiographical narrative of 1938 by providing more historical detail, e.g., on his preaching tour of Latvia with William Fetler in 1924.

1194. Nelson, H. E. "The Flaming Evangel." In *A. B. Simpson Centenary 1843-1943,* 13-16. New York: Christian and Missionary Alliance, 1943.

A poignant reminiscence of Simpson wiping blood and dirt from the face of a street person with whom he, E. D. Whiteside, and Henry Wilson were sharing the Gospel crown this tribute to Simpson the evangelist.

1195. Nelson, Shirley. *Fair Clear and Terrible: The Story of Shiloh, Maine*. Lutham, N.Y.: British American Publishing, 1989. 457 p.

Mentions October 1892 as the time of Frank Sandford's departure from the Alliance.

1196. Neudorf, Eugene. *A Light to All Japan: The Story of Susan Dyck*. The Jaffray Collection of Missionary Portraits, 19. Camp Hill, Pa.: Christian Publications, 1998. 217 p.

A native of Saskatchewan, Susan Dyck served as a C&MA missionary to Japan from 1953 until 1985, when she was diagnosed with Alzheimer's disease and had to return to Canada. Includes reminiscences from the life of her mentor, Mabel Francis.

1197. *The New Crusade Songs: Designed for Use in Evangelistic Campaigns, Bible Conferences, and Missionary Conventions*. Harrisburg, Pa.: Christian Publications, 1940. 100 p.

Includes eight songs by A. B. Simpson and 12 by other Alliance contributors, including Paul Rader.

1198. Newbern, William (C)rawford (1900-1972). *The Cross and the Crown: My View of Alliance Bible Seminary.* Hong Kong: The Alliance Press, 1973. 132 p.

Alliance Bible School founded in 1899 in Wuchow, China, by Robert Hall Glover, was the first Bible school started by the Alliance outside the U.S.A. The name was changed to Alliance Bible Institute in 1938. It was moved to Hong Kong in 1950 and received its present name in 1955.

1199. ———, comp. and ed. *Youth Hymns: 1-2-3-4 Combined.* Hong Kong: Alliance Press, 1966. 1 vol. musical score.

Chinese and English words with music. Six of the 200 hymns are by Alliance hymnists.

1200. Newberry, William Wisdom. *Untangling Live Wires, or Light on Some Problems of Divine Guidance.* New York: Christian Alliance Pub. Co., 1914. 128 p.

The plain sense of Scripture (as interpreted in community) is the final arbiter in discernment, since the Holy Spirit always acts in conformity with the teaching of Scripture. Yet the Spirit's guidance may also come through such diverse phenomena as common sense, dreams, visions, glossolalia, and other direct forms of spiritual communication. But the discerning Christian will also be on guard against the deceitfulness of the devil and the soulish delusions of the human spirit.

1201. Nichol, John Thomas. *Pentecostalism.* New York: Harper and Row, 1966. 280 p.

Claims, with reference to the revivals of 1907, that "one outburst of Pentecostal phenomena which cannot be attributed directly to West Coast influence is the charismatic revival that occurred within the Christian and Missionary Alliance" (p. 37). For a different assessment see 1064.

1202. Nienkirchen, Charles W. (1952-). *A. B. Simpson and the Pentecostal Movement: A Study in Continuity, Crisis, and Change.* Peabody, Mass.: Hendrickson Publishers, 1992. 162 p.

An expansion of 1203. Includes a chapter on the response of Simpson's associates to Pentecostalism, and a lengthy exposé of the revisionist historiography of A. W. Tozer. Cf. 2216. To set the record straight, excerpts from Simpson's Nyack diary (1907-1916), his presidential reports for 1906-1908, and his editorials are included in appendices.

1203. ———. "A. B. Simpson: Forerunner and Critic of the Pentecostal Movement." In *The Birth of a Vision*, eds. David F. Hartzfeld and Charles Nienkirchen, 125-64. Regina, Sask.: His Dominion, 1986.

Simpson's insistence on deriving doctrine from the narratives of Acts influenced the Pentecostal hermeneutic. His educational institutions trained many future Pentecostal leaders; and his writings, doctrines, and polity also profoundly influenced Pentecostalism. However, he vigorously opposed the Pentecostal "evidence doctrine," and he criticized those Pentecostals who either abused spiritual gifts or were preoccupied with them. However, Simpson's private diary for the years 1907-1916 reveals that he had been seeking (albeit unsuccessfully) a deeper, fuller baptism of the Holy Spirit that would include glossolalia. Cf. 1204.

1204. ———. "Albert B. Simpson: Fore-runner of the Modern Pentecostal Movement." In *Azusa Street Revisited: Facts of the American Pentecostal Experience: Society for Pentecostal Studies Conference, Costa Mesa, Calif., November 13-15, 1986*, n.p., 1986. 25 p.

A condensation of 1203.

1205. ———. "'Deep Calleth unto Deep': Stillness in Early Alliance Spirituality." *His Dominion* 14 (summer 1988): 2-22.

A. B. Simpson and his associates pursued active ministries that were rooted in the kind of contemplative stillness advocated by the Quietists. "The practice of stillness was deemed essential to various aspects of early Alliance spirituality, notably, prayer, the Spirit-filled life, healing, education and conventions" (p. 8).

1206. ———. *The Man the Movement and the Mission: A Documentary History of the Christian and Missionary Alliance, Vol. 1*. Regina: by the author, 1987. 383 p.

Most of the documents are either by or about A. B. Simpson. Includes study questions.

1207. Niklaus, Robert L. *To All Peoples: Missions World Book of the Christian and Missionary Alliance*. Camp Hill, Pa.: Christian Publications, 1990. 429 p.

Basically an updated and profusely illustrated version of the narrative portion of 319.

1208. Niklaus, Robert L., John S. Sawin, and Samuel J. Stoesz. *All for Jesus: God at Work in the Christian and Missionary Alliance over One Hundred Years*. Camp Hill, Pa.: Christian Publications, 1986. 322 p.

The most thorough, comprehensive, and up-to-date history of the C&MA, despite the fact that it tends to be long on description and short on evaluation. John Sawin's contribution (1843-1919) is the best available treatment of the early Alliance. An appendix, "The Founder's Team," gives brief biographies of Simpson's associates.

1209. Noel, Michael David, ed. *Church Planting Voices*. Camp Hill, Pa.: Christian Publications, 1998. 287 p.

Six strategy papers and 19 testimonies by C&MA workers.

1210. North American Women's Missionary Prayer Fellowship. Committee on Guidelines Revision. *Women's Ministries in the Christian and Missionary Alliance in Canada: A Handbook*. Harrisburg, Pa.: Christian Publications, 1982. 91 p.

Identical in content to 1211.

1211. North American Women's Missionary Prayer Fellowship. Committee on Guidelines Revision. *Women's Missionary Prayer Fellowship in the Christian and Missionary Alliance: A Handbook*. Harrisburg, Pa.: Christian Publications, 1982. 91 p.

Includes a brief history of the Women's Missionary Prayer Fellowship, the predecessor to Alliance Women.

1212. Oerter (J)ohn (H)enry (1831-1915). *Divine Healing in the Light of Scripture*. New York: Christian Alliance Pub. Co., 1900. 140 p.

All disease is a consequence of the wrath of God against human sin. Therefore, one of the consequences of Christ's atonement is the removal of the manifestation of God's wrath in the bodies of believers, for God did not intend to give life (in the present age) only to the incorporeal part of humanity. "Divine healing is the physical earnest of the coming resurrection" (p.12).

1213. ———. *The Parousia of the Son of Man*. New York: Alliance Press Co., 1902. 225 p.

A thorough exegesis of the biblical passages concerning eschatology. Originally presented as lectures at the Missionary Training Institute. Rejects the idea of a pretribulation rapture: the great tribulation, like all other times of tribulation mentioned in Scripture, will be a tribulation of persecution for believers and of judgment for unbelievers.

1214. *Official Minutes of the First General Assembly of The Christian and Missionary Alliance in Canada, June 3rd to June 8th, 1980.* [Toronto?]: The Alliance, 1980. 28 p.

1215. Oldfield, Mabel Dimock (1878-1965). *With You Alway: The Life of a South China Missionary.* Harrisburg, Pa.: Christian Publications, 1958. 252 p.

This detailed autobiography describes the everyday life of C&MA missionaries in South China and provides biographical information on R. A. Jaffray and the author's husband, Walter. The chapter "Tongues" (p. 84-91) deals with the response of C&MA missionaries in China to the "tongues crisis" of 1907.

1216. Oldfield, Walter (H)erbert) (1879-1958). *Kidnapped by Chinese Bandits.* Harrisburg, Pa.: Christian Alliance Pub. Co., 1930. 30 p.

After an attack during which he narrowly missed being shot, Oldfield, along with the 80 other surviving passengers on a Chinese riverboat, was taken prisoner by Chinese bandits. He managed to escape with both his life and all but $6.00 of the $865.00 he had been carrying.

1217. ———. *Kwang-si: Past Achievements and Present Need.* New York: Christian and Missionary Alliance, 1913. 13 p.

The C&MA entered Guangxi in 1893, following abortive attempts by other missions to establish a work there. Its missionaries were the first to establish permanent residence in this hyper-xenophobic province.

1218. ———. *Over "The Hump" with God.* Toronto: The Christian and Missionary Alliance, [1944?]. 16 p.

Describes the journey of Walter and Mabel Oldfield from China "over the hump" to India, and thence to Canada, for a medical furlough, despite apparently insurmountable obstacles.

1219. ———. *Pioneering in Kwangsi: The Story of Alliance Missions in South China.* Harrisburg, Pa.: Christian Publications, 1936. 208 p.

What little Protestant mission work had been undertaken before the C&MA entered Guangxi province in 1892 was snuffed out by persecution. This account includes geographical and ethnographical observations, a record of the mission work of other societies, and a list of the Alliance missionaries who died on the Guangxi field.

1220. O'Leary, Denyse. "Report Verifies Abuse of Missionary Kids." *Faith Today*, March-April 1998, 15-16.

An independent commission of enquiry established by the C&MA concluded that students at Mamou Alliance Academy in Guinea (which operated from 1921 to 1971) experienced physical, emotional, sexual, and spiritual abuse by staff. Negligence by C&MA administrators allowed the abuse to continue. The Alliance has responded by agreeing to pay for a large share of the victims' past and future therapy bills and by promising to initiate changes in policy to prevent recurrences of abuse.

1221. Oliver, Dennis M. "Christianity and Culture." *Church Growth Bulletin* 10 (January 1974): 327-29.

The Bible, when read in its literary sense, does effectively communicate God's Word, but that communication is more in terms of principles than specifics. Within the context of these principles "there is room for a plurality of theological emphasis."

1222. Olson, Lee. "The Hymnology of Rev. A. B. Simpson, Founder of the Christian and Missionary Alliance." M.S.M. thesis, Union Theological Seminary, 1943. 172 p.

A brief biography of A. B. Simpson, followed by the text of 63 of his hymns, with a brief commentary on each. Includes accounts, by Simpson's daughter Margaret Simpson Buckman, who set many of his poems to music, of how a particular hymn came to be written. Olson directed the School of Sacred Music at the Missionary Training Institute.

1223. Olsson, Emilio. *The Dark Continent—at Our Doors: Slavery, Heathenism and Cruelty in South America*. New York: M. E. Munson, 1899. 89 p.

Recounts Olsson's adventures as a colporteur, including his observations regarding the plight of the indigenous people he encountered. Although this account mentions neither dates nor the mission he was working for at the time, Olsson did embark on journeys similar to the ones described herein during his brief stint as the superintendent of the C&MA's South American mission (mid-1897 until his dismissal in May 1899).

1224. ———. "A Missionary's Experience." *The Examiner*, 22 June 1899, 26-27.

Accuses the Alliance of failing to supply his missionary stipend, and other monies necessary to the furtherance of the C&MA mission in South America, during his final year as field director for South America. For A. B. Simpson's response, cf. *The Christian and Missionary Alliance* 23 (8 July 1899): 87-88.

1225. ———. *La obra en Sud-America del colportor-evangelista Emilio Olsson*. Santiago de Chile: Imprenta Moderna, 1896. 183 p.

Recounts Olsson's experiences as a colporteur-evangelist in South America prior to his joining the C&MA.

———, joint author. *A Plea for South America: The Neglected Continent.* See 1793.

1226. ———. *Rev. A. B. Simpson's Misstatements Refuted.* New York: [by the author?], 1899.

1227. Opperman, Kenn (W)ayne (1926-). "In Debt . . . for Life." *Moody Monthly*, May 1970, 27, 40-42.

Like the Apostle Paul (Rom. 1:14-15) Christians are in debt to unbelievers in the sense that the latter will never achieve right relationship with God apart from the agency of the former. In particular, Christians must live before unbelievers as a correct representation of God the Father and demonstrate what it means to live in right relationship with God.

1228. ———. *My Visit with Pope Paul VI.* n.p., [ca. 1969]. 6 p.

Describes his two audiences with Pope Paul VI. Laments that, despite his experience of conversion, the pope had no assurance of salvation.

1229. Ordóñez, Francisco. *Historia del Cristianismo en Colombia*. Cali, Colombia: La Alianza Cristiana y Misionera, [1956?] 379 p.

Written by a member of the Colombian C&MA to commemorate the 100th anniversary of the arrival of the first evangelical missionary in Colombia. Describes the martyrdom of evangelicals during "la violencia" and contends, against Roman Catholic detractors, that evangelicals are not sectarian opportunists. Includes a lengthy chapter on the C&MA.

1230. Orr, J. Edwin. *Always Abounding!: A Pen Sketch of Oswald J. Smith of Toronto*, 2nd ed. London: Marshall, Morgan and Scott, 1948. 128 p.

Smith regarded the C&MA as one of the formative influences in his life: his wife was a graduate of the Missionary Training Institute; most of his close friends were connected in some way with the Alliance; he admired A. B. Simpson's stress on missions, evangelism, and holy living; and he was impelled by a sense of urgency vis-à-vis missions that he had acquired from the Alliance.

1231. Orthner, Jerry. *Angels: Friends in High Places: Who They Are and What They Do, Plus 40 Amazing Stories*. Camp Hill, Pa.: Horizon Books, 1997. 288 p.

A popular angelology by an Alliance pastor. A few of the 40 testimonies are by Alliance missionaries.

1232. Osborne, Grant R. "Hermeneutics and Hostility: Eschatology as a Test Case for Theological Debate." *His Dominion* 14 (fall 1987): 27-30.

The doctrine of the return of Christ is a cardinal doctrine that must be believed by all Christians, yet the C&MA is justified in making the premillennial position a doctrinal distinctive and wise in not elevating to this status any of the various theories about the timing of the rapture.

1233. *Our Mexican Neighbours: Alliance Home Missions*. New York: The Alliance, 1956. 4 p.

Describes Alliance efforts to evangelize Mexican immigrant workers in Texas.

1234. *Our Most Southern Outpost*. New York: Christian and Missionary Alliance, 1954. 11 p.

Highlights of the Alliance's mission work in Chile.

1235. Overholtzer, Ruth P. (1897-). *Salvation Songs for Children: Number One*. Harrisburg, Pa.: Christian Publications, 1939. 65 p.

1236. ———. *Salvation Songs for Children: Number Two*. Harrisburg, Pa.: Christian Publications, 1943. 65 p.

1237. Owen, Timothy. "Confessions of a Missions Pastor." *His Dominion* 16 (July 1990): 12-19.

When an Alliance pastor applies the same strategy he had used in promoting a building program to promoting the Great Commission (Alliance Missions) Fund in his church pledges more than double.

1238. Oyarzun, Arturo. *Reminiscencias históricas de la obra evangélica en Chile*. Valdivia, Chile: Imprimeria Alianza, 1921. 79 p.

A history of the work of the various evangelical mission agencies in Chile.

1239. Oye, Suteichi. "The Plight of the Lost." In *One Race, One Gospel, One Task: World Congress on Evangelism, Berlin, 1966,* eds. Carl F. H.

Henry and W. Stanley Mooneyham, 2:59-61. Minneapolis: World Wide Publications, 1967.

A sketch of the religious mentality of the Japanese.

1240. Paasonen, Henry A. *Laos: God Visits the Tribesmen*. Harrisburg, Pa.: Christian Publications, [195-?].

1241. Packo, John E. *Coping with Cancer: 12 Creative Choices*. Camp Hill, Pa.: Christian Publications, 1991. 225 p.

Prayer, worship, trust in God (who permits cancer for his glory and the Christian sufferer's spiritual growth), medical treatment supplemented by the healing power of Christ, anointing and prayer for healing by the elders of one's church, a healthy lifestyle, and accepting death as the departure into heaven are the primary strategies advocated.

1242. ———. *Find and Use Your Spiritual Gifts*. Camp Hill, Pa.: Christian Publications, 1980. 117 p.

A manual for use in adult Sunday School classes.

1243. Padilla, Washington. *La iglesia y los dioses modernos: Historia del Protestantismo en el Ecuador*. Biblioteca de Ciencias Sociales, vol. 23. Quito: Corporación Editoria Nacional, 1989. 455 p.

A scholarly analysis of Protestantism in Ecuador with special reference to the sociopolitical implications of a Gospel transmitted by North Americans. Commends the C&MA for its contributions to the education of the children of jungle dwellers.

1244. *Palms of Victory: Designed for Evangelistic Campaigns, Bible Conferences and Missionary Conventions, with Special Emphasis on the Deeper Life*. Harrisburg, Pa.: Christian Publications, 1946. 130 p.

Of the 138 selections (most of which are Gospel songs) only 10 are by Alliance hymnists and only 3 of these are by A. B. Simpson.

1245. Palomino, Miguel Angel. *Lima al Encuentro con Dios: A New Kind of Urban Missiology*. [Lima?]: n.p., 1983. 31 p.

Lima al Encuentro con Dios (LED) is an evangelistic program that originated among the C&MA churches of Lima, Peru. It is based on the following principles: prayer, a focus on urban evangelism, the constant discipling of new believers (often in church-based Bible institutes), a trained leadership team, and highly visible church buildings (often financed by North American Christians). The success of the LED strategy has led to its adoption as the primary church plating strategy of the

C&MA in South America. LED's influence has also extended beyond South America and beyond the Alliance.

1246. ———. *Misión en la ciudad: Enfoque al movimiento Lima al Encuentro con Dios*. Lima, Peru: Nueva Imagen Publicitaria, 1990. 116 p.

A history and critical analysis of LED, a movement which began in the C&MA's Lince church in Lima, Peru, in 1973. This church of 148 members had grown to 12,000 members in 26 churches by 1990.

1247. Pardington, George (P)almer (1866-1915). *The Crisis of the Deeper Life*. New York: Christian Alliance Pub. Co., 1906. 232 p.

Sanctification "involves a radical revolution in personality" (p. 23) as a free gift of grace to the fully surrendered believer. It results in union with God, the appropriation of Jesus' nature, and the indwelling of the Holy Spirit.

1248. ———. *The Crooked Made Straight*, 3rd rev. ed. Nyack, N.Y.: by the author, 1898. 32 p.

A sickly child, Pardington was physically abused by a teacher in 1876. The severe paralysis that resulted became life-threatening by 1880. In 1881, after reading Carrie F. Judd's *The Prayer of Faith*, he became convinced that God would heal him, stopped taking his medicine, and by 1884 was completely well. He began his teaching career at the Nyack Missionary Training Institute in 1897.

1249. ———. "Experiences of Spiritual and Physical Healing." *Triumphs of Faith* 5 (February 1885): 45-48.

A letter to the editor describing his experience of physical healing. This article was reprinted in *Thy Healer* 2 (1885): 104-7, and also forms the basis of 1248.

1250. ———. *The Mind of Christ, or the Gospel for the Intellect*. New York: Christian Alliance Pub. Co., [190-?]. 16 p.

To have the mind of Christ means to have one's intellectual faculties transformed by the Holy Spirit so that Christ can use them in his service. Study is still necessary, but mental toil becomes a luxury and a joy.

1251. ———. *Outline Studies in Christian Doctrine*. New York: Christian Alliance Pub. Co., 1916. 364 p.

The only formal exposition of Christian doctrine from the perspective of the fourfold Gospel. It has been widely used as a textbook in Alliance colleges and seminaries.

1252. ———. *The Still Small Voice*. New York: Christian Alliance Pub. Co., 1902. 244 p.

Twenty-six devotional messages on the spiritual life selected from talks given during the weekly consecration service Pardington conducted for students at the Missionary Training Institute.

1253. ———. *Studies in Christian Doctrine*. Revised by H. M. Freligh. Harrisburg, Pa.: Christian Publications, 1964. 4 vols.

Reprint of 1251, revised for use in group studies.

1254. ———. *Studies in Church History*. New York: Christian Alliance Pub. Co., [ca. 1919]. 165 p.

An annotated outline of church history that advocates a "mystic-missionary" approach to the Christian life, and contends that "with the spiritual insight of the Pietists, the loyalty to truth of the Scotch Covenanters and the self-sacrificing zeal of the Moravians, A. B. Simpson was one of the outstanding spiritual leaders of the [nineteenth] century" (p. 162).

1255. ———. *Twenty-five Wonderful Years: A Popular Sketch of the Christian and Missionary Alliance*. New York: Christian Alliance Pub. Co., 1914. 238 p.

The most useful part of this laudatory history is the 78 p. of memorial tributes to scores of Alliance luminaries, many of whom are not covered in any other biographical source.

1256. Park, Myung Soo. "Concepts of Holiness in American Evangelicalism: 1835-1915 ." Ph.D. diss., Boston University Graduate School, 1992. 299 p.

A. B. Simpson was "the most important holiness preacher outside the Wesleyan camp," and the C&MA is "perhaps the only holiness denomination in the Reformed tradition in America." Simpson's own views were neither Wesleyan nor Keswickian, although they conformed, in general, to those of the Higher Christian Life movement.

1257. Parry, Thomas. *The Indwelling Spirit*. New York: Alliance Press Co., 1906. 230 p.

An explication of the biblical teaching on the person and work of the Holy Spirit in light of Eph. 3:14-21. Emphasizes the ongoing work of the Spirit in the life of the believer.

1258. *The Pastor's Handbook: A Book of Forms and Instructions for Conducting the Many Ceremonies Which Constitute the Pastoral Function*. Harrisburg, Pa.: Christian Publications, 1958-. 102 p.

The revised 3rd edition (1989) includes an appendix on the Christian year not found in previous editions.

1259. Patterson, Alexander. *The Greater Life and Work of Christ: As Revealed in Scripture, Man and Nature*, 2nd ed. New York: Christian Alliance Pub. Co., 1898. 418 p.

An attempt to understand all of Scripture from a Christological perspective, much as A. B. Simpson had done in his Christ in the Bible series.

1260. ———. *The Other Side of Evolution: Its Effects and Fallacy*, 3rd ed. New York: Christian Alliance Pub. Co., 1912. 174 p.

Evolution has no scientific or philosophical basis. It is the doctrine of chance, served up in scientific language. It opposes the teachings of the Bible, for it "originated in heathenism and ends in atheism" (p. xiv).

1261. Patterson, Robert James. "The Life and Thought of A. W. Tozer concerning Sanctification: An Investigation into the Thoughts of Aiden Wilson Tozer concerning Sanctification and the Insights He Received from Some of the Past Mystics of the Church." M.Th. thesis, Regent College, 1989. 580 p.

Tozer was, in effect, a latter day neo-Platonist who was inspired by the Christian mystics' love for and adoration of God, despite the fact that his doctrine and practice often differed considerably from theirs. His tendency to neglect his responsibilities as father and husband makes one wonder how integrated his spirituality really was. Unlike the C&MA in general, he stressed sanctification over evangelism; and although he believed in sanctification-by-crisis, he says little about it in his writings. Includes a chronological listing of Tozer's editorials, an index to the works cited by Tozer, and a compilation of tributes to Tozer by evangelical leaders.

1262. ———. "A Study of the Doctrine of Apostasy Using Galatians 5:4 as a Text—with an Analysis of the Position Held by the Christian and

Missionary Alliance." M.Div. thesis, Northwest Baptist Theological Seminary, 1981. 131 p.

Nowhere do Simpson, Tozer, or modern Alliance writers take a stand on the subject, although all seem to hold positive, Calvinistically oriented views on God's ability to keep the believer from falling away.

1263. Payne, Thomas. *A New Discovery of Jesus Christ, or the Object of a Clarified Vision*. New York: Christian Alliance Pub. Co., [ca. 1916]. 171 p.

A British Holiness perspective on the baptism of the Holy Spirit. Focuses on the illumination wrought by a deeper understanding of the person and work of Christ and the resulting "vision" for missions and evangelism and desire for growth in holiness.

1264. Peak, Giles M. *Christ's Healing Wings: A Series of Talks on Divine Healing*. Alliance Colportage Library, vol. 1, no. 19. Nyack, N.Y.: Christian Alliance Pub. Co., 1899. 152 p.

Thirteen talks given in 1898 and 1899 while the author was pastor of the Gospel Tabernacle Church of Los Angeles.

1265. Pease, Richard B. "Contextualization: The Continuing Search for Relevance." In *Alliance Academic Review 1999,* ed. Elio Cuccaro, 101-17.

Contextualization will be an ongoing challenge for the Alliance because of the burgeoning growth of its ethnic churches and because of its desire to develop effective strategies for presenting the Gospel to resistant cultural groups.

1266. Peña, Gabriel W. *Las buenas nuevas en el Ecuador*. Quito: Imprenta Voz Andes, 1973.

A history of evangelicalism in Ecuador. Includes a twelve-page section on the Alliance.

1267. Pentecost, George F. *The Supreme Claims of Missionary Enterprise*. Living Truths, vol. 1, no. 6. Nyack, N.Y.: Christian Alliance Pub. Co., 1900.

1268. Perkins, Eunice (M)ay (1871-). *Fred Francis Bosworth (the Joybringer): And Continued Story of Joybringer Bosworth, His Life Story*, 2nd ed. River Forest, Ill.: F. F. Bosworth, 1927. 224 p.

Rev. ed. of 1269. Includes an additional chapter and new sermons and testimonies.

1269. ———. *Joybringer Bosworth: His Life Story*. Dayton, Ohio: John H. Scruby, 1921. 232 p.

Biography of (F)red (F)rancis Bosworth (1877-1958), a prominent healer-evangelist who left the Assemblies of God for the C&MA over the tongues controversy. The letter he wrote to the AOG on the issue is reproduced on p. 53-77.

1270. Peters, David John (1945-), and Arlene Mary Peters (1943-). *By an Unfamiliar Path: The Story of David and Arlene Peters*. Camp Hill, Pa.: Christian Publications, 1994. 164 p.

David and Arlene Peters have served as C&MA missionaries to São Paulo, Brazil, since 1986. Prior to this they served with the C&MA in Colombia, working among the Paez Indians (1971-1979), and in Bogotá (1979-1986), where David was field director. Cf. 1016.

1271. Petrie, Arthur (1888-). *The Message of Daniel*. Harrisburg, Pa.: Christian Publications, 1947. 159 p.

A devotional commentary based on classroom lectures given at Simpson Bible Institute.

1272. ———. *Peace?!* New York: Sar Shalom Publications, [195-?]. 19 p.

1273. ———. *The Regathering of Israel*. New York: American Board of Missions to the Jews, 1966. 78 p.

There will be "[two] returns . . . one of part of Israel and in unbelief, the other future and in fullness and in blessing."

1274. Pett, David M. "Divine Healing: The Development of Simpson's Thought." *His Dominion* 16 (March 1990): 23-33.

Simpson's views on healing remained essentially unchanged throughout his ministry: sickness is related to one's spiritual condition, and the divine life of Christ is imparted to the body of the believer by the Holy Spirit for a life of consecrated service. However, certain of his views underwent refinement and clarification. For example, his later writings posit a stronger connection between spiritual preparation and healing. He also became less sanguine in his rejection of medical science, advising believers not to dispense with doctors and medicines unless they sensed Christ specifically directing them to do so.

1275. Philpott (P)eter (W)iley (1865-1957). *A Modern Miracle*. Tracts for the Times. Salvation Series. New York: Christian Alliance Pub. Co., [ca. 1900]. 7 p.

Philpott obeys the Holy Spirit's urging to invite a street corner drunk to a gospel meeting. He leads the man to Christ the next day. The two men meet 14 years later: the former drunkard is now a Christian and a successful businessman.

1276. ———. *Seducing Spirits*. New York: Christian Alliance Pub. Co., [ca. 1919]. 23 p.

The communications that Spiritualist mediums receive may be fraudulent or they may come from evil spirits. Christians should therefore steer clear of spiritualism.

1277. Philpott (P)eter (W)iley (1865-1957), and A. W. Roffe. *New Light: Containing a Full Account of Recent Salvation Army Troubles in Canada*. Toronto: Rose Pub. Co., 1892. 115 p.

Philpott, a brigadier in the Salvation Army in Canada, was fired by General Herbert Booth and vilified by him throughout the Army community in Canada. Not only are the charges against him false, contends Philpott, but the tyrannical leadership, extravagant lifestyle, and unloving conduct of Booth and the Army hierarchy will also undo the work of an otherwise exemplary organization if left unchecked.

1278. Phu, Hoang Le. "The Evangelical Church of Viet Nam during the Second World War and the War of Independence." Master's thesis, Wheaton College, 1967. 147 p.

The ECVN is largely the product of C&MA mission work. Includes a discussion of the Alliance's policy of financial support for overseas churches, and of the factors that have enabled the ECVN to retain its spiritual vitality amid the ravages of war.

1279. ———. " A Short History of the Evangelical Church of Viet Nam (1911-1965)." Ph.D. diss., New York University, 1972. 555 p.

Despite the fact that the ECVN was the first overseas church to fully adopt "three-self" principles it is far from being fully indigenized, for it is deficient in self-nurture and self expression and has yet to develop its own literature and hymnody.

1280. Pierson (A)rthur (T)appan (1837-1911). *Acts of the Holy Spirit*. Camp Hill, Pa.: Christian Publications, 1980. 127 p.

Reprint of *The Acts of the Holy Spirit: Being an Examination of the Active Mission and Ministry of the Spirit of God, the Divine Paraclete As Set Forth in the Acts of the Apostles*, New York: Fleming H. Revell, 1895. According to the (new) foreword by Keith M. Bailey, Pierson was a friend of A. B. Simpson who taught at the Missionary Training Institute, preached at Alliance conventions, and contributed articles to Alliance periodicals.

1281. [———]. "The Christian and Missionary Alliance." *The Missionary Review of the World*, August 1899, 617-21.

In assessing the accusations of Emilio Olsson (cf. 1224), the editors of *The Independent* (cf. 288), and Simpson's countercharges (*The Christian and Missionary Alliance*. 8 July 1899), Pierson, a friend of Simpson, concludes that he can no longer serve as a referee for the C&MA because the Simpsons exercise an unhealthy control over the organization and its finances. The Simpsons must yield their power to others and ensure that missionary candidates are better prepared for the field.

1282. ———. *The Holy Care of the Body*. Harrisburg, Pa.: Christian Publications, 1968. 14 p.

Since the body is sacred, one ought to care for it with reverent discipline. Accordingly, tips on everything from avoiding nervous prostration to proper diet are included.

1283. ———. *How He Lost His Pardon*. New York: Christian Alliance Pub. Co., [ca. 1900]. 4 p.

Unwillingness to forgive will lead to forfeiture of Christ's freely offered pardon.

1284. ———. *Knowing the Scriptures: Rules and Methods of Bible Study*. New York: Gospel Publishing House, 1910. Reprint, New York: Christian Alliance Pub. Co., [1910?]. 459 p.

1285. Pierson, Delavan L. *Why Believe It?* New York: Christian Alliance Pub. Co., [1927?].

1286. *Pioneer Evangelism*. New York: Christian and Missionary Alliance, 1950.

1287. "Pioneers of Religious Broadcasting." *Religious Broadcasting*, January 1979, 25-27, 29-30.

Paul Rader delivered his first radio sermon in 1922. His example had a formative influence on Clarence Jones (1915-1986) founder of HCJB radio. Rader and R. R. Brown (pastor of the Omaha Gospel Tabernacle, who began the nondenominational Radio Chapel service which ran 1927-1977) are both members of the Religious Broadcasting Hall of Fame.

1288. Pippert, Wesley G. "The Untold Story in Vietnam."*Christian Life* (March 1969): 26, 45-50.

The martyrdom of six C&MA missionaries during the 1968 Tet Offensive marked the beginning of increased hostility towards missionaries on the part of the Viet Cong. The president of the Evangelical Church of Vietnam (which was founded by C&MA missionaries) fears that the United States will give away at the Paris Peace Talks whatever military gains it has made.

1289. Pitts, Bill. "Holiness As Spirituality: The Religious Quest of A. B. Simpson." In *Modern Christian Spirituality: Methodological and Historical Essays*, ed. Bradley C. Hanson, 223-48. Atlanta: Scholars Press, 1990.

Simpson responded to the inadequacy of the prevailing Protestant piety of the nineteenth century—conversion experience in a revival setting—with a program of spiritual reform that emphasized personal appropriation of the life of Christ. His message was simple and coherent, and he propagated it effectively through his writings, gospel songs, conferences, and Bible institute.

1290. Plowman, Edward E. "'Candles' in Cambodia: Will They Go Out?" *Christianity Today*, 14 March 1975, 52-53.

A brief history of the Khmer Evangelical Church (a church associated with the C&MA) in the light of the current political upheaval. Cf. 181.

1291. ———. "Suffering in South Viet Nam." *Christianity Today* 11 April 1975, 31-32.

An overview of the current state of the national church and of Protestant and Roman Catholic missionary work in the country in the light of the war.

1292. Plymire, David V. *High Adventure in Tibet*. Springfield, Mo.: Gospel Publishing House, 1959. 236 p.

Victor Guy Plymire (1881-1956) served as a missionary to Tibet with the C&MA (1908-1919) and the Assemblies of God (1920-1949) but no mention is made of his Alliance connections in this rather hagiographic treatment of a trophy of Pentecostalism.

1293. Polding, M. Fred. "Kinshasa, Zaire: An African Strategy for Urban Church Growth." *Urban Mission* 3 (March 1986): 36-38.

The C&MA has succeeded in establishing a strong church in Kinshasa by following the "Boma strategy," i.e., planting prayer cells along tribal lines and using lay leadership. Worship patterns, hymnology, and leadership are strongly African, but the church is beset by dissension and has failed to provide adequate nurture and training for new believers.

1294. Pollard (A)delaide (A)ddison (1861-1934). *Life Lessons in Quatrains*. [191-?]. 9 p.

1295. ———. *The Vision*. New York: Pearl Press, 1912. 24 p.

A florid epic poem in blank verse describing the romance of a Jewish man and woman and their conversion to Christianity.

1296. Pollock, John. "Tuan Change." In *Victims of the Long March*. Waco, Tex.: Word Books, 1970.

A brief biography of Ernest Presswood, C&MA missionary to Kalimantan, Indonesia.

1297. Porcella, Brewster. "The Teaching of the Scriptures on Healing in Relation to the Atonement." Master's thesis, Wheaton College, 1952. 74 p.

Examines the views of A. B. Simpson and others. Concludes that healing is not in the Atonement.

1298. Porter, S. F. *Doctrines of Salvation Outlined, Defined, and Related*. Vermilion, Ohio: by the author, 1990. 141 p.

1299. ———. *Wielding the Sword: Inspirational Bible Sermonettes*. Marion, Ohio: Langley Service, 1934. 39 p.

1300. Porter (W)illiam Curtis (1897-). *Porter-Tingley Debate*. Murfreesboro, Tenn.: G. W. DeHoff, 1947. 275 p

The account of a debate (24 February-1 March 1947) between Porter, a Churches of Christ pastor from Monette, Ark., and Glenn V. Tingley, a C&MA pastor from Birmingham, Ala., on whether the Holy Spirit operates directly in the hearts of sinners (as well as through the Scriptures) and whether the Bible teaches that baptism in water is necessary for salvation. Tingley affirmed the first proposition and denied the second.

1301. Poston, Larry. "Christianity as a Minority Religion." *Alliance Academic Review* (1995): 121-46.

Christianity is a minority religion virtually everywhere in the world and will likely remain such. Evangelicals should embrace this reality, since the church is called to evangelize, not to Christianize. Besides, minority movements have always been more vital, creative, and focused than their majoritarian counterparts. Since the church tends to grow best in the context of secular pluralism, evangelicals should advocate and support this kind of church/state relationship.

1302. Powers, W. E. *Studies in the Book of Genesis*. New York: Christian Alliance Pub. Co., 1928. 128 p.

Attempts to show that "sane science" supports a conservative reading of Genesis.

1303. Pratt, Julius. *Expansionists of 1898: The Acquisition of Hawaii and the Spanish Islands*. Baltimore: Johns Hopkins Press, 1936. 401 p.

The C&MA, along with most other American religious groups, supported the annexation of Cuba, the Philippines, and other Spanish possessions. They regarded the war with Spain as God's way of punishing Spain for her mistreatment of her colonial subjects and of opening Spanish colonies to Protestant missionaries. The Alliance even went so far as to send a representative to present a letter from A. B. Simpson to the secretary of state, urging the latter to do all he could to ensure that the Philippines would be opened to missionaries (see esp. p. 279-316).

1304. *Prayer Warriors: Powerful Portraits of Soldier Saints on God's Front Lines*. Camp Hill, Pa.: Christian Publications, 1998. 115 p.

Extracts from biographies of "Holy Ann" (Anne Preston), Thomas Haire, E. D. Whiteside, and A. W. Tozer.

1305. Price, Roy C. "Adaptations in Christian Higher Education: The Case of the Christian and Missionary Alliance." Ph.D. diss., Oxford Graduate School, 1988. 197 p.

The attitude to higher education in the Alliance has changed little since 1970: some want to give priority to the preparation of ministers, while others want to concentrate on providing a good general post-secondary education for Alliance youth. Includes recommendations for resolving this impasse.

1306. Price, Wendell W. (1926-1987). *Contemporary Problems of Evangelism*. Harrisburg, Pa.: Christian Publications, 1976. 111 p.

Christians should be agents of social change, but not at the expense of their primary calling, which is to evangelize. True social change results from spiritual change. All members of the local church should involve themselves in evangelism, not just a "gifted" few. "Presented as the L. W. Pippert Memorial Lectures, October 1975, Alliance School of Theology and Missions, Nyack, New York."

1307. ———. *Do We Need a New Approach to Our Educational Needs?* n.p., 1970. 30 p.

Alliance colleges have started to increase their liberal arts offerings at the expense of their primary mandate, that of preparing Christian workers. Canadian Theological College has overcome this problem by affiliating itself with the University of Regina. The C&MA ought to expand the Jaffray School of Missions into a seminary and offer courses in practical theology via an extension education program based in C&MA churches.

1308. ———. "The Role of Women in the Ministry of the Christian and Missionary Alliance." D.Min. thesis, San Francisco Theological Seminary, 1977. 276 p.

The current situation, in which women are barred from ordination in the C&MA, needs to change in the light of biblical teaching (especially Gal. 3:28), past C&MA practice (in A. B. Simpson's day women in the Alliance served as evangelists, Bible teachers, and even vice-presidents), and the number of gifted women whose ministry is being stifled by current C&MA policy.

1309. Princell, Josephine (1844-1937). *Frederick Franson, World Missionary*. Chicago: Chicago Bladet, [191-?]. 156 p.

When several Swedes who had taken his Bible courses expressed their desire to become missionaries, Franson (1852-1908) approached A. B. Simpson, who at that time (ca. 1890) had more money than missionaries to support. Franson offered to recruit 200 Swedes for China, and Simpson agreed to raise the money. Late in 1893, with 45 Swedish missionaries already on the field and 155 waiting to be sent, Simpson terminated his support because of complaints by veteran Alliance missionaries in China against Franson's "uneducated and untried workers" (cf. 2104 for a more thorough and somewhat different assessment).

1310. *The Printed Page*. New York: Christian and Missionary Alliance, 1950.

1311. Pruett, W. A. *A Dream That Came True*. The God's Sure Mercies Series. New York: Christian and Missionary Alliance, 1943. 4 p.

The account of a revival that occurred during the early 1940s in French Indochina in churches planted by C&MA missionaries.

1312. Pyles, Franklin Arthur. "The Missionary Eschatology of A. B. Simpson." In *The Birth of a Vision*, eds. David F. Hartzfeld and Charles Nienkirchen, 29-48. Regina, Sask.: His Dominion, 1986.

Because of his historicist interpretation of Revelation, Simpson believed that the only prophecy remaining to be fulfilled with respect to Christ's return is Matt. 24:14. Hence the church must establish a "testimony" in each cultural-linguistic group. The C&MA currently tends toward an "any moment" view of imminence, which has sapped its missionary zeal. For the Alliance to renew its missionary eschatology it must both recognize that the task is much greater than Simpson envisioned it and return to Simpson's more elastic definition of when and how it will be completed. The C&MA must also "honor the King" by combining sanctification, in the form of ministries of social action and justice, with missions.

1313. ———. "Thy Kingdom Come." *His Dominion* 14 (fall 1987): 31-39.

A. B. Simpson's eschatology stressed the "appropriated future kingdom," i.e., that "the blessings of the future kingdom [can] be enjoyed now in a certain measure as they are appropriated by faith" (p. 33).

1314. *Quarter Centennial Forward Movement of the Christian and Missionary Alliance, 1889-1914*. [New York?]: The Alliance, [1914?]. 31 p.

An overview of the work of the Alliance, particularly in missions, followed by an appeal for financial support.

1315. *Questions and Answers for Young Disciples: A Catechism of Christian Truth*. Harrisburg, Pa.: Christian Publications, 1940. 40 p.

Does not refer explicitly to either "healing in the Atonement" or sanctification as a second work of grace.

1316. Quick, L. Bowring. *The Sevenfold Work of the Holy Spirit*. Canoga Park, Calif.: by the author, 1937. 100 p.

Interprets the baptism of the Holy Spirit and spiritual gifts from a Holiness, i.e., anti-Pentecostal, perspective.

1317. Rader, Paul Daniel (1879-1938). *At Thy Word: A Farewell Message*. New York: Christian Alliance Pub. Co., [1920?]. 27 p.

An autobiographical sermon based on 1 Ki.18:36 and preached at Calvary Baptist Church, New York City, 22 October 1920, just prior to his departure on a world tour of mission fields (which is described in 1339, see esp. p. 14).

1318. ———. *Beating Baal, and Other Sermons*. New York: Christian Alliance Pub. Co., 1916. 87 p.

Three somewhat autobiographical evangelistic sermons.

1319. ———. *Breaking Broncos*. Chicago: Chicago Gospel Tabernacle, Chapel Bookstall, 1928. 12 p.

Includes reminiscences from Rader's youth.

1320. ———. *Come See Them Play*. Chicago: Moody Church, 1918. 16 p.

An illustrated promotion for Moody Church's Fresh Air Camp for the poor children of Chicago (Cedar Lake, Ind.)

1321. ———. *The Empty Cottage at Silver Falls, and Another Story*. New York: The Book Stall, 1917. 60 p.

The other story is "The Sheltered Thief," and both are florid in style and evangelistic in intent.

1322. ———. *The Fight for Light, and Other Sermons*. New York: The Book Stall, 1916. 67 p.

Four evangelistic sermons.

1323. ———. *God's Blessed Man: Soul Stirring Sermons*. New York: George H. Doran, 1922. 196 p.

Seventeen sermons on the successful Christian life, compiled and edited by J. Gregory Mantle.

1324. ———. *Harnessing God, Messages with a Method: The Way to "Abundant Life" for Spirit, Soul and Body*. New York: George H. Doran, 1926. 110 p.

1325. ———. *Heavenly Smelling Salts, or Comfort for Troubled Ones*. The Paul Rader Series of Sermons, no. 6. Chicago: Chicago Book Center, [192-?]. 20 p.

Jesus is the healer of the broken hearted and can be trusted to take away our anxieties.

1326. ———. *"Hell" and "How Shall We Escape."* New York: The Book Stall, 1916. 27 p.

Two sermons on the reality of everlasting punishment for unrepentant sinners who do not take Jesus as their "door of escape."

1327. ———. *How to Win, and Other Victory Messages*. New York: The Book Stall, 1919. 99 p.

Eight sermons on self-abandonment (to Christ), the second coming, and evangelism.

1328. ———. *"I Am with You."* The Paul Rader Series of Sermons, no. 2. New York: The Book Stall, 1921. 17 p.

On Matt. 28:20.

1329. ———. *The King's Vision*. The Paul Rader Series of Sermons, no. 3. New York: The Book Stall, 1921. 20 p.

On Ps. 27:4.

1330. ———. *Leaves or Skin?* The Paul Rader Series of Sermons, no. 5. New York: The Book Stall, 1921. 21 p.

Gen. 3:7, 21 reminds us that God longs to give us a "covering of skin" (the righteousness of Christ) to replace our "covering of leaves" (attempts to procure our own righteousness).

1331. ———. *Let Go and Let God*. New York: The Book Stall, 1918. 110 p.

Short stories.

1332. ———. *Life's Greatest Adventure*. London: Victory Press, 1938. 163 p.

Reflections on the Christian life that include the story of his conversion and some information on his years with the Alliance.

1333. ———. *The Man of Mercy*. Chicago: Chicago Gospel Tabernacle, Chapel Book Stall, 1928. 119 p.

Collected sermons on various aspects of the life of Christ. "Trusting through the Stormy Way" includes an account of his travels through Vietnam with his wife and C&MA missionaries R. A. and Minne Jaffray.

1334. ———. *Naaman, or Dipping*. [Chicago?]: n.p., [192-?]. 16 p.
Naaman, who represents those who are too high-minded to "dip," i.e., to receive the cleansing from sin provided by Jesus.

1335. ———. *No Wire Pulling*. The Paul Rader Series of Sermons, no. 5. Chicago: Chicago Book Center, 1920. 19 p.

1336. ———. "Paul Rader Explores Old Memories." *Beta Kappa Journal* 4 (March 1928): 141-43.
Rader was a founding member (1901) of the Beta Kappa fraternity. He attributed his success in communicating the Gospel to men to the time he spent in a fraternity house as a university student.

1337. ———. *Paul Rader's Sermons*. New York: The Book Stall, 1916. 94 p.
Seven sermons preached by Rader while he was pastor of Moody Tabernacle.

1338. ———. *Paul Rader's Stories of His Early Life Interspersed by Spiritual Messages of Priceless Value*. Toronto: The Tabernacle Publishers, [1925?]. 32 p.
"Delivered in the Alliance Tabernacle, Toronto, before audiences numbering 2,500 people with hundreds turned away, January 5th to 12th, 1925." Cf. 1346.

1339. ———. *'Round the Round World: Some Impressions of a World Tour*. New York: Fleming H. Revell, 1922. 248 p.
Describes the world tour of Alliance missions Rader made (October 1920 - May 1921) while he was president of the C&MA.

1340. ———. *"Seeing Things."* The Paul Rader Series of Sermons, no. 4. New York: The Book Stall, 1921. 21 p.
The self-exaltation of Germany that preceded her defeat in World War I reflects the self-exaltation that lies at the root of sin. Each person must repent and believe in the Gospel or face a destruction similar to the one that befell Germany.

1341. ———. *Selections from Tabernacle Hymns, No. 2.* Chicago: Tabernacle Pub. Co., 1921. 32 p.

1342. ———. *The Signs of the Times*. New York: The Book Stall, 1916. 30 p.

The prophecies with reference to the return of Christ are being fulfilled with amazing rapidity. It is time to repent and believe in Christ before that opportunity is taken away.

1343. ———. *Spiritual Words to Popular Songs*. Chicago: Tabernacle Publishing Company, 1919. 42 p.

"Spiritual" lyrics designed to replace the secular words to certain popular songs.

1344. ———. "The Story of Paul Rader—Evangelist."*Missionary Review of the World*, August 1920, 704-11.

Covers his childhood conversion, his lapse under the influence of modernism, and his restoration to confident faith through a crisis experience of sanctification.

1345. ———. *Straight from the Shoulder Messages*. New York: The Book Stall, 1917. 68 p.

A collection of the weekly sermonettes, entitled "A Word for the Weekend," that the *Chicago Daily News* began publishing during the spring of 1916.

1346. ———. *Three Vital Messages: Delivered in the Alliance Tabernacle, Toronto, before Audiences Numbering 2,500 People, with Hundreds Turned Away, January 5th to 12th, 1925.* Toronto: The Tabernacle Publishers, [1925?]. 28 p.

Likely identical in content to 1338.

1347. ———. *The Victorious Life.* The Paul Rader Series of Sermons, no. 1. New York: The Book Stall, 1921. 16 p.

An evangelistic sermon on 2 Cor. 3:18 that contrasts legalism with the freedom of the Gospel, doing with believing, the natural with the supernatural, and reformation with regeneration.

1348. Rader, Paul Daniel (1879-1938), George C. Stebbins, and Lance B. Latham, musical eds. *Tabernacle Hymns No. 2.* Chicago: Tabernacle Pub. Co., published for the Christian Alliance Pub. Co., 1921. 318 p.

Includes 351 hymns, of which 50 are by Alliance hymnists, such as A. B. Simpson, R. Kelso Carter, Albert Simpson Reitz, Paul Rader, Winfield Macomber, and Harry L. Turner.

1349. Raines, Addie B., and Stanton (W)illard Richardson, eds. *Bible Doctrine for Young Christians*. Harrisburg, Pa.: Christian Publications, 1961. 100 p.

A catechetical manual, the doctrinal content of which was determined by the C&MA's Catechism Committee.

1350. Rambo, David (L)loyd (1934-). "The Christian and Missionary Alliance in the Philippines, 1901-1970." Ph.D. diss., New York University 1974. 309 p.

Although the Christian and Missionary Alliance Churches of the Philippines have made the transition from missionary to indigenous control, true indigeneity will not be achieved easily because their members, like all Filipino Protestants, tend to be the most Americanized of all Filipinos. However, the church has adapted ministerial training to local conditions, and their "energetic and unapologetic use of lay leadership" (p. 292) is exemplary.

1351. ———. *Our Hope for the Future*. Camp Hill, Pa.: Christian Publications, 1996. 19 p.

The Alliance needs to reaffirm a contemporized version of the fourfold Gospel. With respect to sanctification, A. B. Simpson believed that "All of the gifts of the Spirit are for the church now" but after formulating its "seek not, forbid not" policy the Alliance went on to depart in practice from Simpson's policy, ending up with a "seek not and better not" approach (to the gift of tongues in particular).

1352. ———. "Training Competent Leaders for the Christian and Missionary Alliance Churches of the Philippines." Master's thesis, Fuller Theological Seminary, 1968. 205 p.

1353. Rambo, Ruth C. "Well-Being of Women Married to Ministers in the Christian and Missionary Alliance." D.Min. diss., Asbury Theological Seminary, 1996. 300 p.

The ministers' wives surveyed were spiritually and emotionally healthy, but under considerable stress. The C&MA needs to provide better pastoral care for its pastors and their wives.

1354. Ratzlaff, Dwayne. "An Old Mediaeval Message: A Turning Point in the Life of A. B. Simpson." In *The Birth of a Vision*, eds. David F. Hartzfeld and Charles Nienkirchen, 165-94. Regina, Sask.: His Dominion, 1986.

Simpson was a true spiritual theologian because the goal of his writings is the spiritual transformation of the reader. He began to pray contemplatively after reading *A Guide to True Peace, or the Excellency of Inward and Spiritual Prayer,* a compilation of the spiritual writings of prominent Quietists. His contemplative prayer included recollection and practicing the presence of God, but Simpson always considered the study of Scripture to be the preeminent means of discerning the will of God.

1355. Ratzloff, Tim. "The Christian and Missionary Alliance." *Evangelical Missions Quarterly* 22 (April 1986): 125-27.

Between 1973 and 1983, the C&MA missionary force increased from 865 to 991. During this time 633 missionaries also left the mission for a variety of reasons, ranging from retirement (97) to moral or marital problems (23). More than a third of those who left did so at the end of their first term.

1356. Rausch, David A. *Zionism within Early American Fundamentalism, 1878-1918: A Convergence of Two Traditions*. New York: Edwin Mellen Press, 1979. 384 p.

Deals at some length with the contributions of C&MA Zionists A. E. Thompson and William E. Blackstone.

1357. Read, William R., Victor M. Monterosso, and Harmon A. Johnson. *Latin American Church Growth.* Grand Rapids: Eerdmans, 1969. 428 p.

Mentions briefly the Alliance work in Colombia, Ecuador, Chile, and Peru. Critiques the C&MA's methods of church planting in South America from the perspective of the church growth movement, e.g., the church in Chile has not grown because the Alliance is "committed to the present sterile methods and approaches."

1358. *Redemption Melodies: Designed for Evangelistic Campaigns, Bible Conferences and Missionary Conventions, with Special Emphasis on the Deeper Life*. Harrisburg, Pa.: Christian Publications, 1951. 123 p.

138 songs, including 20 by A. B. Simpson.

1359. Reed, Jerold F. "A Componential Analysis of the Ecuadorian Protestant Church." D.Miss. diss., Fuller Theological Seminary 1974. 230 p.

A church growth analysis that considers the C&MA along with other Protestant groups.

1360. Rees, Paul S. *Seth Cook Rees: The Warrior-Saint.* Indianapolis: The Pilgrim Book Room, 1934. 203 p.

From 1888 to 1889 or 1890 Rees (1854-1933), a leader in the Holiness movement, and his wife were president and secretary, respectively, of the Michigan Auxiliary of the Christian Alliance. "While never convinced of the accuracy of the movement's slogan-phrase 'The Four-Fold Gospel,' Seth Rees was deeply impressed by Dr. Simpson's ministry, heartily shared his views on missions and the return of the Lord, largely coincided with him on healing and, in consequence, took a keen interest in the work" (p. 25).

1361. *The Regina Chinese Alliance Church.* [Regina, Sask.?]: n.p., [1976?]. 64 p.

Text mostly in Chinese, with English contributions by Ruby Johnston and A. H. Orthner. Commemorates the 45th anniversary of the first Chinese Alliance church in Canada.

1362. Reichert, Richard P. *Daybreak over Ecuador: The Dawning of Evangelical Missions*. Quito: Sunrise Press, 1991. 222 p.

A comprehensive history, by an Alliance missionary, of Protestant missions in Ecuador. The C&MA mission receives extensive treatment.

1363. ———. *Missions Is a Contact Sport: A Survival Manual for Short-term Missions*. Quito, Ecuador: Sunrise Press, 1995. 209 p.

Based on the author's experiences as a C&MA missionary to Ecuador.

1364. Reid, Darrel Robert. "Jesus Only": The Early Life and Presbyterian Ministry of Albert Benjamin Simpson, 1843-1881." Ph.D. diss., Queen's University, 1994. 469 p.

The seeds of both Simpson's deeper-life theology and his mystical Christology were planted in his Reformed youth, and his experience of sanctification was merely an intensification of what he had imbibed from evangelical Presbyterianism. Simpson's independent ministry (which began in 1881) therefore does not represents a complete break with his Presbyterian past.

1365. ———. "Towards a Fourfold Gospel: A. B. Simpson, John Salmon and the Christian and Missionary Alliance in Canada." In *Aspects of the*

Canadian Evangelical Experience, ed. George A. Rawlyk, 271-88. Montreal; Kingston, Ont.: McGill-Queen's University Press, 1997.

Canadians were originally attracted to the C&MA because of its emphasis on holiness and healing, and because it advocated a cooperative relationship with existing denominations. The Canadian Alliance did not emphasize missions to the same degree as its American counterpart, likely because Canadians believed that the mission boards of their denominations were functioning effectively. Lucid description and insightful analysis make this the best short critical treatment of A. B. Simpson, the early Alliance, and the C&MA in Canada.

1366. Reidhead, Paris. *Beyond Believing*. Minneapolis: Bethany Fellowship, 1976. 90 p.

The lordship of Christ transcends the right to all human ambitions, relationships, and possessions.

1367. ———. *Beyond Petition: Six Steps to Successful Praying*. Minneapolis: Dimension Books, 1974. 84 p.

These are: affirmation (of God), confession, thanksgiving, praise, the desire for wisdom, and faith.

1368. ———. "Do You Pray in Faith?" In *Prayer: Its Deeper Dimension: A Christian Life Symposium*, 14-19. Grand Rapids: Zondervan, 1963.

For prayer to be answered one must be in a right relationship to God, eschew sin and selfishness, and make one's requests in the confident assurance that God will answer one's prayer. Originally published in *Christian Life* 20 (May 1958): 14-15.

1369. ———. *Getting Evangelicals Saved*. Minneapolis: Bethany House, 1989. 175 p.

A primer on true conversion for the many American evangelicals who are not Christians at all, but rather have been "converted" to a Gospel of "easy-believism" that minimizes the reality of sin and the need for repentance, faith, conversion, and sanctification (understood as a crisis experience subsequent to conversion).

1370. ———. *Uplifted Gates*. Lubbock, Tex.: Missionary Crusader, [195-?]. 36 p.

Confession of sin is the most important prerequisite for revival.

1371. Reimer, Reginald Eugene. "A Historic Meeting in Vietnam." *Church Growth Bulletin* 8 (May 1972): 225-26.

An account of the first church growth seminar ever conducted in Vietnam.

1372. ———. "The Protestant Movement in Vietnam: Church Growth in Peace and War." Master's thesis, Fuller Theological Seminary 1972. 336 p.

Deals only with church growth among ethnic Vietnamese. The work of C&MA missionaries could have been far more effective if they had had a better understanding of the history and culture of Vietnam. The Vietnamese Protestant church, which is largely made up of converts from animism, has unwittingly adopted American forms of religious expression and is therefore far from being fully indigenized.

1373. ———. "South Vietnam." In *The Church in Asia*, ed. Donald E. Hoke, 565-91. Chicago: Moody Press, 1975.

Discusses the current state of the church in South Vietnam and recounts the history of missionary activity in the country. In 1975, 83% of all Protestants in Vietnam belonged to the Evangelical Church of Vietnam (the South Vietnamese Alliance Church).

1374. Reitz, George W. "A. B. Simpson, Urban Evangelist." *Urban Mission* 8 (January 1991): 19-26.

Simpson was effective as an urban evangelist because of: his vision of the lostness of humankind and the redemptive power of the Gospel; his holistic understanding of the Gospel; his concern for cross-cultural evangelism; his flexibility, e.g., in using theaters, public halls, and tents as meeting places; his ability to mobilize the laity for ministry; and his ability both to learn from other Christian leaders and to recruit them for the ministries of the Alliance.

1375. ———. "Reaching the World through the City." *Alliance Academic Review* (1997): 97-118.

The evangelical church in North America needs to rediscover the city as a worthy object of evangelization. Large cities tend to have large and diverse immigrant populations that are more open to change than they would be in their homeland. Many immigrants eventually return to the country of origin, and if they could return as believers they could do a far more effective job of evangelism than Western missionaries.

1376. *A Remembrance of the Dedication of the Theological Institute, Radio Room and Clinic, Nha-Trang*. [Viet Nam?]: n.p., 1962. 40 p.

An illustrated souvenir of the dedication ceremony (9 July 1961) with text in Vietnamese and English.

1377. Renicks, Philip Marshall. "One Mission's Rationale for Sponsoring a School for MK's." In *Compendium of the International Conference on Missionary Kids: New Directions in Missions: Implications for MK's, Manila, Philippines, 1984,* eds. Beth A. Tetzel and Patricia Mortenson, 265-73. West Brattleboro, Vt.: ICMK, 1986.

Includes a brief history of the Alliance Academy (Quito, Ecuador) and Dalat School (Penang, Malaysia), a ten-point rationale for the C&MA's decision to operate such schools, and the results of surveys (overwhelmingly favorable to the Alliance) of former students and their parents.

1378. *Report of Missionary Conference, Philadelphia, Pa., May 9-11, 1955*. New York: The Christian and Missionary Alliance. Foreign Department, [1955?]. 36 p.

1379. *Report of the Fifth Asia Conference, Bangkok, Thailand, February 18-26, 1969.* New York: Christian and Missionary Alliance, 1969. 259 p.

Consists mostly of reports on evangelistic campaigns, missions ventures, and the state of the C&MA church and mission throughout the world (although the main focus is on C&MA work in South Asia, Hong Kong, and the Pacific Islands).

1380. *Revival Flame: Bosworth Campaign Special*. Oak Park, Ill.: B. B. Bosworth, [ca. 1927]. 128 p.

Rev. ed. of 1381.

1381. *Revival Flame: Bosworth Campaign Special*, 3rd ed. Chicago: Thoro Harris, 1923. 126 p.

A collection of the songs that were sung at the evangelistic campaigns of B. B. and F. F. Bosworth. Many of the songs are by Thoro Harris, some are by B. B. Bosworth.

1382. Reynolds, Lindsay. *Footprints: The Beginnings of the Christian and Missionary Alliance in Canada*. Toronto: Christian and Missionary Alliance in Canada, 1982. 616 p.

Traces the growth of the C&MA in Canada from 1889 until the death of A. B. Simpson in 1919, emphasizing the work of John Salmon, pioneer of the Alliance work in Canada. The final chapter deals with the history of the mother church of much of the subsequent ministry of the Alliance in Canada, the (Toronto) Alliance Tabernacle (now known as First Alliance Church). Cf. 1383.

1383. ———. *Rebirth: The Redevelopment of the Christian and Missionary Alliance in Canada*. Willowdale, Ont.: The Christian and Missionary Alliance in Canada, 1992. 487 p.

The sequel to 1382. Chronicles the revitalization of the C&MA in Canada following its post-World War I doldrums; its inexorable movement towards both denominational status and national autonomy; and its expansion into Western Canada, Quebec, and Canada's immigrant communities.

1384. Richardson, Kenneth. *Garden of Miracles: A History of the Africa Inland Mission*. London: Victory Press, 1968. 255 p.

Peter Cameron Scott (1867-1896) who founded the Africa Inland Mission in 1895, received his theological training at A. B. Simpson's New York Missionary Training Institute, joined the International Missionary Alliance, and served for several months as a missionary to the Congo (1890-1891) before being forced by ill health to return home.

1385. Richardson, Stanton (W)illard. *Praying in the Spirit: Handbook for Missionary Praying*. Minneapolis: Gopher State Litho, 1995. 125 p.

A guide to facilitate intercessory prayer for missionaries.

1386. ———. "The Relation of the Church and Israel to the Millennnium." Master's thesis, Wheaton College, 1946. 81 p.

The early church was premillennial in outlook. The (basically) literal approach of premillennialists accords well with the scriptural teaching that God's special plans for the Jewish people will not be fulfilled until Christ returns.

1387. ———. *Studies in Biblical Theology*. St. Paul, Minn.: St. Paul Bible College, 1969.

Designed as a textbook in biblical theology for the students of St. Paul Bible College. A somewhat uneven treatment of the fourfold Gospel that does not link divine healing with the Atonement, but gives sanctification, premillennial eschatology, and salvation extensive treatment. Includes a procedure for the experiential appropriation of sanctification and a lengthy criticism of the Pentecostal "evidence doctrine." Rejects the Calvinist understanding of predestination in favor of a mediating position (between Calvinism and Arminianism) vis-à-vis the perseverance of the saints.

1388. ———, ed. and comp. *To the Glory of God: Testimonies from Missionaries around the World*. Minneapolis: Gopher State Litho, 1994. 198 p.

Brief testimonies of more than 200 graduates of Crown College and its predecessors who have served as missionaries (most of the 200 are, or have been, Alliance missionaries.)

1389. Riley, William (B)ell (1861-1947). *Christian Science, or Fundamentals of Mrs. Eddy's Faith*. New York: Christian Alliance Pub. Co., 1899. 29 p.

Christian Science is neither Christian nor science, for it denies the existence of a personal God, a personal devil, matter, and sin; and it substitutes a Nirvana-like heaven for the Christian hope of the resurrection of the body.

1390. ———. *Divine Healing, or Does God Answer Prayer for the Sick?* South Nyack, N.Y.: Christian Alliance Pub. Co., 1899. 23 p.

A Baptist believer in divine healing interprets James 5:14-16 as an antidote to the doctrines of Spiritualism and Christian Science: sickness is real, God heals in response to anointing and prayer, and God promises to restore and forgive the sick who pray and have faith.

1391. ———. *The Gospel in Jonah, or Sunday Nights in Soul Winning*. New York: Christian Alliance Pub. Co., [ca. 1900]. 118 p.

1392. ———. *The Menace of Modernism*. New York: Christian Alliance Pub. Co., 1917. 181 p.

The false theology of liberalism leads to the corruption of morality.

1393. ———. *Modern Amusements vs. Church Membership*. New York: Christian Alliance Pub. Co., 1899. 54 p.

1394. ——— . *The Seven Churches of Asia*. New York: Christian Alliance Pub. Co., 1900. 151 p.

A transcript of talks on Rev. 1:1-3:22.

1395. ———. *Theosophy, or Buddhism Abroad*. New York: Christian Alliance Pub. Co., 1899. 29 p.

Theosophy has its origins in Buddhism; exalts intuition over revelation; and has a defective understanding of the nature of humankind, God, and salvation.

1396. Rivard, Eugene Francis. "The Hymnody of the Christian and Missionary Alliance (1891-1978) as a Reflection of Its Theology and Development." D.M.A. diss., Southwestern Baptist Theological Seminary, 1991. 427 p.

The vitality of the early Alliance derived in part from its ability to articulate its distinctive beliefs in its hymnody. After the 4th ed. of *Hymns of the Christian Life* Alliance hymnody declined to such a degree that the 5th ed. (1936) is more a reflection of the evangelical subculture than it is of Alliance distinctives. Subsequent editions have included fewer and fewer hymns by A. B. Simpson (who was by far the most prolific and successful Alliance hymn writer) and very few new hymns reflect Alliance doctrine. To revitalize its hymnody the C&MA must both solicit new (distinctively Alliance) hymns and update the language and music of its traditional hymns. Includes indexes to previously unindexed Alliance hymnals and a complete title and first line index to all of A. B. Simpson's hymns.

1397. ———. "Rediscovering the Music of A. B. Simpson." In *The Birth of a Vision*, eds. David F. Hartzfeld and Charles Nienkirchen, 75-106. Regina, Sask.: His Dominion, 1986.

A. B. Simpson's hymns effectively convey the theology of the "fourfold Gospel." They inspired the first generation of the C&MA and contributed to the movement's success. Yet his hymns are rarely sung in Alliance congregations today because they are written in the archaic Gospel song genre, because the music to which many of them are set is hard to sing, and because many of them are simply too long. The music to some of Simpson's hymns needs to be rewritten, and a new generation of Alliance hymn writers needs to translate the Alliance idiom for the modern churchgoer; yet the lyrics of Simpson's hymns retain a timeless devotional value.

1398. Robb, Alfred Pierce, and Egerton Seitz Robb. *Malembe-Ntaloo: Gentle and Friendly of a Great Price.* n. p.: [198-?]. 28 p.

Biography of Alfred Pierce Robb and Christine Seitz Robb, C&MA missionaries to the Congo (1896-1898). Includes poetry by A. P. Robb.

1399. Robert, Dana L. *American Women in Mission: A Social History of Their Thought and Practice.* Macon, Ga.: Mercer University Press, 1996.

A. B. Simpson's International Missionary Alliance was the first American missionary organization to send sizeable numbers of women to the mission field as faith missionaries. "Simpson's premillennial theology signified a seismic shift in missiology, as it rejected Christian civilization as a rationale for missions" (p. 199). Women were attracted to the International Missionary Alliance because of its premillennial theology, and because it was the first mission to send out women as evangelists under the same terms as men. Women opened Alliance work in Japan, Palestine, and Indonesia. Jenny Fuller of India was considered to be one of the best educated and most articulate faith missionaries of her time. Women held prominent administrative positions in the Alliance, both at home and abroad, and some even served as presidents of branches of the Christian Alliance, "a position tantamount to being pastors of a local church" (p. 204). As the C&MA moved towards acknowledging its denominational status, the number of women in positions of leadership declined steadily (despite the fact that women comprised the bulk of the C&MA's missionary force) so that by mid-century the Alliance's leadership was all male.

1400. Robinson, S. (M)iles. *The Psychology of Saving Faith*. New York: Christian Alliance Pub. Co., 1926. 163 p.

An exposition of the various manifestations of triunity in the Scriptures with respect to salvation and the Christian life.

1401. Robinson, William. *Heart-Throbs: A Book of Verse*. London: Arthur H. Stockwell, 1935. 32 p.

Robinson was an Alliance missionary to Vietnam.

1402. Roffe (A)lfred (W)illiam (1866-1947). *The Divine Touch*. Gravenhurst, Ont.: n.p., 1926. 34 p.

A series of sermons on the book of Daniel, advocating a life of self-effacement and humility as the way to both intimacy with God and the personal appropriation of the power of God.

1403. ———. *Exploring the Faith Realm*. Gravenhurst, Ont.: n.p., 1928. 45 p.

1404. ———. *Five Thousand Miles in Answer to Prayer, or Modern Miracles on the Western Prairies*. Gravenhurst, Ont.: by the author, 1924. 36 p.

A record of the itineration (ca. 1924) throughout the Canadian Prairies of Roffe and Mary Butterfield on behalf of the C&MA. They held missionary and evangelistic meetings and raised money for missions. Personal and place names have unfortunately been omitted from the account.

1405. ———. *God's Method of Developing Faith*, rev. ed. Gravenhurst, Ont.: by the author, [192-?]. 17 p.

A study, based in 1 Ki. 17, of how God developed the faith of the prophet Elijah.

1406. ———. *God's Way Up Is Down: A Deep Lesson from a Familiar Study*. New York: Christian Alliance Pub. Co., 1927. 37 p.

The life of Joseph the patriarch illustrates the spiritual truth that self-abasement is the road to effective service, a rich spiritual life, and, ultimately, exaltation by God.

———, joint author. *New Light: Containing a Full Account of Recent Salvation Army Troubles in Canada.*

See 1276.

1407. Roffe (G)eorge Edward (1905-). "Christianity." *Friendship: Special Supplement: Buddhism and Christianity*. [Laos?]: n.p., [197-?]. 17 p.

An overview of salvation history and Christian doctrine. Text in Lao and English.

1408. ———. "Laos." In *The Church in Asia,* ed.. Donald E. Hoke, 391-409. Chicago: Moody Press, 1975.

A brief but thorough history of the church in Laos, with particular reference to the missionary efforts of the C&MA and to the author's own experiences on the field.

1409. Rohrer, Norman B. *The Remarkable Story of Mom LeTourneau.* Wheaton, Ill.: Tyndale House, 1985. 146 p.

Evelyn Peterson LeTourneau (1900-) was the wife of inventor/industrialist and prominent Alliance layperson R. G. LeTourneau.

1410. Rohrer, Norman B., and Peter Deyneka, Jr. *Peter Dynamite, Twice-born Russian: The Story of Peter Deyneka-Missionary to the Russian World.* Grand Rapids: Baker, 1975. 192 p.

Converted in 1920 through the ministry of Paul Rader, Peter Deyneka

(1898-1987) attended (the C&MA's) St. Paul Bible Training School and went on to found the Slavic Gospel Association.

1411. Rohrick, Lisa M. *Any Road, Any Cost: The Cambodia and Congo Conflicts: Real Life Accounts of Peace in Crisis*. Camp Hill, Pa.: Christian Publications, 1998. 231 p.

The story of the events surrounding the evacuation of Alliance missionaries in 1997 from Cambodia and Congo (Brazzaville) during the civil wars that ravaged both countries. Those missionaries based in Cambodia returned to find their homes and possessions untouched, those based in Brazzaville lost all of their possessions and have yet to return.

1412. ———. *Both Feet on God's Path: The Story of Julie Fehr*. The Jaffray Collection of Missionary Portraits, 16. Camp Hill, Pa.: Christian Publications, 1996. 205 p.

Julie Fehr (1937-1994) served for 30 years as a (Canadian) C&MA missionary to Gabon, working as a Bible translator and church planter. She was also the administrator of theological education by extension programs for the C&MA for all of West Africa.

1413. Ronzheimer, Philip P. *"Trust Me! Trust Me!": Healing and the Sovereignty of God*. Camp Hill, Pa.: Christian Publications, 1992. 17 p.

Those who pray in faith for healing are either healed or empowered to live with their infirmity in such a way that they can fulfill the ministry God has assigned them.

1414. Rose, Darlene Deibler. *Evidence Not Seen: A Woman's Miraculous Faith in a Japanese Prison Camp during World War II.* San Francisco: Harper and Row, 1988. 224 p.

This story of Darlene Deibler's more than two years in Kampili prison camp (1943-1945) is the most frank, well written, and thorough account of the life of Alliance internees in Japanese prison camps (cf. also 766). It also provides illuminating biographical information on R. A. Jaffray.

1415. ———. *The Stone Age Speaks Again*. New York: The Christian and Missionary Alliance, 1948.

1416. Roseberry, Edith M. (1879-1965). *Kansas Prairies to African Forests: The Pioneer Spirit.* n.p.: by the author, 1957. 51 p.

Edith Roseberry (née Plattenburg) joined the Alliance mission to Sierra Leone in 1908. She married R. S. Roseberry in 1914. In 1919 the

Roseberrys became the first Protestant missionaries to open a station in French West Africa (Baro, Guinea). By the end of their missionary service (1953) the C&MA had established 33 mission stations and three Bible schools on this field.

Roseberry (R)obert (S)herman (1883-1976), joint author. *Among the Cliff Dwellers of French West Africa.*

See 1077.

1417. ———. *Black Magic: The Challenge.* Chicago: World Wide Prayer and Missionary Union, 1935. 56 p.

Mostly an anecdotal overview of the progress of missions in West Africa. Despite the title, only one chapter discusses witchcraft, superstition, and other aspects of the animistic cultures of the region.

1418 . ———. *The Niger Vision.* Harrisburg, Pa.: Christian Publications, 1934. 254 p.

A description of the Upper Niger Valley, and a firsthand account of the "pioneer" and "evangelistic" periods of the C&MA mission in "the Soudan." Although Alliance missionaries first arrived in French West Africa in 1890, the mission did not begin significant work in the region until 1919.

1419. ———. *The Soul of French West Africa.* Harrisburg, Pa.: Christian Publications, 1947. 175 p.

Brief biographies of exemplary native Christians (both men and women) who were converted as a result of the C&MA's missionary work in French West Africa.

1420. ———. *Training Men for God in French West Africa.* New York: Christian and Missionary Alliance, 1940. 31 p.

This sequel to 1418 describes "the Bible school period" in Alliance missions in "the Soudan" with reference to the three schools that the C&MA had established in the area by 1939.

1421. Ross, Byron W. *Training Lay Workers.* New York: Christian and Missionary Alliance. Foreign Department, [195-?]. 38 p.

An apologetic for training lay pastors. Includes instructions on how to set up a training program and a sample curriculum. Based on the author's experience as a C&MA missionary to the Philippines.

1422. Rossiter (F)rederick H. (1862-1962). *From Bootblack to Pulpit: The Story of a Homeless Waif.* Spokane, Wash.: Stala Print and Pub. Co., [1960?]. 91 p.

The "rags to spiritual riches" autobiography of an Alliance pastor whose ministry was based in Washington State. Also includes some biographical material on E. D. Whiteside. Introduction by A. W. Tozer.

1423. Rounds (T)ryphena (C)ecilia (1843-1939). *The Broken Lamp, or the Spirit's Victory over Temper*. Chicago: Chicago Hebrew Mission, [ca. 1900]. 8 p.

Her personal testimony.

1424. ———. *God's Judgments upon the Enemies of Israel*. Chicago: Chicago Hebrew Mission, [191-?]. 31 p.

A catalogue of the relevant biblical passages.

1425. ———. *Is the Day of Grace Passed for the Jew?* Chicago: Chicago Hebrew Mission, [191-?]. 16 p.

An apologetic for the evangelization of the Jews.

1426. ———. *The Offerings*. New York: Christian Alliance Pub. Co., 1925. 124 p.

Christ's sacrificial death is the antitype to which all of the sacrifices offered in the Old Testament refer. Certain sacrifices mentioned in Ezek. 40-47 will only be made in a rebuilt temple in Jerusalem when Jesus returns and Israel (i.e., the Jewish people) acknowledges him as Messiah.

1427. ———. *The Stamp Album, or Believe That Ye Have Received.* Chicago: T. C. Rounds, [191-?]. 7 p.

A meditation on trust.

1428. ———. *"Stopped the Mouths of Lions": A True Story*. Chicago: Chicago Hebrew Mission, [192-?]. 4 p.

The "Gospel auto" of the Chicago Hebrew Mission is pelted with projectiles by angry Jews who stop the car. One man puts his ferocious bulldog into the car, but the dog, instead of attacking the occupants (miraculously) becomes so docile that the owner removes it in disgust.

1429. Rudy, Stella M. *Children of China*. Chicago: Rand, McNally and Co., 1937. 64 p.

An illustrated popular ethnography based on the author's 15 years as an Alliance missionary to China.

1430. ———. *More Rainbow Missionary Stories*. Harrisburg, Pa.: Christian Publications, 1946. 187 p.

1431. ———. *New Rainbow Missionary Stories*. Harrisburg, Pa.: Christian Publications, 1943. 192 p.

1432. ———. *Rainbow Missionary Stories*. Harrisburg, Pa.: Christian Publications, 1930. 190 p.

1433. Ryle, John (C)harles (1816-1900). *Prayer*. Harrisburg, Pa.: Christian Publications, 1973. 55 p.

Reprint of a chapter from his *Practical Religion* (London: W. Hunt, 1879).

1434. Sahlberg, Corrine S. (1921-). *Please Leave Your Shoes at the Door: The Story of Elmer and Corrine Sahlberg*. The Jaffray Collection of Missionary Portraits, 5. Camp Hill, Pa.: Christian Publications, 1992. 191 p.

Corinne and Elmer John (1920-) Sahlberg were C&MA missionaries to Thailand (1950-1985). Includes many excerpts from the author's letters describing the Sahlbergs' family life, revealing her concerns for her children in boarding school in war-torn Vietnam, and recounting her oft-repeated experience of being a "widow with a husband." Cf. 738.

1435. Sailor, Ella. *Flame of Freedom*. Regina, Sask.: Canadian Revival Fellowship, 1974. 50 p.

An account of the revival in Western Canada that began in Saskatoon, Sask., on 13 October 1971, at a meeting led by Alliance Evangelists Ralph and Lou Sutera.

1436. Salmon, John. *Fifty-two Years for God*. Toronto: J. J. Gibbons, Limited, 1907.

Salmon's spiritual autobiography.

1437. ———. "Practical Thoughts on the Sixteenth Psalm." *Triumphs of Faith*, July 1887, 158-61.

1438. [———]. *A Work of Faith and Labor of Love*. Toronto: s.n., 1903. On Bethany Orphanage, an Alliance work in Toronto that lasted 1893-1928.

1439. *Sample Pages from Hymns of the Christian Life Nos. 1, 2 and 3 Combined*. New York: Christian Alliance Pub. Co., [1908?]. 66 p.

1440. *Samuel Morris: A Spirit-Filled Life*. n.p., [192-?]. 32 p.

A compilation of reminiscences by Stephen Merritt, T. C. Reade, and Arthur Jordan covering the basic biographical information found in 62.

1441. Saphir, Adolph. *The Epistle to the Hebrews: An Exposition*, 5th American ed. New York: Christian Alliance Pub. Co., [192-?]. 2 vols.

1442. ———. *The Lord's Prayer*. London: James Nisbet, 1869. Reprint, New York: Christian Alliance Pub. Co., [192-?] 420 p.

1443. Sauer, James B. "TEE in Zaire—Mission or Movement." *Evangelical Review of Theology* 2 (October 1978): 290-95.

Mentions the formative role played by the C&MA in establishing theological education by extension in Zaire.

1444. "Saved at Sea: An Octogenarian's Testimony." *The Missionary Witness*, November 1911, 285, 287.

A tribute to John Salmon, patriarch of the Canadian C&MA, on his departure from Toronto.

Sawin, John, joint author. *All for Jesus: God at Work in the Christian and Missionary Alliance over One Hundred Years*.

See 1207.

1445. Sawin, John. "The Fourfold Gospel." In *The Birth of a Vision*, eds. David F. Hartzfeld and Charles Nienkirchen, 1-28. Regina, Sask.: His Dominion, 1986.

"Jesus our Saviour" stresses the need for personal salvation and the mandate of Christians to evangelize; "Jesus our Sanctifier" describes a post-salvation work of grace through which the Christian is separated from sin, becomes dedicated to God, and receives the filling of the Holy Spirit; "Jesus our Healer"(which Simpson considered to be subordinate to the other three "folds") involves the appropriation of the life of Christ as the source of one's bodily life; " Jesus our Coming King" links the personal and premillennial return of Christ with the preaching of the Gospel to all nations.

1446. ———. "Publications of Albert B. Simpson." In *The Birth of a Vision*, eds. David F. Hartzfeld and Charles Nienkirchen, 279-305. Regina, Sask.: His Dominion, 1986.

As an author A. B. Simpson is at his best in the articles and editorials he wrote for the periodicals he edited. The majority of the 116 books he either wrote or edited consist of transcripts of sermons he had preached at the Gospel Tabernacle His oeuvre comprises sermons, commentaries, correspondence courses, devotional literature, doctrinal works, hymn books, poetry, promotional literature, and travelogues. Includes a list of Simpson's published books and a record of the title changes in the periodicals he edited.

1447. ———. "The Response and Attitude of Dr. A. B. Simpson and the Christian and Missionary Alliance to the Tongues Movement of 1906-1920 ." In *Azusa Street Revisited: Facts of the American Pentecostal Experience: Society for Pentecostal Studies Conference, Costa Mesa, Calif., November 13-15, 1986.* n.p., 1986. 72 p.

Simpson believed that the gift of tongues was a legitimate and valuable manifestation of the contemporary outpouring of the Holy Spirit. His diary indicates that he sought the gift fervently, but never received it. His pre- and post-Azusa Street views remained unaltered: the gift is legitimate, but it is not the indispensable evidence of the baptism of the Holy Spirit. Includes extensive indexes to C&MA writings on tongues and 24 p. of extracts from the writings of Simpson and his co-workers.

1448. Schaller, Lyle E. *Tattered Trust: Is There Hope for Your Denomination?* Nashville: Abingdon Press, 1996. 136 p.

The American C&MA's decision, in the mid-1970s, to plant churches among new immigrants led to a doubling of its membership by 1994. The C&MA is thus an example of how missionary passion, coupled with innovative and creative leadership and a flexible organizational structure, can lead to the revitalization of a denomination (p. 38-40).

1449. Schenk, Raymond (W)alter. "A Study of the New Testament Bases for the Teaching of Dr. Albert B. Simpson on Divine Healing." Master's thesis, Wheaton College, 1968. 80 p.

A. B. Simpson believed that it is God's will to heal every Christian, that Christians lacking in faith should avail themselves of some form of medical intervention, and that truly spiritual Christians should seek healing "without means." Although Simpson's views were not always based on accurate exegesis, they were at least logically consistent; and they were for the most part consistent with Simpson's own experience (although he himself used eyeglasses and throat lozenges).

1450. Schiele, David C. *Unity and Rest in Christ Himself.* Kaleden, B.C.: by the author, 1994. 48 p.

A. B. Simpson was mistaken in spending five years of his life seeking a deeper and fuller baptism of the Holy Spirit, since the baptism of the Holy Spirit is not a post-conversion experience. Simpson should rather have rested in the truths embodied in his famous tract *Himself.* Christians may need to "take a crisis action toward God" (p. 48) of recommitment, but they do not need to seek a second baptism of the Holy Spirit.

1451. Schlaizer, Ilse Lefton. *A World Tour with Jesus*. Harrisburg, Pa.: Christian Publications, 1949. 128 p.

Missionary stories for children.

1452. Schneppmueller, Vivian Bosworth. *A Testimony of Salvation and Healing*. St. Paul, Minn.: by the author [192-?]. 16 p.

A biography of C&MA evangelist H. Karl Schneppmueller. His wife Vivian was the daughter of F. F. Bosworth.

1453. *The School That Vision Built: Centennial Review of Nyack College, 1882-1982*. [Nyack, N.Y.]: [Nyack College?], [1982?]. 48 p.

A very thorough account, especially valuable for its many historical photographs. Nyack Missionary Training Institute actually opened in 1883. Cf. 880.

1454. Schoonmaker, Violet. *Christain* [sic] *Schoonmaker: A Man Who Loved the Will of God*. Landour, India: Hyratt Press, 1959. 47 p.

Christian H. Schoonmaker (1881-1919) experienced the Pentecostal revival at Nyack (1905-1907) and in India, where he served as a C&MA missionary from 1907 until he and his wife joined the Assemblies of God in 1914.

1455. Schroeder, David (E)ldon. *The Broken God: Power under Control.* Grand Rapids: Baker, 1994. 134 p.

Meditations on the passion of Jesus Christ. Intended for use in small group ministries devoted to the character formation of men.

1456. ———. *The Centrality of Jesus Christ in the Fourfold Gospel.* Camp Hill, Pa.: Christian Publications, 1994. 18 p.

The genius of the C&MA is not the doctrines of salvation, sanctification, healing, and the second coming, but "Jesus as the Savior, Jesus as the Sanctifier, Jesus as the Healer, and Jesus as the Coming King" (p. 2). This truth needs to be rediscovered if only because "Focusing on the Great Commission has subtly shifted our missiology to being one of duty" (p. 17).

1457. ———. *Ephesians: God's Grace and Guidance in the Church*. The Deeper Life Pulpit Commentary. Camp Hill, Pa.: Christian Publications, 1998. 254 p.

1458. ———. *Follow Me: The Master's Plan for Men*. Grand Rapids: Baker, 1992. Reprint, Camp Hill, Pa.: Christian Publications, 1993. 243 p.

A "strategy for Christian character formation" by the director of higher education for the C&MA.

1459. ———. *Matthew: The King and His Kingdom: God's Rule and Reign in My Life*. The Deeper Life Pulpit Commentary. Camp Hill, Pa.: Christian Publications, 1995. 298 p.

1460. ———. *Solid Ground: Facts of Faith for Young Christians*. Harrisburg, Pa.: Christian Publications, 1982. 255 p.

Attempts to rehabilitate catechetical instruction and to introduce teenagers to Alliance distinctives in a nonthreatening way.

1461. Schultz (D)aniel Y. (1865-1918). *The Paraclete*. New York: Christian Alliance Pub. Co., 1903. 156 p.

A compilation of classroom lectures, and articles in The Christian and Missionary Alliance, on the person and work of the Holy Spirit. Includes instructions on how to be filled with the Spirit.

1462. Scorgie, Glen G. "A. B. Simpson, Modernity and Holiness." In *Studies in Canadian Evangelical Renewal: Essays in Honour of Ian S. Rennie*, eds. Kevin Quast and John Vissers, 137-54. Markham, Ont.: FT Publications, 1996.

Simpson, like other advocates of the deeper life, responded to modernism by stressing the availability of a compelling personal experience of the supernatural. The radical dualism of his theology reflects this preoccupation with the supernatural: the divine life of Christ completely supplants the human element. Hence he preferred divine healing to medical treatment and regarded salvation and sanctification as punctiliar crisis experiences to which human effort could not contribute. His worldview ended up being more dualistic than that of Scripture.

1463. *The Secret That Is Not a Secret*. New York: The Christian and Missionary Alliance, 1960. 7 p.

Describes the Alliance mission in Colombia, 1928-60.

1464. *Seeking Lost Tribes*. New York: The Christian and Missionary Alliance, 1950. 4 p.

Surveys the work of Alliance missionaries among tribal peoples of Asia, Africa, and South America.

1465. Seim, James. "The Alliance Centennial Advance: A Geographical Analysis." *His Dominion* 12 (winter 1986): 2-16.

A statistical analysis of church growth in the C&MA in Canada and the United States in light of the Alliance's goal of doubling its inclusive membership between 1977 and 1987.

1466. Senft, Frederic (H)erbert (1857-1925). "A. B. Simpson's Spirit-Given Gifts: A Study of the Man as Organizer, Author, Editor, Hymn-Writer, Preacher, Friend and Home-Maker." *The Sunday School Times*, 29 November 1919, 696-97.

1467. ———. *Disease and the Divine Remedy*, rev. ed. New York: Christian Alliance Pub. Co., [190-?]. 14 p.

Disease comes via the fall, the direct agency of Satan, the curse of the law, and demonic possession. Healing through prayer can be had by all believers through Christ's redemption. Those who are not healed are deficient in some aspect of godliness.

1468. ———. *Divine Healing: Its Principles and Practice*. New York: Christian Alliance Pub. Co., [190-?]. 14 p.

An apology for "healing in the Atonement." Claims that "there are probably no more failures proportionately among those who claim healing than those who profess to be saved and sanctified."

1469. ———. *How to Keep in Health*. Arlington, Tex.: The Book Room, n.d. 8 p.

The principles are: resting in God, the Atonement, and the indwelling Holy Spirit; daily prayer and Bible study; a healthy lifestyle; a clear conscience; wholesome speech; Christian fellowship; generous giving; and a joyful spirit.

1470. ———. *Making the Best of Things*. Philadelphia: Hebron Tract Society, n.d. 4 p.

The need for cheerfulness in trials is epitomized in the story of a beggar who decorated his crutches for Christmas.

1471. ———. *The Secret and Sense of God's Presence*. Philadelphia: Hebron Tract Society, n.d.. 6 p.

Seven steps towards "maintaining a sense of the presence and joy of God," which is "the secret of the victorious Christian life and fruitful service" (p. 3).

1472. Senft, Ruth (A)nnie. *Jesus. . . My Physician*, 2nd ed. South Nyack, N.Y.: Christian Alliance Pub. Co., 1898. 13 p.

Recounts her miraculous healing and the circumstances surrounding her joining the Alliance.

1473. ———. *Jottings from a Fruitful Life*. Glendale, Calif.: Mission Press, 1930. 25 p.

A biographical sketch, by his wife, of Frederic Herbert Senft (1857-1925) president of the C&MA, 1924-1925.

1474. *Sermons in a Sentence*. Dawson Creek, B.C.: Chapel of Song, 1965. 32 p.

"This booklet commemorates the 10th year of Chapel of Song, broadcast over CJDC, Dawson Creek, B. C." Chapel of Song was a ministry of the Dawson Creek Alliance Church.

1475. *Sermons in a Sentence*. Moose Jaw, Sask.: Tabernacle Tidings, 1955. 39 p.

"This booklet commemorates the 15th year of Tabernacle Tidings, broadcast over CHAB, Moose Jaw, Sask." Tabernacle Tidings was a ministry of the Moose Jaw Alliance Tabernacle.

1476. *Seventy-One Years of World Service*. New York: The Christian and Missionary Alliance, 1959. 10 p.

Rev. ed. of 1861.

1477. Shannon, Jack. "A History of the Christian and Missionary Alliance in Argentina." D.Miss. diss., Trinity Evangelical Divinity School, 1989. 286 p.

This frank analysis of the C&MA's work in Argentina concludes that the church-planting efforts of the mission and the Alianza Cristiana y

Misionera de la Argentina have been less than successful, partly because of poor decisions (made unilaterally) by the leaders of the mission. For example, the mission almost destroyed the church on the eve of the Great Depression by deciding to cut subsidies in order to accelerate indigenization. The most valuable contribution the Alliance has made to the establishment of evangelical Christianity in Argentina is the Bible college it founded and continues to maintain, the Instituto Biblico de Buenos Aires.

1478. ———. "Simpson and Emilio Olssen: The Birth and Death of a Grand Plan." *His Dominion* 16 (March 1990): 15-22.

Simpson's unfortunate decision (1897) to entrust the Alliance's Argentine and South American mission to the footloose and flaky Emilio Olssen stemmed in part from his own philosophy of missions: to preach the Gospel to "every nation," to establish converts in each nation as "a witness," and thereby to usher in the return of Christ. Olssen was relieved of his duties in 1899, but the Alliance did not begin to do serious church planting in Argentina until the 1930s.

1479. *Sharing the Gospel with Brazil*. New York: The Christian and Missionary Alliance, [195-?]. 3 p.

Explains the decision of the Alliance to set up a mission in Brazil.

1480. Shaw, George. *Acquainted with Grief*, 4th ed. n.p.: Caxton Press, 1906. 99 p.

Meditations on Isa. 53 in light of Christ's passion.

1481. ———. *Outside the Gate*. n.p.: The Caxton Press, 1915. 84 p.

A devotional work intended to complement 1480 as an aid to meditation on Passion Week.

1482. ———. *The Spirit in Redemption,* Nyack [i.e., 3rd] ed. New York: Christian Alliance Pub. Co., 1910. 414 p.

A devotional study from a deeper-life perspective by an instructor at the Missionary Training Institute.

1483. *She Hath Done What She Could*. New York: n.p., [1928?]. 10 p.

A tribute to Lizzie K. Brubacher (1856-1928), sister of A. B. Simpson's associate L. Keller Brubacher, who was noted for her work in raising funds for an orphanage in India.

1484. Shell, Richard (L)ee (1955-). "John Wesley and A. B. Simpson on Sanctification." Master's thesis, Asbury Theological Seminary, 1991. 108 p.

Simpson and Wesley both treat sanctification as a post-conversion crisis experience, but Simpson does not share Wesley's emphasis on perfection. He stresses, rather, Christ's indwelling of the sanctified believer and the believer's appropriation of Christ's holiness.

1485. Shepard, Louise (1865-1928). *Heavenly Manna: Bible Messages for a Month.* New York: Christian Alliance Pub. Co., 1898. 119 p.

Meditations on the Christian life.

1486. Shepherd, Jack F. "Church-Mission Relations 'at Home.' " In *Missions in Creative Tension: The Green Lake '71 Compendium,* ed. Vergil Gerber, 124-53. South Pasadena, Calif.: William Carey Library, 1971.

Enumerates and describes tensions between missions and their sending churches. Suggests guidelines for evaluating, modifying, or revising church-mission relationships in the sending country. Proposes changes in how such relationships are structured.

1487. ———. "Mission-and Syncretism." In *The Church's Worldwide Mission: An Analysis of the Current State of Evangelical Foreign Missions and a Strategy for Future Activity*, ed. Harold Lindsell, 85-95. Waco, Tex.: Word Books, 1966.

Enumerates the kinds of syncretism that the church has so far encountered in its missionary activity and suggests a strategy for overcoming the problem.

1488. Shepson, Charles. *A Heart for Imbabura: The Story of Evelyn Rychner.* The Jaffray Collection of Missionary Portraits, 6. Camp Hill, Pa.: Christian Publications, 1992. 183 p.

Minnesotan Evelyn Rychner, who served as a C&MA missionary to Ecuador (1947-1989) played a key role in establishing the evangelical church among the Quechua-speaking Otavalan Indians of Imbabura province. Cf. 734.

1489. ———. *Hidden Manna.* Toccoa Falls, Ga.: Toccoa Falls College Press, 1995. 217 p.

Daily devotionals written by Shepson (a C&MA pastor) for his terminally ill wife.

1490. ———. *How to Know God's Will*. Beaverlodge, Alta.: Horizon House, 1981. 156 p.

God leads in a variety of ways those who seek to know him and his will. Among these ways are: closed doors, specific instructions, sanctified reason, and inner peace.

1491. Short, John N. (1841-1922). *Divine Healing*. Chicago: Christian Witness Co., [189-?]. 39 p.

An announcement in a newspaper indicates that A. B. Simpson will not attend a certain meeting due to illness. Now, if healing is in the Atonement, and if Christ is indeed both his physical and spiritual healer, then Simpson should not be sick, unless he is also spiritually infirm. Since Simpson's experience does not substantiate his theory of divine healing the theory should be rejected.

1492. Shrier, J. Clarence (1910-). *The God of Health*. Harrisburg, Pa.: Christian Publications, 1968. 88 p.

Sermons on healing from the perspective of one who, despite his having suffered a ten-year illness, continues to believe that healing is a dimension of the Atonement.

1493. ———. *I Don't Know What Your God Can Do, but My God Can Do Anything*. Beaverlodge, Alta.: Horizon House, 1975. 93 p.

The autobiography of a pastor of the Christian and Missionary Alliance in Canada.

1494. Sigountos, James G. (1956-). "Did Early Christians Believe Pagan Religions Could Save?" In *Through No Fault of Their Own?: The Fate of Those Who Have Never Heard*, eds. William V. Crockett and James G. Sigountos, 229-41. Grand Rapids: Baker, 1991.

Early Christians may have had a more open-minded attitude to pagan religions than is commonly believed. However, contra the contentions of unitive pluralists such as Paul Knitter, they never considered non-Christian religions to be an alternative path to God, but rather believed that even the most sincere follower of such religions was lost.

1495. Simon, Otto A. (1897-). *The Rock That Followed Me: An Autobiography*. Ann Arbor, Mich.: printed by Cushing Malloy, [197-?]

Simon eventually left the C&MA for the Independent Fundamental Churches of America.

Simpson (A)lbert (B)enjamin (1843-1919), joint author. *A. W. Tozer and A. B. Simpson on Spiritual* Warfare.
See 2219.

1496. Simpson (A)lbert (B)enjamin (1843-1919). *Acts*. Christ in the Bible, vol. 16. New York: Alliance Press Co., 1904. 203 p.

Sermons on selected texts. On Acts 1:8: "we should lead the convert to the altar of consecration and never leave him until he has been sealed and sanctified by the . . . Spirit and saved from backsliding and defeat" (p. 40). Cf. 1837.

1497. ———. *Aggressive Christianity*. Christian Alliance Tracts. Nyack, N.Y.; New York: Christian Alliance Pub. Co., [1899?]. 23 p.

A missionary sermon preached at the close of the Nyack Convention, 10 September 1899. The " distinctive principles of the work of the [C&MA are:] absolute faith in supernatural things and a supernatural God . . . intense aggressiveness in . . . work for God . . . [and outreach] to the regions beyond" (p. 3-4).

1498. ———. *All in All, or Christ in Colossians*. New York: Alliance Press Co., [1901?]. 65 p.

Three sermons on selected passages. "Christ is all in all in the Trinity . . . the Father is pleased to express Himself in the Son, to pour Himself into Christ and stand back while Christ fills the picture and reveals the Father" (p. 9). Cf. 1593 and 1789.

1499. ———. *All Things New*. Living Truths, vol. 1, no. 15. Nyack, N.Y.: Christian Alliance Pub. Co., 1901. 20 p.

A New Year's sermon on Rev. 21:5-7. "Why should it be thought a wild and idle speculation that some day the Bride of the Lamb with her glorious Lord shall be permitted to pass from world to world on some celestial wedding tour " (p. 20).

1500. ———. *The Alliance Missionary Enterprise—What Is It?* New York: Christian Alliance Pub. Co., [1914?]. 4 p.

1501. ———. *An Ancient Pattern for Modern Christian Workers*. Christian Alliance Tracts. Nyack, N.Y.: Christian Alliance Pub. Co., [1899?]. 34 p.

A sermon on Neh. 2:18: "We want just work enough and organization enough to be a scaffolding for the invisible temple and to disappear when He appears and give place to Him" (p. 12).

1502. ———. *Annual Survey of the Christian and Missionary Alliance 1915*. New York: Christian Alliance Publishing Company, 1916. 38 p.

"Submitted by the President at the Annual Council, May 24-28, 1916, at Wheaton, Ill."

1503. ———. *The Apostolic Church*. Nyack, N.Y.: Christian Alliance Pub. Co., [1898?]. 238 p.

Sermons on selected passages in 1 Corinthians. The Lord's Supper "is . . . a means of grace and a channel of actual spiritual impartation from Him to those who are in living fellowship with Him." But "the physical presence of Christ in the Lord's Supper" is experienced in divine healing, which is nothing less than "the actual participation in the physical strength, vitality and energy of our risen Lord" (p. 129-30). Cf. 1603.

1504. ———. *The Apostolic Church*. Alliance Colportage Library, vol. 1, no. 22. Nyack, N.Y.: Christian Alliance Pub. Co., 1899. 118 p.

Cover title: *The Apostolic Church, Part I*. Reprint of p. 1-116 of 1503.

1505. ———. *The Apostolic Church. Part II*. Alliance Colportage Library, vol. 1, no. 23. Nyack, N.Y.: Christian Alliance Pub. Co., 1899. 121 p.

Reprint of p. 117-238 of 1503.

1506. ———. *The Apostolic Church; the Apostolic Testimony*. Christ in the Bible, vol. 18. New York: Alliance Press Co., [1904?] 395 p.

Combines 1503 and miscellaneous sermons on selected passages in 2 Corinthians. The apostle Paul is an example of "victory over self" (p. 276) and of the appropriation of Christ's supernatural life for the body (p. 303). Cf. 1823.

1507. ———. *Are You Living for His Coming?* Tracts for the Times. Lord's Coming Series. New York: Christian Alliance Pub. Co., [ca. 1900]. 8 p.

The practical results of believing in Jesus' imminent return are personal holiness, separation from the world, patience, zeal in evangelistic work, comfort in grief, and fearlessness vis-à-vis death.

1508. [———]. *Are You Ready for His Coming?* Tracts for the Times. Lord's Coming Series. New York: Christian Alliance Pub. Co., [ca. 1900]. 8 p.

Readiness for Christ's return involves: ensuring that one is a Christian, being baptised in the Holy Spirit, sanctification and cleansing, eager expectation, doing work that will stand the test of judgment, and ensuring that one's earthly affairs and personal relationships are in order.

1509. [———]. *Are You Satisfied?* New York: Christian Alliance Pub. Co., [ca. 1900]. 8 p.

Only Christ can satisfy the deepest longings of the human heart—be they physical, intellectual, emotional, or spiritual. The most attractive feature of Christianity is its promise of rest.

1510. ———. *Armageddon.* New York: Christian Alliance Pub. Co., [ca.1918]. 16 p.

A sermon on Rev. 16:16: Christians will not experience Armageddon, but they must be on their guard against the demon spirits that lie behind the spirits of the age (e.g., agnosticism, Romanism, Islam, liberal Protestantism) and must remain morally pure in light of the imminent return of Christ.

1511. ———. *Back to Patmos, or Prophetic Outlooks on Present Conditions.* New York: Christian Alliance Pub. Co., 1914. 103 p.

A meditation, from a premillennialist perspective, on the themes of Revelation. Evidently not, as were most of Simpson's books, a collection of sermons. Chapter 5, the "Parousia and Rapture" posits a rapture of the bride of Christ out of a great tribulation that has already begun. There will be an interval between this coming of the Lord "as a thief in the night" and his final glorious appearing. Simpson's comment that the rapture "will leave much behind. We fear it will leave many Christians" (p. 47) calls to mind his belief in a partial rapture, which is more explicitly set forth in 1661.

1512. ———. *Baptism and the Baptism of the Holy Spirit.* New York: Christian Alliance Pub. Co., [192-?]. 16 p.

Baptism symbolizes "voluntary and profoundly earnest surrender of our life to God in self-crucifixion (p. 6) . . . and that deeper life which comes to us through union with the Holy Spirit" (p. 12). The baptism of the Holy Spirit is both "an enduement of power for service . . ." and "a quickening of spirit for holy living" (p. 12). This experience marks the starting point of Christian experience or "walking in the Spirit," which involves partaking of the Spirit's "Motherhood of love and grace" (p. 15). Includes an account of Simpson's conversion from paedobaptism to believer's baptism.

1513. [———]. *The Baptism of the Spirit.* Tracts for the Times. Deeper Life Series. New York: Christian Alliance Pub. Co., [ca. 1900]. 8 p.

Many Christians know nothing more than John's baptism (Acts 19:21): repentance and a knowledge of forgiveness, but a powerlessness devoid of the fellowship of Christ. "The Holy Spirit is with all Christians, but He is only in those that have opened their hearts, surrendered their beings and wholly received Him" (p. 4). One must wait and prepare for this baptism, as did the apostles.

1514. ———. *The Best of A. B. Simpson.* Compiled by Keith M. Bailey. Camp Hill, Pa.: Christian Publications, 1987. 166 p.

Twelve representative selections from Simpson's works.

1515. ———. *The Best Thing.* [New York?]: [Christian Alliance Pub. Co.?], [189-?]. 32 p.

A sermon on 1 Cor. 13: "The word for love is the same as the word for grace, substantially. It is not an attainment, but an obtainment, not a human quality, but a divine grace . . . divinely wrought and supplied by the Spirit of Jesus Christ" (p. 24). Reprinted as chapter 11 of 1701.

1516. ———. "Bible and Modern Thought." *The Evangelical Christian,* February 1912, 41-42.

The Bible has survived the assaults of the higher critics (of whose writings Simpson seems to have more than a passing knowledge) and remains authoritative and trustworthy.

1517. ———. *But God.* Harrisburg, Pa.: Christian Publications, 1966. 89 p.

Reprint of 1519, with an additional chapter of poetry by A. B. Simpson.

1518. ———. *But God: An Unfolding of the All-Sufficiency and Infinite Variety of the Resources of God That Are Available to His People.* Harrisburg, Pa.: Christian Publications, [193-?]. 112 p.

Reprint of 1519.

1519. ———. *But God: The Resources and Sufficiency of God.* New York: Christian Alliance Pub. Co., 1899. 112 p.

Six sermons on God's providence as exemplified in the lives of Elijah, the Apostle Paul, Jacob, and Esther. Reprinted as Vol. 1, no. 14, of The Alliance Colportage Library. Cf. 1864.

1520. ———. *By His Stripes*. Tracts for the Times. Divine Healing Series. New York: Christian Alliance Pub. Co., [ca. 1900]. 8 p.

A story from the Hindu Scriptures (cf. 1860) precedes this exposition of Isa. 53:5. Christ's atonement covers both the sicknesses and sins of those who believe in Christ and obey him.

1521. ———. *A Call to Prayer*. South Nyack, N.Y.: Christian Alliance Pub. Co., 1897. 23 p.

A sermon on Jer. 33:2-3: "The great lack of Christianity today is the absence of the supernatural working of God. It is being reduced to a science . . . taught as a system . . . pressed as a ceremony and a form of religious culture. . . . God is waiting . . . to show Himself . . . the consuming fire of Pentecost" (p. 23).

1522. ———. *Called to Serve at Home*. Harrisburg, Pa.: Christian Publications, [196-?]. 15 p.

Reprint of 1846.

1523. [———]. *The Calling and Work of the Alliance*. New York: Free Literature Department of the Christian and Missionary Alliance, [ca. 1900]. 9 p.

The Alliance is preeminently a Christ movement: Christ is the source of salvation, holiness, physical healing, and the hope of the consummation of God's healing. The "Christ side" of holiness involves union with God through Christ by the power of the Holy Spirit. It comes through simple self-surrender, not religious toil, so it is neither self-perfection nor the simple "restoration of what Adam lost." The baptism of the Holy Spirit enables Alliance people to work in union with Christ for the evangelization of the world.

1524. ———. *Can the World Be Evangelized in Ten Years?* Missionary Alliance Leaflets. First Series, no. 7. New York: Christian Alliance Pub. Co., 1892.

Yes, if the 5,000 missionaries on the field at present can be matched by another 5,000. In most countries of the world the Gospel can be preached unhindered. Enough potential missionaries should easily be found, with God's help, as should the money to support them.

1525. ———. *The Challenge of Missions: A Selection of Dr. A. B. Simpson's Heart Messages from the Bible on the Necessity of World Evangelism*. New York: Christian Alliance Pub. Co., 1926. 68 p.

Five sermons previously published only in Alliance periodicals. "The Alliance has its place and calling to lead the people of God farther on into all the heights and depths of the life of Christ and further out into all the aggressive work which the children of God have so long neglected" (p. 58).

1526. ———. *The Child Spirit*. New York: Christian Alliance Pub. Co., [1894?]. 28 p.

The true meaning of Christmas is the birth of Christ in the consecrated, receptive, childlike, heart.

1527. ———. *China's Millions*. Tracts for the Times. Mission Series. New York: Christian Alliance Pub. Co., [ca. 1900]. 8 p.

1528. ———. *Christ for the Body: Divine Healing Viewed as a Present Privilege for Believing, Obedient Christians*. New York: Christian and Missionary Alliance, [196-?]. 8 p.

Reprint of 1690.

1529. ———. *Christ in Galatians; Christ in Ephesians*. Christ in the Bible, vol. 19. New York: Alliance Press Co., 1904. 254 p.

Reprint of 1612 and 1669.

1530. ———. *Christ in the Bible*. New York: Word, Work and World Pub. Co., 1886-.

"[A] simple and earnest attempt to unfold the spiritual teachings of the Holy Scriptures, especially with reference to the Person and work of the Lord Jesus Christ, and the development of the plan of Redemption throughout the various Dispensations" (preface to vol. 1). The expository section of each volume was to be followed by homiletical helps and supplementary illustrative material on history, geography, and other related subjects. On the fate of Simpson's lofty intentions for the series, see 1446.

1531. ———. *The Christ in the Bible Commentary*. Camp Hill, Pa.: Christian Publications, 1992-1994. 6 vols.

Reprint of 1530, with added Scripture index and Scripture references, updating of language, and substitution of NIV for AV. Publisher's introduction to vol. 1 provides a literary history of the first series. Vol. 4 (*Gospels and Acts*) reprints the volumes of the 2nd ed. which, except for *The Gospel of John*, consist of sermons. The publisher's foreword to vol.

6 (*Revelation*) includes a disclaimer stating that the C&MA no longer holds to Simpson's idiosyncratic interpretation of that book.

1532. ———. *Christ in the Tabernacle*. Tabernacle Sermons, vol. 9. New York: Christian Alliance Pub. Co., 1888. 158 p.

Seven sermons on the ways in which Christ is the antitype indicated by the multifaceted typological symbolism of the Old Testament tabernacle.

1533. ———. *Christ in the Tabernacle*. Camp Hill, Pa.: Christian Publications, 1985. 98 p.

Updated language and an additional sermon, "God Fills the Tabernacle," distinguish this from 1532.

1534. ———. *Christ in You: The Self-Life and the Christ Life*. Camp Hill, Pa.: Christian Publications, 1997. 133 p.

Reprint of 1537 and 1826.

1535. ———. *Christ Life*. Tabernacle Sermons, vol. 7. New York: Word, Work and World Pub. Co., 1888. 124 p.

Five sermons on the believer's mystical union with Christ: "Not Christ giving us life, but being life to us" (p. 16).

1536. ———. *The Christ Life*. New York: Christian Alliance Pub. Co., [1912?]. 104 p.

Reprint of 1535, with an additional chapter: "Christ the Life."

1537. ———. *The Christ Life*. The Alliance Colportage Series. New York: Christian Alliance Pub. Co., 1925. 121 p.

Includes selected poems by Simpson, an introduction by Walter Turnbull, and three sermons not in 1535. Cf. 1534.

1538. ———. *The Christ Life*. Harrisburg, Pa.: Christian Publications, 1980. 92 p.

Reprint of 1537, with a new foreword and fewer poems.

1539. ———. *The Christ of the Forty Days*. New York: Christian Alliance Pub. Co., [1890?]. 311 p.

Eight sermons on the post-resurrection/pre-ascension life and work of Christ. "For as He gradually and slowly withdrew from earth, lingering those forty days from the Cross to the Throne, so gradually He will return;

and before we see Him in the clouds, we shall be conscious of a nearer presence on the earth below" (p. 73).

1540. ———. *Christ Our Coming Lord*. New York: Christian Alliance Pub. Co., [ca. 1900]. 37 p.

"[T]he coming of the Lord precedes and introduces the millennium" (p. 13). It will bring "the most glorious and complete system of evangelization earth has ever seen" (p. 21). Simpson was also convinced that one of the signs of the Lord's coming that was being fulfilled in his day was the waning of the power of Islam. Reprint of chapter four of 1607.

1541. ———. *Christ Our Sanctifier: Selections from the Writings of the Late Dr. A. B. Simpson Expressing in His Own Words His Teachings on the Doctrine of Sanctification*. Harrisburg, Pa.: Christian Publications, 1947. 14 p.

Sanctification is inviting Christ to occupy the building constructed by the Holy Spirit in regeneration. It involves union with, and sharing the nature of, Christ. The necessary conditions are conviction of unholiness and entire surrender to God through faith. It is not a mark of personal achievement, nor is it a gradual growth in spiritual maturity, nor is it moral improvement or sinless perfection. Rather, it is a second work of grace wrought freely by Christ, which immediately raises one to a higher plane of Christian living. It is a new beginning that must be maintained by conscious dependence on Christ.

1542. ———. *The Christian Alliance Birthday Book: Containing a Scripture Text for Every Day in the Year, with an Appropriate Selection in Verse or Prose from the Writings of Rev. A. B. Simpson*. Compiled and edited by Louise Shepherd. New York: Christian Alliance Pub. Co., 1894. 381 p.

1543. ———. *Christian Courtesy*. Berachah Tracts. Second Series, no. 22. New York: The Word, the Work and the World Pub. Co., [1886?]. p. 199-203.

A sermon on Christian virtue based on Philemon and 1 and 2 John. Reprinted as "Christian Life in the Personal Epistles, or the Courtesies of Christian Life" in 1621.

1544. ———. *A Christian Hero: Life of Rev. William Cassidy*. [New York?]: [Word, Work and World Pub. Co.?], [1888?]. 32 p.

A tribute to the first Alliance missionary to China, who died in 1888 on his way to his posting.

1545. ———. *Christian Science Unchristian.* New York: Alliance Press Company, [189-?]. 16 p.

Christian Science is both un-Christian, in that it denies both the divinity and personality of Jesus, and unscientific.

1546. ———. *Christianity's Crime.* New York: Christian Alliance Pub. Co., [1892?]. 32 p.

Christians have been ignorant of, or indifferent to, the millions of people who are perishing without hope for want of having the Gospel preached to them. Reprinted in 1767.

1547. ———. *The Claims of China As a Mission Field.* Missionary Alliance Leaflets. First Series, no. 6. New York: Christian Alliance Pub. Co., 1892.

It is the most populous nation on earth, there are few native Christians, female children are routinely murdered, women are routinely degraded, and it is Satan's mightiest stronghold.

1548. ———. *The Claims of India.* Missionary Alliance Leaflets. First Series, no. 2. New York: Christian Alliance Pub. Co., [1892]. 9 p.

India is the second most populous nation on earth and the richest and most important of the pagan nations. It has suffered greatly at the hands of the British and from its own heathen practices. Missionary work, though still in its infancy, has been relatively successful.

1549. ———, comp. and ed. *A Cloud of Witnesses for Divine Healing,* 2nd ed. New York: Word, Work and World Pub. Co., 1887. 253 p.

Thirty-seven testimonies, mostly by prominent Alliance people, including George Pardington, whose contribution "The Crooked Made Straight" recounts his experience of physical healing to 1885. This edition contains a few more testimonies than the first edition, of which there are no known extant copies.

1550. ———. *The Coming One.* New York: Christian Alliance Pub. Co., 1912. 228 p.

A selection of 15 of Simpson's eschatological sermons, eight of which have been taken from *The Gospel of the Kingdom.* "[W]e are to preach the Gospel among all nations, not with the expectation that all will be converted. . . . Through us God *is* visiting the Gentiles . . . He is gathering a kind of 'first-fruits of His creatures' from every tribe and tongue" (p. 25-26).

1551. ———. *Committed.* New York: Christian Alliance Pub. Co., [190-?]. 22 p.

Christians must commit their sins, cares, bodies, future, service, and selves to Christ. Such consecration is not "the death knell of . . . their happiness," but rather a seeing, a feeling, and a leaning "upon a person, a great, true, living heart of love" (p. 17-18).

1552. ———. *Concerning Our Brother.* New York: Christian Alliance Pub. Co., [1903?]. 12 p.

A sermon on Gen. 42:21 and Num. 32:23 in which the sinful neglect of the Church to involve itself in the missionary enterprise is compared to Joseph's brothers' sin of not listening to Joseph's anguished cries, and to the shameful refusal of two of the tribes of Israel to help the other ten win their inheritance.

1553. ———. *Count Your Blessings: A Record of Bible Promise and of Answered Prayer.* Nyack, N.Y.; New York: Christian Alliance Pub. Co., [1910?]. 154 p.

A devotional calendar with two Scripture verses (a prayer and a promise) for each day of the year and space to record answers to prayer.

1554. ———. *The Cross of Christ.* New York: Christian Alliance Pub. Co., 1910. 157 p.

Sermons on Christ's atonement and resurrection and their implications for the Christian life. On the implications of the cross for missions to native North Americans: "'the white man's burden . . . means far more than Kipling ever dreamt . . . the millions [sic] of Indian tribes . . . are over against us in the most providential way. We have taken their country from them. We have driven them from their heritage. What have we given them in return?" (p. 84-85).

1555. ———. *Danger Lines in the Deeper Life.* South Nyack, N.Y.: Christian Alliance Pub. Co., 1898. 156 p.

Sermons on selected texts in Judges and Ruth. Deborah exemplifies the proper ministry of women: "she knew that she was called by her spiritual qualifications to lead her people to deliverance from the enemy, yet she took particular pains to find a man to be the executive officer of her plans" (p. 43). Cf. 1724.

1556. [———]. *Darkest Africa.* Tracts for the Times: Mission Series. New York: Christian Alliance Pub. Co., [ca. 1900]. 8 p.

1557. ———. *The Days of Heaven: A New Year's Greeting*. n.p., 1890. 16 p.

A sermon on the possibility that the last decade of the nineteenth century would be the closing age of world history. Cf. 1558.

1558. ———. *Days of Heaven on Earth: A Year Book of Devotional Readings from Scripture Texts and Living Truth*, new ed. rev. Harrisburg, Pa.: Christian Publications, [ca. 1945]. 371 p.

Reprint, with preface, of 1557.

1559. ———. *Days of Heaven upon Earth: A Book of Daily Devotional Readings from Scripture Texts and Living Truth*. Camp Hill, Pa.: Christian Publications, 1984. 369 p.

Reprint of 1560, albeit "carefully edited and contemporized." Includes a new introduction by H. Robert Cowles.

1560. ———. *Days of Heaven upon Earth: A Year Book of Scripture Texts and Living Truths*. New York: Christian Alliance Pub. Co.; Alliance Press Co., 1897. 371 p.

A devotional calendar. The "living truths" are set forth in meditations by Simpson.

1561. ———. *Decision for Christ*. New York: Christian and Missionary Alliance, 1911.

1562. ———. "The Deeper Meaning of Christmas." *The American Holiness Journal*, December 1982, 9-11.

Christ's incarnation and redemption need to be appropriated in devotion and love. As does the baptism of the Holy Spirit, which unites both body and spirit to Christ and gives the believer a foretaste of the complete realization of salvation at the Second Advent.

1563. ———. *Difficulties about Holiness*. n.p., [ca. 1900]. 6 p.

Answers to seven disputed questions about sanctification.

1564. ———. *The Discovery of Divine Healing*. New York: Alliance Press Co., 1903. 146 p.

Nine of the volume's 13 sermons have been reprinted from 1616. Cf. 1751.

1565. ———. *Divine Emblems*. Harrisburg, Pa.: Christian Publications, 1971. 221 p.

Reprint of 1566.

1566. ———. *Divine Emblems in Genesis and Exodus*. New York: Christian Alliance Pub. Co., [189-?]. 396 p.

Reprint of 1569 and 1567.

1567. ———. *Divine Emblems in the Book of Exodus*. New York: Word, Work and World Pub. Co., 1888. 207 p.

Six sermons on the spiritual dimension of the Exodus narrative: "when the pillar of clouds rested, the people rested. . . . The trouble with some of you is that you have gone before the pillar. There are a great many times when God wants us to keep still . . . to be dead to [our] own activity and work and plans" (p. 80). Cf. 1566.

1568. ———. *Divine Emblems in the Book of Genesis*. Tabernacle Sermons, 6th Series, February 1888, vol. 2. New York: Word, Work and World Pub. Co., 1888. 95 p.

Four sermons on the underlying spiritual teaching of the narratives of the creation, fall, and flood, e.g., "the fig leaves may stand . . . for man's self-righteousness, represented in the next chapter by the offering of Cain" (p. 46).

1569. ———. *Divine Emblems in the Book of Genesis*. New York: Word, Work and World Pub. Co., 1888. 194 p.

Includes the four sermons of 1568 and four new sermons on the narratives of Abraham, Isaac, Jacob, and Joseph. Replete with the typological interpretation that would find its full expression in the Christ in the Bible series. Cf. 1566.

1570. ———. *Divine Healing and How to Keep It.* Los Angeles: Free Tract Society, [193-?]. 4 p.

Reprint of 1688.

1571. ———. *Divine Healing and Natural Law.* Tracts for the Times: Divine Healing Series. New York: Christian Alliance Pub. Company, [1894?]. 8 p.

Divine healing is simply a higher spiritual law that supersedes the lower natural laws. "The real secret of Divine Healing is to reach out to the Divine life and become united to the Living One" (p. 6).

1572. ———. *Divine Healing in the Atonement.* New York: Christian Alliance Pub. Co., [1890?]. 14 p.

An exposition of the doctrine based on biblical allusions (most of which are drawn from the Old Testament) e.g., the speech of Elihu (Job 33) illustrates that "sickness is God's second voice to the man who will not hear His first" (p. 6).

1573. ———. *Divine Healing in the Psalms.* Living Truths, vol. 1, no. 25. Nyack, N.Y.: Christian Alliance Pub. Co., 1901. 24 p.

An aid to prayer for physical healing consisting of a compendium, with commentary, of verses from the Psalms.

1574. ———. *Divine Healing: The Vital Touch.* n.p., n.d. 4 p.

A sermon on Luke 8:46 that sets forth the conditions for divine healing: longing, repentance of all known sin, and personal acquaintance with Jesus.

1575. ———. *Divine Providence.* New York: Christian Alliance Pub. Co., [ca. 1900]. 32 p.

A catalogue of biblical examples of the truth that "all things work together for good to those who love God."

1576. [———]. *Do You Want Him to Come?* Tracts for the Times. Lord's Coming Series. New York: Christian Alliance Pub. Co., [ca. 1900]. 8 p.

Christians ought eagerly to expect the Lord's return, for he will return as their friend, end sin and sorrow, make them perfect, bring about the resurrection of their bodies, restore them to dead friends, give them their reward, right the world's wrongs, restore Israel, end the reign of Satan and, most of all, bring himself.

1577. ———. *Does It Pay to Be a Christian?* Christian Alliance Tracts. New York: Christian Alliance Pub. Co., [189-?]. 8 p.

An evangelistic sermon based on Mal. 3:14.

1578. ———. "The Drawings of Divine Love." *The American Holiness Journal*, January 1983, 29-31.

A meditation on Jer. 31:3. God goes out of his way through the Scriptures and through trials to attract us to himself, to make himself necessary to us.

1579. ———. *Earnests of the Coming Age, and Other Sermons*. New York: Christian Alliance Pub. Co., 1921. 222 p.

Twenty representative sermons and articles (selected by Walter Turnbull) including "Evolution or Revolution" in which Simpson caricatures the teaching that sanctification is a form of spiritual evolution: "By a process of growth in grace you will become a saint; and if you do not, you will at least grow old and . . . the power of passion will decay; and if you do not become holy, you will at least become harmless" (p. 20).

1580. ———. *Echoes of the New Creation: Messages of the Cross, the Resurrection and the Coming Glory*. New York: Alliance Press Co., 1903. 166 p.

Nine sermons on selected biblical texts. "While many of the manifestations of [Spiritualism] are mere impostures, yet . . . many are supernatural and real and it is possible for Satan to simulate . . . the form and features of some one we have loved. . . . The only way to overcome this . . . temptation is to tell the devil that this image is not real" (p. 15-16).

1581. ———. *El-Shadai, or the God Who Is Enough, and the Call to Prayer*. South Nyack, N.Y.: Christian Alliance Pub. Co., 1897. 40 p.

Sermons on Gen. 17:1 and Jer. 33:2-3.

1582. ———. *Elim, Its Wells and Palms*. New York: Alliance Pub. Co., 1905. 147 p.

A devotional calendar with readings for the 12 months and 70 years symbolized, respectively, by the 12 wells and 70 palms of Elim (Ex. 15:27).

1583. ———. *Emblems from the Mount*. Nyack, N.Y.: Christian Alliance Pub. Co., 1901. 20 p.

A sermon on Heb. 12:18-24: "Christ hides the law in His heart and puts it in our heart, so that the things that once we hated, we now love" (p. 18).

1584. ———. *Emblems of the Holy Spirit*. Alliance Colportage Library, vol. 3, no. 9. New York: Christian Alliance Pub. Co., 1901. 143 p.

Reprint of the first eight chapters of 1680.

1585. [———]. *The Emergency*. Tracts for the Times. Mission Series. New York: Christian Alliance Pub. Co., [ca. 1900]. 8 p.

An arresting compilation of statistics with respect to the unevangelized: e.g., Americans spend more on artificial flowers than they do on missions.

1586. ———. *The Epistle of James: An Exposition of the Book of James As It Relates to the Practical Life of the Believer*. Christ in the Bible, vol. 22a. Harrisburg, Pa.: Christian Publications, [193-?]. 117 p.

Reprint of 1797.

1587. ———. *The Epistle to the Hebrews*. Harrisburg, Pa.: Christian Publications, [193-?]. 157 p.

Reprint, with new introduction, of 1877.

1588. ———. *The Epistle to the Romans*. Harrisburg, Pa.: Christian Publications, [193-?]. 298 p.

Reprint of 1816.

1589. ———. *The Epistles of Peter, John, and Jude*. Harrisburg, Pa.: Christian Publications, [194-?]. 192 p.

The chapter on Jude cannot be found in any other book by Simpson. The rest is a reprint of 1879 and 1761.

1590. ———. *Epistles of the Advent or, the Blessed Hope in Thessalonians*. [New York]: n.p., [1901?]. 66 p.

Three sermons on eschatological themes. On 2 Thess. 3:5: "The best preparation for Christ's coming is to be faithful in your calling . . . and found at your post. . . . Christ expects us to be always ready and then everything that comes in the way of life's duties is equally sacred and heavenly" (p. 26-27). Cf. 1789.

1591. ———. *The Epistles of Thessalonians, Timothy, and Titus*. Harrisburg, Pa.: Christian Publications, [193-?]. 127 p.

Eleven sermons (with introduction) on selected texts: chapters 1-3 are a reprint of 1590; chapter four is an additional sermon on Thessalonians not found in that volume. On Timothy's need to "stir up the gift of God" (2 Tim. 1:6-7): "There is such a thing as receiving the Holy Ghost at a definite moment and there is such a thing as being filled in the present tense by a continuous experience."

1592. ———. *The Epistles to the Galatians and Ephesians*. Christ in the Bible, vol. 19. New York: Alliance Press Co., 1904. 254 p.

Reprint of 1612 and 1669.

1593. ———. *The Epistles to the Philippians and the Colossians.* Harrisburg, Pa.: Christian Publications, [193-?] 124 p.

Reprint of 1843 and 1498.

1594. [———]. *Errors about His Coming.* Tracts for the Times. Lord's Coming Series. New York: Christian Alliance Pub. Co., [ca. 1900]. 8 p.

It is an error to teach that the Lord has already come, to make unwarranted and presumptuous predictions about when he will return, to believe that the millennium will be realized through the church (without a king) and to regard a restored Israel as the primary agent by which the world will be evangelized.

1595. ———. *Evangelistic Addresses.* New York: Christian Alliance Pub. Co., 1926. 96 p.

"The way to God and Eternal Life made plain by [six] expositions of leading Bible Texts" (t.p.), e.g., Isa. 66:13: "If things are hard, if things are wrong, if things have gone to pieces, there is where we need the mother to comfort us. . . . Oh, I am glad there is not only a Father, but a Holy Ghost, a Comforter and the mother heart of God" (p. 70).

1596. ———. *Even As He.* New York: Christian Alliance Pub. Co., [1891?]. 34 p.

A meditation, based on 1 John 4:17, on the implications of the believer's "intimate and absolute" union with Christ through the Holy Spirit. Also published as a chapter in both 1701 and 1666.

1597. [———]. *Everything for Nothing.* Tracts for the Times. Salvation Series. New York: Christian Alliance Pub. Co., [ca. 1900]. 8 p.

Grace consists in "God's love for the unworthy. . . . God's help for the helpless. . . . [getting] everything for nothing" (p. 3).

1598. ———. *Exodus: A Simple and Earnest Attempt to Unfold the Spiritual Teachings of the Second Book of Holy Scripture, Especially with Reference to the Person and Work of the Lord Jesus Christ.* Harrisburg, Pa.: Christian Publications, [193-?]. 134 p.

Reprint, with a new introduction, of the Exodus portion of 1627.

1599. ———. *Faith and Fanaticism.* Tracts for the Times. Divine Healing Series. New York: Christian Alliance Pub. Co., [ca. 1900]. 8 p.

Faith has the Word of God as its basis, fanaticism relies on something else, "either in addition or opposition to the Bible" (p. 3). Three examples of fanaticism are: Christian Science, Roman Catholic superstitions, and Spiritualism.

1600. ———. "The Faith of God." *Thy Healer* 2 (1885): 157-60.
A sermon on "the faith of God" as faith that has its origin in God and that the believer can trust God to provide.

1601. ———. *The Faith of God.* New York: Christian Alliance Pub. Co., [189-?]. 19 p.
Reprint of 1600.

1602. ———. *Farther on.* New York: Alliance Press Co., [1916?]. 15 p.
A Christmas and New Year's message to the students of the Nyack Missionary Training Institute.

1603. ———. *First Corinthians: The Principles and Life of the Apostolic Church.* Christ in the Bible, vol. 18. Harrisburg, Pa.: Christian Publications, [193-?]. 164 p.
Slightly revised reprint of 1503.

1604. [———]. *The First Resurrection.* Tracts for the Times. Lord's Coming Series. New York: Christian Alliance Pub. Co., [ca. 1900]. 8 p.
The first resurrection will be a resurrection into life for the followers of Jesus. It is for those who share his suffering, appropriate his power, and conform to his death. The second resurrection will be a resurrection into judgment and condemnation for unbelievers.

1605. ———. *Foundation Truths Respecting Divine Healing.* New York: Christian Alliance Pub. Co., [1895?]. 16 p.
A summary of Alliance teaching on the subject.

1606. ———. *Foundation Truths Respecting Sanctification.* Memorial Series, no. 2. New York: Christian Alliance Pub. Co., [1895?]. 21 p.
Sanctification is not the same as regeneration, not the work of death, not our own work, not growth in character or self-perfection, but rather "the receiving of Jesus Christ personally in his perfect life and fullness to reign in our heart and life" (p. 5). This "reckoning of sin and self as . . . dead" (p. 8) occurs in an instant, but the sanctified believer thereafter grows in holiness.

1607. ———. *The Four-Fold Gospel.* New York: Word, Work and World Pub. Co, 1888. 106 p.

Four sermons: Christ as Savior (Rev. 7:10), Sanctifier (John 17:19), Healer (Matt. 8:17, Heb. 13:8), and Coming Lord (Rev. 2:28). "Regeneration is like building a house and having the work done well. Sanctification is having the owner come and dwell in it and fill it with gladness and life, abundantly" (p. 30). Cf. 1540.

1608. ———. *The Four-Fold Gospel*. New York: Christian Alliance Pub. Co., 1925. 128 p.

Introduction by Frederic H. Senft. Includes two additional sermons: "The Walk with God" and "Kept."

1609. ———. *The Fourfold Gospel, or the Fulness of Jesus*. New York: Christian Alliance Pub. Co., 1915. 16 p.

"[There] are four messages in the gospel which sum up . . . the blessings which Christ has to offer us. . . .: Christ our Savior, Sanctifier, Healer and Coming Lord" (p. 3). Cf. 2015.

1610. ———. *The Fourfold Gospel: The Fulness of Jesus*. New York: The Christian and Missionary Alliance, 1937. 8 p.

A slightly edited reprint of 1609.

1611. ———. *The Fourfold Gospel: The Message of the Christian and Missionary Alliance*. New York: The Alliance, 1946. 10 p.

A slightly edited reprint of 1609.

1612. ———. *Free Grace, or Christ in Galatians*. Nyack, N.Y.: Christian Alliance Pub. Co., [1901?]. 65 p.

Three sermons on selected texts. "The end to which the Spirit is always working [is] . . . to form Christ in us. . . . [Sanctification] is not a state, but a relation, a union with a Person " (p. 36) . Cf. 1529 and 1592.

1613. ———. *Friday Meeting Talks, or Divine Prescriptions for the Sick and Suffering*. New York: Christian Alliance Pub. Co., 1894. 187 p.

Condensed versions of twenty talks given at the healing meetings that were held every Friday afternoon at the Gospel Tabernacle for many years. Just as the sanctified person can successfully resist temptation by treating it as a foreign element, so can that same person, having exchanged the natural life for Christ's divine life and strength, treat "old infirmities, symptoms or sufferings, when they reappear, as foreign elements." As a result of this Christ-centered reckoning "the morbid conditions will drop away" (p. 43-45). Cf. 1614.

1614. ———. *Friday Meeting Talks, or Divine Prescriptions for the Sick and Suffering, Series No. 1.* Alliance Colportage Library, vol. 1, no. 15. Nyack, N.Y. : Christian Alliance Pub. Co., 1899. 153 p.

Reprint of 1613.

1615. ———. *Friday Meeting Talks, or Divine Prescriptions for the Sick and Suffering, Series No. 2.* Alliance Colportage Library, vol. 1, no. 18. New York: Christian Alliance Pub. Co., 1899. 135 p.

Twenty-one sermonettes. "By His death He has made . . . complete atonement for our spirit, soul and body, so that these frames are no longer liable on account of sin to the penalty which they have incurred. Disease never need come to us as the penalty of sin and even death is no longer the curse of sin, but the peaceful sleep though which we pass to a higher life" (p. 35).

1616. ———. *Friday Meeting Talks, or Divine Prescriptions for the Sick and Suffering, Series No. 3.* Alliance Colportage Library, vol. 2, no. 9. New York: Christian Alliance Pub. Co., 1900. 111 p.

Nine sermons on divine healing in the Old Testament (Genesis through Psalms). God wants to give us "a converted body. . . . not the repair shop tinkering you up and letting you go on a little longer . . . it is that deep, sweet, love-life of the Lord which He wants to pour into all your being and make you young again" (p. 95-96). Cf. 1511 and 1564.

1617. ———. *From Centre to Circumference: A Special Sermon Preached on His Return from His Missionary Tour.* New York: Christian Alliance Pub. Co., [1893?]. 47 p.

A sermon on Isa. 54:2 preached on his return from his (1893) tour of Alliance missions. Eph. 1:18-23 played a crucial role in Simpson's understanding of the missionary imperative: "What enormous sums of money are squandered on architectural taste and decoration, useless spires, sentimental quartettes, humanitarian schemes of benevolence . . . things . . . which certainly are not God's highest thought for the gospel and the world" (p. 34).

1618. ———. *From Faith to Faith: Exposition of the Epistle to the Romans, Part I.* Alliance Colportage Library, vol. 3, no. 10. Nyack, N.Y.: Christian Alliance Pub. Co., 1901. 122 p.

Reprint of p. 1-123 of 1815.

1619. ———. *From Faith to Faith: Exposition of the Epistle to the Romans, Part II.* Alliance Colportage Library, vol. 3, no. 11. Nyack, N.Y.: Christian Alliance Pub. Co., 1901. 152 p.

Reprint of p. 123-274 of 1815.

1620. ———. *From the Uttermost to the Uttermost: The Life Story of Josephus Pulis*. New York: Christian Alliance Pub. Co., 1914. 80 p.

Josephus Pulis (1831-1913) was a former alcoholic and street person who was one of the seven founding members of the Gospel Tabernacle (1882), a close (lay) associate of A. B. Simpson, and, for Simpson, a model of "the Christ life."

1621. ———. *The Fullness of Jesus: Christian Life in the New Testament.* Tabernacle Sermons, vol. 2. New York: Word, Work and World Pub. Co., [1886?]. 226 p.

Christian life is new, personal, and complete for Christ is our complete justification and sanctification, our faith, our perfect love, our power to will, and the life of our mind and body. Cf. 1543 and 1713.

1622. ———. *The Fullness of Jesus, or Christian Life in the New Testament.* New York: Christian Alliance Pub. Co., 1890. 475 p.

Reprint of 1621.

1623. ———. *The Fullness of Jesus, or Christian Life in the New Testament, Part I.* Alliance Colportage Library, vol. 1, no. 9. New York: Alliance Press Co., 1899. 232 p.

Reprint of p. 1-232 of 1622.

1624. ———. *The Fullness of Jesus, or Christian Life in the New Testament, Part II.* Alliance Colportage Series, vol. 1, no. 10. New York: Alliance Press Co., 1899. 242 p.

Reprint of p. 233-475 of 1622.

1625. ———. *Genesis: A Simple and Earnest Attempt to Unfold the Spiritual Teachings of the First Book of Holy Scripture, Especially with Reference to the Person and Work of the Lord Jesus Christ.* Harrisburg, Pa.: Christian Publications, [193-?]. 136 p.

Reprint of the expository material on Genesis in 1626.

1626. ———. *Genesis and Exodus*. Christ in the Bible, vol. 1. New York: Word, Work and World Pub. Co., 1886. 394 p.

On the Fall: "Sin entered through the Woman. Satan . . . concentrated his forces upon the weaker nature. And often since has he used her simplicity and openness of being as the . . . standpoint from which to attack and destroy man as well" (p. 61).

1627. ———. *Genesis and Exodus*, 2nd ed. rev. Christ in the Bible, vol. 1. New York: Alliance Press Co., 1902. 316 p.

An abridgement of 1626. Lacks biblical text and homiletical helps and illustrations of that edition, but retains the expository material. Cf. 1598.

1628. ———. *The Gentle Love of the Holy Spirit: An Updated and Edited Version of the Former Title Walking in the Spirit*. Camp Hill, Pa.: Christian Publications, 1983.

Reprint, with added foreword, and updated language, of 1853.

1629. ———. "Gifts and Grace." In *The Signs of the Times, or God's Message for To-day: A Symposium on New Theology, Christian Science, the Lord's Coming, the Gift of Tongues, and the Deeper Spiritual Life*, 95-113. New York: Alliance Press Co., 1907.

An exposition of 1 Cor. 13. The work of the Holy Spirit in bestowing gifts ought to be distinguished from the work of the Holy Spirit in saving and sanctifying, so that glossolalia must not be regarded as the necessary evidence of Spirit-baptism. However, even the most spectacular gifts ought to be neither feared nor ignored, but rather welcomed and exercised in the church in an orderly fashion and a spirit of discernment and love.

1630. ———. *Gifts and Grace: A Scriptural Interpretation of the Baptism of the Holy Spirit and Its Relation to the Gift of Tongues*, 10th ed. Harrisburg, Pa.: Christian Publications, [193-?]. 19 p.

A reprint of 1629 that tellingly omits p. 17-21 of the original, which warns against fearing or ignoring the spiritual gifts and provides instruction in their appropriate public use.

1631. [———]. *Go, Give, Pray*. Tracts for the Times. Mission Series. New York: Christian Alliance Pub. Co., [ca. 1900]. 8 p.

A missionary should have good health, a good mind (and preferably a university education) an experience of conversion and the baptism of the Holy Spirit, a passion for evangelism, and the ability to get along with others. Other Christians can be used more effectively by God at home than abroad: these have been entrusted with the ministries of prayer and giving.

1632. [———]. *God's Easy Way of Holiness*. Tracts for the Times. Deeper Life Series. New York: Christian Alliance Pub. Co., [ca. 1900]. 8 p.

God's way of holiness comes through faith rather than works. "God is not blaming you because you do not do better [but] . . . because you do not take the grace that would make you better" (p. 6). The deeper life consists in overcoming evil with good (as opposed to fighting evil).

1633. ———. "The Gospel of Healing." *Thy Healer* 2 (1885): 2: 9-11, 22-25, 32-35, 52-53, 64-66, 79-81, 87-90.

A reprint of "The Gospel of Healing."*The Word, the Work and the World* 3 (April 1883): 57-60; (May-June 1883): 77-80, comprising Simpson's interpretation of the passages of Scripture that refer to divine healing and his practical instructions for those who desire to appropriate it.

1634. ———. *The Gospel of Healing*. New York: Word, Work and World Pub. Co., [1885?]. 11 p.

Traces biblical teaching on divine healing from Exodus to Revelation. Also published as chapter one of 1635.

1635. ———. *The Gospel of Healing*, 4th ed. New York: Christian Alliance Pub. Co., 1890. 283 p.

A five-chapter treatise on divine healing followed by testimonies by Simpson and other Alliance people (including one of Simpson's daughters), an account of the healing ministries being carried out under the aegis of the Gospel Tabernacle, and a refutation of the Christian Science doctrine of healing.

1636. ———. *The Gospel of Healing*, new ed. London: Morgan and Scott, 1915. 154 p.

A reprint of the first five chapters of 1637.

1637. ———. *The Gospel of Healing,* rev. ed. New York: Christian Alliance Pub. Co., 1915. 186 p.

A slightly abridged and updated reprint of 1635.

1638. ———. *The Gospel of Healing*, rev. ed. New York: Christian Alliance Pub. Co., 1926. 193 p.

Identical to 1637, except that it includes the appendix on Christian Science of 1635.

1639. ———. *The Gospel of Healing*. Camp Hill, Pa.: Christian Publications, 1986. 128 p.

A reprint of 1637, but without the chapter on Christian Science. Includes an introduction by John Sawin that gives the publishing history of this, Simpson's first book.

1640. ———. *The Gospel of John*. Christ in the Bible, vol. 15. New York: Christian Alliance Pub. Co., 1904. 301 p.

Rev. ed. (abridged introduction, some new expository notes) of the material on the Gospel of John in 1641. Cf. 1878.

1641. ———. *The Gospel of John and the Acts of the Apostles*. Christ in the Bible, vol. 10. New York: Christian Alliance Pub. Co., 1891. 367 p.

A devotional commentary (i.e., not sermons). The commentary on the Gospel of John covers only chapters 1-17. On Acts 1:4: "An attitude of waiting is one of God's uniform conditions of great spiritual blessing" (p. 259). Cf. 1640.

1642. ———. *The Gospel of Luke.* Christ in the Bible, vol. 14b. New York: Alliance Press Co., 1910. 216 p.

Sermons from 18 selected texts. Jesus' time of testing in the wilderness illustrates that "the baptism of the Holy Ghost is not given to us primarily as an enduement of power for service . . . but . . . for personal character and holiness" (p. 47).

1643. ———. *The Gospel of Mark.* Christ in the Bible, vol. 14. New York: Christian Alliance Pub. Co., 1928. 183 p.

Includes the introduction to 1759 as well as nine sermons on selected passages in Mark 1-8. On 8:22-26: "There was something preliminary to his healing—spiritual preparation, and the Lord was teaching us through him that the sick and suffering nature has to be put to school with God and to be led into those deeper experiences which will fit them to know and touch the Lord and afterwards abide in Him" (p. 92-93).

1644. ———. *The Gospel of Matthew.* Harrisburg, Pa.: Christian Publications, [193-?]. 339 p.

Reprint of 1645 (but lacks poem on p. 340 of that work.)

1645. ———. *Gospel of St. Matthew*, 2nd ed. rev., Christ in the Bible. New York: Alliance Press Co., 1904. 339 p.

Sermons on 19 selected texts. The sermon on Matt. 24- 25 implies a partial rapture: "Most of God's people" will avoid the tribulation "for the

Church will have been withdrawn at the beginning of the tribulation and its watching and holy members caught up to meet the Lord in the air.." (p. 259). Matt. 24:31 "may refer to the final gathering of the tribulation saints, still left on earth after the tribulation" (p. 261). Cf. 1644.

1646. ———. *The Gospel of the Kingdom: A Series of Discourses on the Lord's Coming*. Tabernacle Sermons, 3rd Series. New York: Word, Work and World Pub. Co., [1887?]. 278 p.

Seventeen sermons expressing Simpson's premillennial eschatology. Also includes a twenty-one-point premillennialist manifesto, e.g., the ascension of Christians will precede the great tribulation that will (possibly) last 40 years. There is no hint here of a partial rapture of sanctified Christians. On the signs of the end "the prophetic future is largely filled with the dark figure of the Papacy and God's provident dealings in connection with its overthrow" (p. 127).

1647. ———. *The Gospel of the Kingdom: A Series of Discourses on the Lord's Coming*, rev. ed. New York: Christian Alliance Pub. Co., 1890. 347 p.

Reprint of 1646 that includes a fold-out chart illustrating Simpson's millennial views.

1648. ———. *The Gospel of the Kingdom: A Series of Discourses on the Lord's Coming, Part I.* Alliance Colportage Library, vol. 1, no. 1. Nyack, N.Y.: Christian Alliance Pub. Co., 1899. 164 p.

A reprint of p. 1-164 of 1647.

1649. ———. *The Gospel of the Kingdom: A Series of Discourses on the Lord's Coming. Part II.* Alliance Colportage Library, vol. 1, no. 2. Nyack, N.Y.: Christian Alliance Pub. Co., 1899. 184 p.

A reprint of p. 163-347 of 1647.

1650. ———. *Grace Abounding*. New York: Christian Alliance Pub. Co., [1891?]. 34 p.

A meditation on Rom. 5:20. Grace is reflected in salvation, sanctification, redemption, healing, and the believer's future hope; but above all in the Christian's union with Christ.

1651. ———. *The Grace of Giving*. Christian Alliance Tracts. South Nyack, N.Y.: Christian Alliance Pub. Co., [1899?]. 30 p.

A sermon on financial giving based on 2 Cor. 8:7-9. Simpson finds in this passage a precedent for the use of missionary pledges. Not to be confused with the sermon of the same name in 1767.

1652. ———. *A Great Missionary Movement.* New York: Christian Alliance Pub. Co., 1892. 150 p.

Chapters one to 12 were also published separately as tracts. The last three chapters consist of an introduction to The International Missionary Alliance, the annual report for 1891, and the constitution and bylaws of the IMA.

1653. ———. *Hard Places in the Way of Faith.* New York: Christian Alliance Pub. Co., 1899. 26 p.

A sermon on Acts 27:44. The perils Paul encountered on his journey to Rome illustrate the fact that trials and hardships invariably accompany any decision to trust God. God uses them to deepen this trust; and his providence will enable those who trust in him to endure, and to triumph over any difficulty.

1654. ———. *He Is Risen, or the Principle of Death and Resurrection in Nature and Grace.* New York: Word, Work and World Pub. Co., 1888. 75 p.

Christians have died and risen again in Christ, i.e., they have had their sins reckoned as dead and forgiven and, more importantly, they have renounced their self-will, self-confidence, and all other aspects of the natural life; and they have accepted God's will and appropriated God's strength for their daily lives. One of the aspects of this appropriated Christ-life is physical healing through the prayer of faith.

1655. [———]. *He Saved Others, Himself He Could Not Save.* Tracts for the Times. Salvation Series. New York: Christian Alliance Pub. Co., [ca 1900]. 6 p.

Jesus' sacrificial death provides atonement for all who believe in him. Believers should respond to his love by living lives of sacrificial service.

1656. ———. *He That Baptizeth with the Holy Ghost.* New York: Christian Alliance Pub. Co., [1891?]. 39 p.

A Pentecost sermon on John 1:33 that sets forth Simpson's doctrine of the baptism of the Holy Spirit and his understanding of Jesus' role as dispenser of the Spirit. Also published in 1771.

1657. ———. *Healing through the Holy Spirit.* New York: Christian Alliance Pub. Co., [1891?]. 19 p.

The cruse of oil on the Alliance logo signifies divine healing and symbolizes the Holy Spirit, for "the Lord's healing is imparted to us through the power of the Holy Spirit and His indwelling in the temple of our body" (p. 31).

1658. ———. *Heart Messages for Sabbaths at Home.* Nyack, N.Y.: Christian Alliance Pub. Co., [1899?]. 233 p.

A sermonette for each week of the year. Intended for those who are unable to attend worship services regularly.

1659. ———. *The Heart of God.* Living Truths, vol. 1, no 17. Nyack, N.Y.: Christian Alliance Pub. Co., 1901. 22 p.

God's heart attitude towards sinners is a blend of uncompromising justice and loving mercy.

1660. ———. *Heaven Opened: Expositions of the Book of Revelation.* New York: Alliance Press Company, 1899. 157 p.

Reprint of p. 1-157 of 1661.

1661. ———. *Heaven Opened, or Expositions of the Book of Revelation.* New York: Alliance Press Co., 1899. 298 p.

Fifteen sermons on selected texts. Two of them— "The Firstfruits of the Harvest," and "The Marriage of the Lamb"—develop Simpson's version of the doctrine of the partial rapture: the holy few, the bride of Christ, are translated at the beginning of the Great Tribulation; while the rest, "the friends of the bride," must await the general resurrection.

1662. ———. *Heaven Opened, or Expositions of the Book of Revelation.* New York: Alliance Press Co., 1899. 143 p.

Reprint of p. 158-301 of 1661.

1663. ———. *Heaven Opened, or Expositions of the Book of Revelation, Part I.* Alliance Colportage Library, vol. 1, no. 12. Nyack, N.Y.: Christian Alliance Pub. Co., 1899. 156 p.

Reprint of p. 1-156 of 1661.

1664. ———. *Heaven Opened, or Expositions of the Book of Revelation, Part II.* Alliance Colportage Library. vol. 1, no. 13. Nyack, N.Y.: Christian Alliance Pub. Co., 1899. 143 p.

Reprint of p. 157-299 of 1661.

1665. ———. *Heavenly Robes*. New York: Christian Alliance Pub. Co., [189-?]. 27 p.

A sermon on Isa. 61:10: Christians have been attired in the robe of righteousness, salvation, and power for service; and in the wedding robe of a bride who awaits the return of her husband/Lord.

1666. ———. *The Heavenly Vision*. Nyack, N.Y.: Christian Alliance Pub. Co., 1898. 120 p.

Six sermons on selected passages from the New Testament. "God alone can give the vision, and to know it once is to be lifted out of our petty selfishness and made workers together with God" (p. 17). Cf. 1596.

1667. ———. *Heights and Depths*. New York: Christian Alliance Pub. Co., [189-?]. 28 p.

An Easter sermon on Col. 3:1 and 1 Cor. 2:10 encouraging Christians to move beyond the Resurrection to the Ascension as the focus of their spiritual orientation.

———, joint author. *Henry Wilson, One of God's Best.*

See 2333.

1668. ———. *Higher and Deeper*. South Nyack, N.Y.: Christian Alliance Pub. Co., [1897?] 43 p.

Two sermons: "Higher" (original title: "Forward") on Phil. 3:13-14, advocates radical self-abandonment to Christ; "Deeper," on 1 Cor. 2:10, 12 defines the "deeper life" as "Deeper than the primary truths of the Gospel and the average experience of the Christian" (p. 39-40).

1669. ———. *The Highest Christian Life: Exposition of the Epistle to the Ephesians*. South Nyack, N.Y.: Christian Alliance Pub. Co., 1898. 190 p.

Ten sermons on selected texts. On Eph. 1:17-23: the Holy Spirit is a spirit of wisdom and revelation. "First by giving us knowledge and wisdom of the truth; and secondly, by giving us a direct touch of revelation, a distinct flash of celestial light that makes it all vivid and real to our spiritual senses" (p. 65). Cf. 1529 and 1592.

1670. ———. *The Highest Christian Life: Exposition of the Letter to the Ephesians. Part I.* Alliance Colportage Library, vol. 1, no. 3. Nyack,N.Y.: Christian Alliance Pub. Co., 1899. 80 p.

Reprint of p. 1-80 of 1669.

1671. ———. *The Highest Christian Life: Exposition of the Epistle to the Ephesians. Part II.* Alliance Colportage Library, vol. 1, no. 4. Nyack, N.Y.: Christian Alliance Pub. Co., 1899. 109 p.

Reprint of p. 82-190 of 1669.

1672. ———. *Him That Cometh.* Living Truths, vol. 1, no. 4. Nyack, N.Y.: Christian Alliance Pub. Co., 1900. 21 p.

"This little text [John 6:37] has perhaps brought more souls to Christ than any other. . . . The writer remembers a day a third of a century ago, when, after long struggling . . . at last this little message met him and brought him straight to Christ" (p. 3).

1673. ———. "Himself." *Thy Healer* 2 (1885): 229-34.

The original version of Simpson's famous autobiographical sermon (delivered in June 1885 at the International conference on Divine Healing and True Holiness in Bethshan, London, England) on how he found healing through seeking Christ the healer, rather than healing by itself.

1674. ———. *Himself.* Randleman, N.C.: Pilgrim Tract Society, n.d.. 8 p.

Abridged edition of the original address given at Bethshan, London, 1885. Includes Simpson's poem/hymn "Himself."

1675. ———. *Himself*, new rev. ed. Memorial Series, no. 1. New York: Christian Alliance Pub. Co., [189-?]. 15 p.

The wording at times differs from that of 1673.

1676. ———. *Himself: A Timeless Testimony*. Heritage Series. Camp Hill, Pa.: Christian Publications, 1991. 13 p.

Reprint of 1675, with the addition of the poem *Himself.*

1677. ———. *Himself: An Address Delivered at Bethshan, London, England, June, 1885*, new rev. ed. New York: Christian Alliance Pub. Co., [189-?]. 16 p.

A reworking of the version published in *The Word, the Work and the World* 5 (October 1885): 258-61, which itself was a slight revision of the version published in *Thy Healer*.

1678. ———. *Holy Ghost Ministries*. New York: Christian Alliance Pub. Co., 1900. 148 p.

A reprint of seven chapters from 1727.

1679. ———. *The Holy Spirit, or Power from on High: An Unfolding of the Doctrine of the Holy Spirit in the Old and New Testaments*, new ed. New York: Christian Alliance Pub. Co., 1924. 2 vols.

This edition has an introduction by Walter Turnbull, but is otherwise identical to 1680 and 1681.

1680. ———. *The Holy Spirit, or Power from on High: An Unfolding of the Doctrine of the Holy Spirit in the Old and New Testaments. Part I, The Old Testament.* New York: Christian Alliance Pub. Co., 1895. 394 p.

A collection of 25 sermons, which, along with Part II, provides considerable insight into Simpson's (at times) idiosyncratic pneumatology. For example, on Gen. 1:2, "the great thought in the heart of God is motherhood. . . . Human motherhood has its origin in the Holy Ghost" (p. 21). As far as the ministry of women is concerned, the Holy Spirit has gifted them to prophesy and to teach without restriction, but they are "not called to rule in the ecclesiastical government of the Church of Christ or to exercise the official ministry which the Holy Ghost has committed to the elders or bishops of His church" (p. 149). Cf. 1584.

1681. ———. *The Holy Spirit, or Power from on High: An Unfolding of the Doctrine of the Holy Spirit in the Old and New Testaments. Part II, The New Testament.* New York: Christian Alliance Pub. Co., 1896. 392 p.

A collection of 28 sermons that, like Part I, illustrates Simpson's at times bold pneumatology, e.g., "It was necessary that He should reside for three and a half years in the heart of Jesus of Nazareth, and become, as it were humanized, colored, and brought nearer to us by his personal union with our Incarnate Lord" (p. 15).

1682. ———. *The Holy Spirit: Power from on High*. Edited by Keith M. Bailey. Camp Hill, Pa.: Christian Publications, 1994. 611 p.

Reprint, with added indexes and updated language, of 1680 and 1681. The foreword by Walter Turnbull from 1679 replaces the original foreword by Stephen Merritt.

1683. [———]. *How Easy to Be Lost.* Tracts for the Times. Salvation Series. New York: Christian Alliance Pub. Co., [ca. 1900]. 6 p.

One does not need to be a person of conspicuous wickedness to be lost: one enters life in that condition. One needs to be rescued by Christ, for one is powerless to do anything otherwise about one's condition. Jesus is eager to rescue, but a simple passive response to his offer of salvation is enough to ensure damnation.

1684. [———]. *How Easy to Be Saved.* Tracts for the Times. Salvation Series. New York: Christian Alliance Pub. Co., [ca. 1900]. 6 p.

The story of a train conductor who discovers that Jesus, as pioneer of the faith, has made the way of salvation "easy."

1685. ———. *How God Purges Us.* Guthrie, Okla.: Christian Triumph Co., [1911?]. 24 p.

A meditation on Ps. 139:23-24. God "tries" our sanctification through the trials and temptations of everyday life: these are not random occurrences of which we are victims, but the purifying hand of God at work. God deals with our thoughts by enabling us to replace our own thoughts and mind with the mind of Christ. Also includes instructions by B. Carradine, a Methodist, on how the sanctified ought to deal with moods and spiritual impulses.

1686. ———. *How Long?* New York: Christian Alliance Pub. Co., [1892?]. 43 p.

A sermon on Josh. 13:1 and 18:3, likening the longstanding slackness of the church vis-à-vis missions to the initial reluctance of the Israelites to leave Shiloh and enter Canaan. Like Joshua, contemporary believers must "take possession of the land," i.e., recapture the missionary zeal that is the necessary concomitant of true discipleship.

1687. ———. *How to Help Others.* Tracts for the Times. Divine Healing Series. New York: Christian Alliance Pub. Co., [ca. 1900]. 6 p.

The aim of prayer for healing is to bring the sufferer into a state of complete yieldedness to God. The sufferer must be led to claim Christ for healing just as one would lead an inquirer to claim Christ for salvation.

1688. ———. *How to Keep It.* Tracts for the Times. Divine Healing Series. New York: Christian Alliance Pub. Co., [ca. 1900]. 8 p.

The "it" is divine healing. The keys to retention are: living a life of obedience to God, reckoning on God rather than on symptoms, drawing spiritual nourishment from Christ, not monitoring feelings, and maintaining a cheerful spirit. Cf. 1570, 1689, 1693.

1689. [———]. *How to Receive and Keep Divine Healing.* Springfield, Mo.: Gospel Publishing House, [1934?]. 6 p.

Although no author is given, this tract is an almost verbatim reprint (by a Pentecostal publisher) of 1688.

1690. ———. *How to Receive and Retain Divine Healing*. New York: The Christian and Missionary Alliance, 1959. 11 p.

Reprint of 1691 and 1693. Cf. 1528.

1691. ———. *How to Receive Divine Healing*. New York: Alliance Press Company, [189-?]. 13 p.

An address given at the London Conference of June 1885, emphasizing the need to use the will, rather than to depend on emotions, in taking Christ as one's bodily life. Cf. 1690.

1692. ———. *How to Receive Divine Healing*. New York: The Christian and Missionary Alliance, 1953. 6 p.

Reprint of 1694.

1693. ———. *How to Retain Divine Healing*. New York: The Christian and Missionary Alliance, 1953. 5 p.

Reprint of 1688. Cf. 1690.

1694. ———. *How to Take It*. Tracts for the Times. Divine Healing Series. New York: Christian Alliance Pub. Co., [1900?]. 8 p.

To receive divine healing one must sincerely desire to please God, familiarize oneself with the relevant Scriptures, pursue intimacy with Christ, trust Christ for healing, and act on faith. Cf. 1692.

1695. [———]. *How We Can Haste His Coming*. Tracts for the Times. Lord's Coming Series. New York: Christian Alliance Pub. Co., [ca. 1900]. 8 p.

Since God's conception of time is so different from ours, and since there are references in Scripture to God "shortening the days," contemporary Christians, like the Christians at Pentecost, must be able to do certain things to expedite the Lord's return, including: pursuing personal holiness, engaging in missionary endeavors, and prayer.

1696. ———. *Hymns and Songs of the Four-Fold Gospel and the Fulness of Jesus*. New York: Christian Alliance Pub. Co., 1890. 130 p.

Words only.

1697. ———, comp. *Hymns of the Christian Life*. New York: Christian Alliance Pub. Co., [1914?].

Selections from 1883. Also includes some previously unpublished hymns, including several by A. B. Simpson.

———, joint ed. *Hymns of the Christian Life: New and Standard Songs for the Sanctuary, Sunday Schools, Prayer Meetings, Mission Work and Revival Services.*
See 256.

1698. ———, comp. *Hymns of the Christian Life No. 2.* South Nyack, N.Y.: Christian Alliance Pub. Co., 1897. 300 p.
385 hymns, of which Simpson wrote the lyrics to 72 (and the music to 63 of these). Cf. 772.

———, joint ed. *Hymns of the Christian Life (words only): New and Standard Songs for the Sanctuary, Sunday Schools, Prayer Meetings, Mission Work and Revival Services.*
See 257.

1699. ———. *"I Have Learned the Secret."* New York: Christian Alliance Pub. Co., [189-?]. 31 p.
"It is the great mystery . . . even our union with the spirit and body of the Lord in such a sense that we become partakers of His entire being and nature and draw our spiritual life from His Spirit, our intellectual vigor from His mind, our physical strength from His risen body and our power for service from His omnipotence" (p. 9). Also published in 1703.

1700. ———. *The "I Wills" of God and the Believer.* New York: Christian Alliance Pub. Co., [189-?]. 30 p.
Holy living requires a consecrated and steadfast will that is in union with the will of God.

1701. ———. *In Heavenly Places.* New York: Christian Alliance Pub. Co., 1892. 247 p.
Twelve sermons on the Christian life based on selected biblical texts. "Jesus Only," a sermon on the Transfiguration, preached on the occasion of the departure of missionaries to the Congo, hails St. Cyprian as an example of those who have the beatific vision of "Jesus only" as "their sanctification; . . . their health . . . their providence . . . their joy . . . their power . . . their outfit . . . their infit [sic]" (p. 246). Cf. 1515 and 1596.

1702. ———. *In Step with the Spirit: Discovering the Dynamics of the Deeper Life.* Camp Hill, Pa.: Christian Publications, 1998. 180 p.
Abridged reprint of 1853 (lacks the sermon "Emblems and Aspects of the Holy Spirit").

1703. ———. *In the School of Christ, or Lessons from New Testament Characters concerning Christian Life and Experience.* New York: Christian Alliance Pub. Co., 1890. 250 p.

Twelve sermons. Four of the characters treated are women. On Priscilla: "The ministry of Priscilla . . . was all womanly. It was never apart from her husband . . . but she was no mere cipher. Indeed we can almost infer . . . that she became at last the stronger nature of the two. . . let no man hinder the ministry of women within its true limitations" (p. 177-78).

1704. ———. *In the School of Christ, or Lessons from New Testament Characters concerning Christian Life and Experience, Part 1.* Alliance Colportage Library, vol. 2, no. 1. Nyack, N.Y.: Christian Alliance Pub. Co., 1900. 135 p.

Reprint of p. 1-135 of 1703.

1705. ———. *In the School of Christ, or Lessons from New Testament Characters concerning Christian Life and Experience, Part II.* Alliance Colportage Library, vol. 2 no. 12. Nyack, N.Y.: Christian Alliance Pub. Co., 1900. 136 p.

Reprint of p. 136-272 of 1703.

1706. ———. *In the School of Faith.* New York: Alliance Press Co., [189-?]. 292 p.

Eighteen sermons, inspired by Heb. 11, on the heroes of faith from Abel to Jesus Christ. The first seven chapters are a reprint of 1834. On David: "notwithstanding all his inexcusable faults and glaring sins, the deep and uniform purpose of his heart . . . [was] toward God. His errors were not wilful acts of disobedience, but sudden and passionate outbursts of his own impulsive nature" (p. 175). Cf. 1825.

1707. ———. *In the School of Faith, Part I.* Alliance Colportage Library, vol. 2, no. 23. Nyack, N.Y.: Christian Alliance Pub. Co., 1900. 174 p.

Reprint of p. 1-174 of 1706.

1708. ———. *In the School of Faith, Part II.* Alliance Colportage Library, vol. 2, no. 24. Nyack, N.Y.: Christian Alliance Pub. Co., 1900. 161 p.

Reprint of p. 175-336 of 1706.

1709. [———]. *India's Need.* Tracts for the Times. Mission Series. New York: Christian Alliance Pub. Co., [ca. 1900]. 8 p.

1710. ———. *Individual Responsibility.* [New York?]: [Word, Work and World Pub. Co.?] [1887?].

Reprint of the last chapter of 1727.

1711. [———]. *The Indwelling Christ.* Tracts for the Times. Deeper Life Series. New York: Christian Alliance Pub. Co., [ca. 1900]. 8 p.

A meditation on Col. 1:27. "Christ has two incarnations. The first was when He came to Bethlehem, the second is when He comes into a human heart to dwell there" (p. 3).

1712. ———. "The Indwelling Christ and Divine Healing." *The American Holiness Journal*, February 1983, 28-29.

Divine healing is the life of Jesus dwelling in believers' bodies, the power of the Resurrection made available to fortify them so that they may serve him well and experience his presence in their bodies as well as in their spirits.

1713. ———. *The Infinite Resources of Grace.* Berachah Tracts. Second Series, no. 19. New York: The Word, the Work and the World Pub. Co., [1886?]. 16 p.

A sermon on the nature of the Christian life according to 2 Peter (steadfastness in Christ). Reprinted in 1621.

1714. ———. *Inquiries and Answers.* New York: Word, Work and World Pub. Co., 1887. 137 p.

Answers to 36 frequently asked questions about divine healing, e.g., Paul's thorn in the flesh (not sickness, but "some humiliating and annoying trial") (p. 9) along with three extensive rebuttals to recent criticisms of divine healing: "Divine Healing: Reply to Rev. A. F. Schauffler (likely Adolphus Frederick Schauffler, 1845-1919); "Prayer and the Prayer Cure: A Reply to Dr. Hodge," (likely Archibald Alexander Hodge, 1823-1886); and "Divine Healing Not Identical with Spiritualism: A Reply to Dr. J. M. Buckley," (cf. 204). Cf.1751.

1715. ———. *Inquiries and Answers concerning Divine Healing.* New York: Christian Alliance Pub. Co., [ca. 1895]. 50 p.

Reprint of 35 of the 36 questions and answers in 1714. "How do you explain the cures of Romanism, Spiritualism and the mind cure?" has been omitted.

1716. ———. "'International Conference: Liverpool.'" *Thy Healer* 2 (1885): 217-18.

A sermonette on Mark 11:27-28. Those who reject the fourfold Gospel do so not because it is unscriptural or intellectually untenable, but because they fear the consequences of accepting it.

1717. ———. *Is It God's Will?* Tracts for the Times. Divine Healing Series. New York: Christian Alliance Pub. Co., [ca. 1900]. 8 p.

The Scriptures teach that God desires to heal. But those who pray for healing must will their healing even as God wills it.

1718. ———. *Is Life Worth Living?* South Nyack, N.Y.: Christian Alliance Pub. Co., 1899. 54 p.

Studies in Ecclesiastes: Solomon, seeks to warn his readers against repeating his own follies. He concludes that one ought to live one's life in the light of the following realities: God and moral government exist, there is an eternal afterlife, and God will pass judgment on human activities.

1719. ———. *Isaiah*, 2nd rev. ed. Christ in the Bible, vol. 7. New York: Alliance Press Co., 1907. 401 p.

Sermons on 28 selected texts. Some contemporary examples of the evil described in Isaiah 5:20 are: "the poetry of passion . . . the popular novel . . . the meretricious theatre . . . the suggestiveness of fashion . . . the false teachings of Romanism cloaking over sin through ecclesiastical indulgence" (p. 123).

1720. [———]. *The Islands*. Tracts for the Times. Mission Series. New York: Christian Alliance Pub. Co., [ca. 1905]. 8 p.

A survey of the extent to which the various islands and archipelagos in the tropics have been evangelized.

1721. ———. *Jesus in the Psalms*. New York: Christian Alliance Pub. Co., 1892. 340 p.

Eighteen Psalms are viewed Christologically in these 15 sermons, e.g., Psalm 23, in which the still waters represent "the picture of the Holy Spirit . . . as he brings us into the deepest rest of Jesus" (p. 11).

1722. ———. *Jesus in the Psalms*. Christ in the Bible. Harrisburg, Pa.: Christian Publications, [193-?]. 158 p.

Identical to 1721, except that the sermons have been rearranged in ascending numerical order by psalm.

1723. ———. *Joshua*. Christ in the Bible, vol. 3. New York: Christian Alliance Pub. Co., 1894. 272 p.

Seventeen sermons on selected texts in Joshua and related passages in the New Testament. Israel's entrance into the Promised Land was, for Simpson, a type of the Christian's entrance into the sanctified life; and the later chapters in Joshua represented for him the "highest and best possibilities" (p. 10) of the Christian life. Cf. 1849.

1724. ———. *Judges, Ruth and Samuel*. Christ in the Bible, vol. 4. New York: Alliance Press Co., 1903. 243 p.

Reprint of 1555 and the first five chapters of 1758.

1725. ———. *The Kind of Missionaries We Want*. Missionary Alliance Leaflets. First Series, no. 4. New York: Christian Alliance Pub. Co., 1892.

The International Missionary Alliance is seeking men and women between 21 and 43 years of age who: are thoroughly converted; have been filled with the Holy Spirit; are experienced evangelists; can live simply and endure hardship; can get along well with others; are healthy, joyful, and hard-working; and have a clear call to missions.

1726. ———. *Kings and Prophets of Israel and Judah*. Christ in the Bible, vol. 6. New York: Alliance Press Co., 1903. 291 p.

Seventeen sermons on selected texts from the books of Kings, Chronicles, and prophets. Jonah is both the prototype of the foreign missionary and an illustration of the fact that "God often has to dishonor his servants to save them" (p. 89).

1727. ———. *The King's Business*. New York: Word, Work and World Pub. Co., 1886. 384 p.

Twenty sermons on the Christian life. "Woman too has her ministry . . . 'the beloved Persis labored much in the Lord'; ever of course in a true womanly way and sphere, but with equal liberty in all except the pastoral office and the official ministry of the church. God be thanked for the enlargement and restoration of woman's blessed ministry" (p. 47). Cf. 1678, 1710, 1765, 1795, 1828.

1728. ———. *The King's Business*. Alliance Colportage Library, vol. 2, no. 17. Nyack, N.Y.: Christian Alliance Pub. Co., 1900. 160 p.

Reprint of six sermons from 1727, with new preface.

1729. ———. *Kirjath-Sepher, or the Mind of Christ*. New York: Christian Alliance Pub. Co., [189-?] 26 p.

A sermon on Josh. 15:16-19 emphasizing "the victory of faith over the natural mind and the wisdom of the world" (p. 4). Also published in 1723.

1730. ———. *The Ladder and the Living Way*. New York: Christian Alliance Pub. Co., [189-?]. 23 p.

A sermon on Gen. 28:11-15: Jacob's vision of the ladder is a reminder that Christ is the only living way to heaven.

1731. ———. *The Land of Promise, or Our Full Inheritance in Christ.* New York: Christian Alliance Pub. Co., [1888?]. 273 p.

Twelve sermons in which each phase of the story of Israel's entry into the Promised Land is interpreted allegorically with respect to the deeper life: like Joshua the true Christian will press forward to appropriate sanctification and all of the promises of God recorded in the Scriptures.

1732. ———. *The Land of Promise, or Our Full Inheritance in Christ.* Alliance Colportage Library, vol. 3, no. 2. New York: Christian Alliance Pub. Co., 1901. 170 p.

Reprint of p. 1-170 of 1731.

1733. ———. *The Land of Promise, or Our Full Inheritance in Christ, Part II.* Alliance Colportage Library, vol. 3, no. 3. Nyack, N.Y.: Christian Alliance Pub. Co., 1901. 103 p.

Reprint of p. 171-273 of 1731.

1734. ———. *A Larger Christian Life*. New York: Christian Alliance Pub. Co., 1890. 287 p.

Eleven sermons on the need to abandon mediocrity in the Christian life in favor of a radical dependence on Christ. The result will be empowerment for a breadth and depth of service that would be impossible from a human standpoint. Cf. 1757.

1735. ———. *A Larger Christian Life*. Camp Hill, Pa.: Christian Publications, 1988. 159 p.

Reprint of 1734, with updated language, Scripture passages in the NIV, and an introduction that sets the work in its historical context.

1736. ———. *Larger Outlooks on Missionary Lands: Descriptive Sketches of a Missionary Journey through Egypt, Palestine, India, Burmah, Malaysia, China, Japan, and the Sandwich Islands*. New York: Christian Alliance Pub. Co., 1893. 595 p.

A revised and enlarged version of the corpus of missionary letters Simpson wrote during his world tour of Alliance mission stations, January-July 1893.

1737. ———. "Letters to the Editor." *The Christian*, 20 June 1885. 20.

A rebuttal to "Mr. Simpson's Article" (*The Christian*, 18 June 1885, 5). The Holy Spirit "quickens" the mortal body; full redemption of the body will come only when the Lord returns. The full Gospel includes physical healing, but that doctrine should never receive disproportionate emphasis.

1738. ———. *Leviticus*. Christ in the Bible. Harrisburg, Pa.: Christian Publications, [193-?] 125 p.

Reprint of the first section of 1739.

1739. ———. *Leviticus, Numbers, Deuteronomy*. [New York?]: Alliance Press Co., 1902.

Differs from 1740 in that extensive quotations from Scripture are replaced by references to the passages concerned. Cf. 1738.

1740. ———. *Leviticus to Deuteronomy*. Christ in the Bible, vol. 2. New York: Word, Work and World Pub. Co., 1889. 412 p.

A devotional commentary. The guiding cloud and fire of Num. 9:15-22 illustrates the importance of learning "not only to follow the Spirit when He leads us forward, but also to wait when He holds us in silence" (p. 158). Cf. 1739 and 1778..

1741. ———. *Life More Abundantly*. New York: Christian Alliance Pub. Co., 1912. 134 p.

Thirty-one sermonettes (one for each day of the month) on the Christian life.

1742. ———. *Life of Christ*. Christ in the Bible, vol. 8. New York: Word, Work and World Pub. Co., 1888. 400 p.

A commentary/biography based on the Gospels that includes an appendix of illustrative materials and a fold-out chronology of the life of Christ. On the "hidden life of Christ": "There is still no place where it is so important, and often so difficult to follow Him as in . . . toil, temptation and monotonous, commonplace duties. There the Son of Man fulfilled all righteousness" (p. 48-49).

1743. ———. *The Life of Prayer*. New York: Christian Alliance Pub. Co., 1890. 268 p.

Seven sermons. Prayer "is the converse of a soul with its Heavenly Father, and it is a strange conversation in which the principal party has nothing to say. True prayer listens to God's voice and then adds its 'Amen' to His 'Verily'" (p. 206).

1744. ———. *The Life of Prayer*. The Alliance Colportage Series. New York: Christian Alliance Pub. Co., 1925. 124 p.

Lacks chapters five and six of 1743.

1745. ———. *The Life of Prayer*. Camp Hill, Pa.: Christian Publications, 1989. 89 p.

Reprint of 1744, with updated language and NIV in place of KJV.

1746.———. *The Life of Prayer*, new ed. New York: Christian Alliance Pub. Co., 1915. 163 p.

Reprint of 1744.

1747.———. *Listening*. Cleveland, Ohio: n.p., n.d. 4 p.

A condensation of 1796, with the addition of some new material and two poems by Simpson.

1748. ———. *Look on the Fields*. Christian Alliance Tracts. New York: Christian Alliance Pub. Co., [1899?]. 24 p.

A sermon on John 4:35-36, preached at Carnegie Hall, 15 October 1899. The lostness of the world manifests itself in such things as: intemperance, addiction to opium, immorality (especially polygamy), the degradation of women, slavery, self-torture and fanaticism, cannibalism and human sacrifice, heathen cruelty, the neglect and abuse of the sick, the caste system, ignorance, falsehood and dishonesty, and the religion of heathenism.

1749. ———. *Looking for and Hasting Forward*. South Nyack, N.Y.: Christian Alliance Pub. Co., 1899. 35 p.

A sermon on 2 Pet. 3:11-14. Faith and hope must be based on an understanding of and a longing for Christ's imminent return. Christians can hasten his coming by making sure of their own salvation and sanctification and by seeking to lead as many others into these experiences as possible.

1750. ———. *The Lord for the Body*. Tracts for the Times. Divine Healing Series. New York: Christian Alliance Press Co., [ca. 1900]. 8 p.

Christ has given his body not only for us, but to us. His risen life is the physical source of our bodily strength.

1751. ———. *The Lord for the Body: With Questions and Answers on Divine Healing*. New York: Christian Alliance Pub. Co., 1925. 142 p.

Reprint of 1564 and 1714, along with two additional sermons and the testimony of Simpson's associate, Dr. Henry Wilson. Reprinted by Christian Publications in 1996 without Wilson's testimony and with added Scripture index.

1752. [———]. *The Lord's Coming and Missions*. Tracts for the Times. Lord's Coming Series. New York: Christian Alliance Pub. Co., [ca. 1900]. 8 p.

Belief in the premillennial return of Christ should be an encouragement to missions because it provides a clear objective: finding those in each culture whom the Holy Spirit is preparing to accept the Gospel; an incentive: to accelerate the Lord's return; and a message: the judgment to come.

1753. ———. *The Lord's Day*. Living Truths, vol. 1, no. 41. New York: Christian Alliance Pub. Co., 1901. 19 p.

A sermon on 1 Cor. 16:2 and Rev. 1:10. Christians must honor the first day of the week as the sabbath (Christianity is rest first, then work) and avoid legalistic rigidity in so doing.

1754. ———. *The Love-Life of the Lord*. New York: Christian Alliance Pub. Co., [1891?]. 213 p.

Six sermons (plus introduction) on the Song of Songs. A classic allegorical approach—the romantic and erotic imagery of the book are a symbolic depiction of Christ's love for the church and of the church's love for Christ—with idiosyncratic twists, e.g., the little sister with no breasts (8:8) represents the worldly and immature portion of the church, which will not be raptured with the sanctified but left to be purged by the tribulation. Cf. 1756.

1755. ———. *Lovest Thou Me?* New York: Christian Alliance Pub. Co., [1897?]. 17 p.

A sermon on John 21:15, 17: Peter's failure, like all the failures of Jesus' followers, involved a lack of love. If loving Christ involves feeding his sheep, then the most selfless act of love would be to take the Gospel to an unevangelized people.

1756. ———. *Loving As Jesus Loves: A Devotional Exposition of the Song of Songs*. Camp Hill, Pa.: Christian Publications, 1996. 108 p.

Reprint, with updated language, of 1754.

1757. ———. "Make Your Life a Melody." *Prairie Overcomer* 53 (May 1980): 261-63.

An exposition of 2 Pet. 1:5-8, which was originally published in 1734.

1758. ———. *Making Jesus King*. South Nyack, N.Y: Christian Alliance Pub. Co., 1898. 288 p.

Eighteen typological sermons on the life of David: Samuel's reform prefigures the Protestant Reformation; Saul's "counterfeit kingship" is a type of the false ecclesiastical kingdom that will precede the return of Christ; "the story of [David's] rejection, exile and final triumph freely foreshadows the conflicts and victories that are to usher in the reign of our Lord;" (p. v) and the reign of Solomon prefigures the millennial reign of Christ. Cf. 1724.

1759. ———. *Matthew, Mark and Luke*. Christ in the Bible, vol. 9. New York: Christian Alliance Pub. Co., 1889. 243 p.

A devotional commentary with an appendix of "homiletic hints." On Matt. 24:37-39: "The condition of the world at His coming is finally described. It is certainly not a millennial paradise" (p. 122).

1760. ———. *The Message of Bethlehem*. [New York?]: [Christian Alliance Pub. Co.?] [1908?]. 9 p.

A Christmas poem.

1761. ———. *Messages of Love, or Christ in the Epistles of John*. Alliance Colportage Library, vol. 2, no. 14. Nyack, N.Y.: Christian Alliance Pub. Co., 1900. 160 p.

Nine sermons on selected texts. "[God] always loves and He loves all as much as it is possible under the circumstances for them to receive" (p. 83). Cf. 1589.

1762. ———, comp. *Michele Nardi—the Italian Evangelist: His Life and Work*. New York: Blanche P. Nardi, 1916. 143 p.

A collection of tributes to Nardi (1850-1914), an Italian immigrant to the United States, who studied under Simpson and was unofficially ordained by him before embarking on a life of itinerant evangelism throughout the eastern United States and Italy.

1763. ———. *The Midnight Cry*. [New York?]: n.p., 1914. 19 p.

A sermon on Matt. 25:6. Recent wars and natural disasters, together with the growth of Zionism are all fulfillments of biblical prophecies concerning the second coming of Christ.

1764. ———. *Millennial Chimes: A Collection of Poems*. New York: Christian Alliance Pub. Co., 1894. 155 p.

Includes previously unpublished poems as well as those that had already appeared as hymn lyrics in 772.

1765. ———. *The Ministry of Suffering*. New York: Christian Alliance Pub. Co., [1893?]. 25 p.

A sermon on Phil. 1:29 and Col. 1:24. Suffering can come from various sources and take a variety of forms (even the "spiritual discipline" of the purifying work of the Holy Spirit). It prepares believers for usefulness and gives them opportunities for service. Also published in 1277.

1766. ———. *The Missionary Emergency*. New York: Christian and Missionary Alliance, 1915. 14 p.

Simpson's annual missionary sermon, based on Eph. 5:17 and 1 Cor. 16:8-9, which he preached at the New York convention on 12 October 1913. "Working and praying and sacrificing for the immediate evangelization of the world . . . is the supreme duty of every Christian" (p. 4). Also published in 1767. Cf. 1809.

1767. ———. *Missionary Messages*. The Alliance Colportage Series. New York: Christian Alliance Pub. Co., 1925. 131 p.

Seven collected sermons. "It is usually a woman who reaches the superlative degree . . . no one can do more in promoting the idea of missions at home, no one can be such a recruiting agent for volunteers . . . and no one can give and sacrifice as women do" (p. 51). Cf. 1546, 1765, 1777.

1768. ———. *Missionary Work among the Jews*. Missionary Alliance Leaflets. First Series, no. 10. New York: Christian Alliance Pub. Co., [1892].

Jews are being expelled from Russia and are settling in Palestine. Successful evangelization of Jews is taking place in New York City, southern Russia, and even in Jerusalem.

1769. [———]. *Mother, Has Your Verse Changed?* Tracts for the Times. Salvation Series. New York: Christian Alliance Pub. Co., [ca. 1900]. 8 p.

A reflection on John 5:24: Christians have begun to experience eternal life in this life and will be spared judgment in the next.

1770. ———. *My Medicine Chest.* New York: Christian Alliance Pub. Co., [1913?]. 16 p.

A list of the spiritual counterparts to the various kinds of medical treatments then available. Ninety percent of divine healing is the union of the physical body with Christ its living head. Includes some autobiographical illustrations.

1771. ———. *The Names of Jesus.* New York: Christian Alliance Pub. Co., 1892. 285 p.

Fifteen sermons on selected Christological texts. Although not rigorously theological, these sermons shed considerable light on Simpson's Christology."We are to continually distrust ourselves, and feel our utter inability to think a right thought and to look to Him in utter helplessness and yet in trustful reliance" (p. 236). Cf. 1656

1772. ———. *The Names of Jesus.* Camp Hill, Pa.: Christian Publications, 1991. 197 p.

A revised edition of 1771 in that the language has been updated, KJV quotations have been replaced with NIV, and some archaic examples have been eliminated.

1773. ———. *Natural Emblems of Spiritual Life: Being the Fourth Series of Tabernacle Sermons.* New York: Word, Work and World Pub. Co., [1888?]. 356 p.

Twenty-four sermons that draw spiritual lessons from natural phenomena mentioned in the Bible.

1774. ———. *The Needs of South America.* Missionary Alliance Leaflets. First Series, no. 8. New York: Christian Alliance Pub. Co., [1892?]. 8 p.

South America's people have suffered under the oppression of the Spanish and Portuguese colonizers and the Roman Catholic Church. There are but 5,500 Protestant Christians in the whole continent, and

Bolivia, Nicaragua, Venezuela, and Ecuador have no Protestant presence whatever.

1775. [———]. *Neglected Fields*. Tracts for the Times. Mission Series. New York: Christian Alliance Pub. Co., [ca. 1900]. 8 p.

1776. [———]. *Neglected Warnings*. Tracts for the Times. Salvation Series. New York: Christian Alliance Pub. Co., [ca. 1900]. 6 p.

We refuse at our peril the glorious opportunity inherent in Christ's offer of salvation.

1777. ———. *The New Testament Standpoint of Missions*. New York: Christian Alliance Pub. Co., [1892?]. 33 p.

A sermon that sums up the Alliance position as follows: "we are preaching the gospel not for the conversion of the world, but for a witness unto all nations, and when we shall have accomplished this, He will come" (p. 31). Reprinted as "The New Testament Pattern of Missions" in 1767.

1778. ———. *Numbers and Deuteronomy*. Christ in the Bible. Harrisburg, Pa.: Christian Publications, [193-?]. 293 p.

Reprint, without biblical text, of the Numbers-Deuteronomy portion of 1740.

1779. ———. *The Old Faith and the New Gospels: Special Addresses on Christianity and Modern Thought.* New York: Alliance Press Company, 1911. 161 p.

Topics covered include the theory of evolution, higher criticism, liberal theology, socialism, and non-Christian forms of spiritual healing. Simpson does not completely dismiss the theory of evolution, since in modified form it could describe the way "by which the . . . Creator accomplishes much of His work" (p. 12), but it is a mistake to apply it to the fields of "philosophy, morals and religion" (p. 23). Christians must oppose the increasingly anti-Christian bias of the state-controlled school system by establishing their own educational institutions at all levels.

1780. [———]. *The Opportunity*. Tracts for the Times. Mission Series. New York: Alliance Press Co., [ca. 1905]. 8 p.

Opportunities for missionary work have increased because: certain formerly "closed" countries have opened their borders, transportation and communication have improved, lay people are now free to serve as missionaries, and because America's growing financial prosperity should result in an increase in giving to missions.

1781. ———. *The Opportunity in Japan*. Missionary Alliance Leaflets. First Series, no. 9. New York: Christian Alliance Pub. Co., [1892?].

Japan is a highly civilized country in which the International Missionary Alliance has recently begun to work. The Japanese are naturally inquisitive and are open not only to the Gospel but to other religions as well.

1782. ———. "Our Attitude toward the Coming of the Lord." In *The Signs of the Times: A Symposium on New Theology, Christian Science, the Lord's Coming, the Gift of Tongues, and the Deeper Spiritual Life*, 215-26. New York: Alliance Press Co., 1907.

Postmillennial dreams do not constitute the Christian vision, for "we are building no temple here, but simply quarrying stones and carving timbers for the temple yonder in the New Jerusalem" (p. 226).

1783. ———. *Our Attitude towards the Lord's Coming*. New York: Christian Alliance Pub. Co., [1893?]. 27 p.

"The whole of God's plan for the world has reference to the Lord's coming" (p. 22). "The question . . . is not how many souls we can save, either at home or abroad, but how we can best carry out Christ's work in the gathering in of the elect from all nations and the carrying out of His plans for the hastening of His kingdom" (p. 24).

1784. ———. *Our Land of Promise: A New Year's Message, 1918*. [New York]: [Christian Alliance Pub. Co.?] 1918. 4 p.

Based on Deut. 11:11-12.

1785. ———. *Our Living Lord*. New York: Christian Alliance Pub. Co., [1892?] 16 p.

An Easter sermon based on Rev. 1:18 and 1 Cor. 15:48, 49. As a result of the Resurrection "a new, divine, absolutely foreign and heavenly life [is] implanted directly from the bosom of Christ in the heart of the believer. . ." (p. 12).

1786. [———]. *Pardoned but Guilty*. Tracts for the Times. Salvation Series. New York: Christian Alliance Pub. Co., [ca. 1900]. 8 p.

1787. ———. *Paul: The Ideal Man and Model Missionary*. New York: Christian Alliance Pub. Co., 1896. 73 p.

Five sermons on the apostle who was "a second edition in miniature of the great Pattern life of the Son of man" (p. 5). Paul embodied the fourfold Gospel in his sound conversion, his experience and doctrine of sanctification, his experience and practice of divine healing, and his source of hope: the return of Christ. This Gospel synthesis provided the motive force behind his exemplary missionary consecration and zeal.

1788. ———. "Personal Testimony of Rev. Dr. A. B. Simpson." *The Evangelical Christian*, November 1915, 346-47.

Since his departure from Hamilton, Ont., Simpson has come to a settled conviction regarding his own nothingness, the all-sufficiency of Christ, the hope of the premillennial return of Christ, and the pressing need for the evangelization of the world. (An address delivered in Hamilton, Ont., on the fiftieth anniversary of his ordination.)

1789. ———. *Philippians, Colossians and Thessalonians*. New York: Alliance Press Co., [1903?] 290 p.

Reprint of 1498, 1843, and 1590.

1790. [———]. *The Plan of the Ages*. Tracts for the Times. Lord's Coming Series. New York: Christian Alliance Pub. Co., [ca. 1900]. 8 p.

A catalogue of fulfilled and as yet to be fulfilled prophecies with respect to the return of Christ.

1791. ———. "[Plenary Address at the Anointing Service, 3 June]." In *Record of the International Conference on Divine Healing and True Holiness Held at the Agricultural Hall, London, June 1 to 5, 1885,* 80-86. London: J. Snow and Company, 1885.

Reflections on his four years as a facilitator of divine healing. "The atonement of Christ takes away sin and all the consequences of sin for every believer who accepts him." The prerequisites for healing are resolute appropriating faith, renunciation of selfishness and sin, and dependence on Jesus as one's source of energy and strength.

1792. ———. "[Plenary Address, Evening of 2 June]." In *Record of the International Conference on Divine Healing and True Holiness Held at the Agricultural Hall, London, June 1 to 5, 1885,* 64-69. London: J. Snow and Company, 1885.

An overview of healing and holiness work being carried on in the United States, followed by a brief spiritual autobiography and a synopsis of the "fourfold Gospel."

1793. ———. "[Plenary Address, Morning of 2 June]." In *Record of the International Conference on Divine Healing and True Holiness Held at the Agricultural Hall, London, June 1 to 5, 1885*, 38-41. London: J. Snow and Company, 1885.

A meditation on the references to the Holy Spirit in the Gospel of John. The work of regeneration is the "motherhood" of the Holy Spirit, but the regenerate person must move beyond this to become someone in whom the "Spirit . . . personally [dwells] as at home" (p. 39).

1794. ———. *Portraits of the Spirit-Filled Personality: Guidelines for Holy Living from Philippians*. Camp Hill, Pa.: Christian Publications, 1995. 118 p.

Reprint of 1843.

1795. ———. *Power for Service*. New York: Christian Alliance Pub. Co., [189-?]. 32 p.

A sermon on Eph. 1:19: Mortals are, in their own strength, powerless. Christ and the Gospel are God's power through the Holy Spirit; power to convert, to receive Christ, to repent; power through the now-indwelling Holy Spirit to the consecrated (i.e., Spirit-baptized) believer. Also published in 1727 and 1828.

1796. ———. *The Power of Stillness*. Randleman, N.C.: Pilgrim Tract Society, [189-?]. 3 p.

The listening prayer of contemplation leads to the self-surrender that is the key to spiritual power and effective service for Christ. Includes Simpson's account of how he was introduced to the "old mediaeval message" of contemplative prayer through the book *True Peace*.

1797. ———. *Practical Christianity*. Nyack, N.Y.: Christian Alliance Pub. Co., [1901?]. 162 p.

The assumption underlying these eight sermons on selected passages in the epistle of James is that "The epistles of John and Paul represent the interior, the experimental and spiritual side of Christian life, while that of James represents the practical" (p. 9-10). Cf. 1586.

1798. [———]. *Practical Holiness*. Tracts for the Times. Deeper Life Series. New York: Christian Alliance Pub. Co., [ca.1900]. 8 p.

The deeper life consists of both the mystical and the practical. The mystery of the experience of the indwelling Christ must work itself out in practical righteousness.

1799. ———. *Present Truth*. South Nyack, N.Y.: Christian Alliance Pub. Co., 1897. 151 p.

Seven sermons on the supernatural. "[There] is always some portion of Divine truth which might properly be called present truth, God's message to the times . . . one line of truth . . . seems to be pre-eminently present truth and that is the truth about the supernatural" (p. 6-7). Cf. 1842.

1800. ———. *Present Truths, or the Supernatural*. Harrisburg, Pa.: Christian Publications, 1967. 91 p.

Reprint of 1799.

1801. ———. *Pressure and the Test*. Randleman, N.C.: Pilgrim Tract Society, [ca. 1900]. 4 p.

Divine healing involves considerable struggle since it requires constant dependence on God so that the life of Jesus may be manifested in one's body.

1802. ———. *Principles of Divine Healing*. [New York?]: [Word, Work and World Pub. Co.?], [1888?]. 24 p.

1803. ———. "The Principles of Faith Healing." *The Christian*, 11 June 1885, 10-11.

A précis of Simpson's views on healing. Originally published in *The Word, The Work and The World* 5 (May 1885): 154-58. Cf. 543.

1804. ———. *Providence and Missions*. South Nyack, N.Y.: Christian Alliance Pub. Co., 1899. 44 p.

A sermon on Matt. 16:20 and Judg. 4:14. "Two mighty forces co-operate through the whole history of the missionary church and the ascended Lord, the Divine Spirit and the divine Providence" (p. 5).

1805. [———]. *Put Your Name in It*. Tracts for the Times. Salvation Series. New York: Christian Alliance Pub. Co., [ca. 1900]. 8 p.

Faith in Christ involves not so much believing the truth about Christ as trusting in the person of Christ.

1806. ———. "[Question and Response, 4 June]." In *Record of the International Conference on Divine Healing and True Holiness Held at the Agricultural Hall, London, June 1 to 5, 1885,* 126-29. London: J. Snow and Company, 1885.

A delay in the manifestation of healing can be attributed to such deficiencies as a to failure to "[take] the Lord Himself and [live] on His strength" (p. 126). Includes an account of Simpson's climbing a mountain to personally appropriate his own experience of divine healing from heart trouble.

1807. ———. *Questions and Objections*. Tracts for the Times. Divine Healing Series. New York: Christian Alliance Pub. Co., [ca. 1900]. 8 p.

Various scriptural examples that appear to contradict the doctrine of divine healing: Hezekiah's poultice, Paul's thorn in the flesh, Timothy's dyspepsia, and the cases of Trophimus and Epaphroditus are explained and found not to contradict the principle of childlike faith that is the foundation of both the doctrine and the practice.

1808. ———. *Reasons for the Alliance*. New York: Christian and Missionary Alliance, 1888.

1809. ———. "Redeeming the Time." *The Evangelical Christian*, January 1912, 11.

The text of an address, based on Eph. 5:16 and 2 Sam. 5:24, delivered 6 December 1911, at Central Presbyterian Church, Toronto, at the close of the C&MA mid-winter convention. Similar in content to 1766.

1810. ———. *The Regions Beyond*. Missionary Alliance Leaflets. First Series, no. 11. New York: Christian Alliance Pub. Co., [1892?].

The regions beyond are the completely unevangelized areas of the world, such as: Tibet, Turkestan, Siberia, Russia, Southeast Asia, Afghanistan, Arabia, and significant portions of South America, China, and central Africa.

1811. [———]. *The Responsibility*. Tracts for the Times. Mission Series. New York: Christian Alliance Pub. Co., [ca. 1900]. 8 p.

The evangelization of the world has been given to Christians as a command, a trust, a debt, and a means of responding in gratitude to the grace of God. God will hold those who neglect their duty responsible for the fate of the lost.

1812. ———. *The River from the Sanctuary*. New York: Christian Alliance Pub. Co., [189-?]. 15 p.

A sermon on sanctification based on Ezek. 47-48.: "the temple, both of the past and of the future, is God's special type of the human soul and body as the dwelling-place of Jehovah" (p. 1).

1813. ———. "The River of Life." *Thy Healer* 3 (1886): 104-5, 120-24.

A sermon on the river as a biblical symbol. Christians must let go of their self-consciousness and be borne along by the river of the life of God.

1814. ———. *Rolled Away*. New York: Christian Alliance Pub. Co., [189-?]. 22 p.

A sermon on the Resurrection (Luke 24:3) as it applies to the overcoming of obstacles. On the agency of angels: "they are already here where He is . . . this is the metropolis of His presence and providence, and . . . they [are] all about His person as He stands amongst us through the ages" (p. 15).

1815. ———. *Romans*. Christ in the Bible, vol. 11. New York: Christian Alliance Pub. Co., 1894. 274 p.

Sixteen sermons, with a general introduction, on selected texts from the book of Romans. "The seventh of Romans is the hopeless struggle of the new heart with the old heart in a saved man. The eighth of Romans is the victory of the same man [through] the indwelling presence and power of Jesus Christ" (p. 149). Cf. 1618 and 1619.

1816. ———. *Romans*. Christ in the Bible, vol. 17. New York: Alliance Press Co., 1904. 298 p.

Reprint of 1815. Cf. 1819.

1817. ———. *Salvation Sermons*. The Alliance Colportage Series. Harrisburg, Pa.: Christian Alliance Pub. Co., 1925. 123 p.

Eight sermons, four of which had been published previously. The doctrine of the Atonement is "repugnant to New Thought and the good natured God our modern preachers have made out of the putty of their sentimental brains" (p. 40).

1818. ———. *Sanctification*. Nyack, N.Y.: The Christian and Missionary Alliance, 1983. 11 p.

A sermon originally preached in 1901. Sanctification involves separation from sin; dedicating oneself to God; and surrendering body, soul (the locus of intellect, emotion, and the senses) and spirit (the locus of conscience, will, and trust) to him. God does the sanctification: "It is not a state, but a life . . . not an experience, but a Person" (p. 11).

1819. ———. *Sanctification through the Spirit*. New York: Christian Alliance Pub. Co., [189-?] 33 p.

A sermon on Rom. 8:8-9: "the indwelling of the Holy Spirit in us is practically the indwelling of Christ" (p. 9). Also published in 1816.

1820. ———. *Sanctified Wholly and Preserved Blameless*. Living Truths, vol. 1, no. 27. Nyack, N.Y.: Christian Alliance Pub. Co., 1901. 16 p.

A sermon on 1 Thess. 5:23. Sanctification involves "a definite and voluntary self-dedication to God's ownership, possession, transfiguration and service" (p. 5).

1821. [———]. *Saved and Sanctified*. Tracts for the Times. Deeper Life Series. New York: Christian Alliance Pub. Co., [ca. 1900]. 8 p.

Salvation and sanctification are two stages of the Christian life: "salvation brings us into Christ; sanctification brings Christ into us." "Salvation brings to us the new heart; sanctification brings the Holy Spirit to live in the new heart" (p. 2). "Salvation is 'peace with God'; sanctification is the 'peace of God'" (p. 3).

1822. [———]. *The Second Coming of Christ*. Tracts for the Times. Lord's Coming Series. New York: Christian Alliance Pub. Co., [ca. 1910]. 10 p.

The second coming of Christ is one of the most prominent doctrines of the New Testament. It will be personal, visible, triumphant, powerful, glorious, sudden, and unexpected.

1823. ———. *Second Corinthians: The Principles and Life of the Apostolic Teaching*. Christ in the Bible, vol. 18. Harrisburg, Pa.: Christian Publications, [195-?]. 127 p.

Reprint of the 11 sermons on 2 Corinthians that comprise the second part of 1506.

1824. ———. *The Secret of Divine Healing*. Harrisburg, Pa.: Christian Alliance Pub. Co., [1900?]. 6 p.

The fullest experience of divine healing is a life of unceasing dependence on the power of God supplied by the indwelling Christ.

1825. ———. *Seeing the Invisible: The Art of Spiritual Perception*. Camp Hill, Pa.: Christian Publications, 1994. 240 p.

Reprint of 1706, with updated language.

1826. ———. *The Self Life and the Christ Life*. South Nyack, N.Y.: Christian Alliance Pub. Co., 1897. 89 p.

Five sermons on dying to self-will so as to abandon oneself to Christ. "The great lesson of Jonah's life is the need of crucifixion to the life of self . . . . God lovingly [slays] the selfish prophet and [tries] to put Jonah out of his own way, so that God could bless him as He really wanted to" (p. 80). Cf. 1534.

1827. ———. *The Self-Life and the Christ-Life*. Camp Hill, Pa.: Christian Publications, 1990. 55 p.

Reprint, of 1826, with new introduction, Scripture references, updated language, and NIV in place of KJV.

1828. ———. *Service for the King*. Nyack N.Y.: Christian Alliance Pub. Co., 1900. 181 p.

Reprint of seven chapters from 1727. Cf. 1795 and 1829.

1829. ———. *Serving the King: Doing Ministry in Partnership with God*. Camp Hill, Pa.: Christian Publications, 1995. 121 p.

Reprint of 1828.

1830. ———. *Seven Stars in the Firmament of Faith*. New York: Word, Work and World Pub. Co., 1887. 80 p.

Abel, Enoch, Noah, Abraham, Isaac, Jacob, and Joseph, as types of faith.

1831. ———. *Should We Care for Our Bodies?* Tracts for the Times. Divine Healing Series. New York: Christian Alliance Pub. Co., [ca. 1900]. 8 p.

Christians ought to reject both asceticism and an unhealthy preoccupation with the body. A whole Spirit-filled body is a great aid to spiritual growth: "One hour of divine healing will do more to sanctify you and glorify God than a quarter century of invalidism" (p. 8).

1832. ———. *The Significance of the Lord's Supper*. Living Truths, vol. 1, no. 31. Nyack, N.Y.: Christian Alliance Pub. Co., 1901. 18 p.

The Lord's Supper is a channel of grace and is more than a memorial. It is strength for the body as well as the soul.

1833. ———. "Simpson's First Sermon." *Louisville Courier-Journal*, 5 January 1874, 4.

On the all-sufficiency of Christ, especially as revealed in the Transfiguration (Matthew 17:8). Simpson's first sermon as pastor of Louisville, Kentucky's Chesnut Street Presbyterian Church.

1834. ———. *Songs of the Spirit: Hitherto Unpublished Poems and a Few Old Favorites*. New York: Christian Alliance Pub. Co., 1920. 160 p.

Compiled by Simpson's friends just after his death. Many of the "old favorites" are hymn lyrics from the various editions of *Hymns of the Christian Life*.

1835. [———]. *South America*. Tracts for the Times. Mission Series. New York: Christian Alliance Pub. Co., [ca. 1900]. 8 p.

1836. ———. *Souvenir of the Twentieth Commencement of the Missionary Institute: 1901-1902*. Nyack, N.Y.: The Missionary Training Institute, 1902. 16 p.

1837. ———. *The Spirit-Filled Church in Action*. Harrisburg, Pa.: Christian Publication, 1975. 112 p.

Reprint of 1496 that has been edited, adapted, and revised for adult group study.

1838. ———. *Standing on Faith, and Talks on the Self Life* . London: Marshall, Morgan and Scott, 1932. 121 p.

Sixteen previously published sermons.

1839. ———. *Stories of Salvation*. The Alliance Colportage Library, vol. 1, no. 17. New York: Christian Alliance Pub. Co., 1899. 110 p.

Testimonies of many well-known pastors and evangelists.

1840. [———]. *The Story of the Christian and Missionary Alliance*. [New York?]: The Alliance; Nyack, N.Y.: Alliance Press Co., 1900. 98 p.

An illustrated historical overview of the Alliance and its various ministries, with special emphasis on overseas missions. In essence, an expanded annual report. Published anonymously, but A. B. Simpson is likely the author.

1841. ———. "The Sun of Righteousness." *Thy Healer*. 1 March 1893. p. 57.

Simpson's address (based on Mal. 4:2) at the 1893 Bethshan Healing Conference (London, England). Jesus Christ is the source of life: "I do not know where [physical life] begins and [spiritual life] ends" (p. 49).

1842. ———. *The Supernatural: Making Room for the Power of God*. Camp Hill, Pa.: Christian Publications, 1994. 110 p.

Reprint of 1799, with scripture references, updated language, NIV in place of KJV, and index.

1843. ———. *The Sweetest Christian Life*. Nyack, N.Y.: Christian Alliance Pub. Co., 1899. 159 p.

Sermons on Philippians, which book describes the sweetest Christian life in the sense that it treats of the finer qualities of the essential elements of holy character. Cf. 1593, 1789, 1794.

1844. [———]. *Taking Their Own Brimstone*. Tracts for the Times. Salvation Series. New York: Christian Alliance Pub. Co., [ca. 1900]. 8 p.

Those who reject God will "take [their] own brimstone with [them]" to hell in that they will suffer physical torture in their bodies—and in their psyches the torture of memory, unfulfilled desire, and a bad conscience. Similarly, those who turn their lives over to God can make their own heaven.

1845. ———. *Tarry Till*. New York: Alliance Press. Co., [ca. 1908]. 14 p.

The reception of the Holy Spirit is a definite act, the filling of the Holy Spirit is a process. "Tarrying" (Acts 1:4) involves intense desire, putting aside hindrances, sustained prayer, the surrendering of the will, and faith.

1846. ———. *Tarrying by the Stuff*. [New York?]: [Christian Alliance Pub. Co.?], [1893?] 33 p.

A sermon on 1 Sam. 30:24-25. Supporters of missions are as important as the missionaries themselves. "Tarrying by the stuff" in this sense involves becoming imbued with, and propagating, the cause of missions, supporting missionaries financially, providing voluntary administrative support, corresponding with missionaries, and praying for missions. Cf. 1522.

1847. ———. *Temples of the Holy Ghost*. Tracts for the Times. Divine Healing Series. New York: Alliance Press Co., [ca. 1900]. 7 p.

A reflection on 1 Cor. 6:19: "Divine healing . . . is just the life and power of the Holy Ghost added to the human body and so filling it as to supply motive power to every vital function and physical organ" (p. 3).

1848. ———. *Thankfulness and Healing*. Los Angeles: Free Tract Society, n.d. 4 p.

Divine healing is a reward for obedience, the obedience of faith, of which thankfulness is the prime evidence.

1849. ———. *Thirty-one Kings, or Victory over Self.* New York: Christian Alliance Pub. Co., [189-?]. 42 p.

The 31 kings defeated by Joshua and the Israelites symbolize the 31 subtle aspects of "self-life" (one for each day of the month!) that Christians must overcome through self-surrender to Christ once they have "crossed the Jordan" and entered the "promised land" of the sanctified life. Also published in 1723.

1850. ———. *The Times of David and Solomon: Including Parts of the Books of Samuel, Kings and Chronicles*. Christ in the Bible, vol. 5. New York: Alliance Press Co., 1903. 279 p.

Nineteen typological sermons on selected passages, e.g., 1 Ki. 10 in which the Queen of Sheba's longing to meet Solomon represents "the cry of the nations after God" (p. 237).

1851. ———. *Union with Christ.* New York: Christian Alliance Pub. Co., [189-?] 16 p.

A sermon on Heb. 2:11: the Christian is one with Christ in nature, sonship, spiritual experience, suffering, death, and destiny.

1852. ———. *Walking in Love.* New York: Christian Alliance Pub. Co., [1893?] 270 p.

Nine sermons on selected texts from the New Testament on the theme of love. On love and unity : "We do not believe in attempting at this late day any formal organization, uniting all the churches, although we believe that sectarianism is unauthorized by the Scriptures" (p. 160).

1853. ———. *Walking in the Spirit.* New York: Christian Alliance Pub. Co., [1889?]. 286 p.

Sermons on selected New Testament texts. To walk in the Spirit is "to maintain the habit of dependence upon the Holy Ghost for our entire life; spirit, soul and body" (p. 18). Cf. 1628.

1854. ———. *Walking in the Spirit: A Series of Arresting Addresses on the Subject of the Holy Spirit in Christian Experience.* Harrisburg, Pa.: Christian Publications, [193-?]. 155 p.

Abridged reprint of 1853. (Lacks the chapter "Emblems and Aspects of the Holy Spirit.")

1855. ———. *Walking in the Spirit, Part I.* Alliance Colportage Library, vol. 1, no. 5. Nyack, N.Y.: Christian Alliance Pub. Co., 1899. 150 p.
Reprint of p. 1-150 of 1853.

1856. ———. *Walking in the Spirit, Part II.* Alliance Colportage Library, vol. 1, no. 6. Nyack, N.Y.: Christian Alliance Pub. Co., 1899. 147 p.
Reprint of p. 151-297 of 1853.

1857. ———. *Walking in the Spirit: The Holy Spirit in Christian Experience.* Harrisburg, Pa.: Christian Publications, [195-?]. 155 p.
Reprint of 1853.

1858. ———. *The Way Everlasting.* New York: Christian Alliance Pub. Co., [189-?]. 38 p.
A sermon on Ps. 139:23-24: "This is . . . the meaning of everlasting life. Eternity is not a time, it is a state, and we may live in it now" (p. 36).

1859. ———. *We Would See Jesus: A Scripture Text and Devotional Reading for Each Day in the Month.* New York: Christian Alliance Pub. Co., 1910. 64 p.

1860. ———. *"We Would See Jesus": Part of a Sermon Preached to the Educated Natives of India, March 1893.* New York: Christian Alliance Pub. Co., 1893. 21 p.
An evangelistic address in which a Hindu legend about Vishnu serves as an illustration of the universal need for a sacrifice of atonement. Cf. 1520.

1861. ———. *What Is the Christian and Missionary Alliance?* New York: Christian Alliance Pub. Co., 1914. 4 p.
"Extract from the report of the President, Rev. A. B. Simpson, given at the Annual Council held at Nyack, N.Y., May 1914." Cf. 1476 and 1890.

1862. [———]. *What It Is.* Tracts for the Times: Deeper Life Series. New York: Christian Alliance Pub. Co., [ca. 1900]. 8 p.
Sanctification involves separation from sin in all its forms, dedication of oneself to God, and filling— "the incoming of Jesus by the Holy Spirit to relive his own life in us" (p. 7).

1863. [———]. *What It Is Not.* Tracts for the Times. Deeper Life Series. New York: Christian Alliance Pub. Co., [ca. 1900]. 8 p.

Sanctification is not the formation of character, nor is it something one attains gradually: "It is an Obtainment, not an Attainment" (p. 3). It is not sinless perfection, or a clean heart, or the improvement of the carnal nature: it is the entire crucifixion of the old nature. It is a taking in of Christ (not of "the blessing"): all one has to do is simply walk in the Spirit.

1864. ———. *When God Steps In.* Camp Hill, Pa.: Christian Publications, 1997. 84 p.
Reprint of 1519.

1865. ———. *When the Comforter Came.* New York: Christian Alliance Pub. Co., 1911. 128 p.
Thirty-one meditations on the Holy Spirit (one for each day of the month), e.g., "the heart of Christ is not only the heart of a man, but has in it all the tenderness and gentleness of woman . . . He combined in Himself the nature of both man and woman" (p. 13). Likewise, the Holy Spirit, as comforter and heavenly Mother "assumes our nurture, training and the whole direction of our life" (p. 14).

1866. [———]. *Where Art Thou?* Tracts for the Times. Salvation Series. New York: Christian Alliance Pub. Co., [ca. 1900]. 8 p.
God is posing the same question to all people that he posed to Adam, and he does so as a loving Father who longs to be in fellowship with the lost.

1867. ———. *Wholly Sanctified.* New York: Christian Alliance Pub. Co., 1893. 189 p.
Five sermons on 1 Thess. 5:23-24. "Sanctification is . . . God's own life in the spirit that is yielded up to Him to be His dwelling place and the instrument of His power and will" (p. 43).

1868. ———. *Wholly Sanctified.* Harrisburg, Pa.: Christian Publications, 1925. 136 p.
Identical to 1867, except for an introduction by Alfred C. Snead and an additional sermon ("Even as He," based on 1 John 4:17).

1869. ———. *Wholly Sanctified: The Legacy Edition of an Ageless Christian Classic.* Harrisburg, Pa.: Christian Publications, 1982. 128 p.
Identical to 1868, except for the preface by L. L. King (which replaces the introduction) and the addition of six poems by Simpson.

1870. ———. *Why I Believe.* New York: Christian Alliance Pub. Co., [189-?]. 22 p.

The genuineness of the Scriptures and veracity of their contents, the power of the Gospel to transform society, and above all the test of personal experience, are the foundations of Simpson's apologetic.

1871. ———. *Why Should I Go As a Missionary?* Missionary Alliance Leaflets. First Series, no. 12. New York: Christian Alliance Pub. Co., [1892?]. 4 p.

The Lord commands us to go unless he restrains us by some local imperative. The need is greater overseas, and the potential for affecting large numbers of people is greater as well. Much degradation and cruelty, especially to women and children, can be ended if significant numbers of people become Christians.

1872. ———. *Why Should I Go Now?* Missionary Alliance Leaflets. First Series, no. 5. New York: Christian Alliance Pub. Co., [1892?].

The century is far spent, millions are dying every year without knowing Christ. Elaborate theological and linguistic preparation are unnecessary: all one needs are Jesus and the Holy Spirit, a passion to see people become Christians, and Christian common sense. Moreover, the International Missionary Alliance already has more money than it has missionaries.

1873. ———. *Why Should I Go under the Missionary Alliance.* Missionary Alliance Leaflets. First Series, no. 3. New York: Christian Alliance Pub. Co., [1892?].

Although not inherently superior to any other mission, the International Missionary Alliance is interdenominational, its members and supporters are deeply committed Christians, it aims to send ordinary Spirit-filled Christians to the field, it has no administrative costs, and $300.00-$400.00 will support a missionary for a year.

1874. [———]. *Why We Expect Christ to Come.* Tracts for the Times. Lord's Coming Series. New York: Christian Alliance Pub. Co., [ca. 1900]. 8 p.

His coming will be personal, visible, and premillennial. He has yet to take up his prophesied kingship; and his own predictions of his return, and his instructions to his disciples to watch for his coming, indicate that he plans to return.

1875. [———]. *Why We Expect Christ to Come Soon.* Tracts for the Times. Lord's Coming Series. New York: Christian Alliance Pub. Co., [ca. 1900]. 8 p.

The biblical prophecies pertaining to international politics have been fulfilled, as have those pertaining to the Jews, the church, social and commercial conditions, and morality. The current spiritual awakening, and especially the great missionary movement, are also signs.

1876. ———. *Why You Should Go to Africa.* Missionary Alliance Leaflets. First Series, no. 1. New York: Christian Alliance Pub. Co., [1892?].

Degradation, cruelty, and slavery are a way of life in Africa. The church owes Africa a debt of gratitude for sheltering Jesus and the Patriarchs and for providing a home for many leaders of the early church.

1877. ———. *Within the Vail, or Christ in the Epistle to the Hebrews.* Nyack, N.Y.: Christian Alliance Pub. Co., 1900. 256 p.

Fourteen sermons on selected texts. On Hebrews 12:11: "Trial is not always a blessing. There are trials that are wasted and thrown away. . . . Suffering in itself cannot sanctify. . . . Everything depends upon our attitude toward the trial" (p. 203-4) . Cf. 1587.

1878. ———. *The Word Made Flesh: A Christ-Centered Study of the Book of John.* Camp Hill, Pa.: Christian Publications, 1995. 179 p.

Reprint of 1640.

1879. ———. *Words of Comfort for Tried Ones: Discourses on the Epistles of Peter.* New York: Alliance Press Co., 1903. 130 p.

Seven sermons on selected texts. "It is a soldier's business to be fired at. And so it is your calling to suffer for Jesus' sake. If you do not like it, you should retire from the business of being a Christian" (p. 16-17). Cf. 1589.

1880. [———]. *Ye Must Be Born Again.* Tracts for the Times. Salvation Series. New York: Christian Alliance Pub. Co., [ca. 1900]. 6 p.

A dying boy hears from a sensitive minister about Jesus' offer of a new birth, accepts it, and dies joyfully.

1881. Simpson (A)lbert (B)enjamin (1843-1919), and Emilio Olsson. *A Plea for South America: The Neglected Continent.* New York: Christian and Missionary Alliance, 1897. 22 p.

Following a short commendation by A. B. Simpson (on the occasion of Olsson's departure to found the C&MA mission in South America)

Emilio Olsson promotes his plan for the evangelization of South America in four years.

1882. Simpson (A)lbert (B)enjamin (1843-1919), May Agnew Stephens, and Margaret M. Simpson. *Hymns of the Christian Life No. 3: For Church Worship, Conventions, Evangelistic Services, Prayer Meetings, Missionary Meetings, Revival Services, Rescue Mission Work and Sunday Schools*. New York: Alliance Press Co., 1904. 256 p.

270 hymns, of which Simpson wrote the lyrics to 60 (and the music to 31 of these).

1883. ———. *Hymns of the Christian Life Nos. 1, 2 and 3: For Church Worship, Conventions, Evangelistic Services, Prayer Meetings, Missionary Meetings, Revival Services, Rescue Mission Work and Sunday Schools*. New York: Christian Alliance Pub. Co., 1908. 784 p.

946 hymns, including some not found in the three previous Alliance hymnals. Cf. 1697.

1884. ———. *Selections from Hymns of the Christian Life Nos. 1, 2 and 3: For Church Worship, Conventions, Evangelistic Services, Prayer Meetings, Missionary Meetings, Revival Services, Rescue Mission Work and Sunday Schools*. New York: Christian Alliance Pub. Co., [1908?]. 189 p.

207 hymns.

1885. Simpson, Harold H. *Cavendish: Its History, Its People. . . .* Amherst, N.S.: Harold H. Simpson and Associates, 1974. 261 p.

Cavendish, P.E.I., is the birthplace of A. B. Simpson, whose ancestors emigrated there from Scotland in 1790. Includes a genealogy of the Simpson family, some family history, and a brief biography of Simpson that is based on 2066.

1886. Simpson, Richard G. *Who Changed the Sabbath?* n.p., [1937?] 12 p.

A rebuttal of the teaching that all who do not keep the Jewish Sabbath are lost. It was preached in 1937 at the Alliance Gospel Temple, Houlton, Me.

1887. Simpson (W)illiam (W)allace (1869-1961). *Evangelizing West China*. The Assemblies of God in Foreign Lands. Springfield, Mo.: Foreign Missions Dept., [1931?] 14 p.

Simpson served as a C&MA missionary to western China (1895-1915). His differences with the Alliance over glossolalia as the evidence of the baptism of the Holy Spirit (see p. 5-6) led him to resign from the Alliance and join the missions force of the Assemblies of God.

1888. Sipley, Richard M. *Understanding Divine Healing*. Wheaton, Ill.: Victor Books, 1986. 162 p.

An introduction (by a C&MA pastor) to the theology and practice of divine healing. Refers frequently to the writings of A. B. Simpson and other Alliance luminaries. "[H]ealing in the Atonement" means that "the life of Christ will triumph over sickness in the manner God sees as best" (p. 126), i.e., not all who pray for healing will be healed, but the indwelling Christ will at the very least enable those who are not healed to "live victoriously."

1889. *Sixty-Five Years to the Glory of God: 1923-1988*. Chatham, Ont.: Gregory Drive Alliance Church, 1988. 17 p.

A history of Gregory Drive Alliance Church, Chatham, Ont. Chatham was the home town of A. B. Simpson.

1890. *Sixty-Seven Years of World Service*. New York: The Christian and Missionary Alliance, 1955. 10 p.

Rev. ed. of 1861.

1891. *Sixty-Nine Years of World Service*. New York: The Christian and Missionary Alliance, 1957. 10 p.

Rev. ed. of 1890.

1892. *Seventy-One Years of World Service*. New York: The Christian and Missionary Alliance, 1959. 10 p.

Rev. ed. of 1891.

1893. Slade, Ruth M. *English Speaking Missions in the Congo Independent State (1878-1908)*. Brussels: Academie Royale des Sciences Coloniales, 1958.

Despite grandiose plans for a missionary thrust from Matadi to Lake Tanganyika (a distance of 1,600 km.) the C&MA, because of limited resources, confined its early missionary efforts to the lower Congo. Alliance magazines, like those of other missionary organizations, publicized the poor conditions under which most Congolese lived (because of the mismanagement by the colonial administration). The

C&MA mission was the first (1931) to grant full autonomy to the church it had planted in the Belgian Congo.

1894. Slane, Craig J. "Christ and the Spirit: Fleshing Out the Vision of A. B. Simpson's Imitation of Christ." *Alliance Academic Review* (1997): 135-54.

Simpson's vision of the imitation of Christ accords the Holy Spirit a much more direct role than do those of such authors as Thomas à Kempis, Dietrich Bonhoeffer, or Hilary of Poitiers. He believed that the intimate relationship between Jesus and the Spirit must include the notion of Jesus as one who is indwelt powerfully by the Spirit, and that this experience must be reflected in the lives of Jesus' followers. Unfortunately, Simpson's writings on the Holy Spirit neglect the role played by the Spirit in Jesus' experience of suffering and death.

1895. Smalley, William (A)llen (1923-1997). "My Pilgrimage in Mission." *International Bulletin of Missionary Research* 15 (April 1991): 70, 72-3.

The son of William F. Smalley, C&MA missionary to Palestine, William A. Smalley, along with his wife Jane, served as a C&MA missionary to Laos and Vietnam (1949-1954). He left the mission to become a Bible translation consultant. Despite his appreciation for the warmth and love that characterized the Alliance subculture of his youth, Smalley eventually found its anti-intellectualism and cultural chauvinism intolerable, and so he left the C&MA and became a Presbyterian.

1896. Smalley, William (A)llen (1923-1997), and Marie Fetzer. "A Christian View of Anthropology." In *Modern Service and Christian Faith*, 2nd ed., 98-195. Wheaton, Ill.: Van Kampen Press, 1950.

Applied anthropology has been of great benefit to Christian missions because the proclamation of the Gospel needs to be expressed in terms of the life, thought, and culture of its recipients. To date the branch of anthropology of which Christians have made the greatest use is that of descriptive linguistics.

1897. Smalley, William F., comp. and ed. *Alliance Missions in India*. [Nyack, N.Y.?]: [Christian and Missionary Alliance?], [1973?].1113 p.

A pastiche of field reports, articles from Alliance periodicals, miscellaneous documents, and editorial comments. Includes indexes to persons and subjects, as well as brief biographical notes.

1898. ———, comp. and ed. *Alliance Missions in Indonesia*. [Nyack, N.Y.?]: [Christian and Missionary Alliance?], [1976?]. 3 vols.

Follows the same format as 1897, except that it lacks the brief biographical notes. Includes several letters by R. A. Jaffray.

1899. ———, comp. and ed. *Alliance Missions in Irian Jaya* [Nyack, N.Y.?]: [Christian and Missionary Alliance?], [1976?]. 2 vols.

Similar in format to 1898.

1900. ———, comp. and ed. *Alliance Missions in Palestine, Arab Lands, Israel 1890-1970*. [Nyack, N.Y.?]: [Christian and Missionary Alliance?], [1976?]. 557 p.

Follows the same format as 1898 and 1899, except that the editorial comments are more extensive (Smalley served as a C&MA missionary to Palestine 1919-1935).

1901. ———. *New Voices in the Desert*. New York: Christian and Missionary Alliance, 1939. 20 p.

An account of the establishment of the Alliance mission in present-day Jordan.

1902. Smeltzer, Bertha L., with Bernard Palmer. *Mahaffey: The First Hundred Years*. Camp Hill, Pa.: Christian Publications, 1994. 217 p.

The camp, situated near Mahaffey, Pa., was founded as a Methodist retreat. The Alliance took it over in 1913.

1903. Smith, Alfredo. "Abram, the First Missionary." In *Understanding and Nurturing the Missionary Family: Compendium of the International Conference on Missionary Kids, Quito, Ecuador, January 4-8, 1987*. Vol. 1, eds. Pam Echert and Alice Arathon, 20-24. Pasadena, Calif.: William Carey Library, 1989.

A character study that deals with such issues as separation from one's family.

1904. ———. "The Evangelist's Commitment to the Church." In *The Work of an Evangelist: International Congress for Itinerant Evangelists, Amsterdam, the Netherlands*, ed. J. D. Douglas, 151-55. Minneapolis: World Wide Publications 1984.

Discusses the principles on which the "Lima's Encounter with God" project was based—i.e., cooperation, integrity, and accountability—and demonstrates how they can be used as a model for the relationship between the evangelist and the local church.

1905. ———. "Jesus as an MK." In *Understanding and Nurturing the Missionary Family: Compendium of the International Conference on Missionary Kids, Quito, Ecuador, January 4-8, 1987*, Vol. 1, eds. Pam Echerd and Alice Arathon, 44-48. Pasadena, Calif.: William Carey Library, 1989.

Jesus can identify with the struggles of the children of missionaries because he, too, suffered the loss of identity and personal dignity. His life also demonstrates that learning comes through suffering.

1906. Smith, David John. "Listening Prayer: Listening to God for Life and Ministry." *Alliance Academic Review* (1999): 31-59.

The first generation leaders of the C&MA were contemplatives who always preceded ministry "with prayerful listening to God" (p. 42).

1907. Smith, Dellmer. "Mission Church Relationships." In *Missions and the Indian Church*, 16-21. Cass Lake, Minn.: Alliance Indian Publications, 1972.

Missionaries should relinquish to nationals every task that nationals are capable of taking on. They should also seek to live as simply as they can to minimize the economic gap between themselves and the nationals. They should also become fluent in the local language, adopt local customs, and avoid any hint of paternalism or condescension.

1908. ———. "Principles of the New Testament Church." In *Missions and the Indian Church*, 9-15. Cass Lake, Minn.: Alliance Indian Publications, 1972.

The leaders of an indigenous church must apply biblical principles in a culturally sensitive way to determine church standards, ceremonies, and polity. They must also wean the church as quickly as possible from outside financial support.

1909. Smith, Fred H. "Growth through Evangelism." *Urban Mission* 1 (September 1983): 19-28.

Discusses the strategy of Lima al Encuentro con Dios: evangelism; prayer cells; strong leadership; mass meetings featuring prominent evangelists; intensive catechesis; cooperation among the mission, the local church, and the national church; and highly visible church buildings.

1910. Smith, Gordon Hedderly (1902-). *The Blood Hunters: A Narrative of Pioneer Missionary Work among the Savages of French Indo-China.* Chicago: World Wide Prayer and Missionary Union, 1942. 140 p.

The Smiths served as Canadian C&MA missionaries to Indochina (1929-1955). Having spent 1929 to 1934 in Cambodia, they were relocated to Vietnam, where they worked among the peoples of the interior jungles (many of whom had not had previous contact with Caucasians). The present volume is a mixture of ethnographic description and adventure story. Cf. 1917.

1911. ———. *The Missionary and Anthropology: An Introduction to the Study of Primitive Man for Missionaries*. Chicago: Moody Press, 1945. 160 p.

W. A. Smalley, a former C&MA missionary, calls this a "superficial and somewhat dated plea for the use of anthropology by missionaries." *Occasional Bulletin* 11 (20 January 1960): 34.

1912. ———. *The Missionary and Primitive Man: An Introduction to the Study of His Mental Characteristics and His Religion*. Chicago: Van Kampen Press, 1947. 216 p.

Similar to 1911. Encourages a tactful and sympathetic approach to the "heathen beliefs and practices" of "savages" in combination with a refusal to compromise Gospel morality.

1913. Smith, Gordon T. (1953-). *City Shepherds: The Challenge of Urban Pastoral Ministry*. Manila: Alliance Publishers, 1991. 100 p.

Lectures delivered at Alliance Biblical Seminary, Quezon City, the Philippines, September 1990.

1914. ———. "Religions and the Bible: An Agenda for Evangelicals." In *Christianity and the Religions: A Biblical Theology of World Religions*. Evangelical Missiological Society Series, no. 2, eds. Edward Rommen and Harold Netland, 9-29. Pasadena, Calif.: William Carey Library, 1995.

A former C&MA missionary to the Philippines contends that it is unwise to "make definitive conclusions about those who do not have the opportunity to hear [the Gospel]"(p. 25-26) and that "the glory of God and the saving power of Jesus Christ" (p. 26) should be the motive for missions.

1915. ———. "Re-thinking Conversion." *Canadian Evangelical Theological Association Newsletter* (fall 1993): 1-8.

Proposes a seven-fold understanding of conversion that is intended to incorporate the best of Roman Catholic, classical Protestant, and Holiness views: believing in Jesus; repentance; trust in God for life in general, and forgiveness in particular; surrender to the Lordship of Jesus;

baptism; the reception and experience of the Spirit; and incorporation into the church.

1916. Smith, Laura Irene Ivory. *Farther into the Night*. Grand Rapids: Zondervan, 1954. 247 p.

An account of the resumption, following World War II, of the Smith's ministry among the Raday people of the Banmethuot area of South Vietnam.

1917. ———. *Gongs in the Night: Reaching the Tribes of French Indo-china*. Grand Rapids: Zondervan, 1943. 102 p.

A companion volume to 1910. Includes several chapters on the Smiths' ministry in Cambodia.

1918. ———. *Mawal, Jungle Boy of French Indo-China*. Chicago: Moody Press, 1947. 60 p.

An illustrated children's story that describes how a Vietnamese ethnic group, the Raday, came to hear and believe in the Gospel. Includes much ethnographic detail.

1919. Smith, Oswald (J)effrey (1889-1986). *Back to Pentecost*. New York: Christian Alliance Pub. Co., 1926. 124 p.

A popular treatise on sanctification.

1920. ———. *The Baptism with the Holy Spirit*. New York: Christian Alliance Pub. Co., 1925. 54 p.

An apologetic for the baptism of the Holy Spirit as a post-conversion crisis experience, together with instructions on how to obtain it.

1921. ———. *From Death to Life*, 2nd ed. New York: Christian Alliance Pub. Co., 1925. 127 p.

Ten sermons on eternal life and union with Christ.

1922. ———. *The Great Physician*. New York: Christian Alliance Pub. Co., 1927. 128 p.

A classic Alliance apologetic for healing as a provision of the Atonement. Includes his own and others' testimony of divine healing. Foreword by Kenneth Mackenzie.

1923. ———. *Hymns with a Message*. Toronto: The Tabernacle Publishers, 1927. 97 p.

1924. ———. *Is the Anti-Christ at Hand? What of Mussolini?* 4th ed. Harrisburg, Pa.: Christian Alliance Pub. Co., 1927. 128 p.

The ascendancy of Benito Mussolini presages the revival of the Roman Empire. The seventh and last emperor (Mussolini?) will be assassinated, will be resurrected as the anti-Christ, and then the end will come. These events will happen soon, possibly by 1934.

1925. ———. *The King's Highway No. 2*. Toronto: Tabernacle Publishers, 1924. 54 p.

The story of the founding of the Gospel Auditorium and the Alliance Tabernacle, Toronto.

1926. ———. *The King's Highway No. 3*. Toronto: Tabernacle Publishers, [1925?] 48 p.

Missions and evangelism are the most important work of the church.

1927. ———. *The King's Highway No. 4*. Toronto: Tabernacle Publishers, 1926. 47 p.

Reprint of the first five chapters of 1928.

1928. ———. *The Man God Uses*. New York: Christian Alliance Pub. Co., 1925. 133 p.

Fifteen exhortations on Christian service. Cf. 1927.

1929. ———. *The Revival We Need*. Toronto: The Alliance Tabernacle, 1922. 79 p.

Seven sermons castigating the superficiality of contemporary evangelism and appealing for preaching that relies on the power of the Holy Spirit to produce conviction for sin, repentance, and faith. Includes an account of Smith's own experience of revival.

1930. ———. *The Revival We Need*. New York: Christian Alliance Pub. Co., 1925. 125 p.

Includes three chapters of entries from Smith's personal journal for 1917-1918 and an introduction by Jonathan Goforth.

1931. ———. *Songs in the Night*. Toronto: Alliance Tabernacle, 1922. 95 p.

A collection of devotional poems. Excludes any that have so far been set to music.

1932. ———. *The Spirit-Filled Life*. New York: Christian Alliance Pub. Co., 1926. 126 p.

Six sermons on sanctification: "You and I are no more good to God than [a] wild bronco until we have been broken" (p. 42) .

1933. ———. *The Story of My Life*. Toronto: The Peoples Press, 1950. 104 p.

Smith, when he was forced to resign as pastor in June 1926, had enough congregational support simply to have taken over the Alliance Tabernacle and started an independent work, but he was so committed to the Alliance that the thought never even crossed his mind.

1934. ———. *The Story of My Life and the Peoples Church*. London: Marshall, Morgan and Scott, 1962. 128 p.

The chapter on his years in the Alliance is almost identical to the corresponding chapter in 1938.

1935. ———. *Thou Art the Man*. Toronto: Evangelical Publishers, 1919. 89 p.

Sermons on sin and salvation.

1936. ———. *Voices of Hope*. Toronto: Evangelical Publishers, 1919. 133 p.

Florid poetry on a variety of themes, ranging from the love of God, the spiritual life, and missions, to outrage at Germany's "might is right" philosophy.

1937. ———. *Warning and Entreaty*. Toronto: [Alliance Tabernacle], [192-?]. 144 p.

1938. ———. *"What Hath God Wrought!": Dr. Smith's Life and Ministry: An Autobiography*. 7th ed. Toronto: The Peoples Press, 1946. 149 p.

Smith became pastor of the Alliance Tabernacle in Toronto in January 1921, and left in June 1926, having been "manoeuvred out when the work was at its very peak and all was well" (p. 83). He then served briefly as the C&MA's district superintendent for eastern Canada before departing to pastor the C&MA's Gospel Tabernacle in Los Angeles. He left the Alliance in June 1928 to become Canadian director of Paul Rader's Worldwide Christian Couriers. Smith mentions little about the tensions that led to his departure from the Tabernacle in Toronto (see 1383, p. 148-52, for the Alliance's perspective). He was always grateful to the Alliance for providing him with the openings that led to his being in international demand as a speaker. This is the most thorough of Smith's various autobiographies.

1939. ———. *When Antichrist Reigns*. New York: Christian Alliance Pub. Co., 1927. 148 p.

Sermons on the end times, e.g., the restoration of the Jews to Palestine as a fulfillment of prophecy, Mussolini as the possible leader of a revived Roman Empire, and Bolshevism and the rise of atheism as harbingers of the coming of the Antichrist.

1940. ———. *Working with God*. Toronto: Tabernacle Publishers, 1926. 201 p.

An autobiography covering his evangelistic work among the loggers of B.C., his ministry in Toronto, and his preaching tour of Russia in 1924.

1941. ———. "The World Beats a Path to Her Door." *Bridal Call* 8 (May 1925): 22-23, 34.

Smith's favorable assessment of Aimee Semple MacPherson (1890-1944) indicates the close connection between the C&MA's fourfold Gospel and her foursquare Gospel (cf. 1202, p. 39). Originally published in Smith's *Tabernacle News* (March 1925) and here reprinted in MacPherson's own periodical.

1942. Snead (A)lfred (C)ookman (1884-1961). *Alliance Missions in China: China at the Crossroads*. New York: Christian and Missionary Alliance, [192-?]. 8 p.

1943. ———. *The Eternal Christ: A Bible Study*. Word Studies in the Living Word. Nyack, N.Y.: by the author, 1936. 95 p.

Scripture verses, with accompanying word studies, arranged topically and designed for use in adult Bible classes. Foreword acknowledges the author's debt to A. B. Simpson's Christ in the Bible series.

1944. ———. "From Indo-China to Peru." *World Dominion and the World Today: An International Review of Christian Progress* 31 (July-August 1953): 223-25.

An overview of Alliance missions.

1945. ———. *Missionary Atlas: A Manual of the Foreign Work of the Christian and Missionary Alliance*. Harrisburg, Pa.: Christian Publications, 1936. 127 p.

Rev. ed. of 312.

1946. ———. "Missionary Vision and Policies." In *A. B. Simpson Centenary 1843-1943,* 6-10. New York: Christian and Missionary Alliance, 1943.

A. B. Simpson translated his missionary vision into both extensive ministry, as evidenced by the dramatic growth in the number of C&MA mission fields, and intensive ministry, as can be seen from the numbers of Bible institutes that the C&MA has established overseas.

1947. ———. *Other Cities, Urgent Work, Other Sheep: The Three "I Musts" of Jesus Christ and How the Christian and Missionary Alliance Is Seeking to Fulfill Them*. New York: The Alliance. Foreign Department, [1924?]. 20 p.

A florid description of the missionary activity of the C&MA in various cities throughout the world.

1948. ———. *Poems*. n.p., [196-?].

1949. ———. "Progress and Peril in Indo-China." *World Dominion: An International Review of Christian Progress* 32 (September-October 1954): 279-83.

A account of the C&MA's missionary endeavors in Vietnam, Laos, and Cambodia.

1950. ———. *The War, the Work and the Word*. New York: Christian and Missionary Alliance, [1942?]. 11 p.

An update on the state of Alliance missions and the fate of Alliance missionaries worldwide, especially in light of Japanese incursions into East Asia.

1951. ———. "What Constitutes a Missionary Call?" *United Evangelical Action* 17 (February 1959): 5, 12.

Godliness and compassion should characterize all Christians, and especially those who obey the missionary call to "go." Those who are not called overseas are still called to pray for missions, give to missions, and to bear witness to Christ in their daily lives.

1952. Snead, L. U. *The Bible Student's Cyclopaedia, or Bible Marking and Reading Rapid System of Memorizing Biblical Facts, Treasury for Home Circle in Prose and Verse.* New York: Christian Alliance Press, 1900. 286 p.

1953. Snyder, James L. "A. W. Tozer: A Man in Pursuit of God." *Fundamentalist Journal* 5 (March 1986): 46-48.

A brief but thorough treatment of Tozer as writer, mystic, reader, and preacher.

1954. ———. *In Pursuit of God: The Life of A. W. Tozer.* Camp Hill, Pa.: Christian Publications, 1991. 236 p.

A more personal look at Tozer than 545, although it covers much of the same material. Includes many reminiscences by family and friends.

1955. ———. "The Preaching Ministry of A. W. Tozer." *Preaching* 7 (May-June 1992): 48-50.

Regarded as a prophet and the "conscience of evangelicalism," Tozer was an effective preacher because his sermons flowed out of a life of prayer, Bible study, and the study of the Christian classics. He strove to express himself with precision so as to lead his hearers directly into God's presence. Unfortunately, most of his humor and his colorful illustrations have been edited out of his published sermons.

1956. ———. "A Profile in Devotion: A. W. Tozer." *Wesleyan Advocate*, 19 December 1988, 8-9.

Tozer, who in a sermon referred to Julian of Norwich as his girlfriend, believed that the devotional life could best be nurtured by meditating on Scripture, the classic hymns of the faith, and the writings of the Christian mystics and the Puritans.

1957. ———. "A Prophet to Profit By." *Herald of Holiness*, May 1992, 10-12.

In an imaginary conversation between Tozer and a Bible college student, the former presents his views on such subjects as his own success and accomplishments as a pastor, sermon preparation, prophecy, and spirituality.

1958. *Songs of Grace: A Rare Selection of the Best Gospel Songs for General Use—Songs That Have Sung Their Way into Millions of Hearts.* Harrisburg, Pa.; New York: Christian Alliance Pub. Co., 1927.

The 202 selections are a mixture of classic hymns, contemporary Gospel songs, and works by Alliance hymn writers such as A. B. Simpson, R. Kelso Carter, Oswald J. Smith, and Paul Rader.

1959. Southern, Nellie Kirk. *Radiant: Sketches from the Life of James M. Kirk, Pioneer Member of the C.andM.A., Hymn Writer and Organizer.* Orlando, Fla.: by the author, [1945?]. 48 p.

Kirk (1854-1945), a native of Flushing, Ohio, founded the Alliance branch in that city. He was a member of the Ohio Male Quartette, and a number of his hymns were included in C&MA hymnals.

1960. Spader, Larry L. "The Development of a Theology in the Christian and Missionary Alliance." Master's thesis, Covenant Theological Seminary, 1990. 181 p.

The Alliance has always stressed commitment and action over doctrinal precision. In fact, the C&MA did not formulate a statement of faith until 1965. The statement includes the essential evangelical doctrines, and it expresses Alliance distinctives in such a way that evangelicals from a variety of denominational backgrounds would find it congenial. Further doctrinal change in the C&MA seems unlikely.

1961. Spurgeon, (C)harles (H)addon (1834-1892). *Barbed Arrows.* Harrisburg, Pa.: Christian Publications, 1970. 238 p.

Evidently a reprint of *Barbed Arrows from the Quiver of C. H. Spurgeon*. London: Passmore and Alabaster, 1896.

1962. *A Standard in the Flood.* New York: The Christian and Missionary Alliance, 1942. 8 p.

Describes the terrible effects of World War II on Alliance mission fields, and appeals for increased prayer and financial contributions for Alliance missions.

1963. Stanfield, J. M. *Modernism: What It Is, What It Does, Whence It Came, Its Relation to Evolution.* New York: Christian Alliance Pub. Co., 1927. 217 p.

A controversial work, evidently by a non-C&MA author, that even goes so far as to give the names of suspected modernists in missions, church colleges, and seminaries.

1964. Stanger, Frank Bateman. *The Gifts of the Spirit.* Harrisburg, Pa.: Christian Publications, 1974. 31 p.

A critique of the charismatic movement by the president of Asbury Theological Seminary: God still bestows all of the spiritual gifts mentioned in the Bible, but tongues are not a necessary evidence of the baptism of the Holy Spirit.

1965. *Statutes of the Christian and Missionary Alliance: Enacted by General Councils since the Adoption of the Constitution in 1912.* New York: The Alliance, 1933. 37 p.

1966. Stebbins, Tom. *Evangelism by the Book: 13 Biblical Methods.* Camp Hill, Pa.: Christian Publications, 1991. 337 p.

Stebbins is an Alliance pastor, former C&MA missionary, and professor of evangelism at Alliance Theological Seminary.

1967. ———. *Friendship Evangelism by the Book: Applying First Century Principles to Twenty-First Century Relationships.* Camp Hill, Pa.: Christian Publications, 1995. 351 p.

1968. ———. *Missions by the Book: How to Find and Evangelize Lost People of Every Culture on Every Continent.* Camp Hill, Pa.: Christian Publications, 1996. 339 p.

An elementary textbook on missions. Based on biographical narratives, many of which are taken from the author's own experiences as a C&MA missionary in Vietnam.

1969. ———. *Oikos Outreach 4 Times a Year: The Formula for an Effective Strategy You Can Use to Mobilize Your Entire Congregation for Friendship Evangelism.* Camp Hill, Pa.: Christian Publications, 1992. 65 p.

1970. Stein, Nancy Hopton. *Orrville Alliance Church, 60th Anniversary 1928-1988: The Responders, the History of the Orrville Christian and Missionary Alliance Church.* Orrville, Ohio: Nancy H. Stein 1988. 66 p.

1971. Steiner, Rebecca. *On to Timbuctoo.* [Koutiala, Mali?]: Christian and Missionary Alliance, 1995. 59 p.

A history of the C&MA mission in Mali to the end of World War II.

1972. Steiner, Stephen Merritt. "The Contributions of A. B. Simpson to the Hymnody of the Christian and Missionary Alliance." Master's thesis, Southern Baptist Theological Seminary, 1976. 250 p.

Simpson's hymns, since they were written in the gospel song genre, lack musical and literary polish. Nevertheless, they accurately convey the doctrinal emphases of the early C&MA. Includes a listing of the rhyme schemes, key signatures, melodic ranges, and the time signatures of Simpson's hymns.

1973. Steinkamp, Orrel N. *The Holy Spirit in Viet Nam*. Carol Stream, Ill.: Creation House, 1973. 83 p.

An account of a revival (1971-1972) that took place in the Evangelical Church of Vietnam.

1974. Stephens, George T. *True Revival: Six Messages*. Abingdon, Pa.: Bible Evangelism, Inc., 1961. 134 p.

Includes some biographical material on Harold Lee Stephens, husband of May Agnew Stephens. Toronto-born revivalist George T. Stephens trained at the Missionary Training Institute under A. B. Simpson and George Pardington and served briefly, with his brother H. L. Stephens, as an Alliance evangelist.

1975. Stephens (H)arold (L)ee (1874-1947). *Seven Steps of Faith*. Toronto: Stevenson Printing Company, 1908.

Includes an account of Stephens's ministry in the early days of the Alliance work in Toronto.

1976. Stephens, May Agnew (1865-1935), ed. *Jewels in Song*. Nyack, N.Y.: H. L. Stephens, 1925. 126 p.

Contains 138 songs, many of which were written by May Agnew Stephens.

1977. ———, ed. *Missionary Messages in Song*. Toronto: H. L. Stephens, 1910. 102 p.

Stephens wrote about a third of the missionary hymns and Gospel songs in this collection. Includes the story of her hymn "Have Faith in God," and contributions by other Alliance hymn writers.

1978. Sterling, Tamar Wright. *Miss Carrie Peter and Trophies in India*. Findlay, Ohio: Fundamental Truth Publishers, 1938. 159 p.

Carrie Peter (1872-1937) served as a C&MA missionary to India (1898-1936).

1979. Stevens, Robert Meredith. *Paradise Plantation*. Visalia, Calif.: The McBee and Black Pub. Co., 1958. 136 p.

Evangelistic meditations on Scripture using illustrations drawn from country life.

1980. ———. *The Promised Land*. [Fresno, Calif.?]: Yoke Publications, 1963. 186 p.

Sermons on salvation and sanctification, using the Exodus narrative as a point of departure.

1981. Stevens (W)illiam (C)oit (1853-1929). *The Book of Daniel: A Composite Revelation of the Last Days of Israel's Subjugation to Gentile Powers*. Oakland: Hebron Home Office, 1915. 251 p.

A devotional commentary that applies the prophecies of Daniel to the Jews.

1982. ———. *The Latter Rain*. New York: Alliance Press Co., [1907?]. 22 p.

Recognizes that the current Pentecostal revival is a genuine work of God, despite its unusual character: "It would offend God for us to be unwilling or slow to yield ourselves to the mightier outpouring now upon us, either out of a tenacity for past experiences and methods, or out of a dislike for the mode of the present baptism" [p. 18].

1983. ———. *Mysteries of the Kingdom*. Nyack, N.Y.: by the author, 1904. 133 p.

Messages on the return of Christ delivered at the Berachah Home, Nyack, N.Y., during the author's tenure as dean of the Missionary Training Institute.

1984. ———. *Praying in the Holy Ghost*. Shenandoah, Ia.: by the author, [1920?]. 12 p.

Not a treatise on glossolalia, but rather on praying to the Father, in the name of Jesus, in the Holy Spirit.

1985. ———. *Revelation, the Crown Jewel of Biblical Prophecy*. Harrisburg, Pa.: New York: Christian Alliance Pub. Co., 1928. 2 vols.

A devotional commentary that posits "a divisional and successional rapture instead of a momentary complete one, one both preceding and overlapping the tribulation" (Vol 1, p. 140). Reprinted in one volume (434 p.) ca. 1960 by Christian Publications.

1986. ———. *Triumphs of the Cross*, 2nd ed., San Francisco: M. G. McClinton, 1915. 97 p.

Messages on the implications of Christ's suffering and death for sickness, sanctification, spiritual warfare, suffering, fellowship, and evangelism. Originally delivered in 1903 at Nyack in conjunction with "Waiting Days."

1987. ———. *The Unique Historical Value of the Book of Jonah*. [New York?] : Fleming H. Revell, 1924. 88 p.

Jonah's historical value lies in the fact that it demonstrates the ways in which God has shaped human history, the supreme example of which is the "sign of Jonah," the death and resurrection of Jesus.

1988. ———. *Why I Reject the Helping Hand of Millennial Dawn*. New York: Alliance Press Co., [1911?]. 156 p.

A polemic against the group that eventually became the Jehovah's Witnesses.

1989. ———. *Why I Reject the Helping Hand of Millennial Dawn*, rev. ed. San Francisco: M. G. McClinton and Company, 1915. 132 p.

Revised in light of, among other things, the nonfulfillment of Charles Taze Russell's prophecy that "some time before the end of 1914, the last member of the divinely recognized Church of Christ, the 'royal priesthood,' the 'body of Christ,' will be glorified with the Head" (p. 4).

1990. Stockman (E)dward (A)insley (1821-1901). *Advanced Truth, or the Doctrines of Christian Alliance*. Boston: Advent Christian Publication Society, 1891. 31 p.

The Alliance's understanding of salvation and sanctification is in no way superior to Adventist teaching. Its doctrine of "healing in the Atonement" cannot stand the test of either experience or common sense, and it goes beyond the teaching of Scripture. Adventists should continue to pray for the sick, but they should avoid the Alliance error of equating sickness with sin or sanctification with health. Alliance eschatology also contains scandalous elements, e.g., the advance rapture of a spiritual elite and the literal return of the Jews to Israel.

Stoesz, Samuel J., joint author. *All for Jesus: God at Work in the Christian and Missionary Alliance over One Hundred Years*.

See 1207.

1991. Stoesz, Samuel J. "Canadian Alliance Church Growth: At What Expense?" *His Dominion* 12 (winter 1986): 17-28.

Qualitative growth in discipleship does not appear to be keeping pace with the rapid numerical growth of Alliance churches, and so the denomination is in danger of becoming insipid.

1992. ———. *Church and Membership Awareness: A Text on Church Orientation for Use in a Pastor's Class.* Christian Life and Ministry Series. Harrisburg, Pa.: Christian Publications, 1974. 93 p.

Covers the doctrine of the church; the history and teachings of the C&MA; qualifications for church membership; baptism, the Lord's Supper, and church life; and Alliance polity. A study guide was published separately.

1993. ———. *Church and Missions Alive: A Text on the Biblical and Practical Elements of Missions in the Local Church.* Christian Life and Ministry Series. Harrisburg, Pa.: Christian Publications, 1975. 96 p.

A textbook designed to instruct Alliance churches in the nature and history of Christian missions and to facilitate their involvement in the missions program of the C&MA.

1994. ———. *The Cross and Sanctification.* Heritage Series. Camp Hill, Pa.: Christian Publications, 1994. 24 p.

Reprint of a chapter in 1998: "Sanctification and the Cross."

1995. ———. "The Doctrine of Sanctification in the Thoughts of A. B. Simpson." In *The Birth of a Vision*, eds. David F. Hartzfeld and Charles Nienkirchen, 107-24. Regina, Sask.: His Dominion, 1986.

Simpson's understanding of sanctification differed from the dominant eradicationist and suppressionist views in that it stressed the impartation of the life of Christ, through the mediatorial agency of the Holy Spirit, to the believer. Divine healing is thus the physical expression of sanctification. The joys of the sanctified life are a foretaste of the life to come, yet the purpose of sanctification is empowerment: the sanctified are to carry on the (missionary) work of the one who has given his life for the world.

1996. ———. *The Glory of Christ in His Church.* Camp Hill, Pa.: Christian Publications, 1994. 253 p.

The C&MA was originally a transdenominational society, patterned after the (British) Evangelical Alliance, for the purpose of promoting the "deeper life," fellowship, missions, and cooperation among churches. Simpson's Gospel Tabernacle was an independent church affiliated with the C&MA. Alliance "branches" functioned as supplements to existing traditional churches. Their leaders did not perform baptisms or celebrate communion, and their meeting times were scheduled not to conflict with those of established churches. Yet by 1974 the Alliance had (officially) become a denomination. Every four years, the autonomous national churches of the Alliance send representatives to a gathering of the Alliance World Fellowship, a nonlegislative body whose purpose is to facilitate cooperative endeavors among the various national churches of the C&MA.

1997. ———. *Life Is for Growth*. Christian Life and Ministry Series. Harrisburg, Pa.: Christian Publications, 1977. 115 p.

A guide to Christian discipleship stressing the ministry of the Holy Spirit and the need to appropriate one's positional union with Christ by allowing Christ, through the Holy Spirit, to have complete control of one's life. Study questions conclude each chapter. A leader's guide was published separately.

1998. ———. *Sanctification: An Alliance Distinctive*. Camp Hill, Pa.: Christian Publications, 1992. 142 p.

An expansion of 1995. Historians of evangelicalism who label the Alliance's doctrine of sanctification "Kewsickian" fail to understand that Simpson's understanding of sanctification (which was heavily influenced by the writings of W. E. Boardman) stresses living in union with Christ through the Holy Spirit. In Simpson's view power for service cannot be separated (as in Keswick) from power for being, since Spirit baptism unites the moral and equipping aspects of sanctification with personal knowledge of Christ as sanctifier. Cf. 1994.

1999. ———. *Understanding My Church*. Harrisburg, Pa.: Christian Publications, 1968. 223 p.

An overview of: the biblical teaching on the church's origin, nature, and role; church history, with special reference to the North American Holiness movement; and the history, doctrine, polity, and missionary program of the C&MA.

2000. ———. *Understanding My Church*. Camp Hill, Pa.: Christian Publications, 1983. 216 p.

Reprint of 1999. Includes an additional chapter on the C&MA in Canada.

2001. Stoll, David. *Fishers of Men or Founders of Empire?: The Wycliffe Bible Translators in Latin America*. London: Zed Press, 1982. 351 p.

This journalistic caricature also makes some outlandish allegations about C&MA missions, e.g., that funding supplied to the C&MA by the LeTourneau Foundation came from, among other things, the sale of bomb casings to the U.S. military during the Vietnam War.

2002. Story, Grace Cowles. *Footprints on the Sands of China: The Story of Roy T. Cowles, Sixteen Years a Missionary to China*. n.p.: by the author, 1973. 198 p.

Roy T. Cowles served in China with the Alliance Press (1914-1921). His personal diary comprises much of the present work. It contains a number of anecdotes about R. A. Jaffray, founder of the Alliance Press.

2003. Straton, John Roach (1875-1929). *Divine Healing in Scripture and Life*. New York: Christian Alliance Pub. Co., 1927. 154 p.

Straton, a Baptist, believed, like Simpson, in "healing in the Atonement" and advocated a higher plane of trust in which the believer eschews medical intervention in favor of depending on God alone for healing. Includes a lavish dedication to A. B. Simpson and the C&MA.

2004. Strickland, William J. *J. O. McClurkan: His Life, His Theology and Selections from His Writings*. Trevecca Centennial Collection, vol. 2. Nashville: Trevecca Press, 1998. 164 p.

To the ethos of McClurkan's Pentecostal Alliance, the C&MA "contributed Keswick doctrine, missionary outreach, belief in the premillennial return of Christ, the Eleventh Hour concept, and its preference to be regarded as a movement rather than a denomination" (p. 15).

2005. Strohm, Ruth Elinor. "Alliance Missions in the Philippines." [B.Th.?] thesis, St. Paul Bible Institute, 1951. 44 p.

Includes a chapter on the effect of World War II on the mission.

2006. Stull, Ruth B. (1896-1982). *Campfires on the Trail*, 6th ed. Jungle Trail Series. Philadelphia: Morning Cheer Book Store, 1944. 47 p.

Describes life in the Peruvian jungle from the perspective of both the Stulls and the Indians among whom they ministered.

2007. ———. *Child of Flame*. Wheaton, Ill.: Van Kampen Press, 1955. 207 p.

A Christian romance and adventure novel set mainly in South America.

2008. ———. *Gardens and Gleanings along Life's Way*. Chicago: Moody Press, 1958. 192 p.

2009. ———. *Golden Vessels: Missionary Messages by Ruth (Mrs. R. O.) Stull*. Grand Rapids: Zondervan, 1943. 47 p.

Meditations on Scripture and reminiscences from the author's travels in North and South America.

2010. ———. *Laddie on the Trail: The True Story of a Real Dog*, 2nd ed. Jungle Trails Series. Philadelphia: Morning Cheer Book Store, 1944. 48 p.

The story includes incidents from the Stulls' missionary work among the Indians of the Peruvian jungle.

2011. ———. *Miracles on the Trail*, 2nd ed. Philadelphia: Morning Cheer Book Store, 1944. 44 p.

Reprint of 2012.

2012. ———. *Modern Miracles on the Trail*. Jungle Trail Series. Fort Wayne, Ind.: Temple Publishers, 1938. 64 p.

Recounts the Stull family's journeys to their mission station—one trip over the Andes, by mule, the other on the Amazon, by dugout—and includes an account of Ruth Stull's two-week trip to a hospital to have a gangrenous appendix removed. Cf. 2011.

2013. ———. *Sand and Stars: Missionary Adventure on the Jungle Trail*. Los Angeles: Fleming H. Revell, 1951. 189 p.

This autobiography incorporates much of the material in the Jungle Trail series.

2014. ———. *Service on the Trail*, 3rd ed. Philadelphia: Morning Cheer Book Store, 1944. 46 p.

Recounts the joys and sorrows of the author's life as a C&MA missionary in the jungles of Peru. Also describes the social life and customs of the Indians she and her husband were seeking to evangelize.

2015. *The Sufficiency and Relevancy of Christ*. Nyack, N.Y.: The Christian and Missionary Alliance, [197-?]. 8 p.

An explanation of the symbolism of the Alliance logo, and an abridgement of 1609.

2016. Sumrall, Lester Frank (1913-). *Pioneers of Faith*. Tulsa, Okla.: Harrison House, 1995. 194 p.

Includes a chapter each on Fred Francis Bosworth and Carrie Judd Montgomery.

2017. Sunda, James. *Church Growth in the Central Highlands of West New Guinea*. Lucknow, India: Lucknow Publishing House 1963. 57 p.

Reflects, from a church growth perspective, on the "multi-individual" conversions among the peoples of Irian Jaya. Includes a historical overview, to 1961, of the work of the Alliance and other missions in Irian Jaya.

2018. Sung, Kee Ho. "The Doctrine of the Second Advent of Jesus Christ in the Writings of Albert B. Simpson, with Special Reference to His Premillennialism." Ph.D. thesis, Drew University 1990. 214 p.

Simpson cannot be classified as a historicist, a futurist, or a dispensationalist, although his eschatology includes elements from all those schools of thought. His theory of the partial rapture, for example, sets him apart from the dispensationalists. Simpson considered missions to be the "key to the bridal chamber" (p. 148), i.e., Christ, the Bride-groom, will return when the Bride, the Church, has finished the work of evangelizing the world. Simpson's eschatology and his teaching on divine healing had a profound influence on Charles Elmer Cowman, founder of the Oriental Missionary Society.

2019. Sutherland, Spencer T. "An Expanded Youth Program for the National Evangelical Church of Vietnam." Master's thesis, Fuller Theological Seminary, 1963. 108 p.

Attempts to come to terms with the implications of increasing urbanization and the escalation of the war. Concludes that the youth program should not be funded by the mission.

2020. ———. "Ministerial Training in Bible Study Method by Theological Education by Extension." D.Min. thesis, American Baptist Seminary of the West, 1976. 415 p.

Based on his experiences as an instructor at Nhatrang Biblical and Theological Institute, Vietnam.

2021. ———. "Self-Propagation." In *The Indigenous Church: A Report from Many Fields, 1960*, 59-61. Chicago: Moody Press, 1960.

Uses as his example the Evangelical Church of Vietnam. This chapter was originally published as an article in *The Call of Viet-Nam*.

2022. Sutton, Harold J. *Four Lost Treasures*. Cincinnati: The Revivalist Press, [193-?]. 22 p.

Meditations on sympathy, modesty, meditation, and solitude. Cf. 2024.

2023. ———. *The Last Frontier and Other Papers, Vol. 2*. n.p., 1945. 32 p.

A reprint of miscellaneous columns by "the strolling parson" from *The Ambridge* [Pa.] *Daily Citizen* and *The Beaver Daily Times*.

2024. ———. *The Lost Paradise*. Cincinnati: The Revivalist Press, [193-?] 22 p.

Identical in content to 2022.

2025. ———. *Water to Drink and Rivers to Flow*. West Hartzdale, Pa.: n.p., [193-?]. 15 p.

A sermon on Jesus as the dispenser of the Holy Spirit.

2026. ———. *Wayside Thoughts of a Strolling Parson, Vol. 1*. Ambridge, Pa.: s.n., 1945. 32 p.

A reprint of additional newspaper columns by the "strolling parson."

2027. ———. *What God Hath Joined Together*. Cincinnati: The Revivalist Press, [193-?]. 19 p.

Meditations on yielding to Christ.

2028. ———. *The Witness of the Spirit*. West Hartzdale, Pa.: Primitive Methodist Church, [193-?]. 12 p.

A sermon on Rom. 8:16: "The witness of the Spirit is the supernatural testimony of divine favor, begotten in the believing heart by the Spirit of God" (p. 4).

2029. Talbot, Gordon Gray. "The Bible Institute Movement in the Christian and Missionary Alliance." Master's thesis, Wheaton College, 1956. 134 p.

A. B. Simpson, like contemporary Alliance educators, did not have a well-developed philosophy of education. However, in his training school, he sought to develop the whole person through courses in literary, theological, and practical studies taught by exemplary Christians. Students were expected to put theory into practice by engaging in some form of Christian service. These basic emphases are preserved in the six Alliance

Bible institutes in North America, although these seem to be increasingly emphasizing education in the liberal arts.

2030. ———. *A Study of the Book of Genesis: An Introductory Commentary on All Fifty Chapters of Genesis*. Camp Hill, Pa.: Christian Publications, 1981. 288 p.

2031. *The Talking Stick from Gabon*. New York: The Christian and Missionary Alliance, 1947. 22 p.

A history of the C&MA mission in Gabon, which began in 1934.

2032. Tam, R. Stanley (1915-). *Every Christian a Soul-Winner*. Nashville: Thomas Nelson, 1975. 168 p.

Random thoughts on personal evangelism.

2033. ———. *God's Woodshed*. Camp Hill, Pa.: Buena Book Service, 1991. 185 p.

A didactic spiritual autobiography that updates 2033.

2034. ———. *Witnessing Everywhere*. New York: The Christian and Missionary Alliance, 1955. 10 p.

Principles of personal evangelism presented via personal anecdotes.

2035. Tam, R. Stanley (1915-), and Ken Anderson. *God Owns My Business,* updated ed. Camp Hill, Pa.: Horizon House, 1976. 158 p.

Tam, an Alliance businessman/ lay evangelist legally made God the owner of his business.

2036. Tano, Rodrigo D. "Developing Filipino/Asian Leaders for Theological Schools." In *Theological Education in the Philippine Context*, ed. Lee Warak, 83-95. Manila: Philippine Association of Bible and Theological Schools; OMF Literature, 1993.

A checklist of steps to follow in the process of indigenizing the leadership of Philippine theological schools.

2037. ———. "Theology in the Philippine Context: Some Issues and Themes." In *Theological Education in the Philippine Context*, ed. Lee Warak, 1-20. Manila: Philippine Association of Bible and Theological Schools; OMF Literature, 1993.

Unlike Filipino Catholics, evangelicals in the Philippines have had little success in indigenizing their largely western-oriented theological training. Filipino evangelical theological institutions must begin to offer courses in contextualization.

2038. Taylor, Harry Macartney (1913-), and Miriam Taylor. *Edge of Conflict: The Story of Harry and Miriam Taylor.* Camp Hill, Pa.: Christian Publications, 1993. 206 p.

Harry and Miriam Elizabeth (1914-) Taylor served as C&MA missionaries to Cambodia from 1939 to 1941. They spent most of 1942-1945 in a Japanese internment camp in the Philippines, returning to Cambodia in 1947. After being expelled in 1965, they were appointed to Lebanon in 1966. On their retirement (ca. 1981) they returned to the United States, where they began a ministry to Cambodian immigrants. Includes biographical material on Sami Dagher, noted Lebanese Alliance pastor/evangelist. Cf. 733.

2039. Taylor, John F. "Indigenous Churches of the Christian and Missionary Alliance." Ph.D. diss., New York University, 1965. 710 p.

A historical overview of the development of the C&MA's indigenous churches. Such churches should be encouraged to develop according to the principles of self-government, self-support, and self-propagation.

2040. Teng, Philip (1922-). "The Basis of Missions in Acts: The Holy Spirit and Missions." In *Jesus Christ: Lord of the Universe, Hope of the World*, ed. David M. Howard, 211-24. Downers Grove, Ill.: InterVarsity Press, 1973.

The Holy Spirit is the "author and finisher of missions, promoter of missions . . . power for missions . . . strategist for missions . . . and supplier for missions" (p. 211).

2041. ———. "The Basis of Missions in the Epistles: The Church and Missions." In *Jesus Christ: Lord of the Universe, Hope of the World*, ed. David M. Howard, 225-38. Downers Grove, Ill.: InterVarsity Press, 1973.

The eight images of the church in Ephesians all have a missionary dimension. The apostle Paul was convinced of the urgency of his message and constrained by the love of Christ—as was that exemplary modern-day missionary R. A. Jaffray. The church is currently running the last mile in the race towards her own consummation in the return of Christ.

2042. ———. "The Basis of Missions in the Gospels: Christ and Missions." In *Jesus Christ: Lord of the Universe, Hope of the World*, ed. David M. Howard, 195-210. Downers Grove, Ill.: InterVarsity Press, 1973.

Christ, the proto-missionary, taught that the worldwide kingdom of God is not restricted to Jews, and he sent his followers to fulfill his mission to bring the Gospel to the ends of the earth. Matt. 24:14 makes missionary activity a necessary precondition for the return of Christ.

2043. ———. "The Basis of Missions in the Old Testament." In *Jesus Christ: Lord of the Universe, Hope of the World*, ed. David M. Howard, 181-94. Downers Grove, Ill.: InterVarsity Press, 1973.

"The history of the people of Israel is the history of a mission" (p. 182) that extends from the call of Abraham to Esther's decision to risk her life for the sake of her people.

2044. ———. "Evangelism and the Teaching of Acts." In *One Race, One Gospel, One Task: World Conference on Evangelism, Berlin 1966, Official Reference Volumes, Vol. 2*, eds. Carl F. H. Henry and W. Stanley Mooneyham, 17-19. Minneapolis: World Wide Publications, 1967.

"One would not be exaggerating to say that the Acts of the Apostles is evangelism" (p. 17).

2045. ———. "Failure and Judgment of the Seven Churches." In *Christ Seeks Asia: Official Reference Volume Asia-South Pacific Congress on Evangelism, Singapore, 1968*, 30-36. Hong Kong: The Rock House, 1968.

The seven churches of Rev. 2-3 failed Christ through indifference, lifeless orthodoxy, intellectual apostasy, complacency, materialism, and diminished love.

2046. ———. "God at Work through Men: Ananias and Paul." In *Let the Earth Hear His Voice: International Congress on World Evangelization, Lausanne, Switzerland, Official Reference Volume*, ed. J. D. Douglas, 43-44. Minneapolis: Worldwide Publications, 1975.

Ananias represents the "nobodies" who are engaged in evangelism, Paul represents the great leaders. Paul had to undergo a threefold revolution: in his conception of salvation, sense of value, and understanding of life.

2047. ———. "Mission—and the Church's Endowment." In *The Church's Worldwide Mission: An Analysis of the Current State of Evangelical Missions and a Strategy for Future Activity*, ed. Harold Lindsell, 52-64. Waco, Tex.: Word Books, 1966.

The Holy Spirit has been the power behind missions from the beginning, and so the church must depend on him rather than on technique.

2048. ———. "Opportunities and Challenges of the Seven Churches." In *Christ Seeks Asia: Official Reference Volume Asia-South Pacific Congress on Evangelism, Singapore, 1968*, ed. W. Stanley Mooneyham, 49-54. Hong Kong: The Rock House, 1968.

The seven churches faced the challenge of being a faithful minority among the pagan majority, and of demonstrating that Christianity represents the fulfillment of the best aspirations of pagan culture and religion.

2049. ———. "Problems and Trials of the Seven Churches." In *Christ Seeks Asia: Official Reference Volume Asia-South Pacific Congress on Evangelism, Singapore, 1968*, ed. W. Stanley Mooneyham, 37-42. Hong Kong: The Rock House, 1968.

Each of the seven churches of Asia had at least one of the following problems: worldliness, persecution, popularity, direct Satanic resistance, relativism, conformity to the world, compromise, works at the expense of faith, and unbiblical church traditions.

2050. ———. "Resources and Promises of the Seven Churches." In *Christ Seeks Asia: Official Reference Volume Asia-South Pacific Congress on Evangelism, Singapore, 1968*, ed. W. Stanley Mooneyham, 55-61. Hong Kong: The Rock House, 1968.

Their resources consisted of the Word of God, the Holy Spirit, those who had retained their loyalty to Christ, godly leaders, and the all-sufficiency of Christ.

2051. ———. "Strengths and Victories of the Seven Churches." In *Christ Seeks Asia: Official Reference Volume Asia-South Pacific Congress on Evangelism, Singapore, 1968*, ed. W. Stanley Mooneyham, 43-48. Hong Kong: The Rock House, 1968.

The seven churches experienced victory over limitations, evil, impurity, suffering, and false apostles. They also received strength to grow in good works and to work patiently for the Lord.

2052. Tennent, Timothy C. "Training Missionaries to Reach Resistant Peoples."*Alliance Academic Review* (1998): 31-40.

Those cultures that resist the Gospel do so usually because they are inherently resistant to change or for theological, nationalistic, or political reasons. Toccoa Falls College has redesigned its missions curriculum so as to prepare its missions majors for ministry among resistant peoples.

2053. Terranova, Carmelo B. "Living the Christ Life I: Living Holy." In *Proclaim Christ until He Comes: Calling the Whole Church to Take the Whole Gospel to the Whole World*, ed. J. D. Douglas, 116-18. Minneapolis: World Wide Publications, 1990.

Holiness requires renunciation, for it is the reproduction of the interior life of Christ. "Christ in us" is the model of holiness.

2054. Tewinkel, Joseph M. *Built upon the Cornerstone: A Brief History of the Christian Church.* Camp Hill, Pa.: Christian Publications, 1980. 178 p.

A popular overview that sets the history of the C&MA in the context of the history of the Church as a whole. Leader's guide available.

2055. ———. *Crusaders: A History of St. Paul Bible College.* n.p. [1983?] 176 p.

2056. *Thailand.* Korat, Thailand: The Thailand Mission of the Christian and Missionary Alliance, [196-?]. 16 p.

A brief illustrated history and description of C&MA mission work in Thailand.

2057. Theophilus, Paul. "The Local-Born Chinese and Overseas-Born Chinese: Cooperation in Light of Biblical Concepts of 'Church' and 'Kingdom of God.'" In *Ethnic Chinese Congress on World Evangelization*, ed. Sharon Wai-Man Chan, 75-77. Hong Kong: Chinese Coordination Center of World Evangelism, 1986.

Local-born Chinese tend to be individualistic, while overseas-born Chinese tend to stress the corporate nature of the church. However, a proper biblical understanding of the church and the kingdom of God demands that we be neither dependent nor independent, but interdependent.

2058. *There's a Light in This Valley.* New York: The Christian and Missionary Alliance, 1955. 14 p.

Describes the Alliance mission to the Dani and Kapauku peoples of the Baliem Valley of Irian Jaya.

2059. Thigpen, Jonathan N. "A Brief History of the Bible Institute Movement in America: A Look Back to the Future?" *Journal of Adult Training* 7 (spring 1994): 1-13.

Makes frequent appreciative references to A. B. Simpson's pioneering work.

2060. Thomas, T. V., and Ken Draper. "A. B. Simpson and World Evangelization." In *The Birth of a Vision*, eds. David F. Hartzfeld and Charles Nienkirchen, 195-219. Regina, Sask.: His Dominion, 1986.

Simpson's fourfold Gospel was rooted in evangelism: Christ as Savior calls believers to take his Gospel to the ends of the earth; Christ as Sanctifier brings about a consecrated life that includes both zeal and the power to witness; Christ as Healer provides powerful manifestations of healing to accompany verbal proclamation; and Christ as Coming King can have his advent accelerated by the Church's speedy fulfillment of the Great Commission. Despite his paternalism, Simpson was ahead of his time in advocating the development of indigenous churches instead of the proliferation of mission stations.

2061. Thompson (A)lbert (E)dward (1870-1927). *A. B. Simpson: His Life and Work*. Harrisburg, Pa.: Christian Publications, 1960. 228 p.

Reprint of 2067, without the 10 plates of portraits, and with a new foreword (by R. R. Brown).

2062. ———. "The Capture of Jerusalem." In *Light on Prophecy: A Coordinated, Constructive Teaching, Being the Proceedings and Addresses of the Philadelphia Prophetic Conference, May 28-30, 1918*, 144-63. New York: The Christian Herald Bible House, 1918.

The capture of Jerusalem by the British was the beginning of the end of the Jewish diaspora. The subsequent "regathering of Israel" will precipitate a catastrophic conflict over Palestine that will culminate in the return of the Messiah.

2063. ———. *A Century of Jewish Missions*. Chicago: Fleming H. Revell, 1902. 286 p.

The author, an Alliance pastor, became director of the C&MA's Palestine field in 1903.

2064. ———. "Challenge of the New Near East." *The Evangelical Christian*, January 1912, 14-15.

The rise of the Young Turk movement and the waning of the power of the Sultan of Turkey have led to unprecedented opportunities for the evangelization of Muslims in the Middle East (where the author was serving as a C&MA missionary).

2065. ———. "The Jews and Their King." In *The Victorious Life: Messages from the Summer Conferences at Whittier California . . . Princeton, New Jersey . . . Cedar Lake, Indiana*, 250-61. Philadelphia: The Board of Managers of Victorious Life Conference, 1918.

A sermon on Hos. 3:4-5, with special reference to the plight of the Jews, Zionism, and mission work among the Jews. Includes many illustrations from the author's own experience as an Alliance missionary in Palestine.

2066. ———. *The Life of A. B. Simpson: Official Authorized Edition*. Harrisburg, Pa.; New York: Christian Alliance Pub. Co., 1920. 300 p.

Descriptive and laudatory in nature, yet still the best single biographical source on Simpson. Includes memorial testimonials by Paul Rader, James M. Gray, Kenneth Mackenzie, J. Gregory Mantle, F. H. Senft, R. H. Glover, and W. M. Turnbull.

2067. ———. *The Life of A. B. Simpson: Official Authorized Edition*. Harrisburg, Pa.: Christian Alliance Pub. Co., 1920. 228 p.

A shorter version of 2066. Lacks the six testimonials included in that volume. Cf. 2061.

2068. ———. *Ought the Jews to Have Palestine?* New York: Christian Alliance Pub. Co., 1917. 23 p.

The Bible records that God promised Palestine to the Jews, and that promise has not been revoked. The capture of Jerusalem (1917) by British forces is a fulfillment of biblical prophecy that paves the way for the restoration of the Jewish homeland.

2069. Thompson, David. *Beyond the Mist: The Story of Donald and Dorothy Fairley*. The Jaffray Collection of Missionary Portraits, 21. Camp Hill, Pa.: Christian Publications, 1998. 238 p.

The Fairleys (Donald A., 1905-1990; Dorothy Millicent Knowles, 1907-1982) were pioneer C&MA missionaries to south Gabon (1933-1969). A jack-of-all-trades, Don Fairley oversaw the establishment of the Bongolo mission station, including the construction of a hydroelectric plant. He had several encounters with Albert Schweitzer (1875-1965), and tried (unsuccessfully) to convince Schweitzer of Jesus's divinity. Cf. 542.

2070. ———. *On Call.* The Jaffray Collection of Missionary Portraits, 3. Camp Hill, Pa.: Christian Publications, 1991. 220 p.

Thompson is a medical missionary in Gabon whose parents were martyred while serving as Alliance missionaries in Vietnam. Cf. 390.

2071. Tiénou, Tite. "Biblical Foundations: An African Study." *Evangelical Review of Theology* 7 (April 1983): 89-101.

Reprint of 2072.

2072. ———. "Biblical Foundations for African Theology." *Missiology: An International Review* 10 (October 1982): 435-48.

Theology involves reflection on God's self-revelation in the Bible so as to know God and become more obedient to him. African theology, like any other theology, must be prescriptive, i.e., it needs to indicate what Christianity ought to look like when a particular group of people reflects on the Scriptures within the context of their culture. Cf. 2071.

2073. ———. "The Church and Its Theology." *Evangelical Review of Theology* 7 (October 1983): 243-46.

The obstacles to the development of evangelical theology (or theologies) in Africa are: mistrust of theology, placing excessive trust in specialists, ignorance of church history, and denominational individualism. African Christians need to develop a multifaceted hermeneutic that will enable the whole church to participate in the process of gaining theological understanding.

2074. ———. "The Church in African Theology: Description and Analysis of Hermeneutical Presuppositions." In *Biblical Interpretation and the Church: Text and Context*, edited by D. A. Carson, 151-65. Exeter: Paternoster Press, 1984.

Many African theologians have sought to understand the church as family in the African sense, i.e., as including dead ancestors, the unborn, and the living. However, in including non-Christian ancestors this view fails to do justice to the biblical teaching of the church as the household of faith. The church as family must be understood primarily in the context of the local church where "trust, mutual sharing of burdens, concerns and joys are developed in a spirit of kinship" (p. 164).

2075. ———. "Contextualization of Theology for Theological Education." In *Evangelical Theological Education Today: 2 Agenda for Renewal*, ed. Paul Bowers, 42-52. Nairobi: Evangel Publishing House, 1982.

To theologize is to contextualize. Proper contextualization assumes that Scripture is normative for theology, and that the Scriptures must be interpreted in such a way that Christians can serve God meaningfully in the context of their culture.

2076. ———. "Eternity in Their Hearts?" In *Through No Fault of Their Own?: The Fate of Those Who Have Never Heard*, eds. William V. Crockett, and James G. Sigountos, 209-15. Grand Rapids: Baker, 1991.

Rejects the thesis that general revelation mediated through pagan religions prepares pagans to receive the Gospel, because it makes an overly rigid distinction between general and special revelation, and because it fails to account for Jesus' teaching that few will respond to the Gospel.

2077. ———. "Evangelism and Social Transformation." In *The Church in Response to Human Need*, ed. Tom Sine, 261-70. Monrovia, Calif.: MARC, 1983.

Salvation is actualized by the fruit it bears. Repentance, for example, involves the righting of wrongs, both personal and social. Originally presented at the Wheaton '83 Consultation on the Church in Response to Human Need.

2078. ———. "Evangelism and Social Transformation." *The Church in Response to Human Need,* eds. Vinay Samuel and Christopher Sugden, 175-79. Grand Rapids: Eerdmans; Oxford: Regnum Books, 1987.

A revision of 2077.

2079. ———. "Forming Indigenous Theologies." In *Toward the Twenty-first Century in Christian Mission: Essays in Honor of Gerald H. Anderson*, eds. James M. Phillips and Robert T. Coote, 245-52. Grand Rapids: Eerdmans, 1993.

Christian theology must undergo constant reformulation if it is to remain current. Theology can only be properly indigenized if local theologians realize that Christianity does not have a single cultural center, grass-roots Christians participate in the process, and all those involved discipline themselves to seek the truth.

2080. ———. "In the One Case, a Slow Death, in the Other, Open Warfare." *Evangelical Missions Quarterly* 22 (April 1986): 169-70.

A response to 2339. Wisley's principles for relating to Marxist liberation movements are not directly applicable to the situation in Africa, but he is right in contending that the Scriptures, properly contextualized, ought to undergird any Christian response to Marxism.

2081. ———. "Indigenous African Christian Theologies: The Uphill Road." *Alliance Academic Review* (1995): 83-94.
Reprint of 2082.

2082. ———. "Indigenous African Theologies: The Uphill Road." *International Bulletin of Missionary Research* 14 (April 1990): 73-77.
Many African theologians have simply reacted to the West, while others have sought merely to adapt Western theologies to the African situation. Both groups have tended to produce elitist theologies. Truly African theology must transcend these differences and relate itself directly "to the needs of Africans in their total context" (p. 76), including the worship and prayer life of African churches. Cf. 2081.

2083. ———. "The Invention of the 'Primitive' and Stereotypes in Mission." *Missiology: An International Review* 19 (July 1991): 295-303.
The characterization of Africans as animist, tribal, and poor (with, perhaps, lazy, stupid, and sensual thrown in for good measure) contributes nothing to either the theory or the practice of mission. Yet these stereotypes not only persist but they also continue to provide the impetus for much missionary work. Mission should be conducted on the basis of facts, not dehumanizing fictions.

2084. ———. "The Problem of Methodology in African Christian Theologies." Ph.D. diss., Fuller Theological Seminary, 1984. 234 p.
To do theology properly African theologians must first understand what it is to be African, which their overreliance on Western anthropological theory has so far prevented them from doing. Once they have properly understood the religious and cultural dimensions of African life they will be in a position to correct the life and thought of the African church through a proper application of the Scriptures.

2085. ———. "The Problem of Methodology in African Christian Theologies." *Evangelical Missions Quarterly* 21 (July 1985): 293-95.
Abstract of 2084.

2086. ———. "Recapturing the Initiative in Theology in Africa." *Evangelical Review of Theology* 11 (April 1987): 152-56.
Abridgement of 2090.

2087. ———. "Religion, Revelation or Christ?" *Trinity World Forum* 23 (fall 1997): 1-3.

In discussing the relationship between Christianity and other religions Christian theologians and missiologists must stress the person of Jesus rather than abstract concepts such as revelation, inclusivism, or exclusivism.

2088. ———. "The Right to Difference: The Common Roots of African Theology and African Philosophy." *Africa Journal of Evangelical Theology* 9 (1990): 24-34.

The quest for an African theology, like the quest for an African philosophy, is still in its infancy. Both quests are linked to the continuing search for an African identity. These attempts will become more successful as Africans gain greater control of theological education in Africa.

2089. ———. "Themes in African Theology of Mission." In *The Good News of the Kingdom: Mission Theology for the Third Millennium*, eds. Charles Van Engen, Dean S. Gilliland, and Paul Pierson, 239-43. Maryknoll, N.Y.: Orbis Books, 1993.

An African theology of mission will need to address the need of Africans to consolidate the gains of Christian missions while being active in mission; to formulate a biblical and theological basis for an unashamedly African self-understanding; to evangelize boldly, sensitively, and non-triumphalistically; and to integrate evangelism and social responsibility.

2090. ———. *The Theological Task of the Church in Africa*. Byang H. Kato Memorial Lectures; 1978. Achimoto, Ghana: African Christian Press, 1982. 54 p.

African evangelicals need to divest themselves of both the fear of theology and the individualism that they have inherited from Western missionaries. Instead, they must cooperate to develop a contextualized African theology and to train the African evangelical church to live it out. Cf. 2086.

2091. ———. "The Theological Task of the Church in Africa: Where Are We Now and Where Should We Be Going?" *East Africa Journal of Evangelical Theology* 6, no. 1 (1987): 3-10.

African evangelicals have so far contributed little to African theology, but they are in a better position than any other Christian groups to bridge the gap between academic and popular theology.

2092. ———. "The Training of Missiologists for an African Context." *In Missiological Education for the Twenty-first Century: The Book, the Circles and the Sandals: Essays in Honor of Paul E. Pierson,* eds. J. Dudley Woodbury, Charles Van Engen, and Edgar J. Elliston, 93-100. American Society of Missiology Series, vol. 23. Maryknoll, N.Y.: Orbis Books, 1996.

Missionary efforts in Africa have largely been characterized by a condescending conception of Africa as, in the words of A. B. Simpson, "the land of deepest, darkest heathen night." Mission has been unhealthily linked to charity. Western missiologists need to take seriously the significant Christianization that has already occurred in Africa, while African missiologists need to develop intellectual rigor. Missiological training in Africa must stress both the classical theological disciplines and those humanities courses that facilitate critical reflection on culture.

2093. ———. "Which Way for African Christianity: Westernization or Indigenous Authenticity?" *Evangelical Missions Quarterly* 28 (July 1992): 256-63.

J. Herbert Kane, whose *Understanding Christian Missions* is used as a textbook in many seminaries, seemed to regard Christianity and Western civilization as one and the same. In rejecting this dehumanizing colonialist mentality, African Christians must avoid the temptation to return to traditional African religions. Rather, in committing themselves ultimately to Christ, rather than to any particular historical manifestation of Christianity, they must examine Africa's present situation in the light of the past and with a view to the future.

2094. ———. "The Word and the New Arrogance." In *Text and Context in Theological Education*, ed. Roger Kemp, 53-61. Springwood, N.S.W.: International Council of Accrediting Agencies for Evangelical Theological Education, 1994.

Contextualization must take place in theological education, but the educator must guard against isolationism and the elevation of context above divine revelation.

2095. Tin, Pham-Xuan (1912-). *A Brief Account of the Evangelical Church of Vietnam*. n. p., 1973. 29 p.

Covers the Alliance mission, the process of indigenization, and Mennonite missionary activity in Vietnam since 1957.

2096. ———. *The Gospel First Came to Vietnam*. n.p., 1970. 15 p.
An overview of the history of C&MA missionary work in Vietnam and the development of the Evangelical Church of Vietnam.

2097. Tingley, Glenn V. (1901-1988). *Signs of the Soon Coming of Jesus Christ*. Birmingham, Ala.: Radio Revival Book Room, [1963?] 24 p.
Considers the signs of the imminent Second Advent to be: earthquakes, famines, population explosion, the establishment of the state of Israel, the rise of communism, modernism, and improved transportation.

2098. ———. *What Is the Why of Life, or Come unto Me All Ye That Labour and Are Heavy Burdened—My Burden Is Light*. Birmingham, Ala.: Radio Revival Book Room, [1960?] 22 p.

2099. Tingley, Glenn V. (1901-1988), with Judith Adams. *Against the Gates of Hell: The Story of Glenn V. Tingley*. Harrisburg, Pa.: Christian Publications, 1977. 152 p.
Tingley founded the Alliance Tabernacle in Birmingham, Ala., in 1928, and remained its pastor until 1956. In 1929 he began "Radio Revival," one of the longest running daily religious broadcasts in the U.S.A. During the Depression he worked with a group of concerned citizens to expose crime and corruption in the city, and he was often embroiled in controversy.

2100. Tomatala, Yakob Yonas. "The Dynamic Missionary Leadership of Robert Alexander Jaffray." D.Miss. diss., Fuller Theological Seminary, 1990. 389 p.
R. A. Jaffray's visionary leadership was a crucial contributing factor to the establishment and continuing growth of the C&MA churches in Indonesia, which currently have an inclusive membership of about 500,000. This study identifies the factors that made Jaffray an effective leader, tries to determine the extent of his impact as a leader, and identifies his lasting contributions to the leadership of the church.

2101. Tonks, A. Ronald. "A History of the Christian and Missionary Alliance, with a Brief Survey of the Work in Canada." B.D. thesis, McMaster University, 1958. 125 p.
Heavily dependent on 502, 2066, and 2216.

2102. Torjesen, Edvard (P)aul (1924-). *Fredrik Franson, a Model for Worldwide Evangelism*. Pasadena, Calif.: William Carey Library, 1983. 122 p.

Includes a description of the joint mission to China sponsored by the Swedish Alliance Mission and the C&MA. A more detailed account can be found in 2104.

2103. ———. "The Legacy of Fredrik Franson." *International Bulletin of Missionary Research* 15 (July 1991): 125-28.

A descriptive and uncritical overview of Franson's life and work that mentions his connections to the C&MA only in passing. Includes an extensive bibliography of primary and secondary sources in English, Swedish, and German.

2104. ———. "A Study of Fredrik Franson: The Development of His Ecclesiology, Missiology, and Worldwide Evangelism." Ph.D. diss., International College, 1984. 867 p.

Franson (1852-1908) organized the Scandanavian Alliance Mission (SAM), which later became The Evangelical Alliance Mission (TEAM). Forty-five of his early recruits were sent to China as the "Swedish Mission" of the C&MA. A. B. Simpson had agreed to sponsor an additional 155 missionaries, but financial difficulties prevented this. The C&MA's "Swedish Mission" was later absorbed by the SAM. Includes a copy of the correspondence between Simpson and Franson. Cf. 688 and 2102.

2105. Torry, Frank L., et al. *Ye Shall Be My Witnesses: A History of the First Fifty Years of Delta Tabernacle, Hamilton, Ontario, Canada, 1925-1975.* [Hamilton, Ont.?]: [Delta Tabernacle?], 1975. 62 p.

2106. Towner, D. B., and Arthur W. McKee, eds. and comps. *The Tabernacle Hymns* New York: Christian Alliance Pub. Co., [1916?] 266 p.

About 20 of the 258 hymns are by Alliance hymn writers Paul Rader, A. B. Simpson, and Albert Simpson Reitz.

2107. Tozer (A)iden (W)ilson (1897-1963). *A. W. Tozer, An Anthology.* Compiled and edited by Harry Verploegh. Camp Hill, Pa.: Christian Publications, 1984. 235 p.

Sermons, editorials, and prayers from 11 of Tozer's works, along with three biographical sketches. Cf. 2175.

2108. ———. *The Attributes of God: A Journey into the Father's Heart.* Camp Hill, Pa.: Christian Publications, 1997. 196 p.

Theology, the study of the God who is infinite, immanent, immense, good, just, merciful, gracious, omnipresent, holy, and perfect, is a beautiful thing that ought to issue in reverential awe and a desire for personal holiness. These sermons were originally preached at Southside Alliance Church, Chicago.

2109. ———. *The Best of A. W. Tozer*. Compiled and edited by Warren W. Wiersbe. Grand Rapids: Baker, 1978. Reprint, Camp Hill, Pa.: Christian Publications, 1991. 251 p.

Topically arranged excerpts from twelve of Tozer's books.

2110. ———. *The Best of A. W. Tozer, Volume 2*. Grand Rapids: Baker Books, 1995. 296 p.

Reprint of 2201.

2111. ———. *The Bible: An Unchanging Book in an Ever-Changing World*. Camp Hill, Pa.: Christian Publications, 1991. 12 p.

Reprint of a chapter from 2182. Protestants have accommodated themselves to the secular belief in progress, concluding that the Bible must be reinterpreted in the light of the so-called advancements of this age. Rather, they must choose the way of costly discipleship of "Jesus the Maladjusted," and return to the hermeneutic of their spiritual forebears.

2112. ———. "A Blueprint for Worship." *His Magazine*, October 1963, 1-5, 21.

A meditation on Rev. 1:4-8: Christians must live in the light of the Second Coming despite the failure of prophetic schemata based on the interpretation of current political events. Refers, in passing, to Julian of Norwich as "my little girlfriend" (p. 5).

2113. ———. *Born After Midnight*. Harrisburg, Pa.: Christian Publications, 1959. 142 p.

Editorials from *The Alliance Weekly* and *The Alliance Witness*. "Conversion for those first Christians was not a destination; it was the beginning of a journey. . . . it was a journey, not a bed on which to lie while waiting for the day of our Lord's triumph" (p. 15-16).

2114. ———. "Can Fundamentalism Be Saved?" *Christian Life*, August 1954, 14-16, 74.

Contemporary fundamentalism is afflicted with cold textualism, superficiality, and worldliness. Revival will come if Fundamentalists dedicate themselves radically to God, allow themselves to be guided by the New Testament, renounce dispensationalism, and rediscover the power of the Holy Spirit. Reprinted in 2150.

2115. ———. "Caught Between." *His Magazine*, February 1964, 4-7.
A meditation on worship in the context of Rev. 4.

2116. ———. *Christ the Eternal Son: Sermons on the Gospel of John, Chapters 1-3*, Compiled and edited by Gerald B. Smith. Harrisburg, Pa.: Christian Publications, 1982. 136 p.
" Oh, the wonder of the ancient theology of the Christian church. How little we know of it in our day of lightminded shallowness" (p. 21).

2117. ———, comp. *The Christian Book of Mystical Verse*. Harrisburg, Pa.: Christian Publications, 1963. 152 p.
A selection of poems intended for use in private devotions. The selections are mystical in the sense that they lead the reader to God and that their authors enjoyed deep communion with God.

2118. ———. *The Coming King*. [Bromley, Kent, England?]: STL, 1990. 155 p.
Reprint of 2145.

2119. ———. "The Communion of Saints." In *Foundations of the Faith: Twelve Studies in the Basic Christian Revelation*, ed. David J. Fant, 145-56. Westwood, N.J.: Fleming H. Revell, 1951.
This communion refers to the participation in the life and nature of Christ that all Christians (on earth or in heaven) share, and to the fellowship of the Eucharist. It is also a communion of the truth epitomized in the Apostle's Creed. Protestants rightly reject as unscriptural any attempt to communicate with the saints above, but they ought to take pains to welcome into their hearts all believers, regardless of race, nationality, or denomination. They would also do well to deepen their communion with previous generations of Christians by reading the spiritual classics. Finally, Christians should not try to bring about organizational unity in order to fulfill Jesus' prayer for the unity of his disciples; for this unity, based in sharing Christ's divine nature, already exists.

2120. ———. *The Counselor: Straight Talk about the Holy Spirit from a 20th Century Prophet*. Camp Hill, Pa.: Christian Publications, 1993. 171 p.
Slightly edited reprint of 2213.

2121. ———. "The Deeper Life: What Is It?" *Christian Life*, August 1957, 10-12.

The deeper life is simply the Christian life described by the New Testament. It is doctrine actualized in experience by yearning after God. It is only "deeper" because the spirituality of the average evangelical is so shallow.

2122. ———. *The Divine Conquest*. Harrisburg, Pa.: Christian Publications, 1950. 128 p.

Popular evangelicalism is a carnal rationalistic religion that neglects the Holy Spirit. True religion has its origin in Christ, is essentially interior in nature, takes time to cultivate, and has the power to transform the individual. It requires humility, repentance, and the enlightenment of the Holy Spirit—who alone can transform the intellect and will and restore the emotions. Cf. 2176.

2123. ———. "Do Your Prayers Please God?" in *Prayer: Its Deeper Dimensions: A Christian Life Symposium*, 83-88. Grand Rapids: Zondervan, 1963.

Much prayer is wasted on projects that did not originate with God. Prayer ought to have as its primary object the revelation of God's glory in the world and the purification of the church. Yet one must always guard against the intrusion of false motives, for "selfishness is never so exquisitely selfish as when it is on its knees" (p. 86).

2124. ———. "Doctrine at Work and Going Places." *Moody Monthly*, February 1957, 16-17.

The book of Joshua illustrates the truths that doctrine must be translated into experience and that the Christian life should involve constant spiritual advancement.

2125. ———. *The Early Tozer: A Word in Season: Selected Articles and Quotations*. Compiled by James L. Snyder. Camp Hill, Pa.: Christian Publications, 1997. 121 p.

Selections from the column that Tozer wrote for *The Alliance Weekly* during the 1930s and 40s. On giving lurid testimonies: "Do not overdo your devils. The grace of God will not suffer from your telling the exact truth" (p. 105).

2126. ———. *Echoes from Eden: The Voices of God Calling Man*. The Tozer Pulpit, vol. 8. Harrisburg, Pa.: Christian Publications, 1981. 121 p.

Reprint of 2192.

2127. ———. *Essays on Spiritual Perfection: Selections from His Pulpit Ministry*. Compiled and edited by Gerald B. Smith. The Tozer Pulpit, vol. 4., Harrisburg, Pa.: Christian Publications, 1972. 144 p.

Identical in content to 2142.

2128. ———. *Explaining the Deeper Life*. Chichester, England: Sovereign World, 1991. 31 p.

Originally published as articles in *Christian Life*, ca. 1957. Modern evangelical Christianity is in danger of experiencing a boom, but not a revival. Prayer for revival must be accompanied by a radical reformation of life by means of the internal appropriation of the Scriptures, self-emptying (so as to permit the filling of the Holy Spirit) and a desire for, and an acceptance of, spiritual gifts.

2129. ———. *Extracts from the Writings of A. W. Tozer (1897-1963), a 20th Century Prophet*. Bromley, Kent, England: Send the Light Trust, 1969. 48 p.

Reprint of 2132.

2130. ———. *Faith beyond Reason*. Camp Hill, Pa.: Christian Publications, 1989. 160 p.

Reprint (with some updating of language) of 2189.

2131. ———. *Five Vows for Spiritual Power*. Harrisburg, Pa.: Christian Publications, [1960?]. 16 p.

These are: to deal thoroughly with sin, never to be possessed by possessions, never to defend oneself (and especially one's reputation), never to say anything hurtful about another person, and never to accept any glory. Cf. 2170.

2132. ———. *Gems from Tozer: Selections from the Writings of A. W. Tozer*. Bromley, England: Send the Light Trust, 1969. 96 p

Brief extracts from 22 of Tozer's publications. Cf. 2129.

2133. ———. "Gifts of the Spirit: Are They for Today?" *Christian Life*, October 1957, 24-25.

The spiritual gifts mentioned in the New Testament are available to the church today and should be desired and sought by believers in a spirit of absolute submission to God. No one gift, and especially not glossolalia, should be desired more than the rest. Cf. 2170.

2134. ———. *God Tells the Man Who Cares*. Compiled by Anita M. Bailey. Harrisburg, Pa.: Christian Publications, 1970. 172 p.

Editorials published in *The Alliance Weekly,* 1950-1957 and *The Alliance Witness* 1958-1963. "To divide what should be divided and unite what should be united is the part of wisdom. . . .[but sometimes] Truth is slain to provide a feast to celebrate the marriage of heaven and hell" (p. 47).

2135. ———. *God's Greatest Gift to Man*. Harrisburg, Pa.: Christian Publications, [1960?] 16 p.

Christ is God's greatest gift to humankind, and union with Christ— partaking of the divine nature— is the greatest privilege of humankind.

2136. ———. "How to Be Filled with the Holy Spirit." *Christian Life*, December 1957, 14-15.

Similar in content to (though far less extensive than) 2137.

2137. ———. *How to Be filled with the Holy Spirit*. Harrisburg, Pa.: Christian Publications, [1960?]. 58 p.

The Holy Spirit provides immediate, internal evidence of the presence of God. Not many evangelicals have experienced the filling of the Holy Spirit, despite the fact that God intended it to be a feature of the normal Christian life. To be filled with the Holy Spirit one must desire to be filled, present one's body to God, ask to be filled, obey God, and have faith of the same kind one exercised for salvation. Cultivating the presence of the Holy Spirit involves rejecting worldliness, becoming engrossed with Jesus Christ, living righteously, purifying the mind, meditating on Scripture, and recognizing the Spirit's omnipresence.

2138. ———. "How to Make Spiritual Progress." *The Evangelical Christian*, July 1962, 11, 14.

Instructions on how to overcome spiritual complacency, i.e., seek the filling of the Holy Spirit: "Every man is as full of the Holy Spirit as he wants to be" (p. 14).

2139. ———. "How to Try the Spirits: Not Every New Experience or New Truth Is Valid." *Moody Monthly*, December 1979, 51-55.

Reprint of p. 119-32 of 2154.

2140. ———. *How to Try the Spirits: Seven Ways to Discern the Source of Religious Experiences*. Camp Hill, Pa.: Christian Publications, 1997. 18 p.

Reprint of p. 119-32 of 2154.

2141. ———. *I Call It Heresy: Twelve Sermons in Peter's First Epistle*. Compiled and edited by Gerald B. Smith. Harrisburg, Pa.: Christian Publications, 1974. 159 p.

Reprint of 2205.

2142. ———. *I Talk Back to the Devil: Essays in Spiritual Perfection*. Edited by Gerald B. Smith. Harrisburg, Pa.: Christian Publications, 1972. 146 p.

The essence of the deeper life can be summed up in the teaching of the *Cloud of Unknowing* that God is a jealous lover who demands our undivided attention. Cf. 2127.

2143. ———. "The Impact of God's Holiness." *His Magazine*, March 1961, 10-11, 23-24.

A slightly edited reprint of 2157.

2144. ———. *Jesus, Author of Our Faith*. Compiled and edited by Gerald B. Smith. Camp Hill, Pa.: Christian Publications, 1988. 146 p.

Twelve sermons on Heb. 11-13. A companion volume to 2146. Significantly, the chapter entitled "Enoch: Faith Takes Us to the Rapture," makes no mention of the rapture as an event distinct from the translation of the saints at the return of Christ.

2145. ———. *Jesus Is Victor!* Compiled and edited by Gerald B. Smith. Camp Hill, Pa.: Christian Publications, 1989. 170 p.

Twelve sermons on Rev. 1-10. "Sinful men have entered into that holy place where life begins. . . . Nuclear destruction is out of the bottle. . . . The common people do not really know the extent to which their leaders have mortgaged their futures" (p. 101). Cf. 2118.

2146. ———. *Jesus, Our Man in Glory*. Compiled and edited by Gerald B. Smith. Camp Hill, Pa.: Christian Publications, 1987. 136 p.

Twelve Christological sermons based on selected texts from the first ten chapters of Hebrews. "God does not play on our emotions to bring us to the point of spiritual decision" (p. 83). Cf. 2144.

2147. ———. *Keys to the Deeper Life*. Grand Rapids: Zondervan, 1957. 54 p.

Reprint of the series of articles of the same name that was published in *Christian Life* in 1957.

2148. ———. *Keys to the Deeper Life*. Grand Rapids: Zondervan, 1988. 92 p.

Reprint of 2150.

2149. ———. *The Knowledge of the Holy: The Attributes of God and Their Meaning in Christian Life*. New York: Harper and Brothers, 1961. 128 p.

Most American Christians lead spiritually shallow lives because they have lost the concept of majesty. Reading the Christian classics would facilitate a return to "personal heart religion," but in the current religious climate even educated Christians refuse to do this. Hence this popularized distillation of the teachings of such luminaries as Augustine and Anselm.

2150. ———. *Leaning into the Wind*. Wheaton, Ill.: Creation House, 1984. 94 p.

The contemporary resurgence in interest in spiritual experience will not be satisfied by the shallowness that characterizes much of evangelicalism. For true revival to occur evangelicals must long for intimacy with Christ, reject the dead textualism of fundamentalism (but not the doctrine of inerrancy), earnestly desire the filling of the Spirit and the gifts of the Spirit, and put aside anything that might hinder their effectiveness in prayer. Cf. 2114 and 2148.

2151. ———. *Let My People Go: The Life of Robert A. Jaffray*. Harrisburg, Pa.: Christian Publications, 1947. 127 p.

A somewhat hagiographical biography of the Alliance's most famous missionary. Robert Alexander Jaffray (1873-1945) spent most of his career in China, but he was largely responsible for the establishment of the highly successful Alliance missions in Vietnam and Indonesia. Cf. 389.

2152. ———. *Let My People Go: The Life of Robert A. Jaffray*. The Jaffray Collection of Missionary Portraits, 1. Camp Hill, Pa.: Christian Publications, 1990. 135 p.

Reprint, with updated language, of 2151.

2153. ———. "Making Good in the Christian Life." *The Light of Life* 1 (January 1925): 2-3.

2154. ———. *Man, the Dwelling Place of God*. Harrisburg, Pa.: Christian Publications, 1966. 174 p.

Miscellaneous editorials and articles (mostly from *The Alliance Weekly* or *The Alliance Witness*) that expose and offer correctives to the wrong ideas about God that too often contaminate the practical theology of American evangelicalism. Cf. 2139 and 2140.

2155. ———. "The Man Who Exalted God Above All," *Christian Medical Society Journal,* Autumn 1960, 14-20.

A meditation on Ps. 57:5.

2156. ———. "The Man Who Met God in the Fire." *Christian Medical Society Journal*, Spring 1960, 20-26.

A meditation on Exod. 3:1-6.

2157. ———. "The Man Who Saw God on the Throne." *Christian Medical Society Journal*, summer 1960, 16-22.

A meditation on Isa. 6. Cf. 2143.

2158. ———. "Marks of a Spiritual Man." *Moody Monthly*, September 1963, 79-81.

Truly spiritual people want to be holy rather than happy, to obey God even if it means facing adversity, to see life as God sees it, to avoid moral compromise, to see others advance at their expense, and to make decisions in the light of eternity. (Reprinted from *The Alliance Witness.*)

2159. ———. *Men Who Met God*. Compiled by Gerald B. Smith. Camp Hill, Pa.: Christian Publications, 1986. 128 p.

Sermons on the lives of Abraham, Isaac, Jacob, Moses, Elijah, Isaiah, and Ezekiel originally preached at Avenue Road Alliance Church (Toronto). "There are some people with whom you cannot live in peace and keep your conscience right. Do the best you can and do not worry about them" (p. 45).

2160. ———. *The Menace of the Religious Movie*. Harrisburg, Pa.: Christian Publications, [1950?]. 30 p.

Motion pictures are, per se, immoral. Religious movies, i.e., those which dramatize biblical themes Hollywood-style and which are used as a substitute for an evangelistic sermon are a menace because: they distort the biblical pattern of addressing truth primarily to the ear; they cheapen the Gospel by turning it into a form of entertainment; the actors must act insincerely by simulating holy acts and godly emotions; the movie is not a scripturally sanctioned method for conveying spiritual truth. Cf. 2195.

2161. ———. "Missing Jewel." In *Essays on Prayer: A His Reader on Conversing with God*, A. W. Tozer et al, 1-6. Downer's Grove, Ill.: InterVarsity Press, 1968.
Identical to 2162.

2162. ———. "Missing Jewel." *His* 28 (January 1968): 17-23.
A digest of 2218.

2163. ———. *The Next Chapter after the Last.* Compiled and edited by Harry Verploegh. Harrisburg, Pa.: Christian Publications, 1987. 111 p.
A collection of editorials from *The Alliance Weekly* and *The Alliance Witness*. "Protestants deserve a better sort of Scripture reading than they are now getting in our churches. And we who do the reading are the only ones who can give it to them" (p. 291).

2164. ———. "No Revival without Reformation." *Christian Life*, May 1957, 14-15.
Fundamentalism is beset by a textualism that has bred a moral and spiritual complacency that rivals that of liberalism. But mere prayer for revival is not enough to overcome it: nothing short of a radical amendment of life will do.

2165. ———. *Of God and Men.* Harrisburg, Pa.: Christian Publications, 1960. 133 p.
Editorials from *The Alliance Weekly* and *The Alliance Witness*. "Christianity is basically a religion of meanings. . . . The church by pronouncing certain objects sacred and attributing power to them has turned from the pure freedom of the gospel to a kind of educated magic . . . gravely injurious to the souls of man [sic]" (p. 87).

2166. ———. *The Old Cross and the New.* Harrisburg, Pa.: Christian Publications, [196-?]. 6 p.
A new accommodationist understanding of Christianity which "draws friendly parallels between the ways of God and the ways of men" (p. 3) has begun to infect evangelicalism. The cross, by contrast, represents death, a renunciation of selfish ways, and trust in Christ for forgiveness and the power to live out the Gospel.

2167. ———. "On Fire." *His Magazine*, December 1970, 1, 3.

Moses' experience of God in the burning bush gave him power, purity, distinctiveness, and beauty. These experiential virtues are available to those who are prepared to be completely consecrated to God.

2168. ———. *Out of the Rut, into Revival: Dealing with Spiritual Stagnation*. Compiled by James L. Snyder. London: Hodder and Stoughton, 1993. 178 p.

Reprint of 2182.

2169. ———. *Paths to Power*. Harrisburg, Pa.: Christian Publications, [1964?]. 43 p.

Power is that divine impartation that brings about repentance from sin and belief in Christ. God makes this power available to those who appropriate salvation through radical obedience to Christ.

2170. ———. "Pivots." *His Magazine*, February 1967, 10-14.

Rev. ed. of 2131.

2171. ———. "The Praying Plumber." In *Three Condensed Books*, 3-17. Westchester, Ill.: Christian Readers Club, 1957.

Digest of the articles that comprise 2172.

2172. ———. *The Praying Plumber of Lisburn: A Sketch of God's Dealings with Thomas Haire*. Harrisburg, Pa.: Christian Publications, 1960. 38 p.

Haire was evangelist Leonard Ravenhill's prayer partner. A mystic who was a plumber by trade, Haire devoted three nights a week to intercessory prayer. He did not have the gift of tongues, nor did he feel that he needed to have it in order to pray effectively. The final chapter "The Secret of Successful Prayer" was written by Haire himself. Originally published as a series of articles in *The Alliance Weekly*.

2173. ———. *The Price of Neglect*. Compiled by Harry Verploegh. Camp Hill, Pa.: Christian Publications, 1991. 154 p.

Editorials from *The Alliance Weekly* and *The Alliance Witness*. "The present flair for religion has not made people heavenly-minded; rather, it has secularized religion. . . . Religion is promoted by the identical [sic] techniques used to sell cigarettes" (p. 100).

2174. ———. *The Pursuit of God*. Harrisburg, Pa.: Christian Publications, 1948. 128 p.

The "deeper life" consists in cultivating an active receptivity to the God who predisposes us to pursue him. Each chapter describes a certain attribute of God, laments the ways in which popular evangelicalism has failed to pay attention to it, and concludes with instructions (including a closing prayer) on how to restore this neglected truth to its proper place in the life of faith. Introduction by Samuel Zwemer.

2175. ———. *The Pursuit of God: A 31-day Experience.* Compiled by Edythe Draper. Camp Hill, Pa.: Christian Publications, 1995. 208 p.

Daily meditations from 2174, supplemented by quotations from others of his works, various spiritual classics, and the Bible.

2176. ———. *The Pursuit of Man: The Divine Conquest of the Human Heart.* Camp Hill, Pa.: Christian Publications, 1996. 154 p.

Reprint of 2122.

2177. ———. *The Quotable Tozer: Wise Words with a Prophetic Edge.* Compiled by Harry Verploegh. Camp Hill, Pa.: Christian Publications, 1994. 208 p.

Reprint of 2107 that omits the biographical introduction by L. L. King.

2178. ———. *The Quotable Tozer II: More Wise Words with a Prophetic Edge.* Compiled by Harry Verploegh. Camp Hill, Pa.: Christian Publications, 1997. 228 p.

Quotations are keyed to a bibliography of Tozer's works and indexed. A biographical sketch provides a good introduction to Tozer's life and work.

2179. ———. *Renewed Day by Day: A Daily Devotional.* Compiled by Gerald B. Smith. Camp Hill, Pa.: Christian Publications, 1980. 383 p.

Page-length undocumented excerpts from Tozer's works.

2180. ———. *Renewed Day by Day, Volume 2.* Compiled by Gerald B. Smith. Camp Hill, Pa.: Christian Publications, 1991. 383 p.

Identical in format to vol. 1. The excerpts tend to be from his later writings. "The church that can show an impressive quantitative growth . . . is envied and imitated [but] the Bible [shows] this up for the heresy it is" (7 October).

2181. ———. *The Root of the Righteous.* Harrisburg, Pa.: Christian Publications, 1955. 160 p.

Editorials from *The Alliance Weekly*. Spiritual dry spells, if they are not the result of sin, "demand that we exercise faith. . . . Our watchful Heavenly Father [withdraws] His inward comfort from us to teach us that Christ alone is the Rock upon which we must repose our everlasting trust" (p. 128).

2182. ———. *Rut, Rot or Revival: The Condition of the Church*. Compiled by James N. Snyder. Camp Hill, Pa.: Christian Publications, 1991. 178 p.

Fifteen sermons on renewal from Tozer's ministry at Avenue Road Church in Toronto (1959-1963). Awakened Christians have encountered God and ceased to be mediocre or somnolent "the sleeping saints pay to have [awakened Christians] come and do their work for them. They send people like this out to South Africa or the Far East" (p. 311). Cf. 2168.

2183. ———. "The Saint Must Walk Alone." *Eternity*, August 1956, 14-15.

"The man who has passed on into the divine Presence will not find many who understand him" (p. 15).

2184. ———. *The Set of the Sail*. Compiled by Harry Verploegh. Camp Hill, Pa.: Christian Publications, 1986. 172 p.

Editorials from *The Alliance Weekly* and *The Alliance Witness*. On the communion of saints: "the individual Christian will find in the communion of the local church the most perfect atmosphere for the fullest development of his spiritual life. . . . The religious solitary may . . . escape some of the irritations of the crowd, but he is a half-man . . . and . . . a half-Christian" (p. 22).

2185. ———. *Signposts: A Collection of Sayings from A. W. Tozer*. Wheaton, Ill.: Scripture Press, 1988. 228 p.

The sayings are indexed to the first editions of the 11 works from which they were taken.

2186. ———. *The Size of the Soul*. Compiled by Harry Verploegh. Camp Hill, Pa.: Christian Publications, 1992. 196 p.

This collection of editorials from *The Alliance Weekly* and *The Alliance Witness* includes "The Use and Abuse of Good Books," a five-part series on the value of reading the spiritual classics.

2187. ———. *Success and the Christian: The Cost and Criteria of Christian Maturity*. Camp Hill, Pa.: Christian Publications, 1994. 146 p.

Nine previously unpublished sermons. The first rule of holy living is to "venerate all things," to recapture a sense of wonder so as to "see God in His beautiful world" (p. 101, 105).

2188. ———. *Ten Messages on the Holy Spirit, Selections from His Pulpit Ministry*. Compiled by Gerald B. Smith. The Tozer Pulpit, vol. 2. Harrisburg, Pa.: Christian Publications, 1968. 172 p.

The Holy Spirit does what the intellect by itself cannot do (even if engaged in Bible study!): he reveals and glorifies Christ, brings about the new birth of conversion, and leads believers into a life of holiness. The promise of the Holy Spirit is not a repetition of Pentecost, but a perpetuation of it. The filling of the Holy Spirit occurs instantaneously, and those who are filled know that they are. Cf. 2213.

2189. ———. *Ten Sermons from the Gospel of John, Selections from His Pulpit Ministry*. Compiled and edited by Gerald B. Smith. The Tozer Pulpit, vol. 3. Harrisburg, Pa.: Christian Publications, 1970. 167 p.

Evangelicalism is beset by a rationalism that equates truth with knowledge of the text of Scripture and ignores the (necessary) illumination of the Holy Spirit. The holy inactivity exemplified by Mary of Bethany illustrates the waiting on God that is a prerequisite for a life of service to Christ and his church. Cf. 2130

2190. ———. *Ten Sermons on the Voices of God Calling Man*. The Tozer Pulpit, vol. 8. Compiled and edited by Gerald B. Smith. Harrisburg, Pa.: Christian Publications, 1981. 121 p.

God shows himself to be merciful in the very fact that he calls sinners to repentance and salvation. Cf. 2126.

2191. ———. *That Incredible Christian*. Harrisburg, Pa.: Christian Publications, 1964. 137 p.

Editorials from *The Alliance Witness*. "Many Christians accept adversity or tribulation with a sigh an call it their cross, forgetting that such things come alike to saint and sinner. The cross is an extra adversity that comes to us as a result of our obedience to Christ" (p. 111).

2192. ———. *This World: Playground or Battleground?* Compiled and edited by Harry Verploegh. Camp Hill, Pa.: Christian Publications, 1989. 121 p.

Editorials from *The Alliance Weekly* and *The Alliance Witness*. "The man who refers to one or another act as being 'unfair' to him is not a victorious man. He is inwardly defeated" (p. 79).

2193. ———. *Those Amazing Methodists: A Tribute to the Ministry of John and Charles Wesley*. Camp Hill, Pa.: Christian Publications, 1995. 50 p.

Reprint of six articles published in the *Alliance Weekly* in 1957. Unlike the early Methodists: "Protestant Christians today recoil from discipline . . . because they are in bondage. They . . . understand that God does not require us to save our souls by punishing our bodies. But because they have not received free grace as an emancipating agent within their own hearts, they are not free" (p. 22-23).

2194. ———. *Total Commitment to Christ: What Is It?* Harrisburg, Pa.: Christian Publications, 1960.

It is an attachment that is at once intellectual, volitional, exclusive, inclusive (in that one is attached to the same thing that Christ is, and to the church in particular) and irrevocable.

2195. ———. *Tozer on Worship and Entertainment: Selected Excerpts*. Compiled by James L. Snyder. Camp Hill, Pa.: Christian Publications, 1997. 219 p.

The contemporary evangelical church in North America has emphasized selfishness and entertainment over worship to such an extent that its worship has become insipid and, at times, an offense to God. The final chapter is a reprint of 2160.

2196. ———. *The Tozer Pulpit*. Camp Hill, Pa.: Christian Publications, 1994. 2 vols.

Reprint of 2126, 2127, 2188, 2189, 2197, 2202-2204.

2197. ———. *The Tozer Pulpit: Selections from His Pulpit Ministry*. Compiled by Gerald B. Smith. Harrisburg, Pa.: Christian Publications, 1967. 158 p.

Short extracts from sermons Tozer preached at Southside Alliance Church in Chicago. Churches that exploit Christ's teaching on "treasure in heaven" for fundraising purposes need "to be exposed before the whole world. That is religious racketeering, pure and simple" (p. 46).

2198. ———. *Tozer Speaks to Students: Chapel Messages Preached at Wheaton College*. Edited by Lyle W. Dorsett. Camp Hill, Pa.: Christian Publications, 1998. 168 p.

Eleven messages preached between 1952 and 1954. "American people seldom think. . . . We have our religion dished out for us in fiction form so we never have to grasp an abstract idea. Abstractions are absolutely indispensable to any grasp of spiritual things" (p. 22).

2199. ———. *The Tozer Topical Reader*. Compiled by Ron Eggert. Camp Hill, Pa.: Christian Publications, 1998. 2 vols.

1377 quotations from Tozer's works arranged topically and keyed to Scripture and subject indexes.

2200. ———. *Tragedy in the Church, the Missing Gifts: Ten Sermons Relating to the Life and Ministry of the Christian Church*. Edited and compiled by Gerald B. Smith. Harrisburg, Pa.: Christian Publications, 1978. 155 p.

Reprint of 2204.

2201. ———. *A Treasury of A. W. Tozer: A Collection of Tozer Favorites*. Grand Rapids: Baker, 1980. 296 p.

Excerpts from 14 of Tozer's books. Cf. 2110.

2202. ———. *Twelve Messages on Well-known and Favorite Bible Texts*. Compiled and edited by Gerald B. Smith. The Tozer Pulpit, vol. 6. Harrisburg, Pa.: Christian Publications, 1975. 174 p.

"Pray that I will not come to a wearied end—an exhausted, tired old preacher, interested only in a place to roost" (p. 60). Cf. 2214.

2203. ———. *Twelve Sermons in Peter's First Epistle: Selections from His Pulpit Ministry*. Compiled and edited by Gerald B. Smith. The Tozer Pulpit, vol. 5. Harrisburg, Pa.: Christian Publications, 1974. 159 p.

Each sermon attacks defects in popular evangelical belief and practice. The Alliance, for example, tends to stress the second work of grace for the wrong reason, i.e., because the first has been so watered down in contemporary evangelistic practice. Cf. 2141.

2204. ———. *Twelve Sermons Relating to the Life and Ministry of the Christian Church*. The Tozer Pulpit, vol. 7. Harrisburg, Pa.: Christian Publications, 1978. 155 p.

Though the gifts of the Holy Spirit are still available to the church rationalism prevails to such a degree that 90% of what is done in the church is accomplished by human effort alone. To make matters worse, many churches that do seek the gifts exalt one gift, glossolalia, above all the others. Cf. 2200.

2205. ———. "The Voice of the Spirit." *His Magazine*, October 1965, 1-4, 8.

The voice of the Holy Spirit can be heard by the human conscience as conviction of sin, righteousness, and judgment.

2206. ———. *The Waning Authority of Christ in the Churches*. Harrisburg, Pa.: Christian Publications, [ca. 1960]. 15 p.

Jesus Christ is accorded the functional authority of a constitutional monarch in most evangelical churches. Most evangelicals, having substituted their own broad-minded views for the teaching of Scripture, accept as biblical the prevailing spirituality and morality of evangelicalism. The causes of this decline are mainly the power of habit and tradition and the rise of intellectualism.

2207. ———. *The Warfare of the Spirit: Developing Spiritual Maturity*. Compiled by Harry Verploegh. Camp Hill, Pa.: Christian Publications, 1993. 193 p.

This collection of editorials from *The Alliance Weekly* and *The Alliance Witness* includes a preface in which the children of A. W. and Ada Pfautz Tozer express their appreciation for loving and respectful nurture in things intellectual and spiritual.

2208. ———. "We Are Becoming What We Love." *Eternity*, October 1956, 18-19, 37.

Since we become the sum of our loves, we ought to focus our love on right objects, and above all on God. Christian love begins in the will, not in feeling, but does not consist in sanctified willpower, for it requires a spiritual rebirth that God alone can effect.

2209. ———. *We Travel an Appointed Way*. Compiled and edited by Harry Verploegh. Camp Hill, Pa.: Christian Publications, 1988. 113 p.

Editorials from *The Alliance Weekly* and *The Alliance Witness*. "Civilized man has . . . [associated] love with sex exclusively and then [popularized] this error." True love, by contrast, is not merely an emotion, but rather "a benevolent principle under the control of the will" (p. 42).

2210. ———. *What the Bible Says about God, You and How You Can Know Him*. Camp Hill, Pa.: Christian Publications, 1998. 11 p.

An apologetic for Bible reading that includes a reprint of chapter three of 2209.

2211. ———. *Whatever Happened to Worship?* Compiled and edited by Gerald B. Smith. Camp Hill, Pa.: Christian Publications, 1985. 128 p.

Ten sermons preached at Avenue Road Church, Toronto, in 1962. "I have had people tell me very dogmatically that they will never allow 'feeling' to have any part in their spiritual life and experience. I reply, 'Too bad for you!' . . . because I . . . believe [that] true worship . . . is to feel in the heart!" (p. 82).

2212. ———. *What's in the Bible That People Today Ought to Know About.* Harrisburg, Pa.: Christian Publications, 1962. 10 p.

Attempts to give a jargon-free overview of salvation history, e.g., to believe in Jesus as Lord and Savior is to "attach ourselves to him in loyalty and faith" (p. 7).

2213. ———. *When He Is Come: Ten Messages on the Holy Spirit.* Harrisburg, Pa.: Christian Publications, 1968. 172 p.

Reprint, with new preface, of 2188. Cf. 2120.

2214. ———. *Who Put Jesus on the Cross?: Twelve Messages on Well-known and Favorite Bible Texts.* Edited and compiled by Gerald B. Smith. Harrisburg, Pa.: Christian Publications, 1975. 174 p.

Reprint of 2202.

2215. ———. *Why the World Cannot Receive.* Salisbury, Southern Rhodesia: Word of Life Publications, [195-?]. 11 p.

Reprint of chapter nine of 2122.

2216. ———. *Wingspread: Albert B. Simpson—A Study in Spiritual Altitude.* Harrisburg, Pa.: Christian Publications, 1943. 143 p.

A laudatory spiritual biography that adds little to that of A. E. Thompson, but is nonetheless valuable for the light it sheds on Tozer, e.g., his anti-Pentecostalism: "Mr. Simpson was miles ahead of [the Pentecostals] in his spiritual experience. He did not need anything they had" (p. 133). For a different opinion and a critique of *Wingspread,* see 1202.

2217. ———. *Worship: The Missing Jewel.* Heritage Series. Camp Hill, Pa.: Christian Publications, 1992. 26 p.

Reprint of 2218.

2218. ———. *Worship: The Missing Jewel in the Evangelical Church.* Harrisburg, Pa.: Christian Publications, [196-?] 30 p.

2219. Tozer (A)iden (W)ilson (1897-1963), and (A)lbert (B)enjamin Simpson (1843-1919). *A. W. Tozer and A. B. Simpson on Spiritual Warfare*. Heritage Series. Camp Hill, Pa.: Christian Publications, 1993. 34 p.

Chapters from 2142 and 1734.

2220. Tozer (A)iden (W)ilson (1897-1963), et al. *Essays on Prayer: A His Reader on Conversing with God*. Chicago: Inter-Varsity Press, 1968. 89 p.

Tozer's contribution consists of the essay "Missing Jewel."

2221. *Training National Workers*. New York: Christian and Missionary Alliance, 1950.

2222. *Translation Work*. New York: Christian and Missionary Alliance, 1950.

2223. Travis, Drake W. "Christ Our Healer Today." Master's thesis, Alliance Theological Seminary, 1992. 127 p.

The results of the survey on which this thesis is based are included in 2224.

2224. ———. *Christ Our Healer Today: The Ministry of Healing in the Christian and Missionary Alliance*. Camp Hill, Pa.: Christian Publications, 1996. 239 p.

Written in response to a marked decline in interest in divine healing in Alliance congregations in the United States. Includes testimonies of Alliance people who have been healed within the past 40 years and brief descriptions of the ministry of healing of various Alliance people. Concludes with the results of surveys administered in 1989 and 1994.

2225. *Treasures of Darkness*. New York: The Christian and Missionary Alliance, 1954. 11 p.

A brief history of the Alliance mission to the animist peoples of Côte d'Ivoire.

2226. Trouten, Donald James (1926-). "Changes in Educational Policies in the Christian and Missionary Alliance." Ph.D. diss., New York University, 1962. 505 p.

The C&MA, once indifferent to accreditation, is now actively seeking it for all its Bible colleges. The educational mission of the colleges, i.e., the preparation of ministers and missionaries, remains unchanged, although the length of training and the number of course offerings in the liberal arts have increased.

2227. ———. *Financial Factors in Alliance Higher Education*. n.p.: by the author, 1970. 11 p.

It would be far less expensive for the Alliance to convert an existing Bible college into a liberal arts college than it would be to start one from scratch. The amount of control the C&MA exercises over its colleges is proportionately much greater than the amount of funding it provides them.

2228. Truax, Edgar. *Triumph and Tradition in Miaoland*. New York: [Christian and Missionary Alliance?] [1950?]. 16 p.

Vignettes from the author's 30 years as a C&MA missionary among the Miao (Hmong) of the northeastern corner of Guizhou Province, China. Includes a translation of the Hmong myth of creation.

2229. Tsang, To-hang. *An Awakening: Beginnings of the Gospel in Bali*. Hong Kong: China Alliance Press, 1981. 71 p.

Text in Chinese.

2230. Tucker, Ruth A. "Daisy Smith: Forsaking Ministry for Marriage." In *First Ladies of the Parish: Historical Portraits of Pastors' Wives*, 131-44. Grand Rapids: Ministry Resources Library, 1988.

Daisy Billings, a gifted preacher who had trained at Nyack Missionary College, was serving as the de facto assistant pastor of a Presbyterian church in Toronto. When Oswald J. Smith, the new associate pastor, arrived in 1915 she was "bumped" from her preaching duties and public ministry. After her marriage to Smith in 1916 she was completely preoccupied with domestic responsibilities and often depressed (her husband was often away for months at a time). Her public ministry resumed only after her children had left home.

2231. ———. *From Jerusalem to Irian Jaya: A Biographical History of Christian Missions*. Grand Rapids: Academie Books, 1983. 278 p.

Biographees include A. B. Simpson, Betty Olson and the Vietnam martyrs, and Philip Teng.

2232. ———. *Guardians of the Great Commission: The Story of Women in Modern Missions*. Grand Rapids: Academie Books, 1988. 278 p.

Includes brief biographies of such Alliance notables as A. B. Simpson, Emma Whittemore, Mabel Francis, Betty Olson, and Dorie Van Stone.

2233. ———. "Margaret Simpson: Living with an Impractical Visionary." In *First Ladies of the Parish: Historical Portraits of Pastors' Wives,* 95-103. Grand Rapids: Ministry Resources Library, 1988.

Margaret Simpson (1841-1924) had to do most of the child-rearing, while at the same time enduring the vicissitudes of A. B. Simpson's "near manic-depressive personality." In addition, she disagreed with her husband about their move from Louisville to New York City, and she opposed his desire both to be a missionary to China and to turn their house into a healing home. She later became more reconciled to his ministry and took a greater part in it.

2234. Tucker, Ruth A., and Walter Liefeld. *Daughters of the Church: Women and Ministry from New Testament Times to the Present*. Grand Rapids: Academie Books, 1987. 552 p.

Briefly treats A. B. Simpson's attitude to women in ministry.

2235. Tucker (W)alter Leon (1871-1934). *The Redemption of Paul Rader*. New York: The Book Stall, 1918. 201 p.

A biography that concentrates on the years 1912 (when Rader underwent the crisis that led to his return to faith) and 1917. Includes many photographs and samples of Rader's preaching, as well as a lurid description of Rader's three-day crisis experience.

2236. ———. *"With Him," or Studies in the Epistle to the Ephesians*. New York: The Book Stall, 1917. Reprint, Harrisburg, Pa.: Christian Alliance Pub. Co., 1928. 120 p.

2237. Turnbull, Cora Mae (1879-1928). *The Craft of Soul Winning: A Practical Course of Study in Methods of Christian Service, Especially in Winning Individuals to Faith in the Lord Jesus Christ*. Nyack, N.Y.: Correspondence Bible School, 1925. 215 p.

2238. ———. *Songs of the Trail*. Harrisburg, Pa.: The Evangelical Press, 1928. 66 p.

Her collected poetry, including poems about Nyack and the Missionary Training Institute.

2239. ———. *"Your Hour and the Power of Darkness."* New York: Christian and Missionary Alliance, [192-?]. 8 p.

An exhortation to pray against the spiritual forces of darkness. Stresses the role of spiritual warfare in mission work.

2240. Turnbull, John (R)odney (1890-). *From Head Hunting to Christ: Journeys in Borneo*. Glendale, Calif.: Arthur Mouw, [1940?] 64 p.

The account of his 1939 visit to Alliance mission stations in Borneo (Kalimantan). Author was the brother of Walter M. Turnbull.

2241. ———. *From Human Sacrifice to Christ*. Fort Wayne, Ind.: The Temple Publishers, 1942. 64 p.

The account of a visit made to missions in China, Hong Kong, and the Philippines. Several of the Philippine believers encountered had formerly practiced human sacrifice.

2242. ———. *The Golden Jubilee of Missionary Adventure to India 1916: India Revisited 1966*. New Delhi: Published for the author by Masihi Sahitya Samstha, [1967?]. 187 p.

2243. ———. *In Storied Palestine: Along the Fascinating Highways of the Holy Land*. New York: Christian Alliance Pub. Co., 1927. 101 p.

Recounts the author's extensive travels as an Alliance missionary to Palestine (1926-1927). Some of the chapters are reprints of articles in *The Alliance Weekly*.

2244. ———. *Israel, Land of Glory*. Crawfordville, Ind.: Holy Land Mission, 1969. 72 p.

Reflections in light of the Six-Day War and the author's missionary travels in the Holy Land. The modern state of Israel reflects God's promises to Abraham and his offspring, promises that cannot be broken despite the disobedience of both ancient and modern Israel.

2245. ———. *The River Cassia As It Flows through the Life of Pastor Chao*. New York: Christian and Missionary Alliance, 1937. 16 p.

Pastor L. T. Chao, was a convert of Isaac Hess, C&MA missionary to South China.

2246. ———. *True Stories from Indo-China*. New York: Christian and Missionary Alliance, 1937. 16 p.

Alliance missionaries' accounts of conversions, healings, and miracles.

2247. ———. *With Uncle John in the Holy Land*. Beirut: by the author, [195-?] 58 p.

Retraces Paul's first missionary journey, making explanatory comments on the relevant texts in light of geography, archaeological discovery, and church history.

2248. Turnbull, Ralph G. *A History of Preaching Vol. III: From the Close of the Nineteenth Century to the Middle of the Twentieth Century*. Grand Rapids: Baker, 1974. 586 p.

A. B. Simpson was as a strong doctrinal preacher who emphasized missions, tithing, and the fourfold Gospel (p. 274-78). A. W. Tozer was a scholarly, worshipful, and precise preacher who "invoked the will and sought to capture the mind," made his mysticism subject to revelation, presented a balanced view of the Holy Spirit, and emphasized the sovereignty of God (p. 277-81).

2249. Turnbull, Walter (M)ason (1881-1930). "Bringing Back the King." *Bridal Call* 9 (September 1925): 10-12, 25-26.

A premillennial sermon preached at Aimee Semple McPherson's Angelus Temple by Simpson's successor as pastor of the Gospel Tabernacle. Cf. 1202, p. 39.

2250. ———. "The Founder of the Christian and Missionary Alliance." *Missionary Review of the World* 43 (April 1920): 267-71.

A brief but thorough sketch of Simpson's career as a promoter of world missions.

2251. ———. *The Shadow of the Sun-Dial, or the Destiny of the Jew*. New York: Christian Alliance Pub. Co., [1920?]. 34 p.

An apologetic for Zionism. Laments the blindness of the Jewish people in not recognizing Jesus as their Messiah, and predicts that they will undergo tribulation.

2252. Turnbull (W)alter (M)ason (1881-1930), and C. H. Chrisman, comps. and eds. *The Message of the Christian and Missionary Alliance*. New York: Christian Alliance Pub. Co., [1927?]. 31 p.

A thoroughly Simpsonian explication of the fourfold Gospel, together with a presentation of the C&MA's philosophy of missions.

2253. Turner, Harry L. (1887?-1976). *The Voice of the Spirit*. Harrisburg, Pa.: Christian Publications, [1951?]. 157 p.

A textbook on the Holy Spirit based on the author's classroom lectures at St. Paul Bible Institute. "The Spirit is given to [the] . . . born-again to indwell them, seal them, witness to their salvation, integrate them into . . . the Church" (p. 8). The filling of the Holy Spirit can only be sustained if one continues to live according to the desires and promptings of the Spirit.

2254. *Twenty Days on a Raft*. New York: Christian and Missionary Alliance, 1943. 15 p.

A brief account of the ordeal and rescue of C&MA missionary Ethel Bell and family that is described in more detail in 99.

2255. Tymchak, Michael. "Ethics and the Coming King." *His Dominion* 14 (fall 1987): 2-13.

"The knowledge that the king is coming challenges us to accomplish the ethical mission He has given, not to alter it" (p. 12).

2256. United States. Bureau of the Census. *Census of Religious Bodies: 1926. Christian and Missionary Alliance. Statistics, Denominational History, Doctrine, and Organization. . . .* Washington, D.C.: U.S. Government Printing Office, 1940. 10 p.

Includes comparative statistics based on census reports for 1916, 1926, and 1936.

2257. Urquhart, John. *Roger's Reasons, or the Bible and Science*. New York: Alliance Press Co., [ca. 1900]. 30 p.

"Roger" successfully champions the cause of biblical orthodoxy in a conversation with three other fictitious characters: a liberal theologian, lawyer, and man of letters.

2258. ———. *The Wonders of Prophecy, or What Are We to Believe?* 6th rev. ed. The Alliance Colportage Series. New York: Christian Alliance Pub. Co., [1925?] 2 vols.

The fulfilled prophecies of Scripture provide overwhelming evidence that God's foreknowledge governs history and that humankind ought to respond to God's revelation in loving obedience.

2259. Van Dyck, Howard. *Liberated! Alliance Missionaries' Internment and Release*. New York: Christian and Missionary Alliance, 1945. 15 p.

The story of the internment and release of Alliance missionaries stationed in the Philippines during World War II.

2260. ———. *Paul's Picture of Paganism*. New York: The Christian and Missionary Alliance, 1948. 22 p.

An explication of Rom. 1:19-28 that draws on the author's experiences as a missionary to China.

2261. ———. *Too Many Moons and Their Eclipse*. New York: The Christian and Missionary Alliance, 1940. 8 p.

An apologetic for missions to China. Despite the great need at home "there are no heathen in the [U. S.] like the heathen in foreign lands" (p. 5). Missions should not be regarded as a means of civilizing an already rich culture, like that of China, although "enlightenment, education, healing [and] culture" (p. 6) are by-products of the missionary enterprise.

2262. ———. *William Christie, Apostle to Tibet*. Harrisburg, Pa.: Christian Publications, 1956. 176 p.

After many years as an Alliance missionary to China and Tibet (1892 -1924) Christie went on to serve the C&MA in a number of administrative capacities: as superintendent of the Northwestern District and principal of St. Paul Bible College (1925-1926), as foreign secretary for China and Japan (1926-1930), as treasurer (1930-1947), and as vice-president (1931-1947).

2263. ———. "Wings over New Guinea." *World Dominion: An International Review of Christian Progress* 33 (July-August 1955): 245-51.

In April 1954, with the aid of a flying boat, C&MA missionaries establish contact with the recently discovered primitive tribes of the Baliem Valley. The flying boat, piloted by C&MA missionary Al Lewis, goes missing a year later.

2264. Van Hoogen, Joel. "Premillennialism and the Alliance Distinctives."*Alliance Academic Review* (1998): 41-70.

The five Alliance distinctives, i.e., "the integrity of God, the inerrancy of His Word, the centrality of His Son, the prospects of His sanctification, and the supremacy of His vision" (p. 66) can all be affirmed by both postmillennialists and amillennialists. However, within the Alliance, these distinctives have all arisen because of the movement's premillennial eschatology. This connection needs to be emphasized, understood, and maintained if the C&MA is to sustain its vitality.

2265. Van Stone, Doris Mae (1922-), and Erwin Lutzer. *Dorie: The Girl Nobody Wanted*. Chicago: Moody Press, 1979. 158 p.

Doris Van Stone's experience of the love of God enabled her to overcome the trauma of child abuse and motivated her to become a C&MA missionary to Irian Jaya.

2266. Vencer, Agustin B., Jr. "An International Perspective on Evangelical-Catholic Cooperation." *Evangelical Missions Quarterly* 31 (July 1995): 278-79.

Evangelicals should make common cause with Catholics on sociopolitical issues, but should not cooperate with them in missions and evangelism because significant theological differences between the two groups remain unresolved.

2267. ———. "Raising Financial Support in Asia." In *The Work of an Evangelist: International Conference for Itinerant Evangelists, Amsterdam, the Netherlands*, ed. J. D. Douglas, 439-48. Minneapolis: World Wide Publications, 1984.

Guidelines for fundraising in the Third World, with special reference to the Philippines.

2268. ———. "Relief and Development in Evangelism." In *The Calling of an Evangelist: The Second International Congress for Itinerant Evangelists, Amsterdam, the Netherlands*, ed. J. D. Douglas, 379-83. Minneapolis: World Wide Publications, 1987.

Social concern and evangelism go hand in hand.

2269. Vencer, Agustin B., Jr., and John Allan. *Poor Is No Excuse: The Story of Jun Vencer*. Exeter, England: Paternoster Press; Grand Rapids: Baker, 1989. 108 p.

Vencer, a pastor in the Christian and Missionary Alliance Churches of the Philippines (CAMACOP) has served as leader of both the Philippine Council of Evangelical Churches and the World Evangelical Fellowship. He has also been active in promoting social action projects in the Philippines.

2270. Vergara, Ignacio. *El protestantismo en Chile*, 2nd ed. Santiago: Editorial del Pacifico, 1962. 259 p.

The C&MA church in Chile suffered a large-scale defection to the Baptists in 1909. Undaunted, C&MA missionaries established a printing press and became the most prolific publishing concern in the country. The C&MA gets along well with other Protestant groups in the country, but its publications attack the Roman Catholic Church, which it considers to be the Antichrist.

2271. *Viet Nam: Unfinished Task!* New York: Christian and Missionary Alliance, 1960. 6 p.

An appeal for funds to construct buildings for a Bible school in Nhatrang.

2272. Vilban, Mary. *A Paralytic Cured.* New York: Word, Work and World Pub. Co., [1883?].

A woman who had been a paralytic for eight years, and considered a hopeless case by physicians, is healed in response to prayer during one of A. B. Simpson's Friday meetings. Includes a list of the preparatory instructions Simpson gave her.

2273. Villegas, Ceferino D. (1937-). "Cross-cultural Orientation for Filipino Missionaries of the Christian and Missionary Alliance Churches of the Philippines." Master's thesis, Wheaton College, 1973. 77 p.

2274. ———. "Principles of Lay Leadership." D. Miss. diss., Fuller Theological Seminary, 1982. 297 p.

The Christian and Missionary Alliance Churches of the Philippines are the fastest growing church in the Philippines, largely as a result of the ministry of lay preachers in rural areas.

2275. Vogel, Lester Irwin. "Zion As Place and Past: An American Myth: Ottoman Palestine in the American Mind Perceived through Protestant Consciousness and Experience." Ph.D. diss., George Washington University, 1984. 513 p.

Includes an analysis of American missionary efforts in Palestine to 1917, including those of the C&MA.

2276. Volstad, David K. "The Christian and Missionary Alliance in Lima, Peru." In *Guidelines for Urban Church Planting*, ed. Roger Greenway, 45-56. Grand Rapids: Baker, 1976.

A description and evaluation of the Lima al Encuentro con Dios (LED) evangelistic campaign. A significant number of new converts did not become baptized members of the church, perhaps for lack of trained catechists. Nevertheless, the LED experiment should be considered a success, and the model itself is capable of being contextualized to any culture.

2277. Waite, Montrose (1891-1977). *Waite: A Man Who Could Not Wait.* Detroit: Parker Books, 1988. 166 p.

Waite's father was a C&MA pastor in Jamaica. Waite attended the Missionary Training Institute and served as an Alliance Missionary to Sierra Leone from 1923 to 1937. After the Alliance decided not to send any more black missionaries to Sierra Leone (their white counterparts did not want to work alongside American blacks) and reneged on its promise to support his family during an extended furlough, Waite and other blacks formed the African-American Missionary Crusade, under whose auspices he and his family returned to Sierra Leone in 1946.

2278. Wallbrook, William (1864?-1899). *Diary of, and Poems by, the Late Rev. Wm. Wallbrook.* College Point, N.Y.: A. K. Schultz, 1900. 127 p.

Wallbrook, a Canadian, served as an Alliance missionary to the Congo (1895-1896). Forced to return home because of illness, he pastored churches in the New York City area until his death. His diary recounts his experiences of healing and financial provision, his baptism in the Spirit, his experiences of spiritual power, and his successes in personal evangelism.

2279. Wan, Enoch, ed. *Missions within Reach: Intercultural Ministries in Canada: A Compendium Volume of the Intercultural Ministries National Conference of Canada, 1993.* Hong Kong: China Alliance Press; Edmonton, Alta.: China Alliance Press (Canada), 1995. 190 p.

2280. Ward (C)harles (M)orse (1909-), ed. *Elder A. G. Ward: Intimate Glimpses of My Father's Life.* Pulpit Series, 14. Springfield, Mo.: Assemblies of God, 1955. 43 p.

Alfred George Ward (1881-1960) began his ministerial career around 1901 as a Methodist circuit rider in Alberta. He joined the C&MA a few years later, but left to join the Assemblies of God in 1919. He "came into direct contact with" A. B. Simpson, whom he came to respect deeply. Simpson's *The Gospel of Healing* and Kenneth Mackenzie's *Divine Life for the Body* profoundly influenced his own understanding of divine healing.

2281. Wardle, Terry H. (1952-). *Exalt Him!: Designing Dynamic Worship Services.* Camp Hill, Pa.: Christian Publications, 1988. 154 p.

A textbook developed in the context of the author's experience as an Alliance pastor and as a professor at Alliance Theological Seminary.

2282. ———. *How to Share the Gospel: Presenting the Good News One on One*. Camp Hill, Pa.: Christian Publications, 1997. 26 p.
Reprint of chapter eight of 2283.

2283. ———. *One to One: A Practical Guide to Friendship Evangelism*. Camp Hill, Pa.: Christian Publications, 1989. 204 p.
Cf. 2282.

2284. ———. *Wounded: How You Can Find Inner Wholeness and Healing in Him*. Camp Hill, Pa.: Christian Publications, 1994. 232 p.
Interwoven throughout the book is Wardle's account of how he (a C&MA pastor and college professor) overcame a severe depression through counseling and prayer for inner healing.

2285. Warneck, Gustave. *Outline of a History of Protestant Missions from the Reformation to the Present Time: A Contribution to Modern Church History*. Edited by George Robson; translated from the 7th German ed. Edinburgh: Oliphant, Anderson and Ferrier, 1901. 378 p.
The founder of the Protestant science of missions has this to say about the C&MA: "In . . . eight years this whimsical mission has not . . . sent out more than 330 missionaries, male and female, most of them, it is true, little trained and not equal to their calling. . . . The works of God are not of such hot-house growth, and from such intemperate enthusiasm nothing healthy can be born. . . . Of any results from the past twelve years' work there is nothing to report" (p. 115).

2286. Warren, Edward L. *The Presbyterian Church in Louisville: From Its Organization in 1816 to the Year 1896*. Chicago: n.p., 1896. 36 p.
A. B. Simpson was installed as pastor of the Chestnut Street Church on 2 January 1874. The success of the revival meetings held by Major Whittle and P. P. Bliss in 1875 led to the construction of a new building designed to accommodate 2,000 people. The church was renamed Broadway Tabernacle Presbyterian Church. Simpson resigned on 10 November 1879.

2287. Watson, Eva (M)argaret (1847-). *Holy Ann*. New York: Christian Alliance Pub. Co., [ca 1925]. 32 p.
Ann Preston (1810?-1906) was an illiterate Irish immigrant who worked as a servant in rural Ontario. She became locally famous for her saintly life, the mystical dimension of her relationship to God, and her remarkable powers of insight. She was a Methodist who often attended Alliance meetings.

2288. *We Are Debtors to This Continent Also*. New York; Toronto: The Christian and Missionary Alliance, [196-?]. 8 p.

Describes Alliance home missions to indigenous peoples, Jews, Latin Americans, French Canadians, and mountaineers in Kentucky and the Ozarks.

2289. Webber, Leroy C. *In His Steps: Studies in the Book of I Peter*. New York: The Alliance Hour, [1970?]. 19 p.

Five devotional sermons preached on "The Alliance Hour," the radio ministry of the C&MA.

2290. "Wedding Bells." *Triumphs of Faith*, June 1890, 121-24.

An account of the wedding of Carrie Judd and George Montgomery (14 May 1890) and of the role played by A. B. Simpson in the ceremony and reception.

2291. Wee, Asterio J. "Developing Strategies for CAMACOP's Urban Church Growth and Church Planting." D.Miss. diss, Fuller Theological Seminary, 1989. 217 p.

Includes a two-chapter history of the Christian and Missionary Alliance Churches of the Philippines.

2292. Weideman, C. Donald. "An Evaluation of A. B. Simpson's Idea of Sanctification from the Biblical Perspective." Master's thesis, Wheaton College, 1966. 103 p.

Simpson's doctrine of sanctification is a fusion of forensic (Calvinistic) and Pietistic elements.

2293. Weidman, Mavis, and Daryl Dale. *Teaching Basics: Preschool: A Teacher Certification Book.* Nyack, N.Y.: Education Office, The Christian and Missionary Alliance, 1985. 73 p.

2294. Weld, Wayne C. *An Ecuadorian Impasse*. Chicago: Department of World Missions, Evangelical Covenant Church of North America, 1968. 137 p.

An attempt to understand why church growth in Ecuador has been so slow. Mentions the key role played by the Alliance in establishing an evangelical church in Ecuador. Includes a brief history and evaluation of the work of the C&MA and the other churches and missions operating in the country.

2295. Wenninger, Joseph Carl (1919-). "A Study of Attitudes of Christian and Missionary Alliance Clientele toward Higher Education." Ph.D. diss., University of Minnesota, 1972. 256 p.

A survey-based study that recommends broadening Alliance higher education to include more liberal arts courses, converting some Bible colleges to liberal arts colleges, and the establishment of a C&MA seminary in both the United States and Canada.

2296. Westergren, Timothy D. "Do All Roads Lead to Heaven?: An Examination of Unitive Pluralism." In *Through No Fault of Their Own?: The Fate of Those Who Have Never Heard*, eds. William V. Crockett and James G. Sigountos, 169-82. Grand Rapids: Baker, 1991.

The unitive pluralism of John Hick and Paul Knitter subordinates Christ's uniqueness to the "absolute authority" of religious pluralism. Christians must avoid being culturally imperialistic in their sharing of the Gospel, behave tolerantly towards outsiders, and engage in dialogue with other religious traditions—but they must not compromise the exclusive claims of Christ in so doing.

2297. Westervelt, Josephine Hope. *The Green Gods*. New York: Christian Alliance Pub. Co., 1927. 140 p.

A missionary romance, set in Vietnam, that ends as follows: "David and Mary Lois, happy in each other and happy in the Lord, were a joy to the Christians gathered there and a drawing attraction to the unsaved heathen about them" (p. 140).

2298. Westmeier, Arline M. "Healing and Power in the Protestant Community of Bogotá with Special Emphasis on the Christian and Missionary Alliance Churches." Master's thesis, University of Aberdeen, 1988. 252 p.

Discusses the varieties of folk healing and the various superstitions about physical healing that are prevalent in Colombia—and how these practices and beliefs change once Colombians become Christians and experience divine healing.

2299. ———. *Healing the Wounded Soul: Ways to Inner Wholeness*. Shippensburg, Pa.: Companion Press, 1989. 152 p.

A guide to inner healing, based on the author's 21 years as a C&MA missionary in Colombia.

2300. Westmeier, Karl-Wilhelm. "Evangelical Churches in the Colombian State: The Socio-religious Themes of the Bulletins of the Evangelical

Confederation of Colombia." Masters Studies thesis, Alliance School of Theology and Missions, 1978. 249 p.

Deals with the persecution of evangelical churches, including those of the Colombian C&MA, during "la Violencia."

2301. ———. *Reconciling Heaven and Earth: The Transcendental Enthusiasm and Growth of an Urban Protestant Community, Bogotá, Colombia*. Studies in the Intercultural History of Christianity, vol. 41. Frankfurt am Main: Peter Lang, 1986. 462 p.

A phenomenological study of evangelicalism in Bogotá by an Alliance missionary. Concludes that the enthusiastic Protestantism of the bogotanos studied enables them to cope with the pressures of urban life and to deal effectively with the supernatural.

2302. Weston, Frank S. *New Thought: Its Origin, Nature and Opposition to the Word of God*. New York: Christian Alliance Pub. Co., [193-?]. 8 p.

New Thought is a pantheistic philosophy of "self-salvation through the exercise of one's own will" (p. 3) that is inimical to the Gospel.

2303. Weston, William Todd (1914-). *Wotta Dad I Had!: In Loving Memory of W. G. Weston*. Creve Coeur, Mo.: by the author, [1981?] 158 p.

A folksy laudatory biography, of William G. Weston (1881-1964), a noted C&MA evangelist.

2304. W. F. T. *Culture and Christianity*. New York: Alliance Press Company, [1900?]. 19 p.

Considers the two to be mutually irreconcilable.

2305. *What Is the Christian and Missionary Alliance?* Willowdale, Ont.: The C&MA in Canada, 1987. 12 p.

An overview of the beliefs, history, and governance of the C&MA. Includes the doctrinal statement and the poem "Himself."

2306. Whipple, N. M. "National Leadership in the Laos Church." In *The Indigenous Church: A Report from Many Fields*, 43-51. Chicago: Moody Press, 1960.

A brief description of a self-governing indigenous church of the C&MA.

2307. Whitney, Etta. *God's Faithfulness*. n. p., [1950?] 9 p.

Recounts God's sustenance of C&MA missionaries to Hong Kong during their internment by the Japanese from December 1941 to 29 June 1942.

2308. Whittemore (E)mma (M)ott (1850-1931). "Conquered and Healed." *Thy Healer* 21 (November 1884): 283-85.

Recounts her healing, through the prayers of A. B. Simpson, of a serious spinal injury.

2309. ———. *Delia, the Bluebird of Mulberry Bend*, rev. ed. New York: Fleming H. Revell, 1914. 126 p.

The story of Cordelia Loughlin (d. 1892), a convert of the Door of Hope, who underwent a remarkable transformation and had a fruitful ministry in the 18 months between her conversion and her death.

2310. ———. *Frankie, or the Little Conqueror*. 3rd ed. [New York?]: Door of Hope Repository, 1894. 67 p.

Biography of Whittemore's pious son who died in childhood. A shorter version appears in 2311, p. 289-304.

2311. ———. *Mother Whittemore's Records of Modern Miracles*, ed. F. A. Robinson. Toronto: Missions of Biblical Education, 1931. 301 p.

An autobiography in the form of an anecdotal history of the Door of Hope, a rescue mission for women founded in New York City in 1890 by Mrs. Whittemore, an associate of A. B. Simpson.

2312. ———. *Mother Whittemore's Records of Modern Miracles*, ed. F. A. Robinson. Toronto: Missions of Biblical Education, 1937. 220 p.

An abridgement of 2311.

2313. Whitwell, Cutler B. "The Life Story of W. E. B. — and of 'Jesus Is Coming.'" *The Sunday School Times*, 11 January 1936, 19-20.

A missionary address delivered by Blackstone at the Gospel Tabernacle's 1886 convention (held at Old Orchard Beach, Me.) inspired A. B. Simpson to found the Christian Alliance.

2314. Wick, Robert (S)tanley. "The Alliance Mission in Irian Jaya." Ph.D. diss., California Graduate School of Theology, 1985. 450 p.

The most thorough, comprehensive (1938-1984) and evaluative treatment of the subject. Concludes that the church has achieved full indigeneity because it is self-supporting, self-propagating, and self-governing—and even supplies its own Bible translators. Cf. 2315.

2315. ———. *God's Invasion: The Story of Fifty Years of Christian and Missionary Alliance Work in Irian Jaya.* Camp Hill, Pa.: Buena Book Services, 1990. 225 p.

Essentially a reprint (updated to 1989) of the descriptive portions of 2314.

2316. Widbin, R. Bryan. "Salvation for People outside of Israel's Covenant?" *In Through No Fault of Their Own?: The Fate of Those Who Have Never Heard,* eds. William V. Crockett and James G. Sigountos, 73-83. Grand Rapids: Baker, 1991.

The Old Testament portrays Israel as God's unique people, a light to the nations. However, God initiates an unmediated relationship with some people outside of the covenant community. God fearers such as Melchizedek find salvation in Yahweh apart from the influence of either Israel or the religions of the ancient Near East.

2317. Wiersbe, Warren. "The File-card Mentality." *Good News Broadcaster* 40 (September 1982): 6-7.

A. W. Tozer's warning against "the file-card mentality"—i.e., stereotyping and lack of open-mindedness with respect to the nonessentials of the faith—ought to be borne in mind whenever one feels inclined to pass judgment on a particular person, movement, or idea.

2318. ———. *A. W. Tozer.* In *Walking with the Giants.* Grand Rapids: Baker, 1979.

A brief appreciative bio-bibliographical essay.

2319. Wilkerson, Barbara. "The History and Philosophy of Religious Education in the Christian and Missionary Alliance." Ed.D. diss., Rutgers University, 1989. 440 p.

The official decisions and actions of the C&MA have hindered the progress of Christian education, and the Alliance has yet to clearly articulate its philosophy of religious education. This has led to a blurring of doctrinal distinctives, and especially since 1956, when the Alliance stopped producing its own Sunday School curriculum and opted instead for the generic evangelical Scripture Press curriculum. This decline in distinctiveness also stems from the tendency of world evangelization to overshadow the rest of the fourfold Gospel in Alliance thinking and practice.

2320. Williams, George H., and Edith L. Blumhofer. "A History of Speaking in Tongues and Related Gifts." In *The Charismatic Movement*, ed. Michael P. Hamilton, 61-113. Grand Rapids: Eerdmans, 1975.

An unsubstantiated reference (p. 112, n158) mentions that Mrs. Simpson was opposed to speaking in tongues and implies that her opposition might have accounted for A. B. Simpson's failure to experience the gift.

2321. Williams, Herman. "Goals of the Indian Church." In *Missions and the Indian Church*, 44-63. Cass Lake, Minn.: Alliance Indian Publications, 1972.

Paternalism and cultural insensitivity on the part of the missionary must give way to actions informed by native ways and a desire to foster the establishment of an indigenous church.

2322. Williamson, William B. "Christian and Missionary Alliance." In *An Encyclopedia of Religions in the United States: One Hundred Religious Groups Speak for Themselves*. New York: Crossroad, 1992.

Especially helpful for its definitions of specialized terms that occur frequently in C&MA publications.

2323. Willoughby, W. Robert. *First Corinthians: Fostering Spirituality*. The Deeper Life Pulpit Commentary. Camp Hill, Pa.: Christian Publications, 1996. 262 p.

2324. ———. "Pentecost: An Experience for Today: An Examination of the Baptism of the Holy Spirit in Acts." *His Dominion* 13 (spring 1987): 35-40.

The C&MA has tended to emphasize the sanctifying work of the Holy Spirit to the detriment of the vocational ministry of the Spirit. Spiritual renewal in the Alliance will require the appropriation of the latter without the neglect of the former.

2325. Wilson, Ernest Gerald. "The Christian and Missionary Alliance: Developments and Modifications of Its Original Objectives." Ph.D. diss., New York University, 1984. 596 p.

As the C&MA has progressed from the status of a fraternal organization to that of a denomination a number of changes have occurred: the position and ministry of women have been diminished; the church has become more Baptistic in doctrine and has tended to deemphasize divine healing and sanctification; education has been stressed to the detriment of prayer and evangelism; Christian Publications no longer publishes exclusively fourfold Gospel material, but rather whatever will likely sell well; and, more positively, ministry to the poor is being reemphasized.

2326. Wilson, Henry (1841-1908). *The ABC of Divine Health after 24 Years' Experience.* New York: Alliance Press Co., 1908. 68 p.

Divine healing rests upon the foundations of the Bible, Christ's atonement, the experience of Christians throughout history, and the glorified body of Jesus. Divine healing is God's health "infused into us, physically as well as spiritually" (p. 25), which leads to a physical experience of the mystery of union with Christ.

2327. ———. *Bible Lamps for Little Feet.* New York: Christian Alliance Pub. Co., 1902. 184 p.

Bible stories retold for children, with illustrative vignettes and study questions.

2328. ———. "The Internal Christ." In *The Signs of the Times, or God's Message for Today: A Symposium on New Theology, Christian Science, the Lord's Coming, the Gift of Tongues, and the Deeper Spiritual Life*, 204-14. New York: Alliance Press Co., 1907.

The imitation of an external Christ "calling and charming us to follow Him and by following become like Him" (p. 206), animates most Christian spirituality. The deeper life, the highest Christianity, preaches an internal Christ, who has been reincarnated in believers so that they live "by the force of an energizing power within" (p. 209). Since disease arises from mental or spiritual conditions those indwelt by the living Christ will be delivered from the power of disease. Reprinted as chapter one of 2329.

2329. ———. *The Internal Christ.* New York: Christian Alliance Pub. Co., 1908. 92 p.

The experience of the deeper life can be summed up as "God in me and I in Him so fully that I cannot tell where God begins and I end; . . . and where I begin and God ends."

2330. ———. *The Lord's Healing for the Lord's Body.* Living Truths, vol. 1, no. 37. Nyack, N.Y.: Christian Alliance Pub. Co., 1901. 15 p.

A sermon on 1 Cor. 11:29 linking divine healing to the Incarnation and the Resurrection.

2331. ———. *The Present State of the Church of England in Canada: Its Cause and Cure.* CIHM/IMCH Microfiche series; no. 25957. Kingston, Ontario: [Daily News Office], 1883. 16 p.

The Church of England in Canada ranked fourth in numbers and fifth in rate of increase among Canadian churches in the 1870s. Clerical abuses of privilege, clerical incompetence, and poor administration are the chief causes of this unacceptable state of affairs.

2332. ———. *Talks to Children*. New York: Christian Alliance Pub. Co., [1890?] 95 p.

2333. Wilson, Madèle, and (A)lbert (B)enjamin Simpson (1843-1919). *Henry Wilson, One of God's Best*. New York: Alliance Press Company, 1908. 194 p.

Henry Wilson, a Canadian and a former Anglican clergyman, became Simpson's associate pastor at the Gospel Tabernacle in 1891. From 1901 until his death he served as Field Superintendent for the C&MA. Simpson (who wrote the last five chapters of the present volume) considered him to be the embodiment of the fourfold Gospel and of a spirituality that goes beyond the mere imitation of Christ.

2334. *Wings for Shangri-La*. New York: The Christian and Missionary Alliance, 1953. 5 p.

An appeal for funds to purchase a flying boat to transport missionaries to the Baliem Valley of Irian Jaya.

2335. Winrod, Gerald B. *Christ Within*. Wichita, Kans.: Winrod Publication Center, 1925. Reprint, New York: Christian Alliance Pub. Co., [1927?]. 141 p.

2336. Winter, Ellen M. *Out of the Depths*. New York: Alliance Press Co., 1904. 107 p.

A spiritual autobiography centering on the author's experiences of divine healing.

2337. Winter, Ralph D. "Protestant Mission Societies: The American Experience." *Missiology: An International Review* 8 (April 1979): 139-78.

The C&MA is "an example of a para-church organization that became a denomination against its own will" (p. 166). Its "overseas work has not produced autonomous national churches" (p. 158).

2338. Wisley, Thomas Noel (1939-). "Dynamic Biblical Christianity in the Buddhist/Marxist Context: Northeast Thailand." Ph.D. diss., Fuller Theological Seminary, 1984. 485 p.

Promotes a nonsyncretistic dynamic equivalency Christianity. Uses examples from his experience as a C&MA missionary to Thailand.

2339. ———. "Meeting the Marxist Challenge in the Philippines." *Evangelical Missions Quarterly* 22 (April 1986): 160-67.

Deals with the author's attempts to contextualize his teaching of theology (at Alliance Biblical Seminary) in light of the challenge posed by Marxist liberation movements in the Philippines. Cf. 2080.

2340. ———."Towards a Dynamic Indigenous Church: Thailand and Cambodia: Case Studies of Indigeneity in the Christian and Missionary Alliance." In *Readings in Dynamic Indigeneity*, eds. Charles Kraft and Tom N. Wisley, 207-25. Pasadena, Calif.: William Carey Library, 1979.

A truly indigenous church will take indigenous forms, transform them, adapt them, and use them for Christian ends and to convey Christian meanings. The Cambodian C&MA church is more indigenized than the Thai C&MA church because "the forms and patterns emerged from within Cambodian-ness . . . thus establishing deep meaning and relevance to resultant functions of the church" (p. 223).

2341. Witmer, S. A. *The Bible College Story: Education with Dimension.* Manhasset, N.Y.: Channel Press, 1962. 253 p.

Ruth Miller and W.C. Stevens, both faculty members at Nyack, were among the first Bible college instructors to stress the inductive study of Scripture. Miller began teaching at Prairie Bible Institute in 1923. Includes a brief history of Nyack College.

2342. Woerner, David, ed. *Desde el siglo (1897) y hasta el siglo (1997) tu eres Dios*. Temuco, Chile: Imprenta y Editorial Alianza, 1997. 413 p.

A centennial history of the C&MA in Chile. Includes a list of past missionaries and pastors, and biographical sketches of current missionaries and pastors.

2343. Woerner, Gustave (1896-1978). *What's Up?* Toronto: The Christian and Missionary Alliance, [1943?]. 8 p.

Despite the fact that (as a result of World War II) many C&MA missionaries have either been evacuated or interned the mission is operating unhindered in many fields.

2344. Woodberry, Mrs. (K)ittie C. *Through Blood-Stained Shansi*. New York: Alliance Press Co., 1903. 223 p.

The Woodberrys traveled through Shanxi and other regions in northern China as representatives of the C&MA mission. They sought to verify the number of deaths that had occurred among the Swedish mission of the C&MA during the Boxer Rebellion, and to collect the indemnity that the Chinese government had promised to pay to the survivors of the uprising.

2345. Woodcock, Eldon. "Being Filled with the Holy Spirit." *Alliance Academic Review* (1999): 75-99.

The New Testament does not explicitly state the conditions for being filled with the Holy Spirit. Early Alliance literature was characterized by "some looseness in the handling of pneumatological terminology" (p. 94). A. B. Simpson, for example, "did not always clearly distinguish among the Holy Spirit's reception, baptism, and filling" (p. 99). As a result, "there are some variations in how [these terms] were understood" (p. 94).

2346. Woodward, David B. *Aflame for God: Biography of Fredrik Franson, Founder of the Evangelical Alliance Mission*. Chicago: Moody Press, 1966. 190 p.

Considers the causes of disaffection between the Swedish Alliance Mission and the C&MA to be: lack of funding (on the part of the C&MA) to support the unexpected deluge of Swedish missionary candidates, and, on the field (China) itself, the language barrier and the Swedes' simpler lifestyle.

2347. *Women in the Church: A Discussion Paper for the Consideration of Elders' Boards of the Christian and Missionary Alliance in Canada*. [Toronto?]: [The Christian and Missionary Alliance in Canada?], 1987. 197 p.

This document reflects only the opinions of the three-member commission that prepared it. It concludes that normally only men should serve as senior pastors or elders, although the Holy Spirit may direct a congregation to select a woman for these positions; and that since district and denominational boards and committees have no biblical counterparts no firm judgments can be made about whether women may serve on them.

2348. Wynkoop, Mildred Bangs. *The Trevecca Story: 75 Years of Christian Service*. Nashville: Trevecca Press, 1976. 304 p.

J. O. McClurkan founded a Holiness association, the Pentecostal Alliance, in Nashville in 1898. It "was so closely connected with the Christian and Missionary Alliance . . . that the two were virtually identical" (p. 32). The Pentecostal Alliance severed its official connections with the C&MA in November 1901, apparently over its dissatisfaction with the C&MA's administration of overseas missions work, and changed its name to the Pentecostal Mission.

2349. Yeomans, Lilian B. *Healing from Heaven.* Springfield, Mo.: Gospel Publishing House, 1926. 134 p.

Lectures on divine healing by a Pentecostal physician. Yeomans knew A. B. Simpson personally, and she mentions his healing from a heart condition and the healing of his daughter Margaret from diphtheria as prime examples of the power of God to heal without means.

2350. Ziemer (L)ouis (H)enry (1884-1953). *How Every Man Determines His Own Destiny.* Grand Rapids: Zondervan, 1937. 15 p.

An evangelistic radio sermon.

2351. ———. *The Story of My Conversion and Relative Experiences*, 4th ed. Toledo, Ohio: Toledo Gospel Tabernacle, [1920?]. 40 p.

Zeimer, a Lutheran minister, was converted through reading *The Alliance Weekly*. Shortly after moving to Mansfield, Ohio, he experienced sanctification. After he led a revival, the more conservative members of the church conspired to remove him from office. He went on to found Grace Gospel Tabernacle (of the C&MA).

2352. Zimmerman, Diane Luella. "The Ties That Bind: An Historical Study of the Relationship of the Colleges of the Christian and Missionary Alliance to the Parent Denomination, 1882 - 1992." Ph.D. diss., Michigan State University, 1996. 332 p.

Nyack College, Toccoa Falls College, Crown College, and Simpson College moved from a Bible institute model to a Bible college model to a liberal arts model without departing from either the fundamental commitments of the C&MA or the vision of A. B. Simpson.

Periodical Sources

1. *Action missionaire*. Montpellier, France: L'Alliance Chrétienne et Missionaire. Bimonthly? Vol. 1, no. 1 [1967?]-

2. *Aliança em revista*. Curitiba, Brazil: Aliança Cristã e Missionária do Brasil. Quarterly. Vol. 1, no. 1 (January 1977)-

3. *Alianza en marcha*. Buenos Aires: [Alianza Cristiana y Misionera?] Quarterly. [1962?]-

4. *Alliance Academic Review*. Camp Hill, Pa.: Christian Publications. Annual. 1995-
An anthology of articles, by Alliance scholars, on church history, theology, biblical studies, missions, and pastoral theology.

5. *The Alliance Family*. Zamboanga City, Philippines: The Christian and Missionary Alliance Churches of the Philippines. Quarterly. Vol. 1, no. 1 (1979)- v. 15, no. 2 (1993).

6. *Alliance Life*. Nyack, N.Y.: The Christian and Missionary Alliance. Biweekly. Vol. 122, no. 10 (13 May 1987)-
Continues: *The Alliance Witness*.

7. *Alliance Men in Action*. Altoona, Pa.: Alliance Men International. Quarterly. Vol. 1, no. 1 (spring 1971)-

8. *Alliance News*. Hong Kong: Hong Kong District of the Christian and Missionary Alliance. Monthly. Vol. 1, no. 1 [January 1957?]-
In Chinese.

9. *The Alliance Pulpit Review.* Camp Hill, Pa.: Christian Publications. Annual. 1997-

Articles on homiletics together with outstanding sermons by Alliance preachers.

10. *The Alliance Quarterly*. Wuchang, China: Headquarters of the Alliance Church in China. Semiannual? Vol. 1, no. 1 (192-?)-

Text in Chinese.

11. *The Alliance Teacher*. Nyack, N.Y.: Christian and Missionary Alliance, National Christian Education Office. Quarterly. Vol. 25, no. 2 (spring 1979)-

Continues: *Spotcast.*

12. *The Alliance Weekly: A Journal of Christian Life and Missions*. New York: A. B. Simpson. Weekly. Vol. 37, no. 1 (7 October 1911)-v. 92, no. 52 (25 December 1957).

Continues: *The Christian and Missionary Alliance*. Continued by: *The Alliance Witness.*

13. *The Alliance Witness*. New York: Christian Publications. Biweekly. Vol. 93, no. 1 (1 January 1958)-v. 122, no. 9 (29 April 1987).

Continues: *The Alliance Weekly*. Continued by: *Alliance Life*.

14. *The Alliance World*. Toronto: C&MA Tabernacle. Monthly? Vol. 3, no. 8 (November 1923)-v. 3, no. 9 (December 1923).

Continues: *The Word of Life*. Continued by: *The Prophet*. Oswald J. Smith, editor.

15. *The Alliance World: Churches in Missionary Action*. Harrisburg, Pa.: Christian Publications. Quarterly. (fall 1977)-

Continues: *World Missions Folio.*

16. *Annual Report and List of Officers and Members*. New York: Gospel Tabernacle.1882/83-

A. B. Simpson began the Gospel Tabernacle, the birthplace of the C&MA, shortly after his resignation as pastor of Thirteenth Street Presbyterian Church (7 November 1881) and within a year the church, which "was not designed as a mission to the lowest and vicious classes, but a self-supporting work among the middle classes who have no church home" (1882/83, p. 5), had attracted 235 members and 700 adherents.

17. *Annual Report . . . and Minutes of the General Council.* [New York?]: The Christian and Missionary Alliance. 1947-1983.

Continues: *Annual Report of the General Council.* Continued by: *Minutes of the General Council . . . and Annual Report.*

18. *Annual Report of The Christian and Missionary Alliance.* South Nyack, N.Y.: Christian Alliance Pub. Co. 1897/98-1936.

Continues: *Annual Report of the International Missionary Alliance.* The International Missionary Alliance and the Christian Alliance became the Christian and Missionary Alliance in 1897. Continued by: *Annual Report to the General Council.*

19. *Annual Report of the General Council.* New York: The Christian and Missionary Alliance. 1938-1946.

Continues: *Annual Report to the General Council.* Continued by: *Annual Report and Minutes of the General Council.*

20. *Annual Report of the International Missionary Alliance.* New York: The Alliance. 1892, 1894-1895/96.

Continued by: *Annual Report of the Christian and Missionary Alliance.* Annual reports from 1889 (covering 1887-1888) to 1892 (1890-1891) were published in *The Christian Alliance* and its successor *The Christian Alliance and Missionary Weekly.* Those of the Christian Alliance and the International Missionary Alliance (the renamed [1889] Evangelical Missionary Alliance) were published jointly in 1893 as *Year Book of the Christian Alliance and the International Missionary Alliance.* The reports consist largely of narrative accounts of mission work in the various Alliance fields.

21. *Annual Report to the General Council.* Nyack, N.Y.: The Christian and Missionary Alliance. 1937.

Continues: *Annual Report of The Christian and Missionary Alliance.* Continued by: *Annual Report of the General Council.*

22. *L'Appel de l'Indochine.* Alès, France: [L'Alliance Chrétienne et Missionnaire?]. 1950-

Similar in content to *The Call of Indo-China.*

23. *Arab Lands Arena.* Beirut, Lebanon: The Christian and Missionary Alliance in Arab Lands. Vol. 1, no. 1 (1968)-

24. *The Asian Missionary Trumpet.*
The organ of C&MA indigenous mission agencies in Asia.

25. *AYF Compass*. New York: National Youth Office of the Christian and Missionary Alliance. Quarterly. [Vol. 1, no. 1 (1959?)]-v. 6, no. 1 (winter 1964).
Continued by: *Compass.* The organ of the Alliance Youth Fellowship.

26. *Behind the Ranges.* Kotabaru, Indonesia: West Irian Mission of The Christian and Missionary Alliance. Quarterly. Vol. 1, no. 1 (fall 1963)-[v. 21, no. 2 (fall 1987) ?]
Continued by: *Behind the Ranges of Irian Jaya.*

27. *Behind the Ranges of Irian Jaya*. Jayapura, Indonesia: Irian Jaya Mission of The Christian and Missionary Alliance. Semi-annual. [Vol. 22, no. 1 (spring 1988)?]-
Continues: *Behind the Ranges.*

28. *The Berachah Year Book.* New York: The Word, the Work and the World Pub. Co. [1885-1886?]
Likely continues *Annual Report and List of Officers and Members.* Includes the annual report of The Gospel Tabernacle and the ministries of the fledgling Alliance and a devotional calendar of meditations on themes related to the doctrinal distinctives of the movement.

29. *Betania*. Temuco, Chile: Sociedades Femininas de Chile, Corporación Alianza Cristiana y Misionera. Quarterly. Vol. 1, no. 1 (January 1960)-
The organ of the women's organizations of the C&MA in Chile.

30. *The Bible Magazine.* Wuzhou, China: South China Alliance Press. Quarterly. No. 1 (January-March 1913)-
Text in Chinese. Edited by R. A. Jaffray.

31. *The Bible Magazine*. Shanghai: Alliance Press. Bimonthly. Vol. 1, no. 1 (1947)-
Text in Chinese. Edited by Paul Bartel and Wilson Wong. First issue includes a memorial to R. A. Jaffray.

32. *Biennial Report . . . and Reports and Minutes of the General Assembly*. Willowdale, Ont.: The Christian and Missionary Alliance in Canada. 1998-

Continues: *Minutes of the General Assembly . . . and Biennial Report.*

33. *The Borneo Pioneer*. [Wuzhou, China?]: [Dutch East Indies Mission of the Christian and Missionary Alliance?] 1929.

Continued by: *The Pioneer.* Only two issues were published. All the articles were written by R. A. Jaffray.

34. *Burkina Report*. Elizabethtown, Pa.: The Christian and Missionary Alliance in Burkina Faso. Semi-annual. Vol. 13 (winter 1984)-

Continues: *Upper Volta Report.*

35. *The Call of French Indo-China*. Hanoi, Vietnam: Gospel Press. Quarterly. No. 1 [1922?]- no. 28 (October 1929-March 1930).

Continued by: *The Call of French Indo-China and East Siam.*

36. *The Call of French Indo-China and East Siam*. Hanoi, Vietnam: Gospel Press. Semi-annual. No. 29 (April-June 1930)-[1950?].

Continues: *The Call of French Indo-China*. Split into: *The Call of Indo-China* and *The Task.*

37. *The Call of Indo-China*. Dalat, Vietnam: Imprimerie Évangélique. [1950?]-1952-1953 Conference issue.

Continues: *The Call of French Indo-China and East Siam.* Split into: *The Call of Vietnam*, *Jungle Frontiers*, *Cambodia,* and *The Challenge of Laos*.

38. *The Call of Vietnam: News Magazine of the Vietnam Field of the Christian and Missionary Alliance.* Dalat, Vietnam: Imprimerie Évangélique. Semiannual. Fall 1953-summer 1966.

Continues (in part): *The Call of French Indo-China and East Siam.* Merged with *Jungle Frontiers* to form *Vietnam Today.*

39. *CAMACOP Today*. [Manila?]: Christian and Missionary Alliance Churches of the Philippines. Monthly? 1988-September 1997.

40. *Cambodia*. [Phnom Penh?]: The Cambodia Mission of the Christian and Missionary Alliance. Bimonthly. Vol. 1, no. 1 (1953)-

Continues (in part): *The Call of Indo-China.*

41. *The Canadian Alliance*. Toronto: The Christian and Missionary Alliance. Vol. 1, no. 2 (August 1924)-

Oswald J. Smith, editor. "The official organ of the Canadian District."

42. *Canadian Alliance News*. [Toronto?]: The Christian and Missionary Alliance. Quarterly. Vol. 1, no. 1 (spring-summer 1977)-

43. *The Challenge of Laos*. [Vientiane?]: The Laos Mission of the Christian and Missionary Alliance. Quarterly. Vol. 1, no. 1 (September 1953)- ; January 1956-

Continues (in part): *The Call of Indo-China*.

44. *Chile Missionary Tidings: Organ of the Christian and Missionary Alliance in Chile, South America*. Temuco, Chile: Alliance Mission of Chile, S. A. Quarterly. Vol. 1, no. 1 [1919?]-

45. *Chile Times*. Temuco, Chile: The Chile Mission of the Christian and Missionary Alliance. Semiannual? [1963?]-

46. *China-Hongkong Tidings of the Christian and Missionary Alliance*. Hong Kong: The Christian and Missionary Alliance Hongkong Field. Semi-annual? May 1959-

Continues: *China Tidings of the Christian and Missionary Alliance.*

47. *The China Tidings of the Christian and Missionary Alliance*. Hong Kong: China Missionaries of the Christian and Missionary Alliance. Annual? January 1951-

Continued by: *China-Hongkong Tidings of the Christian and Missionary Alliance.*

48. *The Christian Alliance*. New York: The Word, Work and World Pub. Co. Monthly. Vol. 1, no. 1 (January 1888)-v. 2, no. 6 (June 1889).

Continues: *The Word, the Work and the World*. Continued by*: The Christian Alliance and Missionary Weekly.* Edited by A. B. Simpson.

49. *The Christian Alliance and Foreign Missionary Weekly*. New York: Christian Alliance Pub. Co. Weekly. Vol. 12, no. 1 (5 January 1894)-v. 17, no. 26 (25 December 1896).

Continues*: The Christian Alliance and Missionary Weekly*. Continued by*: The Christian and Missionary Alliance.* Edited by A. B. Simpson.

50. *The Christian Alliance and Missionary Weekly*. New York: Christian Alliance Pub. Co. Weekly. Vol. 1, no. 1 (1 August 1889)-v. 11, no. 26 (29 December 1893).

Continues: *The Christian Alliance*. Continued by: *The Christian Alliance and Foreign Missionary Weekly*. Edited by A. B. Simpson.

51. *The Christian Alliance Year Book*. New York: The Word, Work and World Pub. Co. 1888-

Includes a devotional calendar and readings, the articles of incorporation and the constitution of the Christian Alliance and the Evangelical Missionary Alliance, and reports on the various ministries associated with the Gospel Tabernacle and the two Alliances. Edited by A. B. Simpson.

52. *The Christian and Missionary Alliance*. New York: Christian Alliance Pub. Co. Biweekly. Vol. 18, no. 1 (1 January 1897)-v. 26, no. 26 (30 September 1911).

Absorbed: *Living Truths*. Continues: *The Christian Alliance and Foreign Missionary Weekly*. Continued by: *The Alliance Weekly*. Edited by A. B. Simpson.

53. *Christian and Missionary Alliance Church and School News, Shanghai*. Shanghai, China: [Shanghai Mission of the Christian and Missionary Alliance?] No. 1 (school term ending 28 January 1921)-

Edited by John Woodberry. The schools concerned are Beulah Academy and Mary S. Black Seminary for Girls.

54. *The Christian Messenger*. [189-?]-

Published by D. W. Myland.

55. *Church Growth: Canada: A Bulletin of Evangelism and Church Planting*. Regina, Sask.: Canadian Theological College. Three times per year. Vol. 1, no. 1 (March 1974)-v. 3, no. 3 (fall 1976).

Continued by: *His Dominion*.

56. *Colombia*. Cali, Colombia: The Christian and Missionary Alliance. Semiannual? [May 1971?]-

57. *Colombia*. New York: The Christian and Missionary Alliance. [193-?]-

58. *Colombia Missionary Tidings*. Armenia, Colombia: Colombia Mission of the Christian and Missionary Alliance. Annual? [193-?]-

Continued by: *Colombia Tidings.*

59. *Colombia Tidings*. Cali, Colombia: The Colombia Mission of the Christian and Missionary Alliance. Semi-annual? [1953?]-[fall 1970?].

Continues *Colombia Missionary Tidings.* Continued by: *Colombia.*

60. *Combined Home and Foreign Prayer Calendar and Directory of Mission Fields and Missionaries of the Christian and Missionary Alliance.* New York: The Alliance. Semiannual? [193-?]-

61. *Communicate*. Camp Hill, Pa.: Christian Publications. Quarterly. Vol. 1, no. 1 (1990)-

Includes editorial comments on issues relevant to the C&MA and reprints of articles from early Alliance periodicals.

62. *The Companion*. Manila: Alliance Press. Monthly. [1950?]-

63. *Compass*. New York: National Youth Office of the Christian and Missionary Alliance. Quarterly. Vol. 6, no. 2 (spring 1964)-

Continues: *AYF Compass.*

64. *Congo News Letter*. [Boma, Democratic Republic of the Congo?]: Congo Mission of the Christian and Missionary Alliance. [19–?]-[193-?]

Continued by: *Congo Tidings.*

65. *Congo Tidings*. Boma, Democratic Republic of the Congo: Congo Mission of the Christian and Missionary Alliance. Annual. [193-?]-

Publication suspended 1942-1946. Continues: *Congo News Letter.*

66. *The Co-Worker*. Zamboanga City: The Philippine Mission of the Christian and Missionary Alliance. Quarterly. [19–]-

Continued by: *The Philippine Co-Worker.*

67. *The Criterion*. Nyack-on-the-Hudson, N.Y.: Christian Alliance Pub. Co. Annual. [1913?]

The high school annual of Wilson Memorial Academy. Includes many photographs of Alliance leaders. The 1913 issue was likely the only one published; it is the best source of information on the school, which lasted 1906-1918.

68. *Cross*. Hong Kong: Hong Kong Alliance Mission. Bimonthly. No. 1 (October 1997)-

69. *Echoes from Cathay*. Wuzhou, China: Central China Mission of the Christian and Missionary Alliance. Annual. [19–]-

70. *Echoes from the Valley of Blessing*. College Point, N.Y.: The Berachah Orphanage. Monthly. Vol. 1, no. 1 (February 1894?)-

Newsletter of the Berachah Orphanage, a ministry of the C&MA.

71. *Ecos de la Alianza: Organo oficial del Distrito Argentino de la Alianza Cristiana y Misionera*. General Pico, Argentina: Distrito Argentino. Monthly. Vol. 1, no. 1 [December 1938?]-

The official organ of the Argentine C&MA.

72. *Ecuador*. Quito, Ecuador: Ecuador Mission of the Christian and Missionary Alliance. Quarterly? [194-?]-

73. *Ecuador and Southern Colombia of the Christian and Missionary Alliance*. [Quito, Ecuador?]: [the Alliance?] Irregular. [1930-1940?]

74. *Exploits of Faith*. [Miami Beach, Fla.?]: [F.F. Bosworth?]. Monthly. [192-?]-

Edited by F. F. Bosworth.

75. *Faith Missionary*. Oberlin, Ohio. Quarterly. Vol. 1, no. 1 (January 1882)-

Vol. 7 (1888) has accounts of Alliance conventions. Several issues have letters from Marcus B. Fuller of the North Berar Faith Mission, which joined the International Missionary Alliance in 1892.

76. *Foreign Department: Principles and Rules*. New York: The Christian and Missionary Alliance. Irregular. [19–]-

A revised edition was published in 1922. The Foreign Department was the predecessor to the C&MA's Division of Overseas Ministries.

77. *Foreign Service Manual*. New York: The Christian and Missionary Alliance. Foreign Department. Irregular. [1952?]-

78. *French West Africa Quarterly News*. The French West Africa Mission of the Christian and Missionary Alliance. Quarterly. [193-?]-

79. *The Frontier*: *News Letter of the Kweichow Szechwan Mission of the Christian and Missionary Alliance*. New York: The Mission. Irregular. Vol. 1, no. 1 (January 1936)-

80. *The Full Gospel Messenger*. [St. Paul, Minn.?]: Northwestern District of the Christian and Missionary Alliance. [1918-1936?]
The organ of the Northwestern District.

81. *Gabon Tribes*. Fougamou, Gabon: Gabon Field of the Christian and Missionary Alliance. Annual. 1959-

82. *Gabon Update*. Mouila, Gabon: The Christian and Missionary Alliance in Gabon. [1982?]-

83. *Gleanings from the Argentine*. [Buenos Aires?]: [The Christian and Missionary Alliance?] 1920-

84. *Good News*. Chicago: Moody Church. [1916-1921?]
Published during Paul Rader's tenure as pastor of Moody Church.

85. *The Gospel in All Lands*. New York: Anson D. Randolph and Co. Monthly. Vol. 1, no. 1 (February-May 1880)-
A. B. Simpson was the editor of vol. 1 of this illustrated missions periodical and co-editor with Eugene R. Smith of vol. 2 (July 1881)- v. 4, no. 5 (November 1881).

86. *The Growing Church Newsletter*. Nyack, N.Y.: The Alliance Witness. Irregular. No. 1 (March 1985)-

87. *The Harvest*. [Hiroshima? Japan]: The Japan Mission of the Christian and Missionary Alliance. Annual? [1954?]-
Continued by: *Japan Harvest*.

88. *The Herald*. Hong Kong: [South China Mission of the Christian and Missionary Alliance?] [1939?]-

89. *Himself*. Toronto: The Alliance Tabernacle. Monthly. Vol. 4, no. 11 (November 1924)-v. 5, [no. 4?] (1925).
Oswald J. Smith, editor. "To foster the needs and work of Alliance Tabernacle." Continues: *The Prophet*. Continued by: *The Tabernacle News*.

90. *His Dominion*. Regina, Sask.: The Canadian Church Growth Centre. Quarterly. Vol. 4, no. 1 (spring 1977?)-v. 16, no. 2 (July 1990).

Continues: *Church Growth: Canada*. One of the best sources of scholarly articles on Alliance history.

91. *The India Alliance*. Bombay: The Christian and Missionary Alliance in India. Monthly. Vol. 1, no. 1 (July 1893)-(December 1897); new series: Vol. 2, no. 1 (July 1902)-v. 19, no. 7 (March 1919).

92. *The India Alliance: A Bulletin of the India Mission of the Christian and Missionary Alliance*. Akola, India: The Mission. Quarterly. [192-?]-(fall 1956).

Split into: *The India Alliance. Gujarat Edition* and *The India Alliance. Marathi Area Edition*.

93. *The India Alliance. Gujarat Edition*. Dholka, India: Gujarat Mission of the Christian and Missionary Alliance. Quarterly. [Spring 1957?]-

Continues (in part): *The India Alliance: A Bulletin of the India Mission of the Christian and Missionary Alliance*. Continued by: *Song of India*.

94. *The India Alliance. Maharashtra Field Edition*. Akola, India: Maharashtra Field of the Christian and Missionary Alliance in India. Three times a year. Rainy season 1964/hot season 1965-

Continues *The India Alliance. Marathi Area Edition*.

95. *The India Alliance. Marathi Area Edition*. Akola, India: Marathi Mission of the Christian and Missionary Alliance in India. Three times a year. Bulletin 1 (1957)-hot season 1964.

Continues (in part): *India Alliance: A Bulletin of the India Mission of the Christian and Missionary Alliance*. Continued by: *India Alliance. Maharashtra Field Edition*.

96. *The Indian Christian*. Wheaton, Ill.: Alliance Indian Publications. Bimonthly. Vol. 1 (1969)-v. 11, no. 5 (September-October 1979).

Merged with: *Indian Life Magazine*.

97. *The Ivory Coast Today*. Bouake, Côte d'Ivoire: Ivory Coast Mission of the Christian and Missionary Alliance. Three times a year. Vol. 1, no. 1 (winter 1961)-

98. *Japan Harvest*. [Hiroshima? Japan]: The Japan Mission of the Christian and Missionary Alliance. Semiannual. Vol. 11 (spring 1964)-

Continues: *The Harvest*.

99. *Jian Dao: A Journal of Bible and Theology*. Hong Kong: Alliance Bible Seminary, Hong Kong. Annual. 1994-

Text in English and Chinese. Includes abstracts, in both languages, of every article.

100. *Jungle Frontiers*. Saigon, Vietnam: The Tribes of Viet-Nam Mission of the Christian and Missionary Alliance. Semiannual. No. 1 (April 1954)-no. 23 (summer 1966).

Continues (in part): *The Call of Indo-China*. Merged with: *The Call of Vietnam* to form *Vietnam Today*.

101. *Juventud en marcha*. Buenos Aires: Alianza Cristiana y Misionera Argentina. Bimonthly. [1949?]-

102. *Kalam Hidoep*. Makassar, Indonesia: [Kemah Indjil Geredja Masehi Indonesia?] Seven issues per year? Vol. 1, no. 1 (1930)-

In Bahasa Indonesia; edited by R. A. Jaffray. Continued by: *Kalam Hidup*.

103. *Kalam Hidup*. Bandung, Indonesia: Kemah Indjil Geredja Masehi Indonesia. Monthly? [193-?]-

Continues: *Kalam Hidoep*.

104. *Kansu-Tibetan Border News*. Minchow, China: Kansu-Tibetan Border Mission of the Christian and Missionary Alliance. Semiannual? Vol. 1, no. 1 (1934)-

Likely continued by: *The Regions Beyond*.

105. *Kwikama: Nkanda wa Dibundu dia C. M. A. Boma, Democratic Republic of the Congo: Dimbu Kia Muila y C&MA*. No. 1, [1964?]-[197-?].

The official organ of the C&MA in the Democratic Republic of the Congo. Text in Kikongo.

106. *Living Truths*. New York: Living Truths. Monthly. Vol. 1, no. 1 (July 1902)-v. 7, no. 9 (September 1907).

Each issue consists of an extended article, in tract format, on a theme related to the fourfold Gospel. Edited anonymously by A. B. Simpson, who intended the periodical/tract as an unobtrusive means of disseminating Alliance doctrine beyond the borders of the movement itself. Absorbed by: *The Christian and Missionary Alliance.*

107. *Macedonian Vision.* Hong Kong: Foreign Missionary Society of CC&MA of Hong Kong. Bimonthly. Vol. 1 [1979?]-
Text in Chinese.

108. *The Mali Messenger.* Nyack, N.Y.: Mali Field of the Christian and Missionary Alliance. Semiannual. Vol. 1, no. 1 [1976?]-
Continues (in part): *Mali-Upper Volta Tidings.*

109. *The Mali-Upper Volta Tidings.* Bobo-Dioulasso, Burkina Faso: The Mali-Upper Volta Mission of the Christian and Missionary Alliance. Three times a year. Vol. 1, no. 2 (December 1960)-
Continues: *The Sudan-Upper Volta Tidings.*

110. *Manual of the Christian and Missionary Alliance.* New York: The Alliance. Irregular. 1911-

111. *Manual of the Christian and Missionary Alliance in Canada.* Willowdale, Ont.: The Alliance. Irregular. 1986-

112. *Mbolo: Gabon Greets You.* [Mouila, Gabon?]: Mission Évangélique. Annual. Vol. 1, no. 1 (June 1949)-

113. *The Messenger of the Canadian Bible Institute.* Regina, Sask.: Canadian Bible Institute. Monthly. September 1941-[198-?]

114. *Minutes of the General Assembly . . . and Biennial Report.* [Willowdale, Ont.?]: The Christian and Missionary Alliance in Canada. Biennial. 1982-1996.
Continued by: *Biennial Report . . . and Reports and Minutes of the General Assembly.*

115. *Minutes of the General Council . . . and Annual Report.* Nyack, N.Y.: The Christian and Missionary Alliance. 1984-
Continues: *Annual Report . . . and Minutes of the General Council.*

116. *Missionary Handbook for Global Ministries.* [Toronto?]: The Christian and Missionary Alliance in Canada. Irregular. 1999-

117. *Missionary Handbook for International Ministries*. Nyack, N.Y.: The Christian and Missionary Alliance. Irregular. [1988?]-

118. *Missionary Handbook for Overseas Ministries*. Nyack, N.Y.: The Christian and Missionary Alliance. Irregular. 1976-1987.
Continues: *Policies and Procedures of the Foreign Department*. Continued by: *Missionary Handbook for International Ministries*.

119. *Mundo aliancista*. Buenos Aires: Alianza Cristiana y Misionera Argentina. Bimonthly? [197-?]-

120. *Official Directory*. Colorado Springs: The Christian and Missionary Alliance. Annual. 1999-
Continues in part: *Prayer Directory of the Christian and Missionary Alliance.*

121. *Official Directory of the Christian and Missionary Alliance.* New York: The Alliance. Annual. 1967-
Continues: *Official Directory: The Officers, Board of Managers, and Home and Foreign Workers of the Christian and Missionary Alliance.*

122. *Official Directory of the Christian and Missionary Alliance in Canada*. Toronto: The Alliance. Irregular. 1984-1991.
Continued by: *Prayer Directory of the Christian and Missionary Alliance (Toronto, Ont.)*

123. *Official Directory: The Officers, Board of Managers, and Home and Foreign Workers of the Christian and Missionary Alliance*. New York: The Alliance. Annual. [19–?]-1966.
Continued by: *Official Directory of the Christian and Missionary Alliance.*

124. *Open Line: A Communications Link between the President and Licensed Workers of the Christian and Missionary Alliance*. Nyack, N.Y.: Office of the President. Bimonthly. Vol. 1, no. 1 (May-June, 1982)-

125. *Panorama*. Kankan, Guinea: The Christian and Missionary Alliance of Guinea. Semiannual. Fall 1961-

126. *The Parlor Evangelist.* Audubon, N.J.: William T. MacArthur. Monthly. Vol. 1, no. 1 [1928?]-

Largely the work of William T. MacArthur and Philip Mauro. Vol. 2, no. 7 (August-September 1929) and vol. 2, no. 8 (October 1929) include a personal testimony by MacArthur about A. B. Simpson.

127. *Peru: "Occupy Till I Come."* [Huánuco?, Peru]: The Christian and Missionary Alliance. No. 1 [192-?]-

128. *Peruvian Echoes.* Lima: The Christian and Missionary Alliance in Peru. Semiannual. Vol. 1, no. 1 (July 1949)-

129. *The Philippine Co-Worker.* Zamboanga City, Philippines: The Philippine Mission of the Christian and Missionary Alliance. Semiannual. Vol. 1 (January 1963)-

Continues: *The Co-Worker.*

130. *The Pioneer.* Wuzhou, China: Alliance Press. Quarterly. Vol. 1, no. 1 (1929)-v. 12, no. 45 (December 1941); v. 13, no. 46 (January 1946)-June 1958; September 1964-1975.

Continues: *The Borneo Pioneer.* R. A. Jaffray wrote many of the articles in vols. 1-12.

131. *De Pionier.* Wassenaar, Netherlands: Alliance Zendingscentrum, "Parousia." Monthly. January 1939-

Missionary organ of the Dutch C&MA.

132. *Policies and Procedures of the Foreign Department.* New York: The Christian and Missionary Alliance. Irregular. 1964-1970.

Continued by: *Missionary Handbook for Overseas Ministries.*

133. *Prayer Calendar and Directory of Alliance Work and Workers.* New York: The Christian and Missionary Alliance. [1921?]-1922.

Continued by: *Prayer Calendar and Directory of Home and Foreign Workers of the Christian and Missionary Alliance.*

134. *Prayer Calendar and Directory of Home and Foreign Workers of the Christian and Missionary Alliance.* New York: The Alliance. Semiannual. 1922-

135. *Prayer Calendar and Directory of Mission Fields and Missionaries of the Christian and Missionary Alliance*. New York: The Alliance. Semiannual. [192-?]-

136. *Prayer Calendar and Directory: The Fields and Missionaries of the Christian and Missionary Alliance: Foreign*. New York: The Alliance. Annual. [1932?]-

137. *Prayer Calendar and Directory: The Home and Foreign Work of the Christian and Missionary Alliance: Combined*. New York: The Alliance. Annual. [1932-?]-

138. *Prayer Connection: Guide to Intercession for the Worldwide Work of the Christian and Missionary Alliance.* Colorado Springs: The Alliance, 1999-

Continues in part: *Prayer Directory of the Christian and Missionary Alliance (Nyack, N.Y.)*

139. *Prayer Directory of the Christian and Missionary Alliance (Nyack, N.Y.)* Nyack, N.Y.: The Alliance. Annual. 1985-1998.

Continues: *Prayer Manual of the Christian and Missionary Alliance.* Split into: *Official Directory* and *Prayer Connection: Guide to Intercession for the Worldwide Work of the Christian and Missionary Alliance.*

140. *Prayer Directory of the Christian and Missionary Alliance in Canada*. Toronto: The Alliance in Canada. Annual. 1997-

Continues: *Prayer Directory of the Christian and Missionary Alliance (Toronto, Ont.)*

141. *Prayer Directory of the Christian and Missionary Alliance (Toronto, Ont.)* Toronto: The Alliance in Canada. Annual. 1992-1996.

Split from: *Prayer Directory of the Christian and Missionary Alliance (Nyack, N.Y.)*. Continued by: *Prayer Directory of the Christian and Missionary Alliance in Canada*.

142. *Prayer Manual: A Calendar for Daily Prayer for the Foreign and Home Work of the Christian and Missionary Alliance*. New York: The Alliance. Annual. [194-?]-1966.

143. *Prayer Manual of the Christian and Missionary Alliance*. New York: The Alliance. Annual. 1967-1984.

Continues: *Prayer Manual: A Calendar for Daily Prayer for the Foreign and Home Work of the Christian and Missionary Alliance.* Continued by: *Prayer Directory of the Christian and Missionary Alliance (Nyack, N.Y.)*

144. *The Prophet*. Toronto: Alliance Tabernacle. Monthly? Vol. 3, no 5 (August 1923); Vol. 4, no. 1 (January 1924)-[v. 4, no. 10 (October 1924?)].

Edited by Oswald J. Smith. Continues: *The Alliance World.* Continued by: *Himself.*

145. *Realidades*. Quito, Ecuador: Libreria Realidades. Monthly. Vol. 1, no. 1[1932?]-

146. *The Regions Beyond*. Minchow, China: Kansu-Tibetan Border Mission of the Christian and Missionary Alliance. Vol. 1, no. 1 [1940?]-

147. *Report*. Mansfield, Ohio: Ruth Stull. Monthly. [194-?]-

Continued by: *Trailways*. Issued to promote world missions.

148. *Salud y vida*. Temuco, Chile: Imprimeria y Editorial Alianza. Monthly. 1 August 1913-

Official organ of Corporación Iglesia Alianza Cristiana y Misionera Chile.

149. *La senda antigua*. Saladillo, Argentina: [Alianza Cristiana y Misionera Argentina?] Monthly. March 1916-

150. *Senior Full Gospel Quarterly*. New York: Christian Alliance Pub. Co.. Quarterly. Vol. 1 (1917)-

Likely the first C&MA periodical for youth.

151. *Sidestreets*. Manila: Alliance Publishers. Monthly. Vol. 1, no. 1 (June 1980) - v. 5, no. 2 (March 1984).

152. *Song of India*. Dholka, India: Gujarat Mission of the Christian and Missionary Alliance in India. [195-?]-

Continues: *The India Alliance. Gujarat Edition.*

153. *The South China Alliance Tidings*. Wuzhou, China: The South China Mission of the Christian and Missionary Alliance. Bimonthly. Vol. 1, no. 1 [1907?]-[August 1938?]
Edited by R. A. Jaffray.

154. *South China Tidings*. [Hong Kong?]: South China Mission of the Christian and Missionary Alliance. Annual? Vol. 1, no. 2 (September 1949)-
Continues: *Tidings*.

155. *Spotcast*. New York: Christian and Missionary Alliance. Quarterly. Vol. 1, no. 1 [1954?]-v. 25, no. 1 (winter 1978-79).
Continued by: *The Alliance Teacher*.

156. *The Student Evangel*. [New York?]: [Christian Alliance Pub. Co.?] Monthly. Vol. 1 (1915)- v. 3, nos. 9-10 (January-February 1918).
Cover subtitle: *A Journal of the Nyack Schools of the Christian and Missionary Alliance*.

157. *The Sudan-Upper Volta Tidings*. Bobo-Dioulasso, Burkina Faso: The Sudan-Upper Volta Mission of the Christian and Missionary Alliance. Vol. 1, no. 1 (August 1960)-
Continued by: *The Mali-Upper Volta Tidings*.

158. *The Tabernacle News*. Toronto: Alliance Tabernacle. Monthly? Vol. 5, no. 5 (September 1925)-
Edited by Oswald J. Smith. Continues: *Himself*.

159. *The Target*. [Manila?]: [Christian and Missionary Alliance Churches of The Philippines?] [19–]-

160. *The Task of the Christian and Missionary Alliance in Siam*. Bangkok, Thailand: [Siam Mission of the Christian and Missionary Alliance?] Semiannual? Vol. 1, no. 1 (October 1947)-
Title varies slightly. Continues (in part): *The Call of French Indo-China and East Siam*.

161. *El testigo*. La Plata, Argentina: [Alianza Cristiana y Misionera Argentina?] Monthly. July 1901-

162. *Tidings*. [Wuzhou, China?]: South China Mission of the Christian and Missionary Alliance. Vol. 1, no. 1 (October 1948).

Likely a continuation of *South China Alliance Tidings*. Continued by: *South China Tidings*.

163. *Trailways*. Mansfield, Ohio: Ruth Stull. Monthly. January 1948-
Continues: *Report*.

164. *Triumphs of Faith: A Monthly Journal*. Oakland, Calif.: Office of *Triumphs of Faith*. Monthly. 1881-
Devoted to the promotion of Christian holiness and to divine healing. Includes testimonies by a number of early Alliance people. Edited by Carrie Judd Montgomery.

165. *Upper Volta Report*. Elizabethtown, Pa.: The Upper Volta Mission of the Christian and Missionary Alliance. Semiannual. Vol. 1 (summer 1978)-v. 12 [spring 1984?].
Continued by: *Burkina Report*.

166. *Vietnam Today: News Magazine of the Vietnam Field, Christian and Missionary Alliance*. Saigon, Vietnam: Vietnam Field. Three times a year. No. 1 (October 1966)-no. 13 (summer 1973).
Merger of: *The Call of Vietnam* and *Jungle Frontiers*. Nos. 3-13 entitled *Viet Nam Today*.

167. *Visión aliancista*. Mar del Plata, Argentina: [Alianza Cristiana y Misionera Argentina?] Monthly. Vol. 1, no. 1 (January 1979)-

168. *La voz de la Alianza*. Cali, Colombia: Alianza Cristiana y Misionera Colombiana. Five times per year? Vol. 1, no. 1 [1964?]-

169. *West African Witness*. Kankan, Guinea: French West Africa Field of the Christian and Missionary Alliance. Quarterly. Vol. 1, no. 1 [1951?]-

170. *The Western Christian Alliance*. Boone, Ia.: J. C. Crawford. Vol. 1, no. 1 (July 1909)-[1916?].
Crawford became superintendent of the Western District of the C&MA in 1910. He severed ties with the C&MA in 1916.

171. *The Word of Life*. Toronto: Alliance Tabernacle. Monthly. Vol. 3, no. 6 (September 1923)-v. 3, no. 7 (October 1923).
Edited by Oswald J. Smith. Continues: *The Prophet*. Continued by: *The Alliance World*.

172. *The Word, the Work and the World*. New York: The Word, the Work and the World. Monthly. Vol. 1, no. 1 (January 1882)-v. 9, nos. 5 - 6 (November-December 1887).

Absorbed: *The Work and the World*. Continued by*: The Christian Alliance*. Edited by A. B. Simpson.

173. *The Work and World*. New York: A. B. Simpson. Irregular. Vol.1, no.1 (February 1882)-v. 2, no. 4 (December 1882).

Absorbed by: *The Word, the Work and the World*. A short-lived scaled-down version of *The Word, the Work and the World* that was dedicated exclusively to missions.

174. *World Missions Folio*. New York: The Christian and Missionary Alliance. Quarterly. [1961?]- [summer quarter 1977?]

Continued by*: The Alliance World: Churches in Missionary Action*.

175. *The World Wide Christian Courier*. Chicago: World Wide Christian Couriers. Monthly. June 1926-December 1931; June 1932.

Paul Rader was editor-in-chief. Includes reports from C&MA missionaries.

176. *Year Book of the Christian Alliance and the International Missionary Alliance*. New York: Christian Alliance Pub. Co. 1893-[1896?].

Includes reports from the two Alliances, the Gospel Tabernacle, the New York Missionary Training College, and the other Alliance-affiliated ministries. Continued by*: Annual Report of the Christian and Missionary Alliance*.

177. *The Young People's Full Gospel Quarterly. A New Course of Bible Studies for Young People's Societies of All Denominations*. Harrisburg, Pa.: Christian Publications. Quarterly. [1924?]-

178. *The Youth's Counsellor*. New York: Christian Alliance Pub. Co. Weekly. [192-?]-

179. *Zendingsvisie*. Wassenaar, Netherlands: Alliance Jeugd Beweging der Christian and Missionary Alliance. Quarterly. Vol. 1, no. 1 [1960?]-

A missions periodical for youth.

Personal Name Index

All numbers in the indexes designate entry numbers. Entry numbers in bold indicate works by A. B. Simpson; those in italics indicate works by A. W. Tozer; those preceded by a P indicate sources listed in Periodical Sources.

Aberhart, William (1878-1943), 518
Abraham (Biblical prophet), 958, 1903
Allen, Ethan O., 277, 921
Allen, William E., 15
Anderson, E. M. (1887-1948), 27

Barnes, Samuel G., 69-72
Barnes, Vera F. (1900-1994), 69-72
Barratt (T)homas (B)all (1862-1940), 77
Bartleman, Frank (1871-1936), 78-80
Beckdahl, Agnes N. T. (1876-1968), 95
Bell, Ethel G. (1893-1983), 99-100, 760, 2254
Bell, Robert W., 99-100, 760, 2254
Bibighaus, Alexandria Wasilewska (1908-), 107
Birrel, Francis Catlin (1869-1964), 113
Birrel, Matthew Brown (1869-1957), 114
Blackstone (W)illiam (E)ugene (1841-1935), 901, 2313
Blanchard, Charles (A)lbert (1848-1925), 137, 144
Blumhardt, Christoph Friedrich (1842-1919), 250
Bollback, Anthony G. (1922-), 153
Bollback, Evelyn P. (1921-), 153
Bosworth (F)red (F)rancis (1877-1958), 109-10, 161, 630, 1268-69, 1380-81, 2016, P74
Brainerd, David (1718-1747), 498
Brown, Marie Burgess, 151
Brubaker, Lizzie K. (1856-1928), 1483
Bubna, Donald L. (1929-), 199-202

Carlsen, David Axel, 236
Carter (R)ussell Kelso (1849-1928), 277, 381, 442
Cassidy, Elizabeth, 262
Cassidy, William (d. 1887), 262, **1544**
Catholic Church. Pope (1963-1978: Paul VI), 1228
Chao, T. L., 2245

Jacober, Edward G. (1919-1984), 784
Jacober, Virginia, 784
Jacobson, Alma A. (d. 1965), 785
Jacobson, Gerhard (1889-1972), 785
Jaffray, Margaret, 766, 1414
Jaffray (R)obert (A)lexander (1873-1945), 691, 723, 904-6, 1215, 1333, 1414, 2002, 2041, 2100, *2151-52*, P33, P130
Jeffrey, Ruth Goforth (1898-1972), 788
Johnson, Paul (d. 1952), 382, 567
Johnson, Priscilla (d. 1952), 382, 567
Jones, Clarence W. (1915-1986), 354, 793, 1192, 1287
Jones, Howard O. (1921-), 648, 799, 797, 801
Jones, Wanda (1923-), 799, 801, 862
Joseph (Son of Jacob), 1406

Kenyon (E)ssek (W)illiam (1867-1948), 1074
Kerr (D)aniel (W)arren (1856-1927), 814
Kincaid, Ray L., 818
Kincheloe, Raymond McFarland (1909-1986), 822
King, Louis L. (1915-), 261
Klein, Carol M., 853
Klein, George, 853
Kirk, James M. (1854-1945), 1959
Kuglin, Robert J., 868

Lake, John (G)raham (1870-1935), 871
Larson, Reuben, 354, 793
Lecaro, Miguel, 877
Leno, Patty, 885
Lesko, Basil, 887
LeTourneau, Evelyn Peterson (1900-), 861, 1409
LeTourneau (R)obert (G)ilmour (1888-1969), 5, 888-90, 914
Lewer, Mary E., 891
Lewis, A. Rodger (1923-1999), 892
Lewis, Lelia J. (1927-), 892
Lichtenfels, Sophie (1843-1919), 641-43, 895-97
Lindenberger (S)arah A. (1852-1922), 903
Linn, Jason, 906
Livingston, James Haley (Jim) (1931-), 908
Livingston, Jean Ann (1931-), 908
Lombard, Victor, 911
Long, Charles E. (1935-), 912
Long (E)lma (G)race (1933-), 912
Loughlin, Cordelia (d. 1892), 2309

MacArthur, William (T)elfer (1861-1949), 926, P126
MacPherson, Aimee Semple (1890-1944), 518, 1941
Manning, Preston, 437
Marx, Groucho (1891-1977), 804
Mauro, Philip (1859-1952), 633, 1033, 1036, P126
Maxwell (L)eslie (E)arl (1895-1984), 518
McAuley, Jeremiah (1839-1884), 1142
McClurkan, James (O)ctavius (1861-1914), 2004, 2348
McFedries, Annie, 1060
Meloon family, 524
Meminger, Wilbur (F)iske (1851-1909), 1084
Merritt, Stephen (1834-1917), 60-62, 1092, 1440
Minder, John (1898-1980), 687, 913, 1107
Montgomery, Carrie Judd (1858-1946), 12, 150, 1118, 1121, 1125, 1129, 2016, 2290, P164
Morgan, G. L., 1138
Morris, Samuel (1872-1893), 60-62, 1024, 1093, 1091, 1440
Moseley, Thomas (1886-1959), 1163
Mussolini, Benito (1883-1945), 1924

Myland (D)avid (W)esley (1858-1943), 217, 582, 871, P54

Nardi, Michele (1850-1914), 115, **1762**
Naylor, Henry (Mrs.), 1191

Oldfield, Mabel Dimock (1878-1965), 1215
Oldfield, Walter (H)erbert (1879-1958), 1215-16, 1218
Olsen, Betty (d. 1968?), 724
Olsson, Emilio, 305, 1223-26, 1281, 1477-78, **1881**
Opperman, Kenn (W)ayne (1926-), 1228
Ozman, Agnes Nevada (1870-), 759

Pardington, George (P)almer (1866-1915), 1248-49, **1549**
Paul, the Apostle, Saint, **1787**
Perkin, Noel (1893-), 150
Peter, Carrie (1872-1937), 1978
Peters, Arlene Mary (1943-), 1270
Peters, David John (1945-), 1270
Philpott (P)eter (W)iley (1865-1957), 518, 1275, 1277
Plymire, Victor Guy (1881-1956), 150, 1292
Presswood, Ernest (1908-1946), 766, 1296
Preston, Anne (1810?-1906), 1304, 2287
Pulis, Josephus (1831-1913), **1620**

Rader, Daniel Paul (1879-1938), 108, 533, 571, 1287, 1317-19, 1332-33, 1336, 1338-39, 1344, 1410, 2235, P84, P175
Ramabai Sarasvati, Pandita (1858-1922), 627
Rauschenbusch, Walter (1861-1918), 539
Rees, Seth Cook (1854-1933), 1360
Robb, Alfred Pierce, 1398
Robb, Egerton, Seitz, 1398
Roffe (A)lfred (W)illiam (1866-1947), 549, 1404
Rose, Darlene Deibler, 766, 1414
Roseberry, Edith M. (1879-1965), 1416
Roseberry (R)obert (S)herman (1883-1976), 728, 1416, 1418
Rossiter (F)rederick H. (1862-1962), 1422
Rounds (T)ryphena (C)ecilia (1843-1939), 1423
Rychner, Evelyn Marie (1919-), 1488

Sahlberg, Corinne (1921-), 1434
Sahlberg, Elmer John (1920-), 1434
Salmon, John (1831-1918), 112, 509, 569, 581, 1365, 1382, 1436, 1444
Sandford, Frank W. (1862-1948), 568, 1177, 1195
Saul, King of Israel, 969
Schneppenmueller, H. Karl, 1452
Schoonmaker, Christian (1881-1919), 1454
Schweitzer, Albert (1875-1965), 853, 2069
Scott, Peter Cameron (1867-1896), 1384
Senft (F)rederic (H)erbert (1857-1925), 1473
Senft, Ruth (A)nnie, 1472
Shepard, Louise (1865-1928), 278, 915
Shrier, J. Clarence (1910-), 1492-93
Simon, Otto A. (1897-), 1495
Simpson (A)lbert (B)enjamin (1843-1919), 2, 183, 223, 287-88, 329, 463, 518, 553, 568-69, 611, 681, 710-11, 804, 844, 1076, 1129, 1177, 1194, 1206, 1208, 1254, 1364-65, 1374, 1462, 1466, **1511**, **1673-1677**, **1736**, **1788**, **1870**, 1885, 2060-61, 2066-67, *2216*, 2233, 2286, 2290, 2320, 2349, P4, P12, P16, P18, P20, P28, P48-52, P85, P90, P106, P126, P172-

Subject Index

About the Author

H. D. (Sandy) Ayer was born in New Westminster, British Columbia, in 1952 and grew up in the semi-wilderness of Kitimat, B.C., where he acquired his love of nature. Following his graduation from library school in 1984, he and his wife Diane moved to Regina, Saskatchewan, where Sandy began work as director of library services at Canadian Bible College/Canadian Theological Seminary. His interest in Alliance bibliography stems from his roles as institutional archivist and administrator of the library's special collection in Allianceana and his love of collecting things. The 6' 8" author has the distinction of being perhaps the world's tallest theological librarian.

He and Diane have two children, Adam, fifteen, and Hannah, twelve. Sandy reads to relax and birds for excitement. If he were ever to write another book, it would be about his experiences as a birder.